# PRO FOOTBALL
# HALL OF FAME
# ALL-TIME
# GREATS

# PRO FOOTBALL HALL OF FAME ALL-TIME GREATS

## *Don R. Smith*

### FOREWORD BY PETE ROZELLE

GALLERY BOOKS
An imprint of W.H. Smith Publishers Inc.
112 Madison Avenue
New York City 10016

To the Pro Football Hall of Fame, the all-time greats of the past,
present and future and the millions of fans who have made
pro football a truly world event.

Don R. Smith

First published in 1988 by
Octopus Books Limited,
Michelin House, 81 Fulham Road, London, SW3 6RB

This edition published in 1988 by Gallery Books
An imprint of W.H. Smith Publishers Inc.
112 Madison Avenue, New York, New York 10016

ISBN 0 8317 6300 0

Printed by Mandarin Offset in Hong Kong

Editor Isobel Greenham
Art Editor David Rowley
Designed by Grid Graphics
Picture Research Rachel Duffield
Production Controller Audrey Johnston

# CONTENTS

# FOREWORD

I suppose the wonderful thing about all sports, both amateur and professional, is that they all are basically games. Games appeal to all of us—young and old, big and small, men and women. Games are universal, diverse, amusing, competitive, physical and mental; they stimulate us and make us proud. They make us come alive.

The history of sports is the story of those games and those who played them. Professional football, the game with which I am most familiar and with which I have been emotionally involved for my entire adult life, has a marvelous history. One that is truly American, one that was born in Canton, Ohio, a town in our midlands, expanded to both coasts and to our borders to the north and south, and is now creating new fans throughout the world.

Much of the history of our game that today flies the banner of the National Football League can be found in Canton at the Pro Football Hall of Fame. It opened in 1963 and has grown into a living memorial to our heroes of the past and remains the ultimate athletic goal of our stars of today and tomorrow.

This book, *Pro Football Hall of Fame All-Time Greats*, is a chronicle about our great game and the people who, through personal sacrifice and extraordinary athletic deeds, forged a place for it, nurtured it, and made it a living tribute to the American spirit. This publication will lift you from the sandlots to the modern stadiums and domes, and transform the megaphone announcements of yesteryear into the television camera angles of today. It will flash before your eyes the memories of Nagurski and Grange, Thorpe and Halas, Bell, Baugh and Hein, then—almost like instant replay—record the feats of Namath and Staubach, Unitas and Greene, Sayers and Gifford, Lombardi and Ewbank.

Don Smith has been involved in the modern pro game with teams in both the American and National Football Leagues. Since joining the Pro Football Hall of Fame in 1968, he has been a force in its continual expansion. He is certainly qualified to compile what follows on the pages of this book. I hope that you enjoy it as much as Don has assured me he enjoyed writing it.

Pete Rozelle
Commissioner
National Football League

*Enthusiastic fans, show their support of the Denver Broncos. As Pete Rozelle once said: "Here's to the millions of fans who are, have been, and will be the lifeblood of pro football!"*

# FOOTBALL BEGINS IN AMERICA, 1869–1919

American football, which evolved into something resembling its present form in the 1880s, can trace its roots to both soccer and rugby, sports which are played in most nations of the world but are not particularly popular in the United States. Soccer is history's most popular sport, as well as its oldest. Some form of the game may have been played in the Greek city-state of Sparta or in Rome at least 2000 years ago. Rugby, on the other hand, is a relatively new sport, having been invented in England in 1823, when a student name William Webb Ellis, playing in a soccer game, had the audacity to pick up the ball and run with it. Soccer rules, of course, dictated the ball could be advanced only by kicking but the idea of running with the ball caught on and a new sport was born.

As early as 1860, secondary schools in the Boston area were playing soccer football games and, on November 6, 1869, Rutgers and Princeton played what now stands in history as the first college football game. Each team had 25 players, the ball could be advanced only by kicking or butting with the head and goal posts were placed 25 yards apart. Rutgers won, six goals to four.

In New England, however, Harvard began playing a different sport, one more like rugby, called the "Boston game." McGill University of Montreal in Canada also played rugby so the two schools met in a three-game series in 1874. While most schools still played soccer, Harvard turned to rugby exclusively. Seemingly, every college played by its own set of rules.

Then in 1876, representatives from soccer- and rugby-playing colleges convened at the Massasoit House, a hotel in Springfield, Massachusetts. Playing rules resembling those of rugby were adopted. Yale's representative at the convention, Walter Camp, soon became a rugby football star. He was destined to foster most of the rule changes that transformed rugby into the new sport of American football.

At Camp's suggestion, rules were adopted in 1880 that called for one team to hold undisputed possession of the ball until it voluntarily gave up possession. Thus the scrimmage line marking the start of each new play was born. The number of players on a team was reduced from 15 to 11 and the procedure of transferring or centering the ball from one player to another to start a play was introduced.

When it turned out teams were reluctant to give up the ball after a reasonable period of possession, the "block game" resulted, with each team holding the ball for one full half. Soon, a team was required to gain 5 yards in three plays to maintain possession. Later the rule called for a gain of 10 yards in four plays, as it is today. In 1888, Camp promoted a rule permitting tackling as low as the knees. In the decades ahead, many other Camp innovations continued to shape the evolving game of American football.

Soon after the Civil War, athletic clubs that sponsored a great variety of sports teams became a popular phenom-

enon in the United States. By the 1880s, most athletic clubs had a football team. Competition was heated and each club vowed to stock its teams with the best players available. Toward this end, some clubs obtained jobs for star players. Others "awarded" expensive trophies or watches to their players, who would in turn pawn their awards, only to receive them again and again after each game they played. A popular practice was to offer double expense money to players for their services. All these practices were questioned by the Amateur Athletic Union but for every tactic declared illegal, a new one was developed.

Finally, on November 12, 1892, the Allegheny Athletic Association (AAA) simply gave money to a player to perform in a game against the Pittsburgh Athletic Club (PAC). While the PAC had suspected something illegal was afoot, there was no immediate evidence to back up its belief. Verification, in fact, did not come for almost 80 years until the Pro Football Hall of Fame received and displayed a document—an expense accounting sheet of the Allegheny Athletic Association—that clearly shows a "game performance bonus to W. Heffelfinger for playing (cash) $500." While it is possible that others were paid to play before 1892, the AAA expense account provides the first irrefutable evidence of an out-and-out cash payment. It is appropriately referred to today as "pro football's birth certificate."

Heffelfinger, who had been an all-America guard at Yale

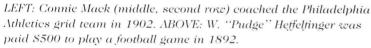

*LEFT: Connie Mack (middle, second row) coached the Philadelphia Athletics grid team in 1902. ABOVE: W. "Pudge" Heffelfinger was paid $500 to play a football game in 1892.*

in 1889, 1890 and 1891, was working as a low-salaried railroad employee in Omaha, Nebraska, when he was granted a leave of absence to play with the Chicago Athletic Association team on a six-game tour of the eastern states. Meanwhile, the PAC, gearing up for its big contest with Allegheny, was seeking a quality player to replace its star back, who was injured. To PAC manager George Barbour, who scouted the Chicago team in a game in Cleveland, Heffelfinger seemed to be the ideal solution but when Barbour offered $250 to play, Heffelfinger turned down the offer because he didn't want to risk his amateur standing.

But a week later, Heffelfinger and two other stars named Ben "Sport" Donnelly and Ed Malley showed up in AAA uniforms as the teams began their warmups. Barbour hastily pulled his PAC players off the field but, after a heated debate, it was agreed that all bets on the game were off and the game would be played simply as an exhibition. Midway through the first half, Heffelfinger forced a fumble, scooped up the ball and ran 25 yards to the end zone. Touchdowns counted four points in those days so the AAA had a 4–0 victory. Despite the comparatively large payment to Heffelfinger, the ledger sheet also showed a $621 profit for the game, thus making pro football's first venture

successful both on the field and at the gate.

Pro football spread rapidly. Donnelly was paid $250 by

## THE FIRST INDOOR GAME

Pro football was played indoors for the first time in 1902 in New York's Madison Square Garden. Seeking a premier attraction to draw crowds over the New Year's holiday, the arena's manager, Tom O'Rourke, hit on the idea of a pro football "world series." He invited teams from Philadelphia, Long Island, Syracuse, N. Y., Orange, N. J., and New York City to participate.

The games were played on a miniature field just 70 yards long and 35 yards wide. The sticky dirt surface that was placed on the arena floor tended to favor the heavier teams and to neutralize the punting game, a major factor in all grid games in the earlier days.

O'Rourke set up a schedule he thought would assure an enthusiastic turnout for a championship game between the New York Knickerbockers and the Orange Athletic Club. However, the Syracuse Athletic Club, which had loaded its roster with stars from several teams, foiled the promoter's master plan. Syracuse edged the favored Knickerbockers, 5–0, and then stunned Orange, 36–0, for the championship.

O'Rourke staged a second indoor tournament in 1903 and then abandoned the idea.

*Jim Thorpe was a crowd-pleasing superstar for the Canton Bulldogs from 1915–20.*

the AAA the very next week. Three players were signed to $50-per-game contracts by the PAC in 1893. Lawson Fiscus, a former Princeton star, openly admitted he had been paid double expense money and $20 a game to play for the Greensburg, Pennsylvania, town team in 1894. In 1895, a young Washington and Jefferson college quarterback, John Brallier, was paid $10 and "cakes" (expenses) to play for the Latrobe, Pennsylvania, town team. For years, Brallier was considered to be the first pro football player but the AAA expense sheet clearly negates this claim.

By the mid-1890s, several western Pennsylvania teams were considered to be out-and-out professional clubs but the pro grid boom didn't last long in the area. The first pro team, the AAA, gave up after the 1897 season. By 1905, most of western Pennsylvania's pro football elevens had disbanded.

By this time, the sport had migrated 100 or so miles west to northeastern Ohio, where it flourished for the first time. The Massillon Tigers became Ohio's first pro team in 1903. Two neighboring teams, the Canton Bulldogs and the Akron Indians, along with several other Ohio clubs, turned pro in 1904. Within a decade, most major Ohio cities could claim a pro football team.

The most heated rivalry, however, pitted Massillon against Canton, located just 7 miles to the east. Today, that

rivalry still exists in the form of one of America's most famous high-school series. Massillon quickly developed into a powerhouse but Canton was determined to make up for its late start by assembling a team that could compete against the Tigers. It was in this intense atmosphere a scandal erupted in 1906 that threatened the very existence of pro football.

A two-game Massillon–Canton series was scheduled to conclude the season. With fanatical determination, the Bulldogs loaded their roster with a host of top stars, including four players from Massillon. Both teams had successful seasons and the year-end showdown was eagerly awaited. Grantland Rice, the premier sports reporter of the time, wrote of the impending battle:

*There have been a few football games before. Yale has faced Princeton. Harvard has tackled Penn, and Michigan and Chicago have met in one or two steamy affairs. But these were not the Real Product when measured by the football standard set by the warring factions of Stark County, Ohio, now posing in the football limelight.*

Canton opened with a 10–5 victory but Massillon retaliated with a 13–6 score. Shortly after the second game, the revelation of a gambling plot stunned the grid world. During the 1906 campaign, Canton players asked their coach, Blondy Wallace, to hold most of their pay in safekeeping lest they lose their money playing poker or on "some other extravagances." Before the first game, they asked Wallace to bet that money on a Canton victory. There was no payoff after the Bulldogs victory, however, because Wallace had not wagered the money, holding it, he claimed, for a bet on the second game. After the second contest, the *Massillon Independent* accused Wallace of trying to rig the outcome of both games. The newspaper produced documented evidence that Wallace and a deposed Tigers player had tried to engineer a deal which called for Canton to win the first game, Massillon the second and a third game to be played "on its own merits."

A Canton player, accused of taking part in the scam, fled town on the first train, still dressed in his playing uniform. Canton fans who had lost heavily on the second game angrily confronted Bulldog players in the Cortland Hotel bar that evening and a full-scale brawl broke out before police arrived. Caught red-handed and disgraced, Canton bowed out of the pro football picture for a half-dozen years.

With Canton on the sidelines and Massillon's program toned down, pro football spread to other areas of Ohio between 1907 and 1911 but the Bulldogs re-emerged in 1912 under a new manager, Jack Cusack, who doubled as a full-time officer of the East Ohio Gas Company. In 1915, Cusack was faced with an ultimatum to give up one job or the other. He chose to continue with football and for the next six years played a most significant role in the sport's development.

Cusack was determined that the mistakes of 1906 must never be repeated but he was also aware of the need for excellent playing talent if the Bulldogs were to be successful at the box office. As the season-ending series with Massillon approached in November, 1915, Cusack made a bold, and at the time controversial, move by signing the fabled American Indian athlete, Jim Thorpe, to a $250-a-game pact to play for Canton.

Fan response was instantaneous. Bulldogs attendance, which had been averaging 1500, ballooned to 8000 for the game in Massillon and 10,000 for the return match in Canton. For the next several seasons, Thorpe performed brilliantly as the Bulldogs became the dominant team of pro football. The fans who watched the magical star in the maroon-and-white jersey were rarely disappointed.

The Bulldogs were undefeated as they embarked on the Massillon series in 1916. The teams fought to a scoreless tie in Massillon but Thorpe led his team to a 24–0 victory in Canton. The Bulldogs claimed the mythical world championship. It was more of the same in 1917. The multitalented Thorpe led the Bulldogs to a 14–3 victory in the first Massillon game and, although the Tigers won the second contest, Canton again claimed the world title.

Because of World War I manpower shortages, pro football was suspended in 1918 but Thorpe and the Bulldogs returned for one last hurrah in 1919. Big Jim led his team in every offensive category as the Bulldogs posted a 9–0–1 record and a third straight unofficial championship. The season marked the end of an age not only for Canton but for pro football as well. The Bulldogs were due for later successes without the talented Indian as their leading light but the ageing Thorpe, with his playing skills steadily waning, was destined for only periodic moments of brilliance with other teams during the rest of his career.

Pro football had existed for 28 years since Pudge Heffelfinger picked up his $500 in that November game in Pittsburgh in 1892. By 1919, the sport had gained a beachhead on the American sports scene but a more organized approach was imperative if pro football were to continue to grow. Before the 1920 season rolled around, pro football would enter a new era.

*Canton claimed world championships in 1916, 1917 and 1919. The Bulldogs regularly played before capacity crowds.*

## THE COLUMBUS PANHANDLES

Several pro football elevens gained prominence in Ohio while the Canton Bulldogs were idle following the gambling scandal of 1906. One was the Columbus Panhandles, who were organized by Joe Carr, a young newspaperman who was destined to become the long-term president of the NFL.

The team, made up of employees of the Panhandle division of the Pennsylvania Railroad, was never outstanding on the field but existed for 20 years because it kept operating costs to a minimum. Players could ride free on the railroad and the Panhandles avoided stadium rental fees by scheduling most of their games out of town.

Whatever success or fame the Panhandles did realize was made possible by the Nessers, an immigrant family from Germany, who provided six talented sons for the team. John, Phil, Ted, Fred, Frank and Alfred all were long-time members and a seventh brother, Charles, also played for a game or two in 1921.

Panhandle lore also records that Mother Nesser kept busy patching team uniforms while Papa Nesser served as the team's water boy. Ironically, the biggest Nesser of them all, 350-lb Pete, was the only non-football-playing member of the family.

# THE NFL'S GROWING PAINS, 1920–32

In spite of its relative success in the Akron-Canton-Massillon triangle of northeastern Ohio, pro football was in a disastrous state of disorganization and confusion as the 1920s approached.

Salaries were soaring out of control. Most players were getting $50 to $75 a game, some stars more than $100 each week and a superstar like Jim Thorpe $250 each time he put on a uniform. A salary cap was impossible because players jumped from team to team, following the highest bidder, on almost a week-to-week basis. The Columbus Panhandles alleged they faced Knute Rockne, the famous Notre Dame coach who was also a star end, on at least six different teams one season. Most business arrangements were slipshod and there were no rules to govern how teams operated against one another.

Another problem involved the use of college students who were still enrolled in school. These players would perform in college games on Saturdays and then with the pros, under assumed names, on Sundays. For a sport fighting to gain acceptance with the public, this practice produced a negative image.

At a meeting in Canton on September 17, 1920, the American Professional Football Association (APFA) was formally organized. Two years later, the APFA changed its name to the National Football League (NFL). The meeting was held in the Hupmobile agency of Ray Hay, the Canton Bulldogs' business manager. Because there were not enough chairs to go around, some delegates had to sit on the show cars' running boards.

Charter memberships were extended to 10 teams from four states—the Canton Bulldogs, Akron Pros, Cleveland Indians and Dayton Triangles from Ohio, the Hammond Pros and Muncie Flyers from Indiana, the Racine (Chicago) Cardinals, Decatur Staleys and Rock Island Independents from Illinois and the Rochester, New York, Jeffersons. To create an aura of respectability, a membership fee of $100 was established but no charter member paid it. With the hope that his magic name would attract attention, Thorpe was elected the league's president.

Organizing a league did not, in itself, eliminate the confusion surrounding pro football. In some ways, it only

increased the chaos. Each club was allowed to draw up its own schedule and there was no set number of games each team needed to play. APFA teams scheduled independent clubs as well as fellow league members and even tried to count the non-league games in the standings. Four more teams joined the league during the 1920 season, which ended with Akron, Canton and the Buffalo All-Americans all claiming the championship.

While Canton, with a 7–4–2 record, had no legitimate claim to the title, Akron (8–0–3) and Buffalo (10–1–2) did. Akron won a four-team playoff series which had an interesting by-product. One of the additional games pitted Canton against Buffalo and attracted 15,000—a remarkable crowd for those times—in the New York Polo Grounds. The next day, Akron and Buffalo played to a scoreless tie, which effectively ended the All-Americans' title hopes. The game also generated the first player trade in APFA history when Akron sold tackle Bob ''Nasty'' Nash to Buffalo for $500 and 5 percent of the gate receipts.

In the spring of 1921, Joe Carr, the Columbus Panhandles' owner, was elected the APFA president to replace Thorpe, who had been only a figurehead in the

*Quarterback Jim McMahon led the Chicago Bears to a Super Bowl XX win, a magic moment in the NFL Charter Member's long history.*

## THE OORANG INDIANS

Perhaps the most unique chapter in NFL history unfolded in 1922 and 1923, when the Oorang Indians football team was organized by Walter Lingo, the owner and operator of the Oorang Kennels in the small town of LaRue in central Ohio. Lingo bought the franchise for the sole purpose of publicizing and selling a special breed of hunting dog known as the Airedale, so named because it was first produced by people living along the dale or valley of the River Aire in Yorkshire, England.

Besides his dogs, Lingo had another great interest—the American Indian. He commissioned the fabled Jim Thorpe to line up a team made up entirely of full- or part-blooded Indians. The Oorang roster included such names as Big Bear, Joe Little Twig, David Running Deer, Red Fang, Xavier Downwind, Dick Deer Slayer, Eagle Feather, Long-Time Sleep, Ted Lone Wolf and War Eagle.

The Oorang Indians were primarily a road team and, at first, proved to be an excellent gate attraction. Halftime entertainment when Oorang played consisted of Indian and dog shows. The team did include two future Pro Football Hall of Famers, Thorpe and Joe Guyon, but it won only three games in two years and disbanded after the 1923 season.

From a playing standpoint, Oorang's two-season highlights were limited to a 75-yard punt by Thorpe and a 96-yard interception return by Guyon plus a history-making play by opponent George Halas of the Chicago Bears. Halas's 98-yard return of a Thorpe fumble stood as an NFL record for 49 years.

inaugural season. The first item on Carr's agenda was to confirm Akron as the 1920 champions. The second was to try to get the APFA house in order.

Under Carr's stern but sure hand, the association slowly gained respectability. The new president, who had wide experience as a minor-league baseball executive, freely borrowed from baseball in drafting an APFA constitution and by-laws. He gave teams territorial rights within the league and restricted player movements. He issued weekly standings so that there would be no question who was the champion. He opened a permanent office in Columbus, Ohio, from where he exerted strong but fair leadership for nearly two decades until his death in 1939.

The league expanded to 21 teams in 1921 and, during its first decade, no fewer than 36 cities were on the membership roster at one time or another. Most of the franchises were based in cities with such small populations they could not support major-league sports teams. When the 1930 season opened, just 10 of the 36 teams were still in

*Red Grange (left) meets with his agent, C. C. "Cash and Carry" Pyle, who skillfully showcased his superstar to the masses.*

business. Today, only four franchises with roots from the 1920s remain—the Green Bay Packers, the New York Giants, the Chicago Bears and the Cardinals, who played in Chicago from 1920 until 1959 and in St Louis from 1960 until 1987. The team was transferred to Phoenix in 1988.

Four cities no longer represented in the NFL had championship teams in the 1920s. Besides Akron in 1920, the Canton Bulldogs were two-time winners in 1922 and 1923. The Frankford Yellowjackets followed in 1926 and the Providence Steam Roller in 1928. Akron and Canton dropped out of the NFL after the 1926 season. Frankford and Providence both quit after the 1931 campaign.

One survivor from the 1920s, the Green Bay Packers, exists today as a sort of sports "dinosaur." The only small-city franchise in major professional athletics, the Packers not only survived but became the sole NFL team ever to win three straight championships. They did it twice, in 1929–31 and in 1965–7.

While Carr's organizational skills produced significant improvements in the league's operations, the NFL still desperately needed a publicity outlet to bring massive attention to the brand of football played in the pros.

The year 1925 proved to be a turning point in the league's fortunes. Two events, the establishment of a franchise in New York City and the signing of Harold "Red" Grange to a Bears' contract, gave pro football the impetus it required.

First came Tim Mara's purchase of an NFL franchise for $500. His team, the New York Giants, provided the league a berth in the nation's largest city and, with it, the national publicity it had craved so long. The signing of Grange, the whirling-dervish runner from the University of Illinois and

the most famous athlete of his time, ensured the sport an unmatched drawing card.

Mara wisely turned to experienced football men who lined up an excellent team. The Giants finished with a fine 8–4 record but they couldn't lure fans away from big-time college football powers such as Yale, Harvard, Princeton and Columbia. Mara's losses steadily mounted.

Still determined and convinced the Giants needed a superstar to attract New York City fans, he set out to sign Grange, only to learn he was too late. Negotiations with Grange and his agent, C. C. "Cash and Carry" Pyle, had provided George Halas of the Chicago Bears with the biggest coup in NFL history to that time. Ten days after his final college game, "The Galloping Ghost" donned a Bears' uniform for a Thanksgiving Day battle with the cross-town rival Cardinals. Showing his respect for the young super-star, Cardinals ace Paddy Driscoll continually punted away from Grange. To the dismay of the fans, the game ended in a scoreless tie.

Halas, Pyle and Grange immediately took the show on the road. The Bears played 18 games on a coast-to-coast barnstorming tour that lasted until January 31 and attracted hundreds of thousands of first-time pro football fans. When Grange and the Bears reached New York, a stunning 73,000 turned out at the Polo Grounds. In one day, Mara recouped all his losses. From that point on, the future of pro football was assured in New York.

After the tour, the hard-dealing Pyle notified Halas he would allow Grange to play with the Bears in 1926 only if the player received a five-figure salary and one-third ownership of the team. When Halas said no, Pyle petitioned the NFL for a second team in New York. Mara rejected this idea and Carr steadfastly reaffirmed territorial rights rules protecting NFL members.

So Pyle and Grange formed a rival league, to be known as the American Football League (AFL). Grange was assigned to play with the AFL's flagship club, the New York Yankees. Seven other new teams were formed and the Rock Island Independents, an NFL charter member, defected to join the AFL. Before the season even began, salaries skyrocketed. Mara paid each Giant $50 more per game and Chicago Cardinals' owner Chris O'Brien experienced se-vere financial problems competing with the rival Chicago Bulls. Pyle hired a politician and former Princeton athlete, Bill Edwards, as commissioner and set his salary at $25,000. Carr, as NFL president, was paid only $2500 annually.

Grange and the Yankees drew well in New York but attendance was disastrously weak everywhere else. Cleve-land and Newark folded in October and Brooklyn, Boston and Rock Island succumbed in mid-November. By season's end, only four teams remained. Pyle obviously had been badly beaten.

Mara, wanting one more crack at his antagonists, agreed to a post-season showdown with the AFL champions, the Philadelphia Quakers. The Giants won, 31–0, but the AFL had accomplished what no other NFL challenger could achieve for 40 years, an inter-league playoff.

As a peace concession, the Yankees were granted an NFL franchise for 1927 but no other AFL team survived. The NFL, whose membership numbered 22 in 1926, reduced its ranks to just 12 teams. The 1927 Giants allowed only 20 points in 13 games, the finest defensive performance in history, while winning the NFL championship with an 11–1–1 record.

The NFL's first dynasty developed when the Green Bay Packers swept to championships in 1929, 1930 and 1931. Boasting such future Hall of Famers as Cal Hubbard, Mike Michalske, Johnny "Blood" McNally, Clarke Hinkle and Arnie Herber, along with their coach, Curly Lambeau, the Packers enjoyed a 34–5–2 record during their three-year romp. They almost won a fourth straight title in 1932, finishing with a 10–3–1 mark and a .769 percentage. Had tie games counted one-half win and one-half loss as they do today, the Packers would have been champions again. As it was, both the Chicago Bears with a 6–1–6 record and the Portsmouth Spartans with a 6–1–4 ledger had identical .857 percentages.

The Bears and Spartans decided to play an extra game for the championship but, when the weather turned bitter cold in midweek, the teams agreed to move the game indoors to Chicago Stadium, a hockey arena that had recently hosted a circus. Because of the close confines of the indoor arena, several special ground rules had to be devised. The field was only 80 yards long and 145 feet wide (standard width is 160 feet) and the sidelines edged close to the stands. Rather than shifting the scrimmage line to simulate a 100-yard field, it was agreed to settle for the 80-yard distance. To reduce the danger of players crashing into the stands, the ball was to be moved inbounds 10 yards after out-of-bounds plays. It was also decided to move the goal posts to the goal line from the back of the end zone.

A crowd of 11,198 turned out to see pro play close at hand for the first time. The fans learned that, contrary to some contentions, the pros did play for keeps. "It was the difference between sitting ringside at a heavyweight fight or

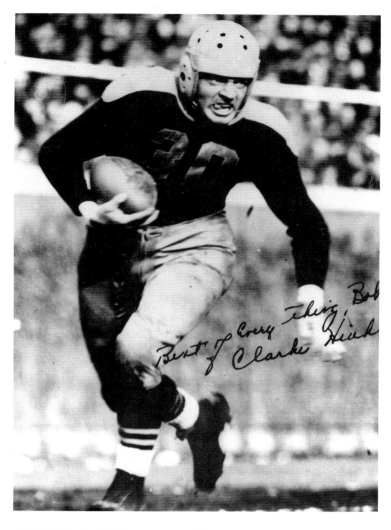

*ABOVE: Clarke Hinkle was one of the finest all-around players in the storied history of the Green Bay Packers. BELOW: The Redskins and Giants have battled annually since 1932.*

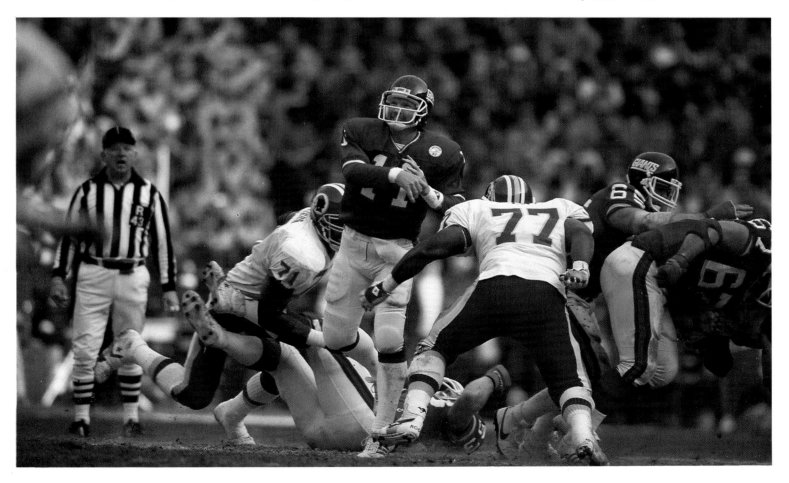

## THE DULUTH ESKIMOS

The NFL desperately needed a new superstar for the 1926 season to replace Red Grange, who had defected to the new American Football League (AFL). Help came from an unusual source, 23-year-old Oluf "Ole" Haugsrud, the co-owner of the financially struggling Duluth Eskimos franchise.

Haugsrud, who earlier had joined with partner Dewey Scanlon to purchase the Eskimos for $1, was a long-time friend of Ernie Nevers, a native Minnesotan. Next to Grange, Nevers had been the nation's finest college star during his all-America season at Stanford in 1925. Ernie agreed to play with Duluth if Haugsrud would match the AFL offer, $15,000 and a 25 percent share of the gate. Urged by other NFL owners, Haugsrud agreed.

To make ends meet, the Eskimos became a road team, playing 28 games during an 111-day trip after an opening contest in Duluth. Nevers more than lived up to his star billing, as the Eskimos, with a meager 13-man squad, compiled a 19–7–3 record. Other Duluth players agreed on a salary scale of $75 for a win, $60 for a tie and $50 for a loss. There were times the club fell behind in its salary payments but eventually all players received their full pay. The Eskimos ended up with a $4000 profit and the knowledge they had played a major role in history's first inter-league war.

Portsmouth 7-yard line. Chicago's battering-ram fullback, Bronko Nagurski, blasted to the 1 on first down and then was stopped cold the next two plays. On fourth down, Nagurski faked a plunge, stopped, moved back a step or two and lobbed a pass to Grange for the game's only touchdown. The Bears won, 9–0.

Rules of the time dictated a forward pass must be thrown at least 5 yards behind the scrimmage line. The Spartans protested, but without success, that Nagurski was not back the required 5 yards when he lobbed the ball to Grange.

The special rules of the game prodded George Preston Marshall of the Boston Braves and Halas, chairman of the NFL rules committee, into fresh new thinking about pro football as a spectator sport. They proposed three new rule changes: (1) to move the goal posts permanently to the goal line; (2) to always place the ball no less than 15 yards inbounds at the start of every scrimmage play; and (3) to make a forward pass legal anywhere behind the scrimmage line. All three rules were adopted.

Marshall, sensing the box-office appeal of matching two top teams in a championship showdown, also championed the idea of splitting the NFL into two divisions, with the winners meeting each year for the league title.

Thus, the NFL entered its fourteenth season in 1933 bolstered by four new landmark guidelines that were destined to make pro football a more exciting game. Particularly remarkable is the fact that all four changes emanated from just one game, the unique contest that would never have been played indoors had the weather in Chicago been a few degrees warmer that December week in 1932.

*The Chicago Bears and Portsmouth Spartans played the 1932 NFL title game indoors on the 80-yard-long field of Chicago Stadium.*

in the last row of the upper deck," one sportswriter noted. "All the awful sounds of human beings smashing other human beings was right there and very real."

Late in the game, the Bears had a first down at the

# THE MATURING YEARS, 1933–45

The three significant rule changes enacted after the 1932 season marked the first time the NFL had departed from college regulations, which had been used in pro football ever since 1892. They were adopted with the specific intention of making the sport more appealing to the fans. While the new rules eventually did do much to liven up the game, the results were not as immediately apparent as was the fourth innovation—the two-division setup with an annual championship showdown—emanating from the 1932 indoor championship game.

The Chicago Bears, with a 10–2–1 record, and the New York Giants at 11–3–0 were easy winners in their respective divisions and the two teams fought a classic duel in the NFL's inaugural championship game. Both coaches, George Halas of Chicago and Steve Owen of New York, opened up with every offensive weapon right from the start. Each team threw two touchdown passes and the lead changed hands six times. Basically an offensive show, the contest was decided by a game-saving defensive play by the famed Bears running back, Red Grange.

Owen opened his bag of tricks early. On one play, the Giants set up with an unbalanced line with five men to the right of center Mel Hein and only the end to his left. Just before the snap, the end took a step back, thus making Hein an eligible receiver. The quarterback, Harry Newman, handed the ball back to Hein and then faded back and fell. Hein started strolling down field but began running too

## THE DEMISE OF THE DROPKICK

In 1934, NFL rule-makers took a full inch off the girth of the football, thus making it easier to pass. The use of a tee for placekicks also was legalized. Although that was not the intention, the two rule alterations also sounded the death knell for the dropkick, which up to that time had been an alternate method to the placekick for scoring field goals and extra points. With the new rules, placekicking became much more accurate—and faster—than the delicate dropkick, which required that the kicker's foot make contact with the football at the precise moment it touched the ground.

Dutch Clark, the Detroit Lions triple-threat tailback, was the last great dropkicker in the NFL. His last active season was in 1938. The final dropkick in pro football action came in the 1941 championship game. With the Chicago Bears on their way to a 37–9 win over the New York Giants, the Bears' Ray McLean, for a lark, dropkicked the extra point after the game's last touchdown.

soon, thus tipping off the Bears. He gained 30 yards but did not score the touchdown Owen had planned.

Borrowing a tactic from the 1932 indoor game, Bronko Nagurski lobbed two touchdown passes. The second one erased a 21–16 New York lead and put the Bears ahead to stay. Nagurski passed to end Bill Hewitt, who lateralled to the other end, Bill Karr, who streaked 14 yards to score.

The Bears' 23–21 nail-biting victory was exactly the kind

*Detroit's Glenn Presnell finds a big hole in the New York Giants line during the Lions' 26–7 win for the 1935 NFL crown. It was Detroit's only title-game appearance until 1952.*

### RADIO AND TELEVISION COVERAGE

The NFL was introduced to national coverage by the electronic media very early in its history.

The first national radio broadcast was the Columbia Broadcasting System's coverage of the 1934 Thanksgiving Day clash which saw the Chicago Bears defeat the host Detroit Lions, 19–16. The famed Graham McNamee called the play-by-play.

Six years later in 1940, an NFL championship game was broadcast nationally for the first time. Red Barber described the Bears' 73–0 victory over the Washington Redskins to 120 stations of the Mutual Broadcasting System, which paid $2500 for the rights to the game.

A year earlier on October 22, 1939, the NFL had a preliminary taste of television coverage. The Brooklyn Dodgers–Philadelphia Eagles game in Ebbets Field was locally televised by the National Broadcasting Company. At the time, there were approximately 1000 television sets in New York.

of dramatic championship finale the master innovator, George Preston Marshall, had envisioned. The rematch between the Bears and Giants in 1934 was just as dramatic.

The Bears had marched through the NFL West with a perfect 13–0–0 record. A big new star for the Bears was Beattie Feathers, a fleet-footed halfback who became pro football's first 1000-yard rusher with 1004 yards in just 101 carries. No other pro back reached this plateau until Steve Van Buren did it for the Philadelphia Eagles in 1947.

In the title game, Chicago was heavily favored over the Giants, who had struggled to win their division. At game time in New York's Polo Grounds, the temperature hovered near zero and a brisk wind had turned the field into a sheet of ice. Feathers and Grange were out of the game with injuries but the Giants also were missing several stars. With Nagurski powering the attack, the Bears held a seemingly secure 10–3 halftime lead.

But in the locker room before the game, the Giants captain, Ray Flaherty, recalled a college game at Gonzaga in Spokane, Washington, when his team used sneakers on an icy field with good results. Owen found a die-hard fan named Abe Cohen, who was dispatched to Manhattan College, where he supervised the athletic storeroom. Cohen was soon back at the Polo Grounds with 19 pairs of sneakers. Owen ordered every player who could find a pair that fit to wear them in the second half. Nine Giants did.

It took a while for the New Yorkers to adjust to the new equipment but when they did, they erupted with a 27-point, fourth-quarter explosion to beat the Bears, 30–13.

The Bears' perfect season had been ruined but, just as was the case in the 1933 finale, pro football once again had been the big winner. The NFL's championship series opened with two games which matched arch-rivals. Each was a classic struggle; each is still remembered today as a highlight of pro football history.

In 1935, the Detroit Lions whizzed past the Giants, 26–7, in a game that was significant simply because the Lions played in it. In the first 12 years of the NFL title series, the Lions' 1935 appearance was the only break in a monopoly that found the Bears or the Green Bay Packers the Western

Division winners and the Giants or the Boston/Washington Redskins the Eastern champions.

At first, it was just the Bears and Giants who reigned as dominant teams and other NFL owners, particularly Bert Bell of the Philadelphia Eagles, were concerned the lack of competitive balance throughout the ranks could eventually damage the league. So Bell proposed that, starting in 1936, the NFL teams stage a draft of college seniors, held in an order that was the inverse of the teams' finish of the previous season. Ironically, the Eagles' 2–9 record was the worst in the NFL in 1935 so the man who proposed the draft, Bell, made the first choice in the first draft. He chose Jay Berwanger, an all-America halfback from the University of Chicago. The Eagles then traded the negotiation rights to the Bears in exchange for tackle Art Buss. Berwanger decided against playing pro football and the Bears were a draft pick down. They chose two Hall of Famers in that first draft, Joe Stydahar and Dan Fortmann.

With the championship series an instant hit and the 1932 rule-change revolution beginning to take effect with steady if not spectacular offensive growth, NFL optimists were beginning to see the light at the end of the tunnel. Tie games, which had come in significant numbers, were no longer a concern and shutouts were steadily diminishing. Still, pro football had not become the game-after-game offensive show the owners had anticipated at the time they altered the game's ground rules.

Just two players, end Don Hutson of the Green Bay Packers and Washington Redskins quarterback Sammy Baugh, were to give the owners everything they dreamed of

*Don Hutson joined the Green Bay Packers in 1935 and immediately became the most sensational receiver in pro football. In 11 NFL seasons, he amassed 488 pass receptions.*

and much more. Hutson as a pass-catcher and Baugh as a pass-thrower joined the NFL with such rare specialized skills that, on the strength of their performances alone, pro football became transformed into a crowd-pleasing offensive spectacle. Before Hutson and Baugh came on the scene, the forward pass was used only sparingly in the NFL. By the time their playing days were over, the pass was an integral part of every pro football game plan.

Hutson was first on hand. He joined the Packers in 1935 and played for 11 seasons. Blessed with superior speed and

*Sammy Baugh fires one of the 2,995 passes he threw during his 16 seasons with the Washington Redskins.*

exceptional faking ability, he caught passes in numbers never previously thought possible. He forced an entire league to change its defensive thinking just to stop him. When he retired after the 1945 campaign, he had 488 receptions. The second-place career receiver at the time, Jim Benton of the Cleveland Rams, had just 190 catches.

While fine passers in Green Bay helped Hutson to display

*Halfback George McAfee bursts over the Redskins line during the Bears' 73–0 victory in the 1940 NFL title game.*

his exceptional receiving abilities, it took a special talent like Baugh to make a lasting imprint on an entire sport. The Redskins had just moved from Boston to Washington when Baugh joined the team in 1937 as the most ballyhooed rookie ever to enter the NFL up to that time. From the very start, he began setting standards for forward passing to which all other passers have since been compared. In his 16 seasons, Baugh won six NFL individual passing crowns. Until relaxed substitution rules were adopted, both Hutson and Baugh were also excellent defensive players and Baugh was perhaps the finest punter in history. The fact they could not concentrate on their offensive specialties alone tends to make their place in history even more remarkable.

Several years before Hutson and Baugh emerged as superstars, Halas had turned over the Bears' coaching reins to Ralph Jones, who introduced such innovations as the man-in-motion, widening the spacing in the backfield and splitting the ends. Severe financial problems forced Halas to replace Jones with himself for the 1933 season because, as he put it, "I came cheap. I would coach for nothing."

But Halas had not forgotten what Jones had done and, by 1938, the Bears' mentor was slowly but surely beginning to acquire the players he felt could contribute to a T-formation juggernaut. His key acquisition was a Columbia tailback named Sid Luckman. Although Luckman had no experience at all with the T, Halas was convinced he would be the perfect passer for his new offense. Luckman developed slowly in 1939 and early in 1940 but by season's end, he was firmly entrenched as the Bears' quarterback.

The Bears just slipped by the Packers to win the NFL West in 1940. Three weeks before the end of the regular season, they suffered a particularly tough and controversial 7–3 loss to Washington. The Redskins and particularly the team owner, Marshall, had called the Bears "crybabies" because they had complained about a couple of close calls at the end of the game. Thus the stage was set for one of the most significant games in history, the NFL title showdown with the same Redskins. The fired-up Bears executed the T-formation to perfection, scored on a 68-yard run the second play of the game, completely shut down the Baugh-led offense and wound up with a 73–0 victory, the most lopsided score in history. Even though this was a showcase game for Luckman as the leader of the T, he threw only six passes, completing four for 102 yards and one touchdown.

Almost immediately, several NFL teams began convert-ing to the T-formation. Some teams held out for a few years—the Redskins stuck with their double-wing attack until 1944, the Detroit Lions kept their short-punt alignment until after World War II, the Giants stayed with the A-formation until 1953 and the Pittsburgh Steelers remained a single-wing team until the 1950s. But, as Halas said, "The game marked the turning point in pro football. The widespread use of all of today's offensive concepts evolved from this game."

Not all teams were as successful as the Bears with the T. This basically was because Halas was loaded with exceptional talent, possibly the best collection of all time had not World War II intervened. In spite of wartime manpower shortages, the NFL kept on playing for the duration, making do in whatever way it could. The Bears, for instance, called Bronko Nagurski back for the 1943 season after he had been in retirement six years. The Cleveland Rams suspended play in the 1943 season and the Eagles and Steelers joined to form the Phil-Pitt team that year. In 1944, the Rams and Eagles were back in action but the Cardinals and Steelers merged for a season.

The German armies surrendered in May, 1945, and the Japanese succumbed three months later. A total of 638 NFL players had served in the war, 69 had been decorated and 19 had died.

Although a few veterans trickled back into the lineup during the 1945 season, the campaign still was staged with depleted rosters. The Cleveland Rams were bolstered by a sensational rookie quarterback, Bob Waterfield, who led them to their first divisional championship.

On a frozen field in the championship game at Cleveland's Memorial Stadium, the Rams edged the Washington Redskins, 15–14. The key play came in the first quarter when Baugh's wind-blown pass from the end zone hit the goal post. It was ruled a safety and was the margin of difference in the game.

NFL rule-makers immediately sensed the unfairness of the situation and quickly altered the rule so that such a pass hitting a goal post would be merely an incomplete pass. The game was the last for the Rams in Cleveland. Not only would they be in a new city for the 1946 season but the NFL as a whole would be facing perilous but exciting new challenges.

# THE RISE TO POPULARITY, 1946–59

As the success of the Allied cause in World War II became increasingly assured, NFL owners looked ahead to the post-war years with a great deal of optimism. Attendance had steadily advanced from an 8211 average in 1934 to 25,408 each game in 1945. With a vast stockpile of player talent coming out of the armed forces, there was every reason to expect a greatly improved caliber of on-the-field action and increased business at the turnstiles.

To a degree, this did happen when NFL attendance zoomed more than 20 percent to 31,493 per game in 1946. The Giants and Bears each made their eighth appearance in 14 years in the championship game, including four games against each other, but other teams were on the verge of breaking the Chicago–New York monopoly in post-season play.

But there was a storm cloud on the horizon that would soon burst over the NFL. On June 4, 1944—just two days before D-Day—representatives from six cities met secretly in a St Louis hotel room to form the All-America Football Conference (AAFC). Charter members included Buffalo, Chicago, Cleveland, Los Angeles, New York and San Fran-cisco. Before the league began play in 1946, Miami and Brooklyn were added to the roster.

The founder of the new league was the noted *Chicago Tribune* sports editor, Arch Ward, who had a decade earlier launched the College All-Star game series. Ward had turned down the NFL commissioner's job in 1940 but he was still dedicated to the growth of football. He decided on the second league plan only after it became apparent the NFL had no intention of expanding.

When he learned of the AAFC's plans, NFL commissioner Elmer Layden issued the following statement: "Over the years, there has always been talk about new professional leagues sprouting up. As far as I am concerned, the All-America Football Conference should first get a ball, then make a schedule and then play a game." Reporters conveniently shortened Layden's statement to "Tell them to get a football first." It was a remark that haunted him for the remainder of his term as commissioner.

The AAFC was the fourth rival league to challenge the NFL in just over 25 years of operation. The first three competing leagues bore the name American Football League and all three, the first in 1926, the second in 1936–7 and the third in 1940–1, quickly succumbed. Such was not to be the case with the AAFC. It did eventually pass out of existence but only after a bitter and costly four-year struggle.

From first game to last, the AAFC produced quality

*Kenny Washington carries for the Los Angeles Rams in 1946 action against Green Bay. In March, 1946, he became the first black in 13 years to sign an NFL team contract.*

football made possible by a host of outstanding players, including more than 100 former NFL stars lured away by fatter contracts. The AAFC signed 40 of the 66 members of the 1946 College All-Star team. NFL teams were forced to raise their salary structure or fall behind. The AAFC pioneered many pro football innovations, including the use of air travel to far-away games. Boldly moving into big stadiums, the AAFC outdrew the NFL in average game attendance, 28,319 to 27,602, during its four seasons.

While the AAFC became the first to establish permanent major-league sports franchises on the West Coast, the NFL was not far behind. Just 12 days into 1946, Rams owner Dan Reeves, totally disenchanted with the fan support in Cleveland, announced he was moving the Rams to Los Angeles. NFL owners were at first opposed to the change but finally agreed when Reeves threatened to withdraw from the league. For the first time, the NFL was truly national in its geographical scope.

To fight the AAFC, the NFL owners tapped Bert Bell, the founder of the Philadelphia Eagles and, since 1940, a co-owner of the Pittsburgh Steelers, to replace Elmer Layden as NFL commissioner. They were looking for a strong leader and Bell proved to be that and much more. In his first season, he was faced with a potential gambling scandal just before the NFL championship game. When he learned two

Giants, Frank Filchock and Merle Hapes, had been offered bribes to fix the game, Bell swung into action. Although the players did not accept the bribe, they failed to report the offer to their coach, Steve Owen. Bell promptly suspended Hapes but allowed Filchock to play. Later, with additional evidence, he also suspended Filchock. All actions were announced immediately and the owners realized they not only had their strong leader but a powerful public relations force as well.

The 1946 championship game marked the last time either the Giants or Bears would appear in the season's finale until 1956, when they met each other for a fifth time. In 1947, the Chicago Cardinals, paced by the famous "Dream Backfield" of Charley Trippi, Elmer Angsman, Paul Christman and Pat Harder, won their first championship since 1925. The next two seasons, the Philadelphia Eagles, with hard-running Steve Van Buren leading the way, were in the throne room. Playing in the snow in the 1948 title game, they whitewashed the Cardinals, 7–0. The next year in the rain in Los Angeles, the Rams were 14–0 victims.

By this time, the AAFC was faced with a unique problem—one of its teams, the Cleveland Browns, simply was too good for the rest of the league. The Browns won all four AAFC championships and amassed a stunning 52–4–3 won–lost record. Fans throughout the league, including

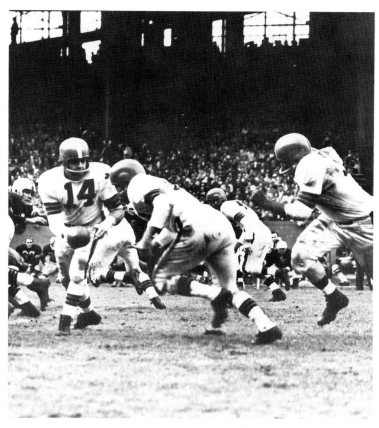

*BELOW LEFT: Steve Van Buren plunges for the only score in the Eagles' 7–0 win over the Cardinals in the 1948 NFL title game. ABOVE: Field general Otto Graham (#14) led the Cleveland Browns to 10 division or league championships in 10 years.*

Cleveland, were simply losing interest. Clearly it was time to end the senseless and costly struggle.

Bell set the terms of the AAFC's surrender. The Browns, the San Francisco 49ers and the Baltimore Colts would be admitted into the NFL and the players from other AAFC squads would be divided by a series of methods among the established NFL teams. But despite its dissolution the AAFC had made a lasting mark in pro football—it had indeed "gotten a football."

Although the Browns had overwhelmed all AAFC foes for four years, most NFL die-hards were convinced they would get their come-uppance once they met a "real" pro football team. Commissioner Bell scheduled the long-awaited confrontation between the Browns and the NFL's best, the 1949 champion Eagles, for the opening game of the 1950 season at Philadelphia's Municipal Stadium. It seemed a perfect matchup. In the last three years when the Eagles won divisional or league titles, their cumulative record was 28–7–1, certainly comparable to Cleveland's 35–2–3 mark the same three years.

A crowd of 71,237—larger than any previous championship game turnout—was on hand. Philadelphia, a six-point favorite, scored first on a field goal but Otto Graham, the Browns' quarterback, countered with three touchdown passes before switching to a grinding ground game in the second half on the way to a rather easy 35–10 victory. "This is as good a team as I have ever seen," Bell exclaimed as he congratulated Paul Brown, the Cleveland coach.

The Browns went on to win their division championship the first six years they were in the NFL. They concluded the 1950 campaign with a 30–28 victory in an epic championship game struggle with the Los Angeles Rams. They also won league titles in 1954 and 1955.

Other teams, however, were capable of challenging the Browns during the early 1950s. One was the Rams, who capped a sensational 1951 season with a clinching touchdown pass from Norm Van Brocklin to Tom Fears in a 24–17 championship win over the Browns. The Detroit Lions, paced by Bobby Layne and Doak Walker, were next in line. They beat Cleveland, 17–7 in 1952 and 17–16 in 1953. The Browns ended their decade of excellence with two solid championship victories, 56–10 over Detroit in 1954 and 38–14 over the Los Angeles Rams in 1955. Graham, who had guided the Browns to 10 divisional or league crowns in 10 seasons, retired after the game. While the Browns remained competitive for many years, they never again were as dominant a team.

The 1950s marked the start of the NFL's first serious involvement with television. In 1950, the Rams became the first NFL team to televise all of its games, both home and away. The sponsor agreed to make up the difference in home-game income if it was lower than it had been the season before. Attendance did fall and the sponsor paid $307,000 to the Rams. The next year, owner Dan Reeves changed the Rams policy so that only road games were televised. Home attendance increased sharply and new fans were made every week through TV exposure.

In 1951, the NFL began to approach television policy as a league-wide matter and Bell once again showed he was firmly in control. He contracted for the NFL title game between the Rams and the Browns to be televised coast-to-coast by the DuMont Network, which paid $75,000 for the rights for the game. In 1955, the National Broadcasting Company (NBC) upped the ante to $100,000 to become

## BLACKS IN PRO FOOTBALL

Black players are prevalent on the roster of every pro football team today but it hasn't always been that way. There was a 13-season span from 1933 to 1945 when there were no blacks playing pro football.

Charles Follis became the first black to play in the pros when he signed a contract with the Shelby, Ohio, Blues on September 25, 1904. Three other blacks played on pre-NFL pro teams and 13 more saw service in the NFL from 1920 to 1933. Two of them, halfback-coach Fritz Pollard of the Akron Pros and tackle Duke Slater of the Chicago Cardinals, proved to be on a par, talent-wise, with all other NFL stars of the 1920s. In 1933, Joe Lillard, a runner from Oregon State, played with the Cardinals while Raymond Kemp, a tackle from Duquesne, performed with the Steelers. Both were blacks.

Then, whether by design or by chance, there were no more black men in the NFL until March 21, 1946, when Los Angeles Rams owner Dan Reeves broke whatever ban might have existed by signing ex-UCLA running back Kenny Washington. A few days later, he also added Woody Strode, a former UCLA end, to the Rams roster. Before the season began, the Cleveland Browns of the new All-America Football Conference added two blacks to their roster. Guard Bill Willis was the first acquisition and fullback Marion Motley the second. They proved to be excellent finds for the Browns. Both are now members of the Pro Football Hall of Fame.

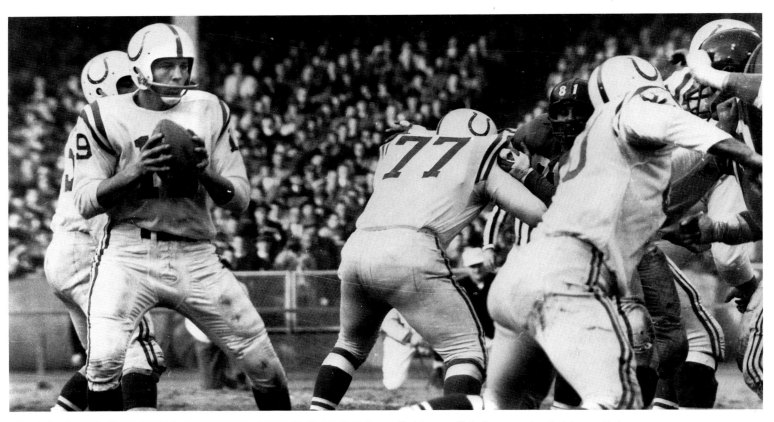

*Baltimore Colts' quarterback Johnny Unitas sets up to pass against the New York Giants in the 1958 NFL championship game.*

### CLEVELAND STADIUM

Cleveland Municipal Stadium, the site of the 1945 NFL championship game between the Cleveland Rams and Washington Redskins, exists today as the longest-lived stadium in continuous use by a pro football team. The Rams moved to Los Angeles after the 1945 title game but the Browns of the new All-America Football Conference became the tenants the next season. The Browns have been in the NFL since 1950 and still play in the 80,098-seat Municipal Stadium.

The massive stadium was first used by the Rams for four seasons starting in 1939. After they suspended play in 1943, they returned in 1944 to call League Park their home. In 1945, only the championship game was played in Municipal Stadium.

The most recent addition to the NFL stadium family is sparkling-new Joe Robbie Stadium, home of the Miami Dolphins. The 75,500-seat stadium, financed entirely by Robbie, the Dolphins' president, was opened in 1987.

the television network for the championship game.

Bell insisted that home games be blacked out and he resisted altering that policy, regardless of pressure. "I refuse to lift the blackout," he said. "It would be an act of bad faith to those who have bought tickets." Bell's policies were challenged in court but he held fast and won.

At the start of the 1950s, the NFL opened the way for modern-day, two-platoon football with the adoption of a free substitution rule. The wide-open action featuring specialists in all phases of the game did much to bring pro football into the public eye. NFL attendance, which averaged 25,356 per game in 1950, had ballooned to 43,617 in 1959. In the 1950 championship showdown, the winning Browns received $1113 each and the losing Rams $686. Nine years later, the champion Colts received $4674

in playoff money and the runnerup Giants $3083. All of this was indicative of the NFL's growing popularity.

One game more than any other, the 1958 championship game between the Baltimore Colts and the New York Giants, raised pro football interest to boiling point. The Colts, who were established just five seasons earlier, and their talented young quarterback, Johnny Unitas, had captured the fancy of the masses. The Giants, on the other hand, were an established NFL power with a host of long-term rooters. Besides the sellout crowd in Yankee Stadium, the game was watched by a national television audience.

Baltimore jumped to a 14–3 lead but the Giants rallied to go ahead, 17–14, in the fourth quarter. With time running out, Unitas coolly marched the Colts 86 yards with a final pass to Raymond Berry, setting up a game-tying field goal by Steve Myhra with seven seconds to play. In the sudden-death overtime period, the first ever in NFL championship play, Unitas marshaled a 13-play, 80-yard drive, which was concluded by Alan Ameche's 1-yard touchdown plunge. The Colts won, 23–16. The dramatic battle captured the imagination of millions. *Sports Illustrated* writer Tex Maule called it "The Greatest Football Game Ever Played."

The Colts were on their way to a second straight championship in 1959 when, on October 12 at a Steelers–Eagles game in Philadelphia's Franklin Field, Commissioner Bell suffered a heart attack and died. He left behind a legacy of progress and accelerated popularity for the league he served so well.

A successor to the beloved Bell had not been named when the 1950s turned into the 1960s. New challenges, such as the formation of still another American Football League, already were close at hand. All any NFL die-hard could hope was that, whoever the new commissioner might be, he would maintain the groundswell of prosperity pro football was at last beginning to realize.

# THE WAR YEARS, 1960–9

Well before NFL commissioner Bert Bell's death on October 11, 1959, Lamar Hunt, a determined young man with oil millions to support his enthusiasm, announced he was organizing a new football league which would begin play in 1960. Bell, in testimony before a congressional committee probing possible monopolistic practices, had on July 29 testified that the NFL welcomed the formation of the new league. "The more teams and the more competition the better," he said.

Hunt had been rejected in an earlier attempt to purchase the Chicago Cardinals of the NFL and reasoned a new league was a viable alternative. "It seemed to me a natural thing," he said. "There had been an American and a National League in baseball, competing side by side for 60 years."

On August 14, 1959, six cities—Dallas, Denver, Houston, Minneapolis, Los Angeles and New York—became charter members of the new American Football League (AFL). Thus, for a fourth time, a challenger to the NFL adopted this name. Buffalo and Boston joined up a short time later and, on November 22, the new league held its first draft with each team picking 33 prospects. Eight days later, war hero and former South Dakota governor Joe Foss was named commissioner.

Bell's testimony to Congress notwithstanding, the NFL didn't exactly welcome the new intruder league. Suddenly, the older league developed expansion plans. Two weeks after the AFL's organizational meeting, NFL expansion chairman George Halas offered NFL franchises to Hunt and K. S. "Bud" Adams Jr, the owner of the Houston AFL team. Hunt and Adams could have jumped ship and avoided costly competition with the NFL but they both agreed they had made a commitment to the other AFL owners and that they had to live up to their promise. This spirit of concern and sacrifice for the common cause would continue throughout the AFL's history.

On January 26, 1960, the Los Angeles Rams' 33-year-

*The original group of AFL owners who took on the gigantic task of combatting the NFL called themselves "The Foolish Club."*

## SIGNING PLAYERS

Once it became apparent the American Football League (AFL) was going to challenge the older league seriously for player talent, the NFL organized Operation Hand Holding, a large task force of scouts, club officials and special agents. With it, the NFL whisked away a number of prized players and had them signed before AFL scouts could even make initial contact.

But the AFL managed a trick or two of its own. One star, Matt Snell from Ohio State, somehow escaped the NFL dragnet. When New York Jets owner Sonny Werblin invited Snell's parents to a game and then personally served them coffee on a cold day, the parents were deeply impressed. Snell soon signed on the dotted line.

Some joined the AFL for unusual reasons. Pittsburgh linebacker Marty Schottenheimer accepted a deal with Buffalo because it included a rear-window defroster for his new car.

Then there was the case of wide receiver Otis Taylor from Prairie View A&M. The Cowboys invited him to spend Thanksgiving in Dallas but, once there, he found he was a virtual prisoner in his motel room. Kansas City Chiefs scout Lloyd Wells learned of Taylor's whereabouts but was foiled by NFL guards when he tried to enter the hotel. Wells jumped a fence behind the motel to locate Taylor's room, tapped on a window and convinced Otis to leave. He then put him on a flight to Kansas City, where he was signed the next day by the Chiefs.

old general manager, Pete Rozelle, was the surprise choice to replace Bell as the NFL commissioner. The new leader already knew about the AFL first hand. He had signed Louisiana State superstar Billy Cannon to a Rams contract on November 30, 1959 but several weeks later, Cannon signed a second contract with the Houston Oilers of the AFL. The courts awarded Houston the rights to Cannon. Thus, a full-fledged war, to be fought with pens, checkbooks, and a plethora of money and other incentives to hordes of young athletes, was declared.

Just one day after Rozelle's appointment, Minneapolis was lured out of the AFL with the promise of an NFL expansion team in 1961. Another NFL expansion franchise, the Dallas Cowboys, was established to begin head-to-head fighting with Hunt's Dallas Texans in 1960. Although no adequate stadium was available, Oakland filled the AFL void created when Minneapolis defected.

By summer 1960 the AFL had some good news. Commissioner Foss announced a five-year television contract with the American Broadcasting Company (ABC) for $1,785,000 as a starter and with graduated increases each subsequent year. Thus, before its first game, the AFL acquired two weapons never available to other NFL challengers—national exposure and guaranteed income for the financially weak teams to stay in the talent battle.

A year later, Congress legalized single-network television contracts by professional sports leagues, thus paving the way for the NFL to arrange its own league-wide TV deal with the Columbia Broadcasting System (CBS) to televise all regular-season games for $4,650,000 annually. Another contract was concluded for championship-game television.

The NFL had made sure it too was financially prepared for whatever lay ahead.

While off-the-field activity dominated the headlines, the gridiron action in both leagues was also deserving of attention. The Houston Oilers, triggered by former Chicago Bears quarterback George Blanda, won the first two AFL championships. Bolstered by the addition of former NFL passer Len Dawson, Hunt's Texans won the 1962 title in their last game under the Dallas banner. The Texans had battled the Cowboys fairly evenly but Hunt decided it would be best to move his team to Kansas City in 1963. There the Chiefs continued as one of the AFL's premier franchises.

The AFL's glamour team in the early 1960s, however, was the Chargers, who played a year in Los Angeles before moving to San Diego. With such exciting stars as Lance Alworth, John Hadl, Keith Lincoln and Paul Lowe providing perpetual excitement, the Chargers won Western Division titles five of the first six years. AFL football was showcased at its explosive best in the Chargers' 53–10 lacing of the Boston Patriots in the 1963 title game.

Meanwhile, the NFL had an internal problem—how to deal with the awesome Green Bay Packers team that was overwhelming all opposition. After years in the doldrums, the once-dynamic Green Bay club became powerful again under the tutelage of Vince Lombardi. Led by Bart Starr, Jim Taylor and Paul Hornung on offense and Willie Davis, Ray Nitschke and Herb Adderley on defense, the Packers won NFL championships in 1961 and 1962 and again in 1965, 1966 and 1967. No other NFL club had achieved that kind of domination over so many seasons. Lombardi was widely acclaimed as pro football's Man of the Decade.

Still, the "war" news continued to share almost equal billing with the playing results on the gridiron. This was particularly true as the competition grew more intense and

*BELOW: One of Pete Rozelle's first major acts was to arrange an NFL television network package. The rival AFL did the same. RIGHT: Television coverage such as this of Super Bowl XVI from the Pontiac Silverdome is standard practice today.*

it became evident the AFL was going to last longer than most NFL supporters had originally believed possible.

In the early stages, there was plenty of evidence to indicate a quick kill by the NFL was imminent. When the badly mismanaged New York Titans franchise was taken over by the AFL in 1962, that sad event marked a low point in the league's history. But the next year, the AFL signed eight number 1 draft choices. Al Davis became head coach–general manager of the weak Oakland team and, in his first year, turned the Raiders into contenders. Sonny Werblin, with solid financial backing, took over the New York franchise and renamed the team the Jets. A year later, in 1964, Werblin moved the Jets into the spanking-new Shea Stadium. The result was record crowds which provided further notice the AFL was not to be taken lightly.

In January, 1964, AFL commissioner Foss announced a five-year, $36 million TV contract with NBC that would begin in 1965. Thus, each AFL team was assured $900,000 a year from TV income. The NFL countered three months

**EXPANSION TEAMS**

In the late 1960s, four new teams came into pro football. The Atlanta Falcons began play in the NFL in 1966 and the same year the Miami Dolphins became an AFL team. As part of the merger agreement, the New Orleans Saints were admitted to the NFL in 1967 and the Cincinnati Bengals to the AFL in 1968.

Two of the expansion teams, the Dolphins and the Saints, got off to the best possible start with touchdowns on the opening kickoff in their first regular-season action. On September 2, 1966, the Dolphins' Joe Auer returned the kickoff 95 yards against the Oakland Raiders. A year later on September 17, 1967, John Gilliam of the Saints took the Los Angeles Rams' opening kick 94 yards to the end zone. Neither the Dolphins nor the Saints were victorious, however. Oakland defeated the Dolphins, 23–14, and the Rams prevailed over New Orleans, 27–13.

later with its own television package that gave the league $14.1 million per year for regular-season games and $1.8 million annually for championshp games in 1964 and 1965. The role of the television networks was increasingly clear—they were providing the financial ammunition to enable both sides to continue to fight.

The AFL did outbid the NFL for some significant stars in the early years. Billy Cannon in Houston, Lance Alworth in San Diego and Bobby Bell in Kansas City are three prime examples of talented stars who opted for the AFL. The senior league, however, could honestly claim it had won the preponderance of the signing battles in the early 1960s.

In January, 1965, the New York Jets' owner, Sonny Werblin, dropped a bombshell by signing the heralded quarterback from Alabama, Joe Namath, to a reported

### HEIDI

Heidi, the fictional mountain girl from Switzerland, pre-empted the final seconds of a crucial American Football League (AFL) game on November 17, 1968, and, in so doing, became a lasting part of pro football folklore.

The game in Oakland matched the Raiders against the New York Jets. Each team was destined to win its divisional race and then meet in the AFL championship game. The Jets led, 32–29, with 1:03 to play when the National Broadcasting Company (NBC) elected to leave the game so the children's movie special on the Swiss miss could begin on time.

The Raiders scored two touchdowns in the last 42 seconds to win, 43–32. Instantly, fans all over the nation bombarded the NBC switchboard with protests, proving that in America's living rooms on a Sunday afternoon, pro football reigned supreme.

$400,000 contract. With one stroke of the pen, Werblin gave the entire AFL instant respectability and provided what historians agree was the turning point in the war.

Still, the hostilities grew even more intense in 1966. Three NFL rookies—Donny Anderson and Jim Grabowski of Green Bay and Tommy Nobis of Atlanta—each signed more lucrative contracts than the one Namath had won from the Jets. The two leagues spent an estimated $25 million to sign their 1966 draft choices. The NFL nabbed 75 percent and the AFL 46 percent of their draftees. Of the 111 common draft picks, 79 went to the NFL, 28 to the AFL and four went unsigned.

The alarming escalation of the spending war had not been lost on the owners in both leagues. As early as January, 1965—about the time of the Namath signing—some informal peace discussions began. Ralph Wilson Jr of the Buffalo Bills and Carroll Rosenbloom of the Baltimore Colts were the first to talk and they laid much of the framework for an eventual agreement before discussions came to an end.

Peace was not yet a reality when the AFL fired its next salvo. On April 8, 1966, the league, seeking more dynamic leadership, named Oakland's Al Davis to replace Foss as commissioner. Davis immediately started to implement his plan to raid the NFL for veteran stars, particularly quarterbacks, by paying exorbitant bonuses to sign contracts that would be effective as soon as they played out their options. In a three-week period, Davis opened negotiations with more than a dozen NFL stars, including San Francisco quarterback John Brodie and Los Angeles Rams passer Roman Gabriel.

But the AFL was moving in two directions. Two days before Davis was named commissioner, Hunt held a secret rendezvous with Tex Schramm of the Cowboys at the airport in Dallas. Their talks were productive and the two continued their discussions even as Davis prepared for all-out war. The defection of kicker Pete Gogolak from the Buffalo Bills to the New York Giants on May 17 brought the desirability of a merger into even sharper focus. Merger talks soon progressed to the finishing stages.

At a New York press conference on June 8, the war officially ended. There were seven major points in the agreement: (1) Pete Rozelle was to be the commissioner of the merged league; (2) the leagues were to play a world championship game; (3) all existing franchises were to remain at their present sites; (4) a combined draft was to be held; (5) two franchises were to be added by 1968, one in each league—the money from each to be paid to the NFL; (6) AFL clubs were to pay an indemnity of $18 million to the NFL over a 20-year period; and (7) inter-league pre-

season games were to be played in 1967 with a single league schedule to commence in 1970.

The AFL had achieved what it had set out to do—gain parity with the NFL. The merger also provided the AFL with the opportunity to prove it had reached the caliber of NFL play in face-to-face confrontation on the field.

The NFL won 13 of 16 inter-league pre-season contests in 1967 but the Denver Broncos stunned the Detroit Lions, 13–7, on August 5 to give the AFL its first-ever win over an NFL team. The Broncos also defeated the Minnesota Vikings a week later. The Kansas City Chiefs, with a 66–24 lashing of the Chicago Bears, accounted for the third AFL pre-season win.

The Chiefs also became the AFL's first representative in the world championship game, which was not officially known as the Super Bowl until its fourth year. The Green Bay Packers handled the Chiefs just as they had most NFL opponents, winning 35–10 in Super Bowl I. The Pack was back for Super Bowl II and was victorious again, 33–14 over the Oakland Raiders.

*LEFT: George Blanda (#16) led the Houston Oilers to the first two AFL championships. BELOW: The San Diego Chargers were paced by this Fabulous Foursome: (left to right) John Hadl, Paul Lowe, Lance Alworth and Keith Lincoln.*

*Joe Namath sets up to pass for the New York Jets. His signing of a $400,000 contract in 1965 was a major triumph for the AFL.*

In 1968, however, the Baltimore Colts ended Green Bay's dynasty with a 13–1–0 regular-season romp and playoff victories over Minnesota and Cleveland. In the AFL title game, the New York Jets edged past favored Oakland, 27–23. The experts looked on the Colts–Jets Super Bowl III confrontation as a mismatch of catastrophic proportions. In some circles, the Colts were favored by as much as 47 points. But Joe Namath, the Jets' talented field leader, followed up the previous week's brash ''guarantee'' of victory with a supreme performance against a surprised Baltimore eleven. The Jets won, 16–7, and, in so doing, erased any doubts about the competitive viability of the Super Bowl series. Along with the Baltimore–New York title game a decade earlier, Super Bowl III ranks as one of the two most significant games ever in generating extreme fan enthusiasm. Weeb Ewbank earned a unique place in history as the winning coach in both landmark games.

The Minnesota Vikings, with swashbuckling Joe Kapp providing the punch, powered their way to the 1969 NFL title and a Super Bowl IV showdown with the Chiefs. Like the Colts a year earlier, the Vikings were heavily favored. Once again, the AFL team pulled off a big upset. The Chiefs, paced by crafty Len Dawson at quarterback and an overpowering defense, stunned the Vikings, 23–7, in the last game ever played by an AFL team. In the four Super Bowl games before the merger was finalized, the AFL broke even, 2–2, with the NFL.

In just one decade, pro football had grown from 12 teams to 26. The NFL's average crowd had increased from 40,106 to 54,430. The AFL average gate, only 16,538 in its first year, more than doubled to 40,610 in 1969.

The AFL went out of business after the 1969 season. In only a few years, the league, which began as an improbable David vs. Goliath challenge, provided impetus for the most dynamic period of growth in the history of any sport.

# AFTER THE MERGER, 1970–PRESENT DAY

Enthusiastic pro football loyalists anticipated the post-merger years as a time when off-the-field turmoil would end and the primary concern once again could be who won or lost on the football field.

NFL football, 1970s-style, did prove to be more exciting than ever and fan interest grew steadily but the modern era also brought new and often unprecedented problems, some of which threatened the very existence of the sport. Such varied topics as television contracts, player strikes, law suits, congressional investigations, yet more rival football leagues, numerous rule changes, and drug and alcohol abuse have captured the headlines in the last 15 years.

The first order of post-merger business was to realign the expanded 26-team NFL. In 1969, the Pittsburgh Steelers, Cleveland Browns and Baltimore Colts agreed to move into the new American Football Conference (AFC) with the 10 existing AFL teams. The AFC's divisional alignment was also quickly decided. The 13 National Football Conference (NFC—formerly the NFL teams) owners could not agree on their divisional setup but commissioner Pete Rozelle ended the debate by drawing up five plans and having his secretary pick the winning alignment out of a hat.

## MOVING TO THE AFC

A couple of years after the merger officially ended the AFL–NFL war, representatives of the two leagues were still hammering out one last detail—the realignment by divisions of the new 26-team National Football League (NFL). To even up the two conferences of the new NFL, it was agreed that three teams would leave the NFL ranks to join what would be known as the American Football Conference. It was a bitter impasse—everyone thought two 13-team conferences was a great idea as long as someone else made the move.

Commissioner Pete Rozelle, determined to get the matter settled once and for all, announced he would keep the meeting in session for days, if necessary, to get three volunteers. At that point, the Pittsburgh Steelers' revered owner, Art Rooney, said, "Well, hell, I'll go!"

Within seconds, Art Modell of Cleveland was on his feet. "If Rooney goes, I go, too." The next voice heard was that of the Baltimore Colts' Carroll Rosenbloom: "Make it three."

Other merger finalities were settled quickly. Two AFL innovations, including players' names on the backs of jerseys and making the stadium clock the official time keeper, were adopted but another AFL rule that permitted a two-point conversion after a touchdown by running or passing was scrapped.

Once the realignment of the 26 teams was determined,

*John Riggins piled up big yardage for the Washington Redskins for a full decade in the 1970s and 1980s.*

## THE PERFECT SEASON

Only one team in pro football history, the 1972 Miami Dolphins, experienced a perfect undefeated, untied season. With quarterbacks Earl Morrall and Bob Griese directing a ball-control offense, the Dolphins set an NFL record for rushing with 2960 yards. Two Dolphins, Larry Csonka and Mercury Morris, rushed for more than 1000 yards.

In the 17 victories, the Dolphins scored first 13 times and had to come from behind with late rallies to win only three games. Buffalo lost to Miami by just one point, 24–23, but in the third quarter the Bills fell behind to stay.

### THE ANATOMY OF A PERFECT SEASON

| Game | Date | Score | Opponent | Winning score, player, quarter |
|---|---|---|---|---|
| | | | Regular Season | |
| 1 | Sept. 17 | 20–10 | Kansas City | Briscoe, 14-yd reception, 1st |
| 2 | Sept. 24 | 34–13 | Houston° | Kiick, 1-yd run, 1st |
| 3 | Oct. 1 | 16–14 | Minnesota | Mandich, 3-yd reception, 4th |
| 4 | Oct. 8 | 27–17 | New York Jets | Kiick, 6-yd run, 2nd |
| 5 | Oct. 15 | 24–10 | San Diego° | Anderson, interception ret., 2nd |
| 6 | Oct. 22 | 24–23 | Buffalo° | Csonka, 10-yd run, 3rd |
| 7 | Oct. 29 | 23–0 | Baltimore | Csonka, 1-yd run, 1st |
| 8 | Nov. 5 | 30–16 | Buffalo | Morris, 22-yd run, 1st |
| 9 | Nov. 12 | 52–0 | New England° | Morris, 4-yd run, 1st |
| 10 | Nov. 19 | 28–24 | New York Jets° | Morris, 14-yd run, 4th |
| 11 | Nov. 27 | 31–10 | St Louis° | Kiick, 2-yd run, 1st |
| 12 | Dec. 3 | 37–21 | New England | Yepremian, 36-yd FG, 1st |
| 13 | Dec. 10 | 23–13 | New York Giants | Yepremian, 37-yd FG, 1st |
| 14 | Dec. 16 | 16–0 | Baltimore° | Yepremian, 40-yd FG, 1st |
| | | | AFC Playoffs | |
| 15 | Dec. 24 | 20–14 | Cleveland° | Kiick, 8-yd run, 4th |
| 16 | Dec. 31 | 21–17 | Pittsburgh | Kiick, 2-yd run, 3rd |
| | | | Super Bowl | |
| 17 | Jan. 14 | 14–7 | Washington | Twilley, 28-yd reception, 1st |

° Game played in Miami

the NFL settled down to a period of unprecedented stability. Unlike any other decade in pro football history, no franchises disbanded or transferred to other cities in the 1970s. Six teams—the New England Patriots, Dallas Cowboys, Detroit Lions, New York Giants, Los Angeles Rams and New York Jets—did move to new stadiums but remained in the same metropolitan area. In 1976, the NFL expanded to 28 teams with the addition of the Tampa Bay Buccaneers, who now play as an NFC team, and the Seattle Seahawks, destined for the AFC.

In 1980, Al Davis, managing general partner of the Oakland Raiders, decided to transfer his team to Los Angeles. When the NFL refused to sanction the move, Davis joined the Los Angeles Memorial Coliseum in an anti-trust suit against the league. Eventually, a United States Federal District Court ruled against the NFL and paved the way for the Raiders' move to Los Angeles for the 1982 season. Two years later, Colts owner Robert Irsay, ignoring league wishes, took his team lock, stock and barrel from Baltimore to Indianapolis. In 1988, Cardinals owner William Bidwell sought and obtained league permission to move his team from St Louis to Phoenix.

Television, a significant factor in the AFL–NFL war, became even more important after the leagues merged. For the first time, three networks were involved in the TV pact signed in 1970. NBC-TV was awarded rights for all AFC games and CBS-TV got the NFC package, with the two networks televising the Super Bowl in alternate years. A third network, ABC-TV, contracted to air one NFL game every Monday night during the regular season. "Monday Night Football" immediately took the nation by storm.

With NFL television attracting more viewers than ever before, the league's blackout policy, which had been upheld

*BELOW LEFT: Bob Griese was a long-time fixture for the Dolphins. ABOVE: The New Orleans Saints (light jerseys) clashed with the Philadelphia Eagles in a 1978 pre-season game in Mexico City.*

in the courts in the 1950s, came under fire once again. In 1973, Congress settled the issue by passing legislation that required any NFL game that was sold out 72 hours prior to kickoff to be made available to local TV channels.

New television pacts were signed in 1974 and again in 1978. Each contract called for higher rights fees. The airing of other events, such as selected pre-season games, selected Sunday and Thursday contests, the Hall of Fame game and the Pro Bowl, was added to the agreements.

Then came a five-year, three-network, $2.1 billion package in 1982 that exceeded everyone's wildest expectations. During the period of the pact, the league would be paid an average of $420 million annually. A lengthy player strike during the first year of the contract temporarily eroded the TV ratings and did much to slow the influx of television money when the contract came up for renewal in 1987.

The NFL's television committee negotiated a $1.428 billion, three-year package in 1987. The $476 million per year income for the 28 NFL teams, which represented a slight increase over the 1982 contract, was made possible by the addition of the ESPN cable network to televise selected pre-season contests, eight Sunday night regular-season games and the Pro Bowl.

## BLOCKBUSTER TRADES

The startling trade on October 31, 1987, that sent ace running back Eric Dickerson to the Indianapolis Colts in a three-team deal involved four players and six first- or second-round draft choices. Another key figure in the massive player transfer was linebacker Cornelius Bennett, who wound up with the Buffalo Bills. Assuming the draft choices are converted into blue-chip players, it may go down as the most important swap in history.

In terms of sheer numbers it had previously been surpassed by three other trades and equaled by a fourth: **March 26, 1953**—15 players. Tackle Mike McCormack and four other players from Baltimore were traded to Cleveland for 10 players, including defensive back Don Shula, who later became the Baltimore coach.
**January 28, 1971**—15 players. Linebacker Marlin McKeever and seven draft choices from Washington were traded to the Los Angeles Rams for linebackers Maxie Baughan and Jack Pardee, plus four other players and a draft choice.
**June 13, 1952**—12 players. Selection rights to linebacker Les Richter from the Dallas Texans were traded to the Rams for 11 players.
**March 23, 1959**—10 players. Running back Ollie Matson from the Chicago Cardinals was traded to the Rams for seven players, a draft choice and a player to be delivered during training camp.

*Pete Rozelle presents the Vince Lombardi Trophy to the Pittsburgh Steelers' Art Rooney.*

Since 1970, each new television contract has prompted renewed and usually tempestuous negotiations with the NFL Players Association (NFLPA), which demands that players receive their fair share of any television revenue.

The NFLPA, which was first organized in 1956, was relatively inactive until 1968 when a lengthy dispute turned into a combination players' strike/owners' lockout that lasted two weeks. The players staged pre-season strikes again in 1970 and 1974. In 1974, they returned to work without a contract. The five-year agreement signed in 1977 made some player benefits retroactive to the 1974 season.

Neither the players nor the owners were as fortunate in 1982 when a strike which lasted 57 days interrupted the regular season. In the new collective bargaining agreement that followed, the free-agent system was left unchanged but a minimum salary schedule based on years of experience was established. A severance-pay schedule was introduced and medical, retirement and insurance benefits increased. The teams wound up playing a nine-game regular season and a special playoff tournament was devised to determine the teams that would meet in Super Bowl XVII.

Between 1982 and 1987, a player's average salary increased from $90,000 annually to $230,000. So in 1987, unfettered free agency became the principal issue. As in 1982, an in-season strike began after the second week of the regular campaign but the owners retaliated by staging games between hastily organized replacement teams with the results counting in the final standings. The tactic met with better results than expected. After three weeks, the strike ended. No agreement was reached and the players continued to perform under most of the terms of the 1982 agreement while the NFLPA pursued an anti-trust suit.

The NFL, which had been challenged by rival leagues five times in 50 years, faced competition from two more new leagues in the 1970s and 1980s. Soon after the World Football League (WFL) announced it would begin play in 1974, its Toronto team shocked the world-champion

Miami Dolphins by signing three major stars, Larry Csonka, Jim Kiick and Paul Warfield, in a reported $3 million deal. The three played out their options in 1974 and joined their WFL team, which had become the Memphis Southmen, the next season. Six weeks into the 1975 season, the WFL folded but the damage had been done. Several NFL teams lost players to the WFL but the Dolphins suffered most severely, both financially and on the field.

Eight years later, in 1983, the United States Football League (USFL), armed with an ABC-TV contract, was organized as a spring league but after two mildly successful spring seasons, the USFL shifted its schedule to the fall in 1985. When it was unable to negotiate a major-network television contract, the USFL sued the NFL on anti-trust charges. After a lengthy trial, a jury acquitted the NFL on nine of 10 monopoly counts.

In spite of these distractions, NFL fans were enjoying some of the finest football ever played. Many long-time NFL fanatics still questioned whether the old AFL teams belonged in the faster company. For the first two years, the NFC had the best of it in the 40 inter-conference games played each season but the AFC quickly caught up and, after 18 seasons, led the NFC in inter-conference skirmishing by a 413–367–8 margin.

The AFC's strength was even more evident in the Super Bowl. AFC teams won eight of 10 Super Bowls in the 1970s—only the Dallas Cowboys with victories in games VI and XII challenged the AFC's domination.

Baltimore got the AFC started with its victory over Dallas in Super Bowl V. In 1972, the Miami Dolphins enjoyed an unprecedented perfect season. They finished their 17–0–0 campaign with a Super Bowl VII victory over the Washington Redskins and came back the next year to beat the Minnesota Vikings in Super Bowl VIII.

Then it was Pittsburgh's turn. The Steelers, who had not won a championship in 42 years of NFL football, had steadily built a powerhouse over several years by skillful use of the annual college draft. Starting in 1974, they won six straight AFC Central Division titles and four Super Bowl championships. Their 16–6 win over the Minnesota Vikings in Super Bowl IX got them started. Then they edged Dallas in Super Bowls X and XIII and the Los Angeles Rams in Super Bowl XIV. The Raiders added to the AFC string with a 32–14 romp over Minnesota in Super Bowl XI. By the end of the 1970s, the AFL/AFC held a 10–4 Super Bowl series lead.

In the 1980s, however, the NFC bounced back with six wins in eight Super Bowls. Two teams from the NFL's early years—the Chicago Bears in XX and the New York Giants in XXI—won for the first time in the series. The Washington Redskins were victorious in Super Bowls XVII and XXII. The San Francisco 49ers captured Super Bowls XVI and XIX for the NFC. Only the Raiders, representing Oakland in XV and Los Angeles in XVIII, held up the AFC's end.

Over the past two decades, the NFL adopted numerous new rules designed to make the game more appealing for the masses. A 1972 alteration moved in the hashmarks (or inbound lines) from 20 yards to 23 yards, 1 foot, 9 inches. The running backs responded to the new rule with a record 10 players rushing for 1000 yards or more.

In 1974, even more significant changes were adopted. Sudden-death overtime for all games, instead of just playoff games, was introduced. To discourage field goals and encourage touchdowns, the goal posts were moved to the back of the end zone. The spot for kickoffs was shifted from the 40-yard line to the 35. Defensive players were allowed to "chuck" or bump a pass receiver only once. The offensive holding penalty was reduced from 15 to 10 yards. The results of the rule changes were a considerable increase in touchdowns, fewer field goals and longer punt and kickoff returns. Future rule changes also emphasized player safety.

In recent years, the NFL also turned its attention to other nations. The St Louis Cardinals and San Diego Chargers, who met in a 1976 pre-season game in Tokyo, became the first NFL teams to play on another continent. Two years later, the New Orleans Saints and Philadelphia Eagles squared off in Mexico City. In 1983, the Minnesota Vikings and St Louis Cardinals staged a contest in London.

The NFL owners made their international interest official in 1985 by agreeing to stage at least one pre-season game every year in Europe and/or Asia. The Chicago Bears and Dallas Cowboys played in London's Wembley Stadium in the 1986 pre-season. The Denver Broncos and Los Angeles Rams staged an encore at Wembley a year later. The Minnesota Vikings and Chicago Bears played in Gothenburg, Sweden, and the San Francisco 49ers and Miami Dolphins squared off in Wembley in 1988.

While serious problems remain to be resolved, several positive factors indicate NFL football is still the most popular of all sports. Attendance, which averaged more than 55,000 per game since 1971, soared over the 60,000 mark both in 1981 and 1986. Eight of the 10 most-watched television programs of all time involve Super Bowl games. Only the "MASH" special in 1983 (number 3 in the ratings) and "Roots, Part 8," in 1977 (number 8) break into the Super Bowl sweep. Super Bowl XX was viewed by an estimated 127 million in 59 nations and on the QE II luxury ocean liner. Two months later, an estimated 300 million Chinese excitedly watched a tape of the "Gan Lan Qui" (olive ball) game matching the "Ju Xiong" (Giant Bear) against "Ai Guo Zhe" (Patriot) teams. The next year, some 12 million people in England sat up until 2:30 in the morning to view Super Bowl XXI live.

## CAPSULE HISTORY OF THE 28 NATIONAL FOOTBALL LEAGUE FRANCHISES

| Team | First year of play* | Other cities/names for teams |
|---|---|---|
| Phoenix Cardinals | 1920 | Chicago Cardinals, 1920–59 |
| | | St Louis Cardinals, 1960–87 |
| Chicago Bears | 1920 | Decatur Staleys, 1920 |
| | | Chicago Staleys, 1921 |
| Green Bay Packers | 1921 | |
| New York Giants | 1925 | |
| Detroit Lions | 1930 | Portsmouth Spartans, 1930–3 |
| Washington Redskins | 1932 | Boston Braves, 1932 |
| | | Boston Redskins, 1933–6 |
| Philadelphia Eagles | 1933 | |
| Pittsburgh Steelers | 1933 | Pittsburgh Pirates, 1933–40 |
| Los Angeles Rams | 1937 | Cleveland Rams, 1937–45 |
| Cleveland Browns | 1946† | |
| San Francisco 49ers | 1946† | |
| Indianapolis Colts | 1953 | Baltimore Colts, 1953–83 |
| Dallas Cowboys | 1960 | |
| Buffalo Bills | 1960‡ | |
| Denver Broncos | 1960‡ | |
| Houston Oilers | 1960‡ | |
| Kansas City Chiefs | 1960‡ | Dallas Texans, 1960–2 |
| New England Patriots | 1960‡ | Boston Patriots, 1960–71 |
| New York Jets | 1960‡ | New York Titans, 1960–2 |
| Los Angeles Raiders | 1960‡ | Oakland Raiders, 1960–81 |
| San Diego Chargers | 1960‡ | Los Angeles Chargers, 1960 |
| Minnesota Vikings | 1961 | |
| Atlanta Falcons | 1966 | |
| Miami Dolphins | 1966§ | |
| New Orleans Saints | 1967 | |
| Cincinnati Bengals | 1968§ | |
| Seattle Seahawks | 1976 | |
| Tampa Bay Buccaneers | 1976 | |

* In some cases, franchise was granted before team began play.
† Charter members of All-America Football Conference. Joined NFL in 1950
‡ Charter members of American Football League. Joined merged NFL in 1970
§ American Football League member. Joined merged NFL in 1970

But this showcase of pro football is much more than just overwhelming figures measuring world-wide interest. The Super Bowl has become a ritual and a legend that permeates the lives of individuals of every rank. In 1970 when the Chiefs were playing in Super Bowl IV, the first question a burglar apprehended by Kansas City police asked was: "What's the score?" In 1974, Skylab 3 astronauts saw the game from outer space. Georgetown University hospital installed TV sets in the labor rooms to prevent expectant fathers from waiting too long to bring their wives to the hospital. US Secretary of State George Schultz, on a diplomatic mission in Japan, awakened at 3 o'clock in the morning to watch a Super Bowl telecast in Tokyo.

As *Time* magazine once wrote, the Super Bowl is "The Great American Time-Out." One day, it may truly become "The Great World Time-Out."

# THE PRO FOOTBALL HALL OF FAME

An NFL quarterback rifles a 35-yard bullet into the waiting hands of a teammate in the end zone. A massive defensive tackle barrels over two blockers to sack a passer for a critical loss.

In the television booth, the sportscaster calling the action exclaims, "Now there is some kind of football player. He's a cinch to wind up in Canton!" It is the highest compliment that can be paid to any NFL player.

"Winding up in Canton," in pro football jargon, means being elected to the Pro Football Hall of Fame, which happens to be located in Canton, a bustling mid-size city in northeastern Ohio. It was here in 1915 that Jim Thorpe, the first big-name American athlete to play pro football, signed with the Bulldogs.

It was also here the American Professional Football Association, which soon changed its name to the National Football League, was organized on September 17, 1920. The Canton Bulldogs then became the first two-time champions of the new league with undefeated seasons in both 1922 and 1923.

In spite of these impressive historical credentials, Canton was originally bypassed as a home for a Pro Football Hall of Fame. In 1947, NFL owners, incorrectly believing Latrobe, Pennsylvania, was the site of the first pro football game in 1895, awarded Hall of Fame location rights to the city. But Latrobe did not follow through and, a decade later, Hall of Fame site designation was still an open issue.

So it was on December 6, 1959, the *Canton Repository* ran an eight-column editorial with the declaration: "Pro Football Needs a Hall of Fame and the Logical Site is Canton." Civic leaders quickly accepted the *Repository's* challenge and, within four years, a sparkling new Pro Football Hall of Fame became a reality on September 7, 1963. Expansion projects in 1971 and 1978 have made pro football's eye-catching showplace what it is today, a 51,000 square-foot pantheon in a sprawling four-building complex.

The Pro Football Hall of Fame is filled with dynamic and entertaining exhibitions that recapture every phase of pro football's almost 100-year-old history and at the same time pay homage to the great players, coaches and contributors who have been accorded membership into the Hall. The most memorable events of the sport's history are chronicled in dynamic memento, picture and story form in four bright and colorful exhibition areas. Exciting NFL action films are shown hourly in a 350-seat movie theater. A special gem for the serious football student is the research library, the "heart" of the Hall from which all historical activities emanate. For souvenir-minded fans, there is a bustling museum store with a wide range of football gifts.

The first sight for every visitor is the 7-foot bronze statue of Jim Thorpe, located in the lobby directly under the 52-foot dome that some describe as a football rising out of the unique circular entrance building. Those who have seen the Hall from the air say the first edifice looks more like an orange-juice squeezer. From the statue, the guest ascends a

*ABOVE: Pro Football Hall of Fame members are appropriately honored in the regal splendor of the twin enshrinement galleries. BELOW LEFT: The Top Twenty display ranks the leading 20 individuals in rushing, passing, scoring and pass receiving.*

gently sloping ramp to the original Exhibition Rotunda. Here the history of almost 100 years of pro football unfolds in a roughly chronological display format, starting with the first game in 1892 and continuing to the present NFL season. Some of the most unusual mementoes in the Hall's collection are to be found here, including such items as a football from the 1890s, a complete uniform worn in 1902, a football-shaped trophy made of anthracite coal, battered shoulder pads worn by Y. A. Tittle, a Duluth Eskimos great coat and Jim Thorpe's Canton Bulldogs sidelines blanket. A highlight of the Rotunda is the "Professional Football Today" display, a collection of 28 individual team panels which are updated every year.

On the outer perimeter of the next two pie-shaped buildings are the twin enshrinement galleries, regally carpeted in royal blue, where each enshrinee is honored in an individual niche complete with bronze bust, action mural and basic biography. In the center of the second building is the Pro Football Photo-Art Gallery, featuring winning photographs from the Hall's prestigious annual professional photographers contest. The Pro Football Adventure Room in the third building details such varied subjects as "The Story of Blacks in Pro Football," "The 1972 Miami Dolphins' Perfect Season" and "The Evolution of the Uniform from 1920 to the Present Day."

Two major exhibitions dominate the final building. In the colorful Enshrinee Mementoes Room, Hall of Fame members are segregated into displays of the teams for which they played. Included in the exhibitions are selections of prized relics of each team's enshrinees.

In the Super Bowl area, the Vince Lombardi trophy that is awarded to winning Super Bowl teams and exact replicas of the rings that go to winning team members are included in a futuristic display. Picture panels of each Super Bowl and a special videotape of all the games are also featured.

## A CAPSULE HISTORY OF THE PRO FOOTBALL HALL OF FAME

**December 6, 1959** The *Canton Repository* issues an editorial challenge: "Pro Football Needs a Hall of Fame—and Logical Site is Here."

**January 23, 1960** Detroit makes a strong initial bid to the National Football League for the Hall of Fame site designation. The Pittsburgh Steelers remind the NFL of the site rights already given to Latrobe. Paul Brown of the Cleveland Browns reveals Canton's interest.

**February 25, 1960** Canton's Chamber of Commerce, the Jaycees, service and civic clubs and industries strongly endorse the *Repository*'s challenge. A steering committee is appointed.

**January 25, 1961** William E. Umstattd of the Timken Roller Bearing Company makes a formal bid to the NFL on Canton's behalf.

**April 20, 1961** An NFL committee made up of Paul Brown, George Halas and Edwin Anderson visits Canton to inspect the proposed site.

**April 27, 1961** In a roll-call vote of the NFL clubs, Canton wins official recognition as the Hall of Fame city.

**February 8, 1962** The Hall of Fame building fund-raising culminates in the announcement that pledges have reached $378,026. The Timken Company makes the largest donation of $100,000. One citizen pledges $300 to be paid in $6.25 monthly installments.

**April 4, 1962** Dick McCann, long-time general manager of the Washington Redskins, is appointed the Hall's first director.

**August 11, 1962** Hall of Fame ground-breaking ceremonies are held. The same day, the St Louis Cardinals and New York Giants play to a 21–21 tie in the first Hall of Fame game.

**September 7, 1963** The Pro Football Hall of Fame is formally dedicated. The charter class of 17 members is enshrined.

**May 10, 1971** The first expansion, which adds a third building to the Hall, is opened.

**November 20, 1978** Gala ceremonies are held at the completion of the second expansion, which adds a fourth building and increases the size of the complex to 51,000 square feet.

**September 4, 1986** The four millionth visitor is welcomed to the Hall.

*The Modern Era Display is updated regularly to keep pace with the changing NFL scene.*

Throughout the Hall, the visitor may participate in his tour by activating videotape monitors, hear-phone recordings of famous gridiron moments, selective slide machines and quiz games. The Hall prides itself on keeping up to date with the changing pro football scene. Toward this end, between 40 and 50 displays are amended to include the newest information each year. One prime attention-getter is the Top Twenty display, an 8-foot, back-lit pylon that statistically ranks the individual lifetime leaders in passing, receiving, rushing and scoring. The display is changed every week during the NFL season.

More than four million visitors have passed through the Hall's doors in the 25 years since it first opened. All 50 American states and 65 or more foreign nations are represented on the guest register each year. The Hall is open every day except Christmas.

The annual highlight comes in late July or early August when the Pro Football Hall of Fame enshrinement ceremonies are held on the front steps of the grid shrine. More than 10,000 watch and listen as the sport's greatest heroes dramatically share their innermost emotions in their acceptance speeches. A short time later, across the street in Fawcett Stadium, two NFL teams kick off in the AFC–NFC Hall of Fame game. Televised nationally on ABC–TV, the contest annually opens the pro football pre-season schedule. Each NFL team appears in Canton every 13, 14 or 15 years and Hall of Fame games already are scheduled through the 1998 season.

Many sports halls of fame feature an enshrinement and an exhibition game each year but the civic celebration that augments those events in Canton sets the Pro Football Hall of Fame's annual festival apart from all others.

Preliminary events are staged for most of the week before the traditional Football's Greatest Weekend activities begin on Friday morning. That day's schedule includes a mayor's breakfast, a women's fashion show and an enshrinees' civic dinner. All three activities attract more than 3500 football fanatics. A festival parade, which is rated as one of the top 10 in America and draws 200,000, precedes the enshrinement on Saturday morning. Thousands of volunteers work endless hours to make sure that Canton puts its best foot forward as the sports world focuses for one weekend a year on the Pro Football Hall of Fame and its home city.

For the new enshrinees, it is a rewarding but emotional time as they reflect on their careers and the awesome honor they are receiving. They can glory in the realization their special place in history is assured.

As Forrest Gregg, a member of the Hall's 1977 class, said: "If you are a player or a coach—I have been both—you are always aware that some day your career will end. But once you are in the Pro Football Hall of Fame, you know your name is there forever!"

# MEMBERS OF THE
# PRO FOOTBALL HALL OF FAME

The pages that follow contain personalized biographies of the careers of every Pro Football Hall of Fame member.

The prototype Hall of Famer is the athlete who enjoyed exceptional success from the moment he first put on pads in junior high school until his very last game as a professional. Others, perhaps not blessed with exceptional natural abilities, had to work their way to excellence.

The road to the Pro Football Hall of Fame is unique for everyone. No two careers are alike. The only common denominator is that every enshrinee has been judged by a panel and deemed to be the best pro football has produced.

*The new entrance to the Pro Football Hall of Fame.*

# The SIXTIES

The Pro Football Hall of Fame dream became a reality with the
formal opening ceremony on September 7, 1963. The charter class
of 17 members included many of the players and contributors who
gave strength and credibility to the sport in its earliest years.
Before the 1960s were over, 42 more enshrinees increased the
membership count to 59.

# SAMMY BAUGH

*Quarterback*
*6 ft 2 in, 180 lb*
*Born in Temple, Texas, March 17, 1914*
*Texas Christian University (TCU)*
*1937–52 Washington Redskins*

*A multi-talented superstar, Sammy Baugh was a "landmark" forward passer who played a major role in the offensive evolution of pro football. He was also history's finest punter.*

Sammy Baugh, a lean, lanky and highly publicized forward passer from Texas, first arrived on the NFL scene in 1937. Washington Redskins owner George Preston Marshall badly needed a promotional bonanza to make pro football go in the nation's capital. He was pinning his hopes on the Texas Christian all-America and the number 1 pick in the 1937 NFL draft.

When Baugh retired 16 years later, pro football was firmly established in Washington. More significantly, NFL football had evolved from a rock-'em, sock-'em infantry battle, played largely on the ground, into a far more crowd-pleasing, wide-open offensive show that featured the pass as an anywhere-on-the-field weapon.

A three-sport star in high school, "Slinging Sammy" attended TCU on a baseball scholarship and had even signed with the St Louis baseball Cardinals by the time Marshall lured him into the NFL with a $5000 contract offer.

Baugh started his NFL career as a single-wing tailback and didn't make the switch to the T-formation until midway through his career in 1944. His six NFL passing titles were broken up evenly, three coming as a tailback and three as a quarterback. Yet Baugh also is remembered as the best punter in history and he still dominates the NFL record book with his punting feats. The "Texas Tornado," who played both ways the first half of his career, also led the NFL with 11 interceptions in 1943, a year when he also won passing and punting crowns.

Not surprisingly, the good-natured cowboy with the quick hands and whiplike arm enjoyed many exceptional afternoons in his 16 years but two deserve special mention. Sammy concluded his 1937 rookie season with three long touchdown passes to give the Redskins a 28–21 NFL title victory over the Chicago Bears.

Eleven seasons later in 1947, he was given a special day in Washington and, among other gifts, he received a new station wagon. Baugh responded by passing for 355 yards and 6 touchdowns as the Redskins upset the title-bound Chicago Cardinals, 45–21.

Obviously, the great changes brought about in pro football during Baugh's career could not have been generated solely by one person but, without question, Baugh was the major catalyst in the dramatic offensive evolution. As a noted rival, Sid Luckman of the Bears, insisted: "Sammy Baugh was the best. Nobody is ever going to equal him. Not anybody!"

PASSING RECORD

| Year | Attempts | Completions | Percentage passes completed | Yards | TD | Interceptions |
|---|---|---|---|---|---|---|
| 1937† | 171° | 81° | 47.4 | 1127° | 7 | 14 |
| 1938 | 128 | 63 | 49.2 | 853 | 5 | 11 |
| 1939 | 96 | 53 | 55.2 | 518 | 6 | 9 |
| 1940† | 177 | 111 | 62.7° | 1367° | 12° | 10 |
| 1941 | 193 | 106 | 54.9 | 1236 | 10 | 19° |
| 1942 | 225 | 132 | 58.7° | 1524 | 16 | 11 |
| 1943† | 239° | 133° | 55.6° | 1754 | 23 | 19 |
| 1944 | 146 | 82 | 56.2 | 849 | 4 | 8 |
| 1945† | 182 | 128° | 70.3° | 1669 | 11 | 4 |
| 1946 | 161 | 87 | 54.0 | 1163 | 8 | 17 |
| 1947† | 354° | 210° | 59.3° | 2938° | 25° | 15 |
| 1948 | 315° | 185° | 58.7° | 2599° | 22 | 23° |
| 1949† | 255 | 145 | 56.9° | 1903 | 18 | 14 |
| 1950 | 166 | 90 | 54.2 | 1130 | 10 | 11 |
| 1951 | 154 | 67 | 43.5 | 1104 | 7 | 17 |
| 1952 | 33 | 20 | 60.6 | 152 | 2 | 1 |
| TOTALS | 2995 | 1693 | 56.5 | 21,886 | 186 | 203 |

Career passing rating: 72.0

° Led NFL                    † Official NFL passing champion

INTERCEPTION RECORD

| Year | Number | Yards | Average | TD |
|---|---|---|---|---|
| 1937–40 | No records available | | | |
| 1941 | 4 | 83 | 20.8 | 0 |
| 1942 | 5 | 77 | 15.4 | 0 |
| 1943 | 11° | 112 | 10.2 | 0 |
| 1944 | 4 | 21 | 5.2 | 0 |
| 1945 | 4 | 114 | 28.5 | 0 |
| 1946–52 | Did not play defense | | | |
| TOTALS | 28 | 407 | 14.5 | 0 |

Punting: 338 punts, 44.9-yard average

Punt returns: 11 returns, 99 yards, 9.0-yard average, 0 touchdowns

Rushing: 318 attempts, 324 yards, 1.0-yard average, 6 touchdowns

Scoring: 9 touchdowns, 1 extra point, 55 points

# BERT BELL

*League administrator, owner*
*Born in Philadelphia, Pa., February*
*25, 1895; died October 11, 1959,*
*at age of 64*
*University of Pennsylvania*
*1933–40 Philadelphia Eagles;*
*1941–6 Pittsburgh Steelers;*
*1946–59 National Football League*

It wasn't long after Bert Bell was elected the NFL's commissioner in January, 1946, that the rotund man with the gravelly voice showed he would be the fearless, tireless dynamo who would guide the league through some of its darkest days to new heights of popularity.

Bell's first order of business was to prepare his league for the costly four-year struggle with the rival All-America Football Conference (AAFC). Steadfastly rejecting any settlement that would leave the AAFC intact, Bert finally presided over a "merger" after the 1949 season that erased all but three AAFC teams.

In Bell's first year as commissioner, he suspended two New York Giants stars, Frank Filchock and Merle Hapes, just hours before the NFL title game in which they were to play. Their sin was that they had been offered a bribe by gamblers to "fix" the point spread and, while neither had accepted the overtures, neither

reported the attempt to the proper authorities. The incident marked the start of tough anti-gambling codes in the NFL.

Another far-sighted action was Bell's handling of the television situation. "You can't give fans a free game on TV and expect them to pay for the same game at the ball park," he insisted. So the policy, undoubtedly critical to the growth of NFL fan interest, was formulated to permit only road games to be televised back to home cities.

Bell exhibited a rare fortitude when he first recognized the NFL Players' Association. Confronted by angry owners, he simply referred to the league's constitution which permitted him to act on any matter "in the best interests of pro football."

Born to a Philadelphia Main Line family, Bert turned his back on life among the élite to pursue a career in football. He bought the Philadelphia Eagles franchise in 1933 and struggled with overwhelming financial adversity for the rest of the decade. A unique franchise shift in 1940 found Bell moving to Pittsburgh as part-owner of the Steelers, a status he maintained until he was selected as commissioner.

On October 11, 1959, while watching his "two teams," the Eagles and Steelers, play at Philadelphia's Franklin Field, Bert suffered a fatal heart attack. The fact he succumbed at an NFL game seemed appropriate for a man who had made pro football his entire life and had contributed to his sport as few ever had.

*Bert Bell (right) became the NFL commissioner in 1946. Almost immediately, he proved to be the dynamic leader the league badly needed in the challenging post-World War II years.*

# JOE CARR

*League administrator*
*Born in Columbus, Ohio, October 22, 1880; died May 20, 1939, at age of 58*
*No college*
*1921 American Professional Football Association; 1922–39 National Football League*

No one better understood the necessity of bringing some order to early-day professional football than Joe Carr, a former Columbus, Ohio, newspaperman who had managed the Columbus Panhandles football team since 1904. Carr's persistence finally paid off when, in September, 1920, the American Professional Football Association (APFA) was organized in Canton, Ohio.

Jim Thorpe, the best-known name of pro football in 1920, was named the APFA's first president. But a year later, after Thorpe had proven to be only a figurehead, Carr replaced him in the leadership role and established the league's headquarters in Columbus. The next year, in 1922, the league changed its name to the National Football League.

Joe strongly felt the public had the inherent right to know the league was being run honestly and capably. He insisted that players, as well as owners, receive fair treatment at all times.

Immediately, he established a standard player contract modeled on the one used in baseball. He cracked down sharply on the hiring of collegians under assumed names. When the Green Bay Packers, a new team in 1921, ignored Carr's edict, he quickly forfeited the franchise and then renewed it under new ownership a few months later.

In 1925, Red Grange stunned the football world by joining the Chicago Bears just 10 days after his final game with the University of Illinois. Sensing that resentment in college circles was certain to persist if such practices continued, Carr ruled, in the future, no NFL team could sign a college player until his eligibility was completed. Violators were promised a stiff fine or loss of franchise or both.

Carr soon recognized that, to survive, the NFL needed teams in the big cities of America. His first target was New York City and, through Joe's efforts, the New York Giants were born in 1925. The 70,000 crowd that turned out at the Polo Grounds later that year to see the Red Grange-led Bears proved big-city fans, given a good enough attraction, would support pro football.

A dedicated, no-nonsense administrator, Carr also served in executive positions in minor-league baseball and professional basketball during his tenure as NFL president. Neither gold nor glory interested Carr, he simply had the devotion of a missionary. A well-operated sports endeavor was the gospel he spread during his 18 years as the NFL's peerless leader.

*Joe Carr, the NFL President from 1921 to 1939, is pictured (third row, right) with the 1921 Columbus Panhandles.*

# EARL (DUTCH) CLARK

*Quarterback*
*6 ft 0 in, 185 lb*
*Born in Fowler, Colo., October 11,*
*1906; died August 5, 1978, at age*
*of 71*
*Colorado College*
*1931–2 Portsmouth Spartans;*
*1934–8 Detroit Lions*

There are many things about Earl "Dutch" Clark that do not fit the ordinary picture of an all-time great. Tiny Colorado College has produced just one all-America football player—that surprising honor was accorded Clark by Associated Press in 1929. Yet Dutch didn't play his first pro football game until almost two years later when he joined the Portsmouth Spartans for the 1931 season. After two campaigns, Clark retired to become head coach at another small college, the Colorado School of Mines.

By the time he returned to the NFL in 1934, the Spartans had become the Detroit Lions. Even before the year's layoff, Clark was considered to be one of the slowest players on his team. He was so humble and unassuming that, even though as tailback he would ordinarily be expected to carry the ball a high percentage of the time, Dutch hesitated to call his own signal, lest his teammates think he was trying to hog the limelight.

In his seven NFL seasons, Clark still established a legend of invincibility. In his five years with the Lions, he was the mastermind behind Detroit's famed infantry attack that set a team rushing record in 1936 that stood for 36 years. He was called the quarterback because he called the plays—in fact, he was named the all-NFL quarterback six times. Dutch was actually one of a quartet of powerful runners but he was the Lions' true triple-threat, who once completed 53.5 percent of his passes in a season when the league average was just 36.5 percent. He also led the league in scoring three times and, as the NFL's last great dropkicker, was Detroit's conversion and field goal specialist.

Clark had the uncanny knack of being in the right place at exactly the right time and his teammates swore that no one could follow his blockers as well as he did. They claimed, on a 40-yard scoring scamper, Clark might well cover 100 yards following his interference back and forth across the field.

"Dutch is like a rabbit in a brush heap," coach Potsy Clark (no relation) used to say. "When he gets into the secondary, he has no plan, just instinct. Just when you expect him to be smothered, he's free of his tacklers."

Yet if any one trait of Clark's stood out above the rest, it was his genius for quick thinking on the gridiron. "If Clark stepped on the field with Red Grange, Jim Thorpe and George Gipp," a rival coach once said, "Dutch would be the general."

*"Dutch" Clark was one of the most brilliant all-around backs ever to play in the NFL. He was particularly outstanding as a field general who earned the lasting respect of his teammates.*

RUSHING RECORD

| Year | Attempts | Yards | Average | TD | |
|------|----------|-------|---------|-----|---|
| 1931° | No records available | | | | |
| 1932° | 111 | 461 | 4.2 | 2 | |
| 1933 | Did not play | | | | |
| 1934† | 123 | 763 | 6.2 | 6 | |
| 1935† | 120 | 412 | 3.4 | 4 | |
| 1936† | 123 | 628 | 5.1 | 6 | ° With Portsmouth |
| 1937† | 96 | 468 | 4.9 | 5 | Spartans |
| 1938† | 7 | 25 | 3.6 | 0 | |
| TOTALS | 580 | 2757 | 4.8 | 23 | † With Detroit Lions |

44

# HAROLD (RED) GRANGE

*Halfback*
*6 ft 0 in, 185 lb*
*Born in Forksville, Pa., June 13, 1903*
*University of Illinois*
*1925 Chicago Bears; 1926 New York Yankees (AFL); 1927 New York Yankees (NFL); 1929–34 Chicago Bears*

In the early 1920s, George Halas was desperately seeking a special gate attraction to help draw attention not only to his Chicago Bears but to the NFL as a whole. In those same years at the University of Illinois, Harold "Red" Grange, a whirling-dervish halfback who ran with ghostlike speed and elusiveness, became the most noted American athlete of the decade.

Although college stars rarely turned to pro football in those days, the wily Halas pondered just how much Grange could do for pro football. Grange, who worked as an iceman in Wheaton, Illinois, during his college summers, agreed to play for the Bears. On Thanksgiving Day, 1925, just 10 days after Grange's last college game, 36,000 filled Wrigley Field to see Red's pro début against the Chicago Cardinals.

Sensing that a rare opportunity was at hand, Grange's agent, C. C. "Cash and Carry" Pyle, quickly lined up an 18-game coast-to-coast barnstorming tour that saw the Bears kick off with nine games in 17 days and continue to play until January 31, 1926. Drawn by the magic of his famous name and the number 77 he wore both in college and the pros, more than 400,000 fans saw the fabled "Galloping Ghost" in action. Enthusiastic crowds of more than 70,000 in New York's Polo Grounds and 75,000 in the Los Angeles Coliseum highlighted the tour.

When Pyle and Halas could not agree on terms for the 1926 season, Pyle formed a rival American Football League with a team in New York called the Yankees and featuring Grange. While the Yankees had moderate success, the rest of the league failed. Pyle was allowed to move his team into the NFL in 1927 but Grange suffered a crippling knee injury during a game against the Bears. "I didn't play at all in 1928," Grange remembers. "I was just an ordinary ball-carrier after that. I did develop into a pretty good defensive back, however."

Halas invited Grange back to the Bears in 1929 and he remained with them through the 1934 season. In the 1933 NFL championship game, Grange was a defensive hero with a difficult touchdown-saving tackle in the final seconds.

To be sure, Grange's on-the-field achievements in the NFL were minimal. Yet the mere presence of his name in an NFL lineup at a critical point in history played a major role in the league's survival and eventual prosperity.

*By putting on a Chicago Bears uniform in 1925, "Red" Grange did much to assure the eventual success of pro football. Massive crowds turned out to see the fabled running back in action.*

# GEORGE HALAS

*Founder, owner, coach*
*Born in Chicago, Ill., February 2,*
*1895; died October 31, 1983, at*
*age of 88*
*University of Illinois*
*1920 Decatur Staleys; 1921*
*Chicago Staleys; 1922–83 Chicago*
*Bears*

*George Halas enjoyed many memorable moments during his 64 years in the NFL but none was more joyous than the celebration in the Chicago Bears locker room after their stunning 73–0 defeat of the Washington Redskins in the 1940 NFL championship game.*

The only person to participate in the NFL from its organization in 1920 (as the American Professional Football Association) until his death in 1983, George Halas at one time or another during his incredible career filled the shoes of owner, general manager, player, promoter, ticket manager and influential rule maker.

But it was as a coach that he excelled. The indefatigable Halas coached for 40 years and led his teams to 325 victories, far more than any other coach. His Chicago Bears teams won six NFL titles, the first coming in 1921 after his Decatur Staleys moved to Chicago. George's Bears won three other divisional titles and finished second 15 times. Only six of Halas' 40 teams finished below the .500 mark.

Halas, the "Mr Everything" of pro football, had a profound effect on Halas, the coach. One's efforts led to the other's success and vice versa. Even when George was not the official on-the-field leader, there was little doubt who was running the show.

Halas divided his 40-year coaching term into four 10-year segments. When he retired as a player in 1930, he "fired" himself but three years later was back on the sidelines because the Bears were in financial difficulty and, as Halas said, "I came cheap." His second tenure was terminated by a Navy call in 1942 and he aborted his third term in 1955 to give his old friend, Paddy Driscoll, a chance to run the team. His final 10-year hitch terminated in 1968 when George was 73.

As a coach, Halas was first in many ways: the first to hold daily practice sessions, to utilize films of opponents' games for study, to schedule a barnstorming tour, and to have his team's games broadcast on radio. With his players, George maintained tight control. Disobedience and insubordination were not tolerated. The fact that 20 former Bears in addition to Halas are Hall of Fame members attests to his talents as a recruiter.

Along with Ralph Jones, his coach from 1930 through 1932, and consultant Clark Shaughnessy, Halas perfected the T-formation attack with the man in motion. It was this destructive force that propelled the Bears to their stunning 73–0 NFL title win over Washington in 1940 and sent every other league team scurrying to copy the Halas system. To George, this was his greatest thrill in 64 incomparable years of pro football.

COACHING RECORD

| Year | Won | Lost | Tied | Division finish§ | Year | Won | Lost | Tied | Division finish§ |
|---|---|---|---|---|---|---|---|---|---|
| 1920* | 10 | 1 | 2 | 2nd | 1951‡ | 7 | 5 | 0 | 4th |
| 1921† | 9 | 1 | 1 | 1st | 1952‡ | 5 | 7 | 0 | 5th |
| 1922‡ | 9 | 3 | 0 | 2nd | 1953‡ | 3 | 8 | 1 | 4th |
| 1923‡ | 9 | 2 | 1 | 2nd | 1954‡ | 8 | 4 | 0 | 2nd |
| 1924‡ | 6 | 1 | 4 | 2nd | 1955‡ | 8 | 4 | 0 | 2nd |
| 1925‡ | 9 | 5 | 3 | 7th | 1956–57 | Did not coach | | | |
| 1926‡ | 12 | 1 | 3 | 2nd | 1958‡ | 8 | 4 | 0 | Tie 2nd |
| 1927‡ | 9 | 3 | 2 | 3rd | 1959‡ | 8 | 4 | 0 | 2nd |
| 1928‡ | 7 | 5 | 1 | 5th | 1960‡ | 5 | 6 | 1 | 5th |
| 1929‡ | 4 | 9 | 2 | 9th | 1961‡ | 8 | 6 | 0 | Tie 3rd |
| 1930–2 | Did not coach | | | | 1962‡ | 9 | 5 | 0 | 3rd |
| 1933‡ | 10 | 2 | 1 | 1st | 1963‡ | 11 | 1 | 2 | 1st |
| 1934‡ | 13 | 0 | 0 | 1st | 1964‡ | 5 | 9 | 0 | 6th |
| 1935‡ | 6 | 4 | 2 | Tie 3rd | 1965‡ | 9 | 5 | 0 | 3rd |
| 1936‡ | 9 | 3 | 0 | 2nd | 1966‡ | 5 | 7 | 2 | 5th |
| 1937‡ | 9 | 1 | 1 | 1st | 1967‡ | 7 | 6 | 1 | 2nd |
| 1938‡ | 6 | 5 | 0 | 3rd | TOTALS‖ | 325 | 151 | 31 | |
| 1939‡ | 8 | 3 | 0 | 2nd | | | | | |
| 1940‡ | 8 | 3 | 0 | 1st | | | | | |
| 1941‡ | 10 | 1 | 0 | Tie 1st | | | | | |
| 1942‡ | 6 | 0 | 0 | ¶ | | | | | |
| 1943–5 | Did not coach — in US Navy | | | | | | | | |
| 1946‡ | 8 | 2 | 1 | 1st | | | | | |
| 1947‡ | 8 | 4 | 0 | 2nd | | | | | |
| 1948‡ | 10 | 2 | 0 | 2nd | | | | | |
| 1949‡ | 9 | 3 | 0 | 2nd | | | | | |
| 1950‡ | 9 | 3 | 0 | Tie 1st | | | | | |

POST-SEASON RECORD

1933 NFL Championship: Chicago Bears 23, New York Giants 21

1934 NFL Championship: New York Giants 30, Chicago Bears 13

1937 NFL Championship: Washington Redskins 28, Chicago Bears 21

1940 NFL Championship: Chicago Bears 73, Washington Redskins 0

1941 NFL Divisional Playoff: Chicago Bears 33, Green Bay Packers 14

1941 NFL Championship: Chicago Bears 37, New York Giants 9

1946 NFL Championship: Chicago Bears 24, New York Giants 14

1950 NFL Divisional Playoff: Los Angeles Rams 24, Chicago Bears 14

1963 NFL Championship: Chicago Bears 14, New York Giants 10

* With Decatur Staleys

† With Chicago Staleys

‡ With Chicago Bears

§ No division play in NFL until 1933

¶ Left for US Navy after sixth game of 1942 season

‖ Career totals include post-season games

46

# MEL HEIN

*Center*
*6 ft 2 in, 225 lb*
*Born in Redding, Calif., August*
*22, 1909*
*Washington State University*
*1931–45 New York Giants*

Mel Hein, a fixture at center for the New York Giants for 15 seasons, was one of the most durable players in NFL history. In the early days, there was no platoon football and players went 60 minutes every game. Yet he called for a timeout just once in his career—for hasty repairs to a broken nose in 1941. Even in his final campaign at the age of 36, Mel was still playing every game from the first kickoff to the final gun.

Mel combined great stamina, a cool head, mental alertness and simply superior ability to become an exceptional star. He was named the official all-NFL center eight straight years from 1933 through 1940. In 1938, he was named the league's most valuable player, a rare honor for a center. He was the team captain for 10 seasons. When he retired after the 1945 season, Mel's number 7—the luckiest seven in Giants history—was retired.

"Cappy" could do everything expected of a center and a linebacker and quite a bit more. He was adept at snapping the ball—to a tailback, not a T-quarterback—and, on defense, he used pass-jamming tactics still employed by today's finest defenders. Mel was one of the few NFL stars who had the speed and agility to contain Green Bay's premier receiver, Don Hutson, by bottling him up on the sidelines so he could not maneuver into the open.

Although Mel was thoroughly aggressive and coldly ferocious when it came to blocking and tackling, he was a gentleman player. He rarely lost his temper and gouging, kneeing and other similar misdeeds simply were not in his repertoire.

Hein settled on one position in the NFL but in high school he played guard, center, halfback and tackle. He led Washington State to a Rose Bowl bid in 1930 and was named to Grantland Rice's all-America team as a utility lineman but as a tackle, guard or center on several other selections.

Yet Mel had to write to three NFL teams offering his services in 1931. Providence bit first, offering $135 a game. Hein signed and mailed the Steam Roller contract. Then he learned that he could get $150 from the Giants so he hastily wired the Providence postmaster, described the letter he had sent and asked him to return it. When Mel and his new wife, Florence, arrived dead broke in Gotham just before training camp opened, the Giants agreed to advance him $200. Hein also had to beat out two veteran performers to be included on the 25-man squad. He never had to worry about winning a job again and, in his final season, he was the NFL's best-paid lineman at $5000 a year!

*Mel Hein had to write to three NFL teams offering his services after his graduation. Hein finally signed with the New York Giants, with whom he excelled as a center-linebacker over a 15-season span.*

# WILBUR (PETE) HENRY

*Tackle*
*6 ft 0 in, 250 lb*
*Born in Mansfield, Ohio, October
31, 1897; died February 7, 1952,
at age of 54*
*Washington and Jefferson College
1920–3, 1925–6 Canton Bulldogs;
1927 New York Giants; 1927–8
Pottsville Maroons*

Wilbur "Pete" Henry signed with the Canton Bulldogs the same day—September 17, 1920—that the American Professional Football Association, the direct forerunner of the NFL, was being organized in Canton, Ohio. In the *Canton Repository* the next day, the Henry acquisition was banner-headline news while the birth of the new pro football league was relegated to page three.

It is understandable that the newspaper editor could not have grasped the significance of the league meeting. Under any circumstance, Henry was an established superstar, a valuable addition to the Canton team and worthy of headline attention.

At first glance, however, Henry did not look like a football player. Roly-poly in appearance, seemingly both short and pudgy, he looked soft and fat at 6 ft 0 in and weighing 250 lb. But his flesh was tightly packed, as if riveted by steel. He gave the impression of slowness but he had the swift reflexes of a man-eating tiger. Good-natured, easy-going and prone to laughter off the field, he was an uncompromising competitor on the gridiron.

For the Bulldogs, who won NFL championships in both 1922 and 1923, Henry was a major contributor, playing 60 minutes every game. He did much more than just block and tackle with monotonous efficiency. He had been a fullback in high school and, in the NFL, he was used occasionally on a "tackle over tackle" play. "Fats," as Henry was also known, was a superior punter, placekicker and dropkicker and, for many years, he held a spot in the NFL record book for exceptional feats with his kicking foot. In 1922, he dropkicked a 50-yard field goal against Toledo, the next year a 94-yard punt against Akron. His 40-yard field goal tied Akron, 3–3, and preserved Canton's unbeaten season in 1922.

As multi-talented as Pete was on offense, he was even more devastating on defense. Coach Tommy Hughitt of the Buffalo All-Americans devised a game plan that called for his team to run straight at Henry on every play so as to "show him who's boss!" On the first play, Henry flattened several Buffalo blockers and then rocketed into the backfield to throw the ball-carrier for a substantial loss. Hughitt quickly abandoned his game plan.

*"Pete" Henry was a superior tackle but his outstanding punts and dropkicks put him in the NFL record book.*

# ROBERT (CAL) HUBBARD

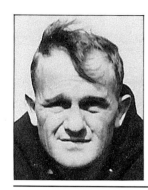

*Tackle*
*6 ft 5 in, 250 lb*
*Born in Keytesville, Mo., October*
*31, 1900; died October 17, 1977,*
*at age of 76*
*Centenary College, Geneva College*
*1927–8 New York Giants;*
*1929–33, 1935 Green Bay*
*Packers; 1936 New York Giants;*
*1936 Pittsburgh Pirates*

"Cal" Hubbard, a Missouri farm boy, developed an early love affair with the sport of football. His local high school did not have a team so he went to school in a neighbouring town. He then enjoyed three fine college years at Centenary in Louisiana and a final 1926 all-America season at Geneva in Pennsylvania. Three NFL teams offered him a contract but his boyhood idol and college coach, Bo McMillin, advised him to sign with the Giants. "At least they are sure to pay you," Bo counseled.

At all levels of football, Hubbard was always the biggest man on the field. An outstanding blocker, he played both end and tackle on offense. As a defensive linebacker, he could stymie the opposition running attack on his side of the line almost single-handed. With his great height, he became proficient at blocking passes just as they were thrown.

Early-day grid teams usually had a "policeman," an even-tempered but dominating personality whose job it was to convince a dirty-playing opponent he should clean up his act. Cal was ideal for the role because he was highly respected by players, fans and officials alike.

Hubbard joined the 1927 Giants as a $150-a-game rookie and quickly set the league on fire. It took the pros a long time to realize that a man of Hubbard's size could also be so fast. Cal continually plugged holes other linemen could not have reached. The Giants won the NFL title and set an all-time record by permitting just 20 points in 13 games.

The next year, Hubbard played unusually well in Green Bay and caught the envious eye of Packers coach Curly Lambeau. Cal liked the small-town atmosphere of Green Bay. In the off-season, he bluntly told the Giants' general manager, "Trade me to Green Bay or I quit."

When Hubbard moved to Green Bay, Lambeau shifted him into the tackle spot full-time. It was a great career move for Cal, who was the NFL's all-league tackle the next five years.

By 1936, Hubbard realized his football days were numbered and it was time to turn to another career for which he had been preparing, that of baseball umpire. He eventually became one of the great umpires of all time. Today, he is the only person to be enshrined in both the Pro Football and the Baseball Halls of Fame.

*"Cal" Hubbard starred as a two-way tackle in the 1920s and 1930s. When his football days were over, he embarked on a career of baseball umpiring that made him famous in another sport.*

# DON HUTSON

*End*
*6 ft 1 in, 180 lb*
*Born in Pine Bluff, Ark., January 31, 1913*
*University of Alabama*
*1935–45 Green Bay Packers*

D on Hutson scored against the Chicago Bears on an 83-yard pass from Arnie Herber his very first scrimmage play as a Green Bay Packers rookie and he wound up with 99 touchdown receptions, a record that still stands today. When he retired in 1945 after 11 superb seasons, he led all receivers with 488 catches. The number 2 man that year trailed Don by 298 receptions!

Although Hutson had been an all-America at Alabama in 1934, there were plenty who doubted the string-bean slim speedster could stand the pace of pro football. But it wasn't long before his mere presence on the field had changed the defensive concept of pro football. As the prime target for two excellent quarterbacks, Herber in the early years and Cecil Isbell later, Don could outmaneuver and outrace virtually every defender in the NFL. Such measures as double coverage and triple-teaming were unheard of until Hutson came on the scene.

There were skeptics among his opponents but they usually paid the price. Jock Sutherland, the Brooklyn coach, scoffed at the thought of putting more than one man on *any* receiver, but in Don's first game against the Dodgers, he had six sensational catches, two of them for touchdowns, as the Packers sped to an easy victory. Sutherland was stunned but also convinced.

Like everyone in the days before free substitution, Hutson was a 60-minute player who spent most of his career as a very fine safety on defense. In his final four seasons, he swiped 23 passes, including one returned 85 yards for a touchdown.

In the 1940s, Don was the Green Bay placekicking specialist, and scored almost 200 points by kicking. He also scored once on an end-around play and another time he passed for a touchdown. Like the baseball pitcher who is elated when he hits a home run, Hutson, ordinarily quiet and subdued, remembers these plays as special moments in a highlight-filled career.

Had it not been for a unique decision by NFL President Joe Carr before he played his first pro game, Hutson might never have become a landmark pass-catcher. Don signed with the pass-

minded Packers but also with the Dodgers, who rarely went to the air. Carr ruled the team that mailed its contract first would be awarded the rights to Hutson. The Packers' contract had been postmarked at 8:30 a.m., the Dodgers' pact at 8:47 the same day. Thus by a mere 17 minutes, Hutson became a Packer. He later admitted it was the luckiest break of his life.

## RECEIVING RECORD

| Year | Number | Yards | Average | TD |
|------|--------|-------|---------|-----|
| 1935 | 18 | 420 | 23.3 | 6* |
| 1936 | 34* | 536* | 15.8 | 8* |
| 1937 | 41* | 552 | 13.5 | 7* |
| 1938 | 32 | 548 | 17.1 | 9* |
| 1939 | 34* | 846* | 24.9 | 6 |
| 1940 | 45 | 664 | 14.8 | 7* |
| 1941 | 58* | 738* | 12.7 | 10* |
| 1942 | 74* | 1211* | 16.4 | 17* |
| 1943 | 47* | 776* | 16.5 | 11* |
| 1944 | 58* | 866* | 14.9 | 9* |
| 1945 | 47* | 834 | 17.7 | 9 |
| TOTALS | 488 | 7991 | 16.4 | 99 |

* Led NFL

## INTERCEPTION RECORD

| Year | Number | Yards | Average | TD |
|------|--------|-------|---------|-----|
| 1935–40 | No records available | | | |
| 1941 | 1 | 32 | 32.0 | 0 |
| 1942 | 7 | 71 | 10.1 | 0 |
| 1943 | 8 | 197* | 24.6 | 1 |
| 1944 | 4 | 50 | 12.5 | 0 |
| 1945 | 4 | 15 | 3.7 | 0 |
| TOTALS | 24 | 365 | 15.2 | 1 |

Rushing: 42 attempts, 236 yards, 5.6-yard average, 1 touchdown

Scoring: 105 touchdowns, 172 extra points, 7 field goals, 823 points

*Don Hutson was truly a player ahead of his time when it came to the art of pass receiving. His great speed and exceptional maneuverability forced defenses to make drastic alterations. His 99 touchdown receptions still rank as a pro football record.*

# EARL (CURLY) LAMBEAU

*Founder, coach*
*Born in Green Bay, Wisc., April 9,*
*1898; died June 1, 1965, at age of*
*67*
*Notre Dame University*
*1919–49 Green Bay Packers;*
*1950–1 Chicago Cardinals;*
*1952–3 Washington Redskins*

*"Curly" Lambeau led the Packers to seven NFL titles during his long tenure in Green Bay. Pictured here (right) with Don Hutson, one of the many stars that helped to make his teams successful.*

Earl "Curly" Lambeau founded the Green Bay Packers in 1919 and was the team's first playing star and its coach for 31 years. More than any other person, he is responsible for the existence today of the Packers' unique small-town franchise in the big-city world of professional sports. His life story is strictly a Green Bay saga that started with his birth there in 1898 and ended with his death near Green Bay in 1965.

Curly suffered his only football injury, a broken ankle, as an eighth-grader. He became the first real football hero at Green Bay's East High School and then played fullback as a Notre Dame freshman in 1918 before a tonsil infection forced him to leave school. Back in Green Bay, he was offered $250 a month to work for the Indian Packing Co. which, a year later, organized a football team called the "Packers." Lambeau became the team's coach and playing captain.

In 1921, the Packers joined the American Professional Football Association but their franchise was cancelled after the season because the team used college players performing under assumed names. Green Bay got its team back when Lambeau promised to obey all rules. He used $50 of his own money to buy the franchise and led a fund-raising drive that netted $2500 to put the Packers back on the field for the 1922 season.

Curly was the first pass-minded coach in the NFL and his teams were like their leader, impatient and explosive. He was an excellent passer in his own right and, after he retired as an active player, he made sure his Packers were always fortified with a talented aerial arm. Passers such as Arnie Herber and Cecil Isbell and receivers such as Don Hutson were joined by excellent players at all positions to make the Packers a powerhouse for almost three decades. The Packers were the first team to win three straight NFL titles in 1929, 1930, and 1931. After the league split into two divisions in 1933, they won three more NFL

championships, four divisional titles and finished second six times during Curly's tenure.

Green Bay fortunes took a sharp downturn in the late 1940s and in February, 1950, "The Bellicose Belgian," frustrated at his loss of one-man control of the franchise, resigned. Two-year coaching terms with both the Chicago Cardinals and the Washington Redskins followed without success. It was evident to all Lambeau had left his heart in Green Bay. It couldn't have been any other way.

## COACHING RECORD

| Year | Won | Lost | Tied | Division finish§ | Year | Won | Lost | Tied | Division finish§ |
|------|-----|------|------|-------|------|-----|------|------|-------|
| 1921° | 3 | 2 | 1 | Tie 6th | 1940° | 6 | 4 | 1 | 2nd |
| 1922° | 4 | 3 | 3 | Tie 7th | 1941° | 10 | 1 | 0 | Tie 1st |
| 1923° | 7 | 2 | 1 | Tie 3rd | 1942° | 8 | 2 | 1 | 2nd |
| 1924° | 7 | 4 | 0 | 6th | 1943° | 7 | 2 | 1 | 2nd |
| 1925° | 8 | 5 | 0 | 9th | 1944° | 8 | 2 | 0 | 1st |
| 1926° | 7 | 3 | 3 | 6th | 1945° | 6 | 4 | 0 | 3rd |
| 1927° | 7 | 2 | 1 | 2nd | 1946° | 6 | 5 | 0 | Tie 3rd |
| 1928° | 6 | 4 | 3 | 4th | 1947° | 6 | 5 | 1 | 3rd |
| 1929° | 12 | 0 | 1 | 1st | 1948° | 3 | 9 | 0 | 4th |
| 1930° | 10 | 3 | 1 | 1st | 1949° | 2 | 10 | 0 | 5th |
| 1931° | 12 | 2 | 0 | 1st | 1950† | 5 | 7 | 0 | 4th |
| 1932° | 10 | 3 | 1 | 3rd | 1951† | 2 | 8 | 0 | ¶ |
| 1933° | 5 | 7 | 1 | 3rd | 1952‡ | 4 | 8 | 0 | Tie 5th |
| 1934° | 7 | 6 | 0 | 3rd | 1953‡ | 6 | 5 | 1 | 3rd |
| 1935° | 8 | 4 | 0 | 2nd | TOTALS‖ | 229 | 134 | 22 | |
| 1936° | 10 | 1 | 1 | 1st | | | | | |
| 1937° | 7 | 4 | 0 | Tie 2nd | | | | | |
| 1938° | 8 | 3 | 0 | 1st | | | | | |
| 1939° | 9 | 2 | 0 | 1st | | | | | |

## POST-SEASON RECORD

1936 NFL Championship: Green Bay Packers 21, Boston Redskins 6

1938 NFL Championship: New York Giants 23, Green Bay Packers 17

1939 NFL Championship: Green Bay Packers 27, New York Giants 0

1941 NFL Divisional Playoff: Chicago Bears 33, Green Bay Packers 14

1944 NFL Championship: Green Bay Packers 14, New York Giants 7

° With Green Bay Packers

† With Chicago Cardinals

‡ With Washington Redskins

§ No division play in NFL until 1933

¶ Resigned after 10 games in 1951

‖ Career totals include post-season games

# TIM MARA

*Founder, administrator
Born in New York City, July 29, 1887; died February 17, 1959, at age of 71
No college
1925–59 New York Giants*

Early in 1925, it was apparent the NFL desperately needed the publicity attention a team in America's largest city could provide. League president Joe Carr went to New York to offer a local fight manager, Billy Gibson, a franchise. Gibson wasn't interested but he introduced Carr to a bookmaker friend, Tim Mara.

When Mara learned he could get a franchise for $500, he commented: "A New York franchise to operate anything ought to be worth $500." Mara immediately turned his new team over to an experienced football executive, Dr Harry March, who signed a name coach from Navy and several all-America collegians.

The 1925 Giants went 8–4 and finished fourth in a 20-team league but they couldn't dent the fans' enthusiasm for big-time college football in New York. By late-season, Mara's losses reached $40,000. Undaunted, the genial man with the big smile tried to sign college superstar Red Grange only to find the Bears had beaten him to the punch.

Still, Grange was important to Mara's future in football. When the Grange-led Bears played in the Polo Grounds in December, 1925, more than 70,000 saw the game and Mara netted $143,000. The future of pro football in New York was assured.

Mara's euphoria was short-lived because, in 1926, Grange and his manager, C. C. "Cash and Carry" Pyle, formed a new league with a New York Yankees franchise set to do battle with the Giants. Mara lost heavily, but the Yankees lost more and the new league went out of business. The next year, the Giants went 11–1–1 and Tim had his first NFL championship.

Mara was born on the lower East Side of New York and had known hard times as a youngster so, when New York Mayor Jimmy Walker approached him in the depression year of 1930 about playing a charity exhibition game, Tim quickly agreed. The Giants defeated the Notre Dame All-Stars, 21–0, and Mara turned over a check for $115,153 to the New York City Unemployment Fund.

In the next two decades, the Giants were among the perennial challengers in the NFL. In the late 1940s, Mara again had to endure another inter-league war, this time with the All-America Football Conference. Once again, Mara and the NFL won.

Mara died in 1959 but his sons followed in his footsteps and today, the Giants still prosper in their seventh decade under the Mara banner.

*NFL President Joe Carr (fourth from left) presents the 1934 league championship trophy to Tim Mara, owner of the New York Giants (center). Mara bought the Giants in 1925.*

# GEORGE PRESTON MARSHALL

*Founder, administrator*
*Born in Grafton, W. Va., October 13, 1897; died August 9, 1969, at age of 71*
*Randolph-Macon College*
*1932 Boston Braves; 1933–6 Boston Redskins; 1937–69 Washington Redskins*

George Preston Marshall was operating a laundry in Washington, DC, when he made the fateful decision to become part-owner of the new Boston Braves franchise in the NFL in 1932. His three partners dropped out when the Braves' first-season losses reached $46,000 but Marshall stayed to contribute to pro football in a unique and most valuable way.

Renamed the Redskins in 1933 and moved to Washington in 1937, Marshall's teams, particularly in the 1936–45 decade, were very successful. They won NFL championships in 1937 and 1942 and divisional titles four other times during that period.

But as successful as Marshall's elevens were, the flamboyant owner left his biggest mark in areas not directly associated with the team on the field. He introduced the idea of a team band and a gala halftime show. He was also the first genuinely to promote his team through the use of professional public relations methods. As early as 1933, he had his club line up for the team photo dressed in war paint, feathers and full headdress. Marshall's publicity campaign in 1937 made Sammy Baugh the most famous pro player before he threw his first NFL pass.

The energetic leader was also a force in improving the playing rules to open up the game and make it more crowd-pleasing. He championed the decision in 1933 to split the NFL into two divisions, with a playoff game to determine the title. Always controversial, Marshall became unhappy with fan support of the 1936 Redskins divisional title team and moved the NFL championship game to the neutral Polo Grounds in New York. By 1937, the Redskins had moved to Washington.

Marshall's total involvement in all team matters undoubtedly played a major role in the Redskins' stunning 73–0 loss in the 1940 title game. When the Redskins beat the Bears, 7–3, three weeks earlier, the Bears complained bitterly about the officiating and Marshall countered by calling the Bears "front-runners," "cry-babies" and "quitters." His remarks, carefully magnified by Bears boss George Halas, inflamed the Bears to a fever pitch and history's greatest rout was the result.

At Marshall's funeral in 1969, Commissioner Pete Rozelle summed up the master showman's unusual gift to the NFL: "Mr Marshall was an outspoken foe of the status quo when most were content with it. We are all beneficiaries of what his dynamic personality helped shape over more than three decades."

*George Preston Marshall was the first to recognize the importance of making pro football more entertaining for the fans. He introduced the idea of a team band and a halftime show.*

# JOHN (BLOOD) McNALLY

*Halfback*
*6 ft 0 in, 185 lb*
*Born in New Richmond, Wisc.,*
*November 27, 1903; died*
*November 28, 1985, at age of 82*
*St John's College of Minnesota*
*1925–6 Milwaukee Badgers;*
*1926–7 Duluth Eskimos; 1928*
*Pottsville Maroons; 1929–33,*
*1935–6 Green Bay Packers; 1934,*
*1937–9 Pittsburgh Pirates*

John McNally still had a year of college eligibility remaining when he decided to take a shot at pro football. To protect his eligibility, he needed an alias, a common practice in the 1920s. He and a friend passed a theater where the movie, *Blood and Sand*, was playing. Suddenly, McNally exclaimed to his friend: "That's it. You be Sand. I'll be Blood." So "Johnny Blood" it was, through 15 seasons in the NFL.

Blood was unbelievably fast, a superb running back and the finest receiver in the league. He could throw passes and punt with the best. On defense he was a ball hawk and a deadly tackler. Johnny played on five pro teams but his finest years came with the Green Bay Packers, with whom he was a major contributor to four championship juggernauts.

His off-the-field antics, however, constantly drew attention away from his exceptional playing skills. When the Packers were ahead, he tended to coast and clown. He broke training rules and ignored curfews. Green Bay Coach Curly Lambeau once offered "The Magnificent Screwball" $10 more per game if he would give up drinking. Johnny refused the extra money but did agree to drink only until Wednesday each week. Another time, he missed the team train but caught up with it by driving his car on the track and then gleefully joining his teammates aboard.

A precocious youngster, Johnny graduated from high school at 14, an age when he was small and immature and could not compete athletically. At St John's College, however, he began to grow and his natural athletic talents burst into full bloom. He was the basketball team captain and a letter winner in three other sports—football, baseball and track—in his junior year.

Blood was also known as "The Vagabond Halfback," and for good reason. At one time or another, he was an Air Force sergeant and cryptographer in China, an overnight prisoner in a Havana jail, a bartender, a hotel desk clerk, a seaman, an excellent debator and an accomplished poet.

Some say Blood clung so fiercely to boyhood he never grew up, at least not until after his pro football days which ended when he was player-coach with the 1939 Pittsburgh Pirates. He didn't marry until he was in his mid-forties and it was his wife, Marguerite, who described him most accurately. "Even when Johnny does the expected," she said, "he does it in an unexpected way."

*Johnny McNally adopted the nickname "Blood" to disguise the fact he was playing as a pro even though he had college eligibility remaining. He was one of the early-day NFL's most talented stars.*

# BRONKO NAGURSKI

*Fullback*
*6 ft 2 in, 225 lb*
*Born in Rainy River, Ontario,*
*November 3, 1908*
*University of Minnesota*
*1930–7, 1943 Chicago Bears*

All who saw the Chicago Bears' Bronko Nagurski bulldoze his way through enemy lines in the 1930s speak of him in the most glowing terms. "There was something strange about tackling Nagurski," long-time teammate Red Grange remembers. "When you hit him at the ankles, it was like getting an electric shock. If you hit him above the ankles, you were likely to get killed." New York Giants coach Steve Owen insisted the only way to defense Nagurski was "to shoot him before he leaves the dressing room."

Thus grew the legend of the intimidating fullback with the barrel chest and tree-trunk legs, the symbol of terrifying, crushing power on NFL gridirons. Bronko may be best remembered for his bull-like ball-carrying but he was a peerless blocker and a bone-jarring tackler. He was even a threat as a passer.

On his pet aerial play, Nagurski would fake a plunge, then step back a yard or two, jump and lob a pass to a waiting receiver. His pass to Grange gave the Bears a victory over Portsmouth in the 1932 championship game but the Spartans protested bitterly "The Bronk" was not the required 5 yards behind the scrimmage line when he threw the pass.

NFL owners saw the potential crowd appeal of the play, whether it was legal or illegal by 1932 standards, and changed the rule to allow a pass to be thrown anywhere behind the line of scrimmage. As if to show his appreciation, Nagurski threw two scoring passes in Chicago's 23–21 win in the 1933 title game.

Born in Ontario to Ukrainian immigrants, Bronko moved with his parents to International Falls, Minnesota, as a young boy. He played high-school football but the nearest opponent was 100 miles away and International Falls never won a game while Bronko was in school. He arrived at the University of Minnesota as a virtual unknown but soon became a hero. In 1929, he was an all-America pick, both as a tackle and a fullback.

Bruised and battered after eight years of NFL football, Nagurski left for a more profitable wrestling career after the 1937 season. But he returned in 1943 when the manpower shortages of World War II prompted an SOS from the Bears. Even after the unprecedented six-year layoff, Bronko still could contribute. He played primarily as a tackle but carried the ball on key plays. In the 1943 NFL title game against Washington, Nagurski ended his career by scoring the touchdown that put the Bears ahead to stay.

| RUSHING RECORD | | | | |
| --- | --- | --- | --- | --- |
| Year | Attempts | Yards | Average | TD |
| 1930–1 | No records available | | | |
| 1932 | 111 | 496 | 4.5 | 4 |
| 1933 | 128 | 533 | 4.2 | 1 |
| 1934 | 123 | 586 | 4.8 | 7 |
| 1935 | 37 | 137 | 3.7 | 1 |
| 1936 | 122 | 529 | 4.3 | 3 |
| 1937 | 73 | 343 | 4.7 | 1 |
| 1938–42 | Retired | | | |
| 1943 | 16 | 84 | 5.3 | 1 |
| TOTALS | 610 | 2708 | 4.4 | 18 |

*Bronko Nagurski was a legend by the time he joined the Bears in 1930. As a linebacker on defense and a fullback on offense, he was the epitome of the raw power of NFL football.*

# ERNIE NEVERS

*Fullback*
*6 ft 1 in, 205 lb*
*Born in Willow River, Minn., June 11, 1903; died May 3, 1976, at age of 72*
*Stanford University*
*1926–7 Duluth Eskimos; 1929–31 Chicago Cardinals*

Ernie Nevers was an 11-letter athletic star at Stanford but was best known for his exceptional performance in the 1926 Rose Bowl. Playing on what amounted to two broken ankles, the blond powerhouse ran for 114 yards and was named the outstanding man on the field, although his Stanford team lost to Notre Dame. That performance naturally led to comparisons of Nevers' talents to those of other great backs. Stanford's coach, Glenn "Pop" Warner, had also coached the great Jim Thorpe at Carlisle. Warner was frank in his appraisal: "Nevers can do everything Thorpe could do and he always tries harder. Ernie gives 60 minutes of himself every game."

After graduation, he signed both pro basketball and pro baseball contracts and, in fact, was destined to throw two gopher balls to Babe Ruth in his historic 60-homer season in 1927.

But pro football also beckoned and Ole Haugsraud of the Duluth Eskimos signed him to a $15,000 contract. It was big money for those days but the NFL, faced with the loss of Red Grange to a rival league, desperately needed a new superstar.

To make the Nevers investment pay off, it was necessary literally to put the show "on the road." The 1926 Eskimos played 29 games, 28 of them away from Duluth. With a 13-man squad, they traveled 17,000 miles but wound up with a 19–7–3 record. In a 1740-minute season, Nevers played all but 27 minutes. Even in the one game doctors ordered him to miss, Ernie, frustrated by the inaction, returned to throw a winning touchdown pass.

Possessed with inexhaustible stamina and an indomitable will, this most iron of all iron men of the early NFL could do everything on a football field. Nevers ran with crashing authority, he passed, returned kicks, punted, placekicked, called signals, played outstanding defense and eventually became a player–coach. He had only one weakness—he simply could not believe anything he tried would not work. If a play failed, he would try and try again, regardless of the consequences.

Nevers played a second year in Duluth and then sat out the 1928 season with a broken transverse process. He returned in 1929 as player–coach of the Chicago Cardinals. Later in the season, "The Blond Bull" enjoyed his finest game, a 40-point outburst in a 40–6 win over the cross-town Bears. A week later, Ernie tallied all 19 points in a 19–0 victory over Dayton. Thus, in two weeks, he scored 59 straight points for his team, possibly the most exceptional accomplishment in sports history.

Nevers, who wound up his career in 1931, played only five seasons in the NFL, less than any other member of the Pro Football Hall of Fame. Ernie claimed he had crammed 10 seasons of football into his five years. It was a hard but quick road to pro football immortality!

*Ernie Nevers played only five seasons but many claim he crammed 10 years of activity into his short NFL career. Nevers was outstanding with both the Duluth Eskimos and Chicago Cardinals.*

# JIM THORPE

*Halfback   6 ft 1 in, 190 lb*
*Born in Prague, Okla., May 28,*
*1888; died March 28, 1953, at age*
*of 64*
*Carlisle Indian School*
*1915–17, 1919–20 Canton*
*Bulldogs; 1921 Cleveland Indians;*
*1922–3 Oorang Indians; 1924*
*Rock Island Independents; 1925*
*New York Giants; 1926 Canton*
*Bulldogs; 1928 Chicago Cardinals*

Just before the season-ending series between the Canton Bulldogs and the arch-rival Massillon Tigers in 1915, Bulldogs general manager Jack Cusack signed the most famous American athlete of the age, Jim Thorpe, for the princely sum of $250 a game. The fabled Indian was everything Cusack expected him to be—an exceptional talent and an unparalleled gate attraction. With Thorpe leading the way, the Bulldogs claimed unofficial world championships in 1916, 1917, and 1919.

While Thorpe's exploits tend to be exaggerated with the passing years, there is no question he was superb in every way. He could run with speed as well as bruising power. He could pass and catch passes with the best, punt long distances and kick field goals either by dropkick or placekick. He blocked with authority and, on defense, was a bone-jarring tackler.

His one weakness was his relaxed approach to the game. Thorpe claimed it was just plain foolishness to practice something he knew he could do supremely well. He seemed to perform at his best only when he was angered.

Thorpe was born in a one-room cabin in Oklahoma. He had some French and Irish blood but he was of mostly Sac and Fox Indian heritage. His Indian name was Wa-Tho-Huk, meaning "Bright Path," something he was destined to follow in the sports world. He was excellent at every sport he tried. He gained his greatest fame by winning the decathlon and pentathlon events at the 1912 Olympics, only to have his medals taken away because he had earned $15 a week playing minor-league baseball one summer. He did play major-league baseball from 1913 to 1919.

But football was his favorite sport. His gridiron reputation was firmly established in 1912 when Thorpe scored 25 touchdowns and 198 points in leading his Carlisle Indian School team to a national collegiate championship. Jim captured the fancy of an entire nation and was a unanimous all-America pick.

Although his magic name was of inestimable value to pro football, Thorpe's best athletic days were behind him when he joined the Bulldogs at the age of 27. He played with six different teams but was rarely effective after the NFL was organized in 1920.

Fortunately, he lived long enough to relish the greatest of his honors, his selection by the nation's press in 1950 as the most outstanding athlete of the first 50 years of the twentieth century!

*The first big-name American athlete to play pro football, Jim Thorpe was a superstar in the pre-NFL years.*

# JIMMY CONZELMAN

*Quarterback, coach, owner*
*6 ft 0 in, 180 lb*
*Born in St Louis, Mo., March 6,*
*1898; died July 31, 1970, age 72*
*Washington University of St Louis*
*1920 Decatur Staleys; 1921–2*
*Rock Island Independents; 1923–4*
*Milwaukee Badgers; 1925–6*
*Detroit Panthers; 1927–30*
*Providence Steam Roller; 1940–2,*
*1946–8 Chicago Cardinals*

**M**ulti-talented Jimmy Conzelman was an outstanding quarterback who spent most of his active years in the dual role of player–coach. He was the player–coach–owner of the Detroit Panthers for two seasons. Off the field, he was even more versatile. At one time or another, he was a middleweight boxing champion, a successful song-writer, an actor, singer and pianist and a newspaper editor and publisher.

Conzelman's post-college career began with the Great Lakes Navy team that won the 1919 Rose Bowl. One of his Great Lakes teammates was George Halas, who recruited him for his 1920 Decatur Staleys pro team. Two seasons later, while Jimmy was playing for the Rock Island Independents, his coaching career began in a most unusual fashion. In one game, the opposition was gaining big yardage through the right tackle spot manned by the team's player–coach. Early in the second half, a substitute entered the game to tell Jimmy: "The owner says you are the new coach. So get busy!"

Conzelman moved to Providence in 1927 and produced an NFL title team in 1928. That year, he suffered a knee injury that ended his playing career. By 1930, realizing that all he had to show for his pro football endeavors was "a bantam-sized bank account and a bum knee," Jimmy decided to try his hand at other careers.

The popular Irishman was lured back into the NFL with the Chicago Cardinals in 1940 but after a pretty dismal 8–22–3 three-year record, he left to join the St Louis Browns baseball team. By 1946, Conzelman was back with the Cardinals and this time things fell quickly into place. The Chicago team improved from a 1–9 mark the previous year to a 6–5 finish in 1946 and then took the NFL championship in 1947 and a second straight division title in 1948.

A key to the Cardinals' success was Jimmy's handling of his players. "I remember best the warmth about him and the way he treated us all," halfback Charlie Trippi said. "He gave me a

feeling I was wanted. I couldn't play hard enough for him."

An exceptional string of circumstances dimmed what should have been Jimmy's happiest years. Owner Charlie Bidwill died in April, 1947, and later that year, Cardinal halfback Jeff Burkett was killed in a plane accident. After the 1948 season opener, tackle Stan Mauldin collapsed and died in the dressing room. A heart-broken Conzelman retired after the 1948 NFL title game.

COACHING RECORD

| Year | Won | Lost | Tied | Division finish‖ |
|------|-----|------|------|------------------|
| 1922* | 4 | 2 | 1 | 5th |
| 1923† | 7 | 2 | 3 | Tie 3rd |
| 1924† | 5 | 8 | 0 | 12th |
| 1925‡ | 8 | 2 | 2 | 3rd |
| 1926‡ | 4 | 6 | 2 | 12th |
| 1927§ | 8 | 5 | 1 | 5th |
| 1928§ | 8 | 1 | 2 | 1st |
| 1929§ | 4 | 6 | 2 | 8th |
| 1930§ | 6 | 4 | 1 | 5th |
| 1931–9 | Did not coach | | | |
| 1940¶ | 2 | 7 | 2 | 5th |
| 1941¶ | 3 | 7 | 1 | 4th |
| 1942¶ | 3 | 8 | 0 | 4th |
| 1943–5 | Did not coach | | | |
| 1946¶ | 6 | 5 | 0 | Tie 3rd |
| 1947¶ | 9 | 3 | 0 | 1st |
| 1948¶ | 11 | 1 | 0 | 1st |
| TOTALS** | 89 | 68 | 17 | |

POST-SEASON RECORD

1947 NFL Championship: Chicago Cardinals 28, Philadelphia Eagles 21

1948 NFL Championship: Philadelphia Eagles 7, Chicago Cardinals 0

* With Rock Island Independents

† With Milwaukee Badgers

‡ With Detroit Panthers

§ With Providence Steam Roller

¶ With Chicago Cardinals

‖ No division play in NFL until 1933

**Career totals include post-season games

*Jimmy Conzelman served pro football as an outstanding quarterback, a successful coach and even as an owner. His playing career ended in 1928. He was out of pro football in the 1930s but returned to coach the Chicago Cardinals in 1940. His 1947 Cardinals also won an NFL title.*

# ED HEALEY

*Tackle*
*6 ft 3 in, 220 lb*
*Born in Indian Orchard, Mass.,*
*December 28, 1894; died*
*December 9, 1978, at age of 83*
*Dartmouth College*
*1920–2 Rock Island Independents;*
*1922–7 Chicago Bears*

After graduation from Dartmouth College, where he had only average success as an end, Healey headed "for the wide open spaces of the west" and soon was loading meat into railroad cars in Omaha, Nebraska. When he heard of a new football league being formed, he took an overnight train to Rock Island, Illinois, to try out with the Independents. He faced the Chicago Tigers in his first game and, although he took a physical beating, he was given $100 and asked to join the team on a permanent basis. "The $100 I received just about took care of the doctor's bills," Healey quipped.

Late in the 1922 season, tackle Ed Healey of the Rock Island Independents lined up against George Halas, the player–coach of the Chicago Bears. Healey had dominated their previous meetings so Halas decided to try a new block, which involved, by his own admission, "some holding." Big Ed first yelled "foul" and then took a vicious swing at Halas but missed.

Right there and then, Halas decided it would be better to have Healey as an ally rather than an enemy. After the game, he bought Healey for $100, which happened to be the exact amount the Rock Island team owed the Bears on back gate receipts.

Healey was elated to get a raise to $100 a game but was most excited that the Bears had a clubhouse. "At Rock Island," Ed explained, "we had no showers and seldom a trainer. At Wrigley Field, we had a nice warm place to dress and nice warm showers."

Throughout his NFL career, Healey was a true warrior, one who enjoyed the violence of the game. To him, tackling—any body contact for that matter—was high pleasure. Halas often called him "the most versatile tackle in history." He was an unofficial all-NFL pick five years.

Even today, tackles experience a somewhat obscure life on the field but Healey was involved in at least two unforgettable plays as a Bear. In 1924, "Big Ed" ran more than 30 yards to nail his own teammate, who had run the wrong way with an intercepted pass, just short of the wrong goal line. Two years later, during the Bears' long barnstorming tour that featured the famous Red Grange, Healey made a touchdown-saving play before 60,000 fans that he called his greatest pro football thrill. Los Angeles All-Stars running ace George Wilson broke through the Bears line and into the open but Healey hurdled several of his own teammates and caught Wilson from behind after a long chase.

Walter Camp, who was considered the foremost authority on football in the early years of the twentieth century, watched the Bears play on several occasions in 1924. During one game, he couldn't take his expert eyes off one man.

"Who is that magnificent tackle?" he inquired.

"Ed Healey," he was told. "Ed Healey from Dartmouth."

Camp was flabbergasted. Over and over in his mind, he pondered how he could have missed Healey at Dartmouth.

The answer, of course, was that it wasn't until Healey turned professional and changed positions that he developed into a giant both in stature and ability.

*When Chicago Bears player-coach George Halas faced Ed Healey of the Rock Island Independents, he always came out second-best. Halas decided to solve the problem by buying Healey. The sale price of $100 was the exact amount Rock Island already owed Halas.*

# CLARKE HINKLE

*Fullback*
*5 ft 11 in, 201 lb*
*Born in Toronto, Ohio, April 10,*
*1910*
*Bucknell University*
*1932–41 Green Bay Packers*

*Clarke Hinkle was noted for his duels with Bronko Nagurski. He was extremely versatile, equally adept both on offense and defense and a long-time inspirational leader of the Packers.*

Clarke Hinkle did many things extremely well during his 10 years with the Green Bay Packers but he is best remembered for his head-to-head duels with another great fullback–linebacker, Bronko Nagurski of the Chicago Bears. Nagurski was the prototype power runner of the 1930s but the rugged Hinkle, 30 lb lighter, was determined to hold his own with anyone on an NFL gridiron. Hinkle's creed was "get to the Bronk before he gets to me," a tactic he used to perfection one day in 1934. Trapped on the sidelines by Nagurski, Clarke escaped his tackle by driving directly into and over him. The Bears' superstar was helped from the field with a broken nose and a fractured rib.

Hinkle was more than a hard-nosed player who loved to challenge the top stars. He was one of the finest all-round players in NFL history. Clarke was a pile-driving runner but he could turn the corner as well as hit the middle. He blocked savagely and his protection of the passer was outstanding. Hinkle could catch the ball and even throw it adequately in option situations. He was also the Packers' punter and placekicker. When he retired in 1941, he clogged the NFL record book with marks that only a new-style game of modern times has obliterated.

As brilliant as the four-time all-NFL star was on offense, he may have been even deadlier on defense. Backing up the Packers line, he was a vicious tackler against the run and yet adept on pass defense—Hinkle proudly claimed he let only one receiver get behind him during his decade of pro football.

Although Hinkle was an all-America at Bucknell, he probably would not have been "discovered" by the primitive pro scouting techniques of the 1930s had it not been for a trip Curly Lambeau, the Packers founder and coach, took to the East-West Shrine game in San Francisco in 1932. Clarke was the top ball-carrier that day and Lambeau immediately signed him for $125 a game.

Hinkle, with his burning desire to compete and willingness to play in spite of painful injuries, always enjoyed the lasting respect of friend and foe alike. Nagurski himself turned out to be Clarke's staunchest press agent and even presented him for induction into the Pro Football Hall of Fame in 1964. "They said I was hard to tackle, but here was a guy who didn't have too much trouble," Nagurski said of his Green Bay foe.

RUSHING RECORD

| Year | Attempts | Yards | Average | TD |
|------|----------|-------|---------|-----|
| 1932 | 95 | 331 | 3.4 | 2 |
| 1933 | 139 | 413 | 2.9 | 4 |
| 1934 | 144 | 359 | 2.4 | 1 |
| 1935 | 77 | 273 | 3.5 | 2 |
| 1936 | 100 | 476 | 4.7 | 4 |
| 1937 | 129 | 552 | 4.2 | 5 |
| 1938 | 114 | 299 | 2.6 | 3 |
| 1939 | 135 | 381 | 2.7 | 5 |
| 1940 | 109 | 383 | 3.5 | 2 |
| 1941 | 129 | 393 | 3.0 | 5 |
| TOTALS | 1171 | 3860 | 3.3 | 33 |

Passing: 54 attempts, 24 completions, 316 yards, 2 touchdowns

Punting: 87 punts, 43.4-yard average

Scoring: 42 touchdowns, 31 extra points, 28 field goals, 367 points

# WILLIAM ROY (LINK) LYMAN

*Tackle*
*6 ft 2 in, 252 lb*
*Born in Table Rock, Nebr.,*
*November 30, 1898; died*
*December 16, 1972, at age of 74*
*University of Nebraska*
*1922–3, 1925 Canton Bulldogs;*
*1924 Cleveland Bulldogs; 1925*
*Frankford Yellowjackets; 1926–8,*
*1930–1, 1933–4 Chicago Bears*

Modern-day defensive football involves players constantly shifting from side to side, jumping a step forward or two paces backward, anything to confuse the offense as it comes to the line of scrimmage. Many old-timers insist such sophisticated maneuvers had their beginnings more than six decades ago when a sensational 252-lb tackle, William Roy "Link" Lyman, pioneered a sliding, shifting style of defensive line play that confused his opponents and made him one of the most respected players of his time.

Steve Owen, an opponent who later coached the New York Giants, was one of the first to fall foul of Lyman's tactics. "Link was the first lineman I ever saw who moved from his assigned defensive position before the ball was snapped," Owen said. "It was difficult to play against him because he would vary his moves and no matter how you reacted, you could be wrong."

Lyman explained he happened on the idea of shifting almost unconsciously as an instinctive move to fool a blocker. He had a unique ability to diagnose a play and many times he would make his move just as the ball was snapped.

Link did not play football at McDonald Rural Federated High School in Pawnee County, Nebraska, because only seven boys attended the school. He quickly adjusted to the game, however, when he entered the University of Nebraska in 1917 and eventually became a superstar on the outstanding 1921 Cornhusker team. Another Nebraskan, player–coach Guy Chamberlin of the Canton Bulldogs, lured Link into pro football in 1922. The Bulldogs won championships in Canton in 1922 and 1923 and again in Cleveland in 1924. In January, 1926, Lyman joined the Chicago Bears for their long barnstorming tour and remained with the Bears the rest of his career. He did take two one-year leaves of absence to play semi-pro football in 1929 and to settle business problems in 1932.

In his last two seasons, the Bears won the 1933 NFL championship and the 1934 divisional crown. Link played on just one losing team in 16 seasons of high school, college and professional football and was a contributor to the very end. Bears coach George Halas insisted Lyman was stronger and tougher in those last two seasons than when he first joined the team eight years earlier.

*"Link" Lyman became the first lineman to adopt a shifting, sliding style of defense that thoroughly confused the opposition.*

# MIKE MICHALSKE

*Guard*
*6 ft 0 in, 209 lb*
*Born in Cleveland, Ohio, April 24,*
*1903; died October 26, 1983, at*
*age of 80*
*Pennsylvania State University*
*1926 New York Yankees (AFL);*
*1927-8 New York Yankees (NFL);*
*1929-35, 1937 Green Bay Packers*

For 12 years, Mike Michalske was pro football's premier guard, a position many insist was the toughest job of all in the 1920s and 1930s. A guard in those days was expected to block the biggest opposing linemen head-on. He also had to pull from the line and lead interference for the ball-carrier. When the other team had the ball, the guard was the key man in stopping the enemy running attack. But he also had to be capable of storming into the backfield to thwart a pass.

Michalske was particularly adept at going after the passer. "We called it blitzing in those days, too," he once said. "It may not have been exactly ethical but it was legal in those days to rough the passer, even after he got rid of the ball. We worked him over pretty good."

Obviously mixing more than a little brainpower with his brawn, Michalske also pioneered the idea of using former fullbacks at guard because they were fast and explosive. He sold the idea to

Green Bay Packers coach Curly Lambeau and thus it was no accident that many fine Green Bay guards had cut their football teeth as fullbacks.

Christened August at birth, Michalske became known as "Iron Mike" because, while he played 60 minutes every game, he simply never was injured. "I just didn't get hurt," he explained. "The players used to say I must be getting paid by the minute."

Michalske played fullback and guard, and also end and tackle, in high school and at Penn State, where he was an all-America pick in 1925. He first turned pro with the new American Football League in 1926 but that league folded after one year. When his New York Yankees NFL team disbanded two seasons later, Michalske waived the $400 salary due him for his free agency.

Mike promptly signed with the Packers, where he remained for eight highly successful seasons, both for him and his team. The Packers won NFL titles in 1929, 1930, and 1931 and Michalske was named all-league four times.

Years later in the 1960s when another Packers dynasty was dominating the NFL, Green Bay fans speculated how Mike would have fitted into Vince Lombardi's plans. Buckets Goldenberg, a Michalske teammate, had the answer: "Mike would be a line-backer with the speed, reflexes and smartness of the very best. He would have been outstanding in any age of football at almost any position."

*Mike Michalske was both an iron-man performer and an on-the-field innovator. He was outstanding on the Packers' championship teams of 1929, 1930, and 1931 and was named all-NFL four times.*

# ART ROONEY

*Founder, administrator*
*Born in Coulterville, Pa.,*
*January 27, 1901*
*Georgetown University, Duquesne*
*University*
*1933–present day Pittsburgh*
*Steelers (Pirates)*

In January, 1975, the Pittsburgh Steelers won their first NFL championship by beating the Minnesota Vikings in Super Bowl IX. In the locker room after the game, celebrating Steelers gathered around the team founder Art Rooney to present him with the game ball. NFL Commissioner Pete Rozelle followed up with the Vince Lombardi Super Bowl trophy. With the possible exception of the vanquished Vikings, the entire sports world rejoiced for the revered Mr Rooney, who at long last had won the championship which he had sought so diligently for so long.

In the years since 1933, when he paid $2500 for the Pittsburgh Pirates NFL franchise, the cigar-smoking Rooney has achieved millionaire status through his non-football interests. Before he entered the NFL, he sponsored such western Pennsylvania semi-pro teams as the J. P. Rooneys, the North Side Majesties and Hope Harveys. He once said his semi-pro teams were comparable to early-day NFL teams. Despite considerable effort on Art's part, his first Pirates elevens—the team name was changed to Steelers in 1940—were not much better. Their first winning season came in 1942 and a tie for the Eastern Division title in 1947 was the nearest thing to a championship the Steelers experienced in their first 40 seasons.

It was not that Rooney didn't try. In 1938, for instance, he shocked the sports world by signing Byron "Whizzer" White, the Colorado all-America, to a then unthinkable $15,000 contract. Such faith in pro football was demonstrated repeatedly by Rooney and it was something that proved to be a guiding light for the NFL during the dark depression years.

The Steelers didn't win and they didn't draw, either. Mr Rooney never complained. "I'll tell you something from the bottom of my heart," Art told a reporter years later. "I'd pay to lose money to keep in this game. I love it that much."

Finally, in the 1970s, the Steelers hit on the right combination, Chuck Noll as coach and a series of brilliant college drafts that made the Steelers the dominant team of an entire decade. They wound up with four Super Bowl championships, something no other team has ever accomplished.

The Steelers of the 1970s were armed with exceptionally talented athletes but, spiritually and emotionally, what they accomplished was a win for Mr Rooney, a win for love, warmth and kindness, all rare traits that "The Chief" has exhibited in more than half a century of NFL football.

*Art Rooney founded the Pittsburgh franchise in 1933 and did much to keep pro football alive in the Depression years. He had to wait 42 years until the Steelers gave him his first title in Super Bowl IX.*

# GEORGE TRAFTON

*Center*
*6 ft 2 in, 235 lb*
*Born in Chicago, Ill., December 6, 1896; died September 5, 1971, at age of 74*
*Notre Dame University*
*1920 Decatur Staleys; 1921 Chicago Staleys; 1922–32 Chicago Bears*

In the early years of the NFL, teams were founded and disbanded and players shifted from club to club in helter-skelter fashion, but there was one notable exception to this general pattern of confusion. It was George Trafton, who played with just one team, the Chicago Bears (who began as the Decatur Staleys in 1920), for the first 13 years of the NFL.

There were no official all-league teams until 1931, but press accounts claim Trafton was the all-NFL center eight times in 13 seasons. Without doubt, George, whose brief Notre Dame career was aborted when coach Knute Rockne caught him playing semi-pro football, was an excellent pro player with a deserved reputation as a superior competitor. He also was recognized as a scrimmage-line ruffian of the first magnitude.

Fabled halfback Red Grange once opined that "Big George" was "the toughest, meanest, most ornery critter alive." One writer reported that Trafton was strongly disliked in every NFL city, with the exception of Green Bay and Rock Island. In those places, "he was hated."

One 1920 afternoon, Trafton was accused of putting four Rock Island players out of action in 12 plays. Another day Big George broke a Rock Island halfback's leg on an out-of-bounds tackle against a fence. When the final gun sounded, he raced from the field, hailed a taxi and eventually thumbed a ride in his mad dash to safety. The next time the Bears played in Rock Island, coach George Halas entrusted the team's $7000 guarantee to Trafton. "I knew if trouble came," Halas explained, "Trafton would be running for his life. I would only be running for $7000."

Trafton, however, was far more than just a roughneck. He was a skilled defensive player who had the moves of a halfback to go with his size and strength. He was one of the first centers to rove on defense and the very first on offense to center the football with only one hand. The Bears' press book once claimed their dynamic team captain never made a bad snap "in 201 games or 158 hours of actual competition."

Consistent with his personality, Big George defiantly wore the supposedly unlucky number 13 jersey and rarely let protocol or tradition stand in his way. When Halas did not offer him a contract in 1930, he simply reported to new coach Ralph Jones. By the time the season opened, Trafton was back in his familiar spot in the middle of the line.

*George Trafton had great speed and agility, as well as size and strength. Unlike most players of his day, Trafton played for just one club in his 13-year NFL career.*

# GUY CHAMBERLIN

*Coach, end   6 ft 2 in, 210 lb*
*Born in Blue Springs, Nebr.,*
*January 16, 1894, died April 4,*
*1967, at age of 73*
*University of Nebraska*
*1919 Canton Bulldogs (pre-NFL);*
*1920 Decatur Staleys; 1921*
*Chicago Staleys; 1922–3 Canton*
*Bulldogs; 1924 Cleveland Bulldogs;*
*1925–6 Frankford Yellowjackets;*
*1927–8 Chicago Cardinals*

Guy Chamberlin played and coached in the earliest years of the NFL when the only statistic kept was the teams' won–lost record. Winning was a category in which Chamberlin excelled. Of those coaches with 50 or more victories, Guy's 56–14–5 record and .780 winning percentage is the absolute best. In his six coaching seasons, five of which were spent as a player–coach, Chamberlin also won four NFL championships.

As a player, he was one of the finest ends of his time. When George Halas began lining up players for his first Decatur Staleys team in 1920, Chamberlin was his prime recruit. He was big, tall and fast, excellent on both offense and defense and a 60-minute player every game.

Guy was a constant threat as a game breaker. In a crucial Staleys game in 1920, Chamberlin scored the winning touchdown on a 70-yard reception. A year later, against the Buffalo All-Americans, Chamberlin contributed the only touchdown in a 10–7 Staleys victory on a 75-yard interception return.

*Guy Chamberlin pictured here with a Canton fan, was a premier end as well as a championship-winning coach with the Canton Bulldogs, Cleveland Bulldogs and Frankford Yellowjackets.*

Although Chamberlin's high school in Blue Springs, Nebraska, was not big enough to field a football team, he became a two-time all-America at the University of Nebraska. Jim Thorpe, who had always been his idol, lured Guy into pro football with the pre-NFL Canton Bulldogs in 1919.

After two seasons with Halas and the Staleys, Chamberlin came back to Canton as player–coach of the Bulldogs. Thorpe was no longer with the team but Chamberlin assembled one of the powerhouse elevens of the 1920s. Canton, with undefeated seasons in both 1922 and 1923, became the NFL's first two-time champion. The Bulldogs were sold to a Cleveland promoter in 1924 but Chamberlin, with a different cast of players, led his team to a third straight championship.

In 1925, Chamberlin joined the Frankford Yellowjackets and a year later won another title with a 14–1–1 record. Guy concluded his career as a player only with the 1927 Chicago Cardinals and as a coach only in 1928. The 1–5–0 mark of the 1928 Cardinals was the lone "smear" on an otherwise almost-perfect coaching record.

As a player or a coach, Guy Chamberlin, in the words of the long-time New York Giants coach Steve Owen, can be remembered appropriately by the description "The Winningest!"

| COACHING RECORD | | | | | |
|---|---|---|---|---|---|
| Year | Won | Lost | Tied | Finish | |
| 1922° | 10 | 0 | 2 | 1st | ° With Canton Bulldogs |
| 1923° | 11 | 0 | 1 | 1st | † With Cleveland Bulldogs |
| 1924† | 7 | 1 | 1 | 1st | ‡ With Frankford Yellowjackets |
| 1925‡ | 13 | 7 | 0 | 6th | |
| 1926‡ | 14 | 1 | 1 | 1st | § With Chicago Cardinals |
| 1927 | Did not coach | | | | |
| 1928§ | 1 | 5 | 0 | 9th | |
| TOTALS | 56 | 14 | 5 | | |

# JOHN (PADDY) DRISCOLL

*Quarterback*
*5 ft 11 in. 160 lb*
*Born in Evanston, Ill., January 11, 1896; died June 29, 1968, at age of 72*
*Northwestern University*
*1919 Hammond Pros (pre-NFL); 1920 Decatur Staleys; 1920–5 Chicago Cardinals; 1926–9 Chicago Bears*

The term "franchise player" is used to describe a star who, by the excellence of his play on the field, plays a major role in his team's success or, in some cases, its very existence. Early in the 1920 season, John "Paddy" Driscoll proved himself to be a franchise player of the rarest kind.

The Chicago Cardinals, a new American Professional Football Association member, were challenged in the Windy City by the non-league Tigers. The owners of both teams, recognizing that such a rivalry would be financially devastating, agreed to play one game. The winner would continue to play and the loser would disband. The Cardinals won, 6–3, their triple-threat quarterback, Driscoll, scoring the game's only touchdown. Team owner Chris O'Brien immediately offered Driscoll the then-princely sum of $300 a game to continue to play for the Cardinals.

Even by 1920 standards, Paddy was not big but he was a brilliant field general who was good at everything but exceptional at punting and dropkicking. Against the Columbus Tigers in 1925, he dropkicked field goals of 23, 18, 50, and 35 yards. For years, his 50-yard field goal stood as an NFL record. Earlier, in 1923, Driscoll scored 27 points against Rochester on four touchdowns and three extra points.

After the Bears moved to Chicago in 1921, they quickly became arch-rivals of the Cardinals. Driscoll seemed always to be at his peak when the two teams played. In 1922, he scored all the points on dropkicked field goals as the Cardinals beat the Bears, 6–0 and 9–0. When the famed Red Grange made his pro début against the Cardinals in 1925, Driscoll angered the large crowd by continually punting away from the whirling-dervish runner. Grange could return only three of Paddy's 23 kicks and the game ended in a scoreless tie. Paddy explained his tactics: "I decided if one of us was going to look bad, it wasn't going to be me. Punting to Grange is like grooving a pitch to Babe Ruth."

The possibility that Driscoll might defect to a new league being formed in 1926 prompted his trade to the Bears, where he continued to subdue the opposition single-handed. Whether it was by a long run, a scoring or a booming kick, team after team, until Driscoll retired after the 1929 season, continued to fall victim to the many talents of pro football's first genuine "franchise player."

*"Paddy" Driscoll was the Chicago Cardinals' leading player in the early 1920s and was then traded to the cross-town Bears in 1926.*

# DAN FORTMANN

*Guard*
*6 ft 0 in, 210 lb*
*Born in Pearl River, N. Y.,*
*April 11, 1916*
*Colgate University*
*1936–43 Chicago Bears*

The NFL staged its first draft of college seniors in 1936 but the nine NFL teams, not recognizing the significance of what was taking place, were armed only with a few newspaper clippings and perhaps a random tip on some local college star.

So it was that Chicago Bears owner George Halas stared blankly at his dwindling list of names when the ninth round of the draft began. On a hunch, he selected a guard from Colgate named Dan Fortmann. "I like that name. I'll take him," Halas exclaimed as he made the selection.

On the surface, it appeared at first that Halas had made a mistake. At 6 ft 0 in and 210 lb, Fortmann was too small for line play in the NFL. He was just 19 and a Phi Beta Kappa scholar, not the ordinary credentials for someone who was supposed to knock down enemy ball-carriers or lead the interference.

By the time his rookie season started, Danny had turned 20 but was still the youngest starter in the NFL. He had determination and talent, however, and soon was excelling as a little man in a big man's game. On offense, he called signals for the linemen and was a battering-ram blocker. On defense, he was a genius at diagnosing enemy plays and a deadly tackler. For seven seasons, Fortmann and Chicago's number 1 pick in the historic 1936 draft, tackle Joe Stydahar, were a formidable combination on the left side of the powerful Bears line.

The Bears were a dominant team during Fortmann's career. From 1936 to 1943, the Monsters of the Midway finished first in their division five times, second twice and third once, and Fortmann was the top man at his position in pro football. He earned all-NFL honors six straight years from 1938 to 1943.

Fortmann and the man who brought him to the Bears, Halas, developed a strong rapport over the years. Danny respected the head man's coaching ability but praised him for another most important reason.

"George made it possible for me to pursue my medical studies while playing football," Fortmann remembers. "He allowed me to miss two weeks of summer practice each year while I finished up in school. Without his understanding and cooperation, I could never have prepared for my future."

*Dan Fortmann combined determination and native ability to become a Chicago Bears all-time great. He was all-NFL six times in eight seasons. Here he opens a hole for Bears' fullback Bill Osmanski.*

# OTTO GRAHAM

*Quarterback*
*6 ft 1 in, 195 lb*
*Born in Waukegan, Ill.,*
*December 6, 1921*
*Northwestern University*
*1946–55 Cleveland Browns*

When Paul Brown began organizing the Cleveland Browns team to play in the new All-America Football Conference (AAFC), the first player he signed was Otto Graham, a tailback from Northwestern University and the Chapel Hill, North Carolina, Pre-Flight team. Brown eyed Graham as the perfect quarterback for his new pro team.

This was a curious choice because Graham, a music major who played the cornet, violin and French horn, planned to concentrate on basketball at Northwestern. He was "discovered" playing intra-mural football as a freshman and although he became a fine passer in three varsity seasons, he had no experience in the T-formation.

Brown never wavered in his decision. "Otto has the basic requirements of a T-quarterback—poise, ball-handling and distinct qualities of leadership." It turned out the coach was right. Once Graham joined the Browns, he not only quickly mastered the mechanics of the T but he became the heart of a dynamic football machine. As center Moe Scarry said, "He's the kind of guy you want to do your best for."

With Graham throwing touchdown passes at a sizzling pace with relatively few interceptions, the Browns won four straight AAFC titles and compiled an awesome 52–4–3 record. Still, pro football "experts" theorized Otto and the Browns would get their comeuppance once they faced the "real pros" in the NFL in 1950, but both the quarterback and the team proved more than equal to the occasion. In the Browns' 30–28 victory over the Los Angeles Rams in the NFL title game, Graham threw four touchdown passes. His finest title-game performance came three years later when he scored three touchdowns and threw for a trio of scores in a 56–10 lacing of Detroit.

Graham retired after that game but responded magnificently to Paul Brown's SOS early in 1955. In the final game of his career, the NFL championship against the Los Angeles Rams, he ran for two touchdowns and passed for two more in a 38–14 victory. For the ninth time in 10 seasons, Otto was named the all-league

*Otto Graham piloted the Cleveland Browns to 10 divisional or league championships in 10 seasons.*

quarterback. He went out as the champion he had always been throughout his pro career.

While Graham was guiding the Browns, the Cleveland team played in 10 straight title games and had four AAFC and three NFL championships. It is a record no other quarterback has ever matched.

| PASSING RECORD | | | | | | |
|---|---|---|---|---|---|---|
| Year | Attempts | Completions | Percentage passes completed | Yards | TD | Interceptions |
| 1946° | 174 | 95 | 54.6 | 1834 | 17§ | 5 |
| 1947° | 269 | 163 | 60.6§ | 2753§ | 25§ | 11 |
| 1948° | 333 | 173 | 52.0 | 2713§ | 25 | 15 |
| 1949° | 285 | 161§ | 56.5 | 2785§ | 19 | 10 |
| 1950† | 253 | 137 | 54.2 | 1943 | 14 | 20 |
| 1951† | 264 | 147 | 55.5 | 2205 | 17 | 16 |
| 1952† | 364‡ | 181‡ | 49.7 | 2816‡ | 20‡ | 24‡ |
| 1953†¶ | 258 | 167 | 64.7‡ | 2722‡ | 11 | 9 |
| 1954† | 240 | 142 | 59.2‡ | 2092 | 11 | 17 |
| 1955†¶ | 185 | 98 | 53.0‡ | 1721 | 15 | 8 |
| TOTALS | 2626 | 1464 | 55.8 | 23,584 | 174 | 135 |

Career passing rating: 86.8

° With Cleveland Browns (AAFC)

† With Cleveland Browns (NFL)

‡ Led NFL    § Led AAFC

¶ Official NFL individual passing champion

Rushing: 405 attempts, 882 yards, 2.2-yard average, 44 touchdowns

Interceptions: 7 interceptions, 102 yards, 14.6-yard average, 1 touchdown

Punt returns: 23 returns, 262 yards, 11.4-yard average, 0 touchdowns

Scoring: 46 touchdowns, 276 points

# SID LUCKMAN

*Quarterback*
*6 ft 0 in, 195 lb*
*Born in Brooklyn, N. Y.,*
*November 21, 1916*
*Columbia University*
*1939–50 Chicago Bears*

In his 12 seasons with the Chicago Bears, Sid Luckman became the first successful T-formation quarterback. One game in Luckman's second season—the 1940 NFL title game which saw the Bears annihilate the Washington Redskins, 73–0—showcased the explosive possibilities of the T attack. Almost immediately, many other pro teams began to adopt the new formation.

Not all teams had the instant success with the T the Bears enjoyed. Loaded with outstanding players, the Bears, during Sid's tenure, won four NFL championships, just missed a fifth and finished second six times. He was all-NFL five times between 1941 and 1947 and the league's most valuable player in 1943.

The modest and mannerly Brooklyn native not only made the Bears a winner but he became a big-play and big-game man as well. Sid is best remembered for the 73–0 game but, because the Bears forged ahead early, he had to pass only six times, completing four of them for 102 yards and a touchdown.

Luckman had many more outstanding games but possibly two, both in 1943, stand out above the rest. On November 14, Sid Luckman Day at the Polo Grounds, he passed for a record-tying seven touchdowns in a 56–7 massacre of the New York Giants. Later that year, in the championship game against the Redskins, he threw for 276 yards and five touchdowns in a 41–21 triumph.

Making Sid's pro career even more remarkable is the fact that he was a triple-threat tailback at Columbia with running as his strongest point. George Halas, who had seen Luckman as the leader of his emerging powerhouse, first presented Sid with a Bears T-formation playbook when he was practicing for the College All-Star game in 1939. Astonished and somewhat alarmed by the complexities of the new system, Sid was not an instant success. He fumbled frequently, had trouble with handoffs, and in general flunked his first T test. Halas shifted Luckman to halfback for a while before making another effort which, on the second try, paid dividends.

Because of Halas' patience, Luckman developed a tremendous

loyalty to the Bears. In 1946, when the Chicago Rockets of a rival league offered him a too-good-to-turn-down $25,000 to serve as player–coach, Sid quickly said "no." "How could I possibly have taken it?" he asked. "How could I quit a club that has done so much for me?"

*Sid Luckman had been a triple-threat tailback in college but George Halas acquired him to run the T-formation attack for the Bears. Here, Halas (left) offers a few pointers to his prized field leader.*

## PASSING RECORD

| Year | Attempts | Completions | Percentage passes completed | Yards | TD | Interceptions |
|------|----------|-------------|------------------------------|-------|-----|---------------|
| 1939 | 51 | 23 | 45.1 | 636 | 5 | 4 |
| 1940 | 105 | 48 | 45.7 | 941 | 4 | 9 |
| 1941 | 119 | 68 | 57.1° | 1181 | 9 | 6 |
| 1942 | 105 | 57 | 54.3 | 1023 | 10 | 13 |
| 1943 | 202 | 110 | 54.5 | 2194° | 28° | 12 |
| 1944 | 143 | 71 | 49.7 | 1018 | 11 | 11 |
| 1945† | 217 | 117 | 53.9 | 1725° | 14° | 10 |
| 1946 | 229 | 110 | 48.0 | 1826° | 17 | 16 |
| 1947 | 323 | 176 | 54.5 | 2712 | 24 | 31° |
| 1948 | 163 | 89 | 54.6 | 1047 | 13 | 14 |
| 1949 | 50 | 22 | 44.0 | 200 | 1 | 3 |
| 1950 | 37 | 13 | 35.1 | 180 | 1 | 2 |
| TOTALS | 1744 | 904 | 51.8 | 14,683 | 137 | 131 |

Career passing rating: 75.0

° Led NFL

† Official NFL individual passing champion

Rushing: 204 attempts, 209 yards, 1.0-yard average, 2 touchdowns

Interceptions: 14 interceptions, 293 yards, 20.9-yard average, 1 touchdown

Punting: 230 punts, 38.4-yard average

Punt returns: 11 returns, 107 yards, 9.7-yard average, 0 touchdowns

Scoring: 6 touchdowns, 1 extra point, 37 points

# STEVE VAN BUREN

*Halfback*
*6 ft 1 in, 200 lb*
*Born in La Ceiba, Honduras,*
*December 28, 1920*
*Louisiana State University (LSU)*
*1944–51 Philadelphia Eagles*

Steve Van Buren answered to a lot of names during his eight-year career in the NFL—"Wham Bam!" . . . "Supersonic Steve!" . . . "Blockbuster!" . . . and several more. Translated, they all meant that even his contemporaries recognized Van Buren as an exceptional football player.

To be sure, Steve's pro career was distinctive. He surpassed 1000 yards rushing twice, won four NFL rushing titles and a rare Triple Crown for rushing, scoring and kickoff returns in 1945. He was all-NFL as a rookie and four more times in his first six seasons.

Van Buren lined up as a halfback but played more like a fullback as the battering ram of a powerful Eagles squad that dominated the NFL in the late 1940s. Philadelphia had never finished above fourth place until Steve came on the scene in 1944. That year they finished second, were runners-up two more years and then won three straight divisional titles. In 1948 and 1949, they won NFL championships.

Van Buren provided the offensive punch in both championship victories. In 1949, playing in the mud against the Los Angeles Rams, Steve carried 31 times for a record 196 yards as the Eagles won 14–0. He may have been even better in the 7–0 shutout of the Chicago Cardinals on a snow-covered field a year earlier. Van Buren rushed for 98 yards and scored the game's only touchdown. The Cardinals had only 96 yards total offense.

Steve's early years were not particularly happy ones. Born in Honduras where his father was a fruit inspector, Van Buren was orphaned when he was very young and sent to New Orleans to live with his grandparents.

He was turned down for football as a high school sophomore because he weighed only 125 lb. For the next two years, he worked in an iron foundry. When Steve returned to school, he played well enough to earn a scholarship to LSU. With the Tigers, Van Buren played blocking back during his first two seasons but, in a splendid senior season, he rushed for 832 yards. Unfortunately, he did not win the all-America acclaim which many felt he deserved. As a result, not too many NFL teams had a book on Steve but the Eagles, tipped off by LSU coach Bernie Moore, drafted him number 1 in 1944. It was a break for Van Buren and, for the Eagles, possibly their most fortunate move ever!

*The Philadelphia Eagles' Steve Van Buren breaks around right end for good yardage in a 1950 clash with the Washington Redskins.*

| RUSHING RECORD | | | | |
| --- | --- | --- | --- | --- |
| Year | Attempts | Yards | Average | TD |
| 1944 | 80 | 444 | 5.5 | 5 |
| 1945 | 143 | 832* | 5.8 | 15* |
| 1946 | 116 | 529 | 4.6 | 5 |
| 1947 | 217* | 1008* | 4.6 | 13* |
| 1948 | 201* | 945* | 4.7 | 10* |
| 1949 | 263* | 1146* | 4.4 | 11* |
| 1950 | 188* | 629 | 3.3 | 4 |
| 1951 | 112 | 327 | 2.9 | 6 |
| TOTALS | 1320 | 5860 | 4.4 | 69 |

| KICKOFF RETURN RECORD | | | | |
| --- | --- | --- | --- | --- |
| Year | Number | Yards | Average | TD |
| 1944 | 8 | 266 | 33.3 | 1* |
| 1945 | 13 | 373 | 28.7 | 1* |
| 1946 | 11 | 319 | 29.0 | 0 |
| 1947 | 13 | 382 | 29.4* | 1 |
| 1948 | 15 | 292 | 19.5 | 0 |
| 1949 | 12 | 288 | 24.0 | 0 |
| 1950 | 5 | 110 | 22.0 | 0 |
| 1951 | 0 | 0 | 0.0 | 0 |
| TOTALS | 77 | 2030 | 26.4 | 3 |

Pass receiving: 45 receptions, 503 yards, 11.2-yard average, 3 touchdowns

Punt returns: 34 returns, 473 yards, 13.9-yard average, 2 touchdowns

Interceptions: 9 interceptions, 81 yards, 9.0-yard average, 0 touchdowns

Scoring: 77 touchdowns, 2 extra points, 464 yards

* Led NFL

# BOB WATERFIELD

*Quarterback*
*6 ft 2 in, 200 lb*
*Born in Elmira, N. Y., July 26,*
*1920; died March 25, 1983, at age*
*of 62*
*University of California at Los*
*Angeles (UCLA)*
*1945 Cleveland Rams; 1946–52*
*Los Angeles Rams*

In the 1945 NFL championship game, Bob Waterfield threw 37- and 53-yard touchdown passes to lead the Cleveland Rams to a 15–14 victory over the Washington Redskins. He was a unanimous all-NFL choice and the league's Most Valuable Player, the first rookie ever to win the award.

Rams owner Dan Reeves had signed the prized newcomer from UCLA for $7500. After his spectacular campaign, Reeves presented Waterfield with a new three-year pact at $20,000 a year. "I wouldn't trade Bob for the Brooklyn Bridge," the Rams leader said, "even with any player you can name thrown in."

Early in 1946, Reeves moved the Rams to Los Angeles and Waterfield moved with him back to his college territory. For the next seven seasons, the Rams were pro football's most feared offensive team and Waterfield was the brilliant field general and precision passer who put points on the scoreboard in massive doses. Always calm against even the greatest odds, he often led his team from far behind with patented aerial rallies.

Bob was exceptionally versatile, a passing whiz to be sure, but also a dangerous runner and a sensational punter and place-kicker. He also played defense his first four years and wound up with 20 career interceptions to prove it.

Waterfield, who was once considered too small and too weak for even college football, proved to be a durable and determined competitor in the pros. In a crucial game against Detroit in his rookie season, he played with painful rib injuries in freezing cold but completed 10 passes to Jim Benton for a stunning 303 yards. In a playoff game against the Bears in 1950, he threw three touchdown passes despite a severe case of the 'flu.

In his last five seasons, Bob was forced to divide his playing time with another premier passer, Norm Van Brocklin. Perhaps because he got fed up with the booing fans who favored Van Brocklin in the quarterback derby, he retired after the 1952 season.

Future play could have done little to enhance his sterling reputation. As teammate Elroy Hirsch said very simply: "Bob Waterfield is the best football player I've ever seen."

*Bob Waterfield, an outstanding passer, punter and placekicker for the Cleveland/Los Angeles Rams, scores one of his 13 career rushing touchdowns.*

## PASSING RECORD

| Year | Attempts | Completions | Percentage passes completed | Yards | TD | Interceptions |
|------|----------|-------------|----------------------------|-------|-----|---------------|
| 1945° | 171 | 89 | 51.4 | 1609 | 14‡ | 16‡ |
| 1946†§ | 251‡ | 127‡ | 50.6 | 1747 | 18‡ | 17 |
| 1947† | 221 | 96 | 43.4 | 1210 | 8 | 18 |
| 1948† | 180 | 87 | 48.3 | 1354 | 14 | 18 |
| 1949† | 296 | 154 | 52.0 | 2168 | 17 | 24‡ |
| 1950† | 213 | 122 | 57.3‡ | 1540 | 11 | 13 |
| 1951†§ | 176 | 88 | 50.0 | 1566 | 13 | 10 |
| 1952† | 109 | 51 | 46.8 | 655 | 3 | 11 |
| TOTALS | 1617 | 814 | 50.3 | 11,849 | 98 | 127 |

Career passing rating: 62.0

° With Cleveland Rams     † With Los Angeles Rams

‡ Led NFL     § Official NFL individual passing champion

Rushing: 75 attempts, 21 yards, 0.3-yard average, 13 touchdowns

Interceptions: 20 interceptions, 228 yards, 11.4-yard average, 0 touchdowns

Punting: 315 punts, 42.4-yard average

Scoring: 13 touchdowns, 315 extra points, 60 field goals, 573 points

# BILL DUDLEY

*Halfback*
*5 ft 10 in, 176 lb*
*Born in Bluefield, Va.,*
*December 24, 1921*
*University of Virginia*
*1942, 1945–6 Pittsburgh Steelers;*
*1947–9 Detroit Lions; 1950–1,*
*1953 Washington Redskins*

Bill Dudley was nicknamed "Bullet Bill" but that was misleading. Not only was Bill small and slow—he once finished 15th in a 15-man pre-game exhibition sprint—but he passed with a jerky motion that frustrated his coaches. His placekicking style was unorthodox. He took no steps but merely swung his foot into the ball pendulum-style. He once was denied a tryout because his high school had no uniform small enough for him.

Still, the moniker "Bullet" was appropriate because he was super-effective on the gridiron. With fiery determination and exceptional versatility, Bill became an elusive runner, a fierce tackler and a dependable punter and placekicker.

Dudley was feared as a game-breaker who could go all the way. With the 1947 Detroit Lions, he scored 13 touchdowns on one punt return, one kickoff return, seven receptions and four rushes. He also threw two touchdown passes.

Bill was Virginia's first all-America and the number 1 draft pick of the Pittsburgh Steelers in 1942. Right from the start, he dispelled any thoughts he was too small to play with the "big boys" of the NFL. He ran for a 55-yard touchdown in his first game and tallied on a kickoff return in his second. He won the NFL rushing title with 696 yards and was named to the official all-league team.

Dudley entered the Army Air Corps after his rookie season and played service football for the next two years in between his bombing runs as a B-29 pilot in the South Pacific. He played briefly in 1945 but a year later became the last of only three NFL players ever to win the coveted Triple Crown, with individual statistical championships in rushing, punt returns and interceptions. He was named the NFL's Most Valuable Player.

Before the 1947 season, Dudley, who had been in Steeler coach Jock Sutherland's doghouse, was traded to Detroit where he was rewarded with a princely $25,000 contract. Three years later, Bill moved to Washington where he played for a further three years.

To the very end, Dudley remained a game-breaker. In a 1950 game against the Steelers, Bill faked, dodged and followed his blockers perfectly on a 96-yard punt return. Many say it was the most exceptional play of a career filled with remarkable accomplishments.

RUSHING RECORD

| Year | Attempts | Yards | Average | TD |
|---|---|---|---|---|
| 1942° | 162§ | 696§ | 4.3 | 5 |
| 1943–4 | On military service | | | |
| 1945° | 57 | 204 | 3.5 | 3 |
| 1946° | 146 | 604§ | 4.1 | 3 |
| 1947† | 80 | 302 | 3.8 | 2 |
| 1948† | 33 | 97 | 2.9 | 0 |
| 1949† | 125 | 402 | 3.2 | 4 |
| 1950‡ | 66 | 339 | 5.1 | 1 |
| 1951‡ | 91 | 398 | 4.4 | 2 |
| 1952 | Did not play | | | |
| 1953‡ | 5 | 15 | 3.0 | 0 |
| TOTALS | 765 | 3057 | 4.0 | 20 |

° With Pittsburgh Steelers

† With Detroit Lions

‡ With Washington Redskins

§ Led NFL

Receiving: 123 receptions, 1383 yards, 11.2-yard average, 18 touchdowns

Punt returns: 124 returns, 1515 yards, 12.2-yard average, 3 touchdowns

Kickoff returns: 78 returns, 1743 yards, 22.3-yard average, 1 touchdown

Interceptions: 23 interceptions, 459 yards, 20.0-yard average, 2 touchdowns

Punting: 191 punts, 38.2-yard average

Passing: 222 attempts, 81 completions, 985 yards, 6 touchdowns, 17 interceptions

Scoring: 44 touchdowns, 121 extra points, 33 field goals, 484 points

*Bill Dudley divided his nine-year NFL career evenly among three teams, the Pittsburgh Steelers, the Detroit Lions and the Washington Redskins. In this 1946 action shot, Dudley picks up good yardage against the Chicago Bears.*

# JOE GUYON

*Halfback    6 ft 1 in. 180 lb
Born on White Earth Indian
Reservation. Minn.. November 26.
1892: died November 27. 1971. at
age of 79
Carlisle. Georgia Tech
1919–20 Canton Bulldogs: 1921
Cleveland Indians: 1922–3 Oorang
Indians: 1924 Rock Island
Independents: 1924–5 Kansas City
Cowboys: 1927 New York Giants*

Joe Guyon, a full-blooded American Indian from the Chippewa Tribe, was born O-Gee-Chidah on the White Earth Indian Reservation in Minnesota. He received only a sixth-grade education from the American government. "It was hard trying to make something of yourself," Guyon once said. "Sports were one of the few ways a youngster could pull himself up."

So Guyon did the only thing he could do. He used his athletic skills to gain a college education and a satisfying professional career. He played on two national championship collegiate elevens, Carlisle Indian School in 1912 and Georgia Tech in 1917. Joe signed to play pro football with the Canton Bulldogs in 1919.

After the NFL was organized in 1920, Guyon played seven more seasons with six different teams. From 1919 to 1924, Joe teamed with another outstanding Indian halfback, the fabled Jim Thorpe. Both were talented players but the better-known Thorpe grabbed all the headlines. Thorpe is still remembered as the player–coach of the Oorang Indians teams of 1922 and 1923 but few, even at the time, knew that Guyon was the team's offensive star and leading scorer.

The paths of the talented Indian pair finally parted late in the 1924 season when Guyon left the Rock Island Independents to go to the Kansas City Cowboys. Guyon stayed with the Cowboys in 1925 while Thorpe, then 37, moved on to the New York Giants. To all intents and purposes, that was Thorpe's last pro stop.

But two years later in 1927, Guyon himself became a Giant and he played a major role in leading the New Yorkers to the 1927 NFL championship. Not surprisingly, Joe, with the big-city exposure and away from the shadow of Thorpe for the first time, enjoyed one of his finest seasons and gained the first significant publicity he had enjoyed since his college days.

The 1928 Giants compiled an 11–1–1 record largely on the strength of a superior defensive team. New York opponents failed to score in 10 of 13 games and tallied only 20 points—never more than seven a game—in the entire season. But Guyon, flashing all of his many abilities—passing, running, punting, tackling and blocking—played a leading role in putting the necessary points on the scoreboard for his team.

In a crucial late-season game against the Chicago Bears, Guyon's touchdown pass gave the Giants a 13–7 win. Joe's quick thinking was as important as his playing skill in the winning touchdown drive that day. George Halas, the Bears' player–coach, zeroed in on Guyon as he set up to pass. Just as Halas leaped to strike, Guyon whirled and swung a knee that caught George in the chest, breaking four ribs. The chipper Chippewa then fell backwards, screaming that he had been clipped. The ruse worked, the Bears were penalized 15 yards and the Giants marched on to their first NFL championship.

As Halas was carried from the field, Steve Owen of the Giants admonished the fallen Bear: "George, you should know better than to try to sneak up on an Indian."

*Joe Guyon was an outstanding all-around star. He played a leading role for six different teams in the NFL's first decade. He and Jim Thorpe are the only full-blooded American Indians who are Hall of Fame members.*

# ARNIE HERBER

**Quarterback**
**6 ft 0 in, 200 lb**
**Born in Green Bay, Wisc., April 2,**
**1910; died October 14, 1969, at**
**age of 59**
**University of Wisconsin, Regis**
**College**
**1930–40 Green Bay Packers;**
**1944–5 New York Giants**

Arnie Herber was a basketball and football star at Green Bay's West High School who sold programs as a teenager so that he could see the Packers play. He eventually migrated to tiny Regis College in Denver where coach Red Strader had visions of a football dynasty. The stock market crash of 1929 ended those dreams and also Arnie's college days.

Herber was working as a handyman in the Packers clubhouse when coach Curly Lambeau decided to give the inexperienced 20-year-old a tryout. For the price of $75 a game, the Packers inherited the first pro quarterback who could use the forward pass with game-winning effectiveness. Handicapped by short fingers, Herber defied standard practice by placing his thumb over the laces to prevent the ball from wobbling and to assure plenty of spiraling action. His passes quickly became noted for two qualities: distance and accuracy.

Arnie threw a touchdown pass to give the Packers a 7–0 victory in the first game of his rookie 1930 season. The Packers won NFL titles in both 1930 and 1931 and remained in a perpetual contending position throughout Herber's 11-year tenure. Herber's passes were always a dominating factor but he could also run, catch passes and punt with the very best. In one game in 1932 against Staten Island, Arnie did all the punting, ran for 85- and 45-yard touchdowns and threw three scoring passes.

Herber won NFL passing championships three of the first five seasons such records were kept and was already an established superstar when the fabled Don Hutson from Alabama joined the team in 1935. The two formed pro football's first lethal pass-catch team, clicking for an 83-yard touchdown on the first play of the 1936 season and providing trouble in massive doses for NFL defenses until Arnie retired after the 1940 campaign.

After four years of retirement, Herber joined the manpower-short New York Giants who advanced to the 1944 NFL title game before losing to Green Bay. One year later in 1945, Herber left

the active NFL scene with his reputation as football's first great long-distance passer intact.

As one Green Bay enthusiast wrote: "Arnie Herber was the Babe Ruth of pro football. Like the Babe, he specialized in the 'long ball,' was highly popular with the fans and left a lasting mark on the sport he played."

PASSING RECORD

| Year | Attempts | Completions | Percentage passes completed | Yards | TD | Interceptions |
|---|---|---|---|---|---|---|
| 1930–1° | No records available | | | | | |
| 1932°‡ | 101 | 37 | 36.6 | 639 | 9 | 9 |
| 1933° | 126 | 56 | 44.4 | 656 | 4 | 12 |
| 1934°‡ | 115 | 42 | 36.5 | 799 | 8 | 12 |
| 1935° | 106 | 40 | 37.7 | 729 | 8 | 6 |
| 1936°‡ | 173 | 77 | 44.5 | 1239 | 11 | 13 |
| 1937° | 104 | 47 | 45.2 | 676 | 7 | 10 |
| 1938° | 55 | 22 | 40.0 | 336 | 4 | 4 |
| 1939° | 139 | 57 | 41.0 | 1107 | 8 | 9 |
| 1940° | 89 | 38 | 42.7 | 560 | 5 | 7 |
| 1941–3 | Retired | | | | | |
| 1944† | 86 | 36 | 41.9 | 651 | 6 | 8 |
| 1945† | 80 | 35 | 43.8 | 641 | 9 | 8 |
| TOTALS§ | 1174 | 487 | 41.5 | 8033 | 79 | 98 |

° With Green Bay Packers    † With New York Giants    ‡ Official NFL individual passing champion

*Arnie Herber spent 11 of his 13 pro football seasons as a quarterback with the Packers. When he first started with the Packers he was instrumental in leading his team to the NFL title. In his sixth season, he joined with Don Hutson to form history's first great pass-catch combination.*

# WALT KIESLING

*Coach, guard   6 ft 2 in, 245 lb
Born in St Paul, Minn., May 27,
1903; died March 2, 1962 age 58
St Thomas (Minn.) College
1926–7 Duluth Eskimos; 1928
Pottsville Maroons; 1929–33
Chicago Cardinals; 1934 Chicago
Bears; 1935–6 Green Bay Packers;
1937–9 Pittsburgh Pirates;
1940–2, 1954–6 Pittsburgh
Steelers (coach)*

Except for the incomparable George Halas, Walt Kiesling devoted more years—34—to the NFL as an outstanding player and a multi-assignment coach than any other Hall of Famer. "Big Kies," as he was affectionately known by all his associates, spent 13 seasons playing guard for six different NFL elevens from 1926 through 1938. He was a player–coach in 1937 and 1938 and then a full-time coach for the 23 years that preceded his untimely death in 1962.

A fun-loving giant of a man who some viewed as a "physical duplicate of Babe Ruth," he spent the final two seasons of his playing career and all but four years of his coaching tenure in Pittsburgh. While he was primarily an assistant coach, he did experience three separate head-coaching terms in Pittsburgh.

He first took over when Johnny "Blood" McNally literally walked off the job in 1939 and then became the head man again late in 1941. A year later, he led the Steelers to a 7–4 record.

Manpower shortages brought on by World War II forced the Steelers to merge with other NFL teams the next two years. In 1943, Big Kies and Philadelphia Eagles coach "Greasy" Neale combined their talents to lead the Phil-Pitt "Steagles" to a 5–4–1 mark, just one game shy of the division leaders, Washington and New York. In 1944, the Steelers joined forces with the Chicago Cardinals with much less success. The talent-shy Card-Pitt eleven, co-coached by Kiesling and Phil Handler, suffered a 10-game season with no wins.

In 1945, Kiesling joined his old friend, "Curly" Lambeau, as an assistant coach with the Green Bay Packers but, four years later in 1949, he was back in Pittsburgh, once again as an assistant. Just before the 1955 season got under way, Big Kies was given the head coaching job for a third time. The 1955 Steelers started out with four wins in five games but slumped badly after that. After a 5–7 record in 1956, Kiesling retired, because of failing health, to a sort of "coach emeritus" assistant's status.

To say the least, Kiesling's up-and-down status between an assistant-coaching and head-coaching role was unusual. Walt's best friends insisted, however, that, while he was happy to help in any way possible, he preferred being an assistant.

Kiesling, who teammates insisted played best "when he had some belly on him," had remarkable speed in spite of his size. He was adept at pulling from the line to lead a play. He was a rookie with the 1926 Duluth Eskimos and enjoyed his finest playing years with the Chicago Cardinals. Kiesling's biggest thrill came with the 1934 Bears who were undefeated in regular season. Two years later with the Green Bay Packers, Big Kies was part of a championship team for the only time as a player or a coach.

The hallmark of Kiesling's career is that he participated in the growth of pro football from its rag-tag days of the mid-1920s to the early 1960s, when the sport was bursting with popularity. As one historian noted, "Walt Kiesling didn't just watch pro football grow from the rocky sandlots. He shoved it along the way!"

*Walt Kiesling played as a guard for 13 seasons and then served both as a head coach and assistant coach the rest of his career.*

HEAD COACHING RECORD

| Year | Won | Lost | Tied | Division finish |
|------|-----|------|------|--------|
| 1939* | 1 | 6 | 1 | Tie 4th |
| 1940 | 2 | 7 | 2 | 4th |
| 1941* | 1 | 0 | 1 | 5th |
| 1942 | 7 | 4 | 0 | 2nd |
| 1943† | 5 | 4 | 1 | 3rd |
| 1944‡ | 0 | 10 | 0 | 5th |
| 1954 | 5 | 7 | 0 | 4th |
| 1955 | 4 | 8 | 0 | 6th |
| 1956 | 5 | 7 | 0 | 5th |
| TOTALS§ | 25 | 39 | 4 | |

\* Coached part of season

† Merged Phil-Pitt team, Kiesling co-coach

‡ Merged Card-Pitt team, Kiesling co-coach

§ Career totals do not include 1943–4 merged-team records

# GEORGE MCAFEE

*Halfback*
*6 ft 0 in, 177 lb*
*Born in Ironton, Ohio, March 13,*
*1918*
*Duke University*
*1940–1, 1945–50 Chicago Bears*

Lombardi promoted so intensely two decades later. It was called "run to daylight." Throughout his NFL career, George McAfee lived that theory to the fullest.

*In his first pro football game, George McAfee returned a punt 75 yards for a touchdown. From that moment on, he was respected as a big-play threat every time he touched the football.*

George McAfee did not have the physique of a future Pro Football Hall of Famer. Even George Halas, who made the Duke all-America the Chicago Bears' number 1 draft choice in 1940, wondered if he had made the right decision after seeing the 177-lb rookie line up against the Monsters of the Midway for the first time. But just one play, which saw McAfee whirl away from a linebacker and into the open field, convinced the Bears' mentor his new halfback would indeed become a superstar.

McAfee's pro career was not a particularly long one. The Bears of 1940 and 1941 were loaded with outstanding talent so George's playing time was limited to about 25 minutes a game. Then he joined the Navy and did not return until late in the 1945 season. Injuries cut his playing time in 1946. He followed with full campaigns in 1947 through 1950 but, altogether, his NFL career consisted of six full seasons and two partial seasons, with his potentially finest years being spent in the service.

As a result, his career statistics are not particularly impressive until a closer look clearly points out that McAfee did just about everything a player can do with a football. He was a mercury-footed runner, a dangerous pass-receiver and one of history's finest kick return specialists. His 12.8-yard average on 112 punt returns stood as an NFL career mark for many years. George also played defense and wound up with 21 interceptions.

Right from the start, McAfee established himself as a game-breaker. In his first exhibition game, he returned a punt 75 yards with 37 seconds left to beat the Brooklyn Dodgers. In the regular-season opener that same year, he ran back a kickoff 93 yards and threw a touchdown pass in a 41–10 Bears victory. George's contribution to the 73–0 rout of the Redskins in the 1940 NFL title game was a 34-yard interception return.

George, whether running wide or up the middle, either as a pass-receiver or a decoy, was known as "One-Play McAfee," a constant headache to the defense. McAfee pioneered the use of low-cut shoes to boost his speed and increase his elusiveness because he realized in his first Bears training camp that it was imperative for someone of his stature to avoid contact whenever possible. He thus ran with the same goal Green Bay's Vince

## PUNT RETURN RECORD

| Year | Number | Yards | Average | TD |
|------|--------|-------|---------|-----|
| 1940 | No records available | | | |
| 1941 | 5 | 158 | 31.6 | 1* |
| 1942–4 | In US Navy | | | |
| 1945 | 1 | 8 | 8.0 | 0 |
| 1946 | 1 | 24 | 24.0 | 0 |
| 1947 | 18 | 261 | 14.5 | 0 |
| 1948 | 30* | 417* | 13.9 | 1 |
| 1949 | 24 | 279 | 11.6 | 0 |
| 1950 | 33* | 284 | 8.6 | 0 |
| TOTALS | 112 | 1431 | 12.8 | 2 |

*\* Led NFL*

## RUSHING RECORD

| Year | Attempts | Yards | Average | TD |
|------|----------|-------|---------|-----|
| 1940 | 47 | 253 | 5.4 | 2 |
| 1941 | 65 | 474 | 7.3 | 6 |
| 1942–4 | In US Navy | | | |
| 1945 | 16 | 139 | 8.6 | 3 |
| 1946 | 14 | 53 | 3.8 | 0 |
| 1947 | 63 | 209 | 3.3 | 3 |
| 1948 | 92 | 392 | 4.3 | 5 |
| 1949 | 42 | 161 | 3.8 | 3 |
| 1950 | 2 | 4 | 2.0 | 0 |
| TOTALS | 341 | 1685 | 4.9 | 22 |

Receiving: 85 receptions, 1357 yards, 16.0-yard average, 10 touchdowns

Passing: 22 attempts, 6 completions, 94 yards, 1 touchdown, 1 interception

Punting: 39 punts, 36.9-yard average

Interceptions: 21 interceptions, 294 yards, 14.0-yard average, 1 touchdown

Kickoff returns: 11 returns, 265 yards, 24.1-yard average, 0 touchdowns

Scoring: 39 touchdowns, 234 points

# STEVE OWEN

*Tackle, coach*
*6 ft 2 in, 235 lb*
*Born in Cleo Springs, Okla.,*
*April 21, 1898; died May 17,*
*1964, at age of 66*
*Phillips University*
*1924–5 Kansas City Cowboys;*
*1926–53 New York Giants*

In three contests with the New York Giants in 1950, the high-powered Cleveland Browns managed just 21 points. In the first game, the Giants shut out the Browns, something that didn't happen again in regular-season play for 11 years.

The architect of the whitewashing was Steve Owen, who devised a new formation soon to be acclaimed as the "umbrella defense." It was basically a 6–1–4 alignment with two ends dropping back to cover on passing plays. From this, the 4–3–3 defense, so popular in modern times, evolved.

Owen was born in Indian territory which is now Oklahoma. His mother was a schoolmarm and his father was a Cherokee strip farmer. Steve's first sports interests involved horse riding—he even had aspirations to become a jockey—but his size soon dictated that football would be his sport.

As an NFL player, Owen was a standout NFL tackle with the Kansas City Cowboys and the Giants for nine seasons. His credo was that "football is a game played down in the dirt and it always will be. There's no use getting fancy about it." That was the way he played the game. As captain of the 1927 Giants, the big tackle led a championship team that conceded an all-time low of 20 points in 13 games.

When Steve became the Giants' player–coach in 1931, he coached the game the same way. For the next decade and a half, the Giants were one of the most feared elevens in the NFL. Almost always, it was the defense that paved the way. Owen, who coached the Giants for 23 years without a contract—a handshake with the Mara family was good enough—engineered 154 coaching victories, two NFL and eight divisional championships.

While Owen often was criticized for being too conservative, he did prove to be one of the game's great innovators. The umbrella defense is a prime example but there are many others. In 1937, he introduced the new A-formation offense and developed a total two-platoon system in which each unit was equally adept at both

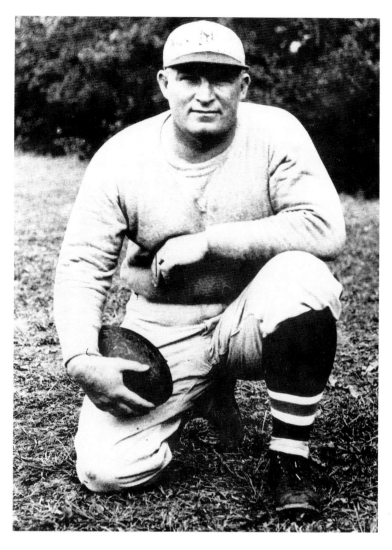

*Steve Owen, who began his pro football career as a standout tackle, became the New York Giants' head coach in 1931. He held the post for 23 years.*

offense and defense. The idea worked well. The players didn't tire as easily and became less susceptible to injuries.

When Owen resigned in 1953, George Halas praised his long-time rival. "Steve was the first to stress the importance of defense and the advantage of settling for field goals instead of touchdowns. Every team strives today to do what Owen was doing 20 years ago."

## COACHING RECORD

| Year | Won | Lost | Tied | Division finish | Year | Won | Lost | Tied | Division finish |
|------|-----|------|------|-----------------|------|-----|------|------|-----------------|
| 1931 | 7 | 6 | 1 | 5th | 1947 | 2 | 8 | 2 | 5th |
| 1932 | 4 | 6 | 2 | 5th | 1948 | 4 | 8 | 0 | Tie 3rd |
| 1933 | 11 | 3 | 0 | 1st | 1949 | 6 | 6 | 0 | 3rd |
| 1934 | 8 | 5 | 0 | 1st | 1950 | 10 | 2 | 0 | Tie 1st |
| 1935 | 9 | 3 | 0 | 1st | 1951 | 9 | 2 | 1 | 2nd |
| 1936 | 5 | 6 | 1 | 3rd | 1952 | 7 | 5 | 0 | Tie 2nd |
| 1937 | 6 | 3 | 2 | 2nd | 1953 | 3 | 9 | 0 | 5th |
| 1938 | 8 | 2 | 1 | 1st | TOTALS* | 153 | 108 | | |
| 1939 | 9 | 1 | 1 | 1st | | | | | |
| 1940 | 6 | 4 | 1 | 3rd | | | | | |
| 1941 | 8 | 3 | 0 | 1st | | | | | |
| 1942 | 5 | 5 | 1 | 3rd | | | | | |
| 1943 | 6 | 3 | 1 | Tie 1st | | | | | |
| 1944 | 8 | 1 | 1 | 1st | | | | | |
| 1945 | 3 | 6 | 1 | 3rd | | | | | |
| 1946 | 7 | 3 | 1 | 1st | *Career totals include post-season games | | | | |

## POST-SEASON RECORD

1934 NFL Championship: Chicago Bears 23, New York Giants 21

1935 NFL Championship: New York Giants 30, Chicago Bears 13

1936 NFL Championship: Detroit 26, New York Giants 7

1938 NFL Championship: New York Giants 23, Green Bay 17

1939 NFL Championship: Green Bay 27, New York Giants 0

1941 NFL Championship: Chicago Bears 37, New York Giants 9

1943 NFL Divisional Playoff: Washington 28, New York Giants 0

1944 NFL Championship: Green Bay 14, New York Giants 7

1946 NFL Championship: Chicago Bears 24, New York Giants 14

1950 NFL Divisional Playoff: Cleveland 8, New York Giants 3

# HUGH (SHORTY) RAY

*Technical Advisor on Rules,*
*National Football League*
*Supervisor of Officials*
*Born in Highland Park, Ill.,*
*September 21, 1884; died*
*September 16, 1956, at age of 71*
*University of Illinois*
*1938–52 National Football League*

Hugh "Shorty" Ray stood only 5 ft 6 in and weighed just 138 lb but many insist Ray is pro football's "unknown hero" who saved a dull game from extinction half a century ago and played *the* major role in making the sport the fast-paced, wide-open game of today.

At the urging of the Chicago Bears' George Halas, Ray brought his expertise to the NFL in 1938 but the groundwork for his unique role in pro football was laid years earlier both at the high school and college level. Football in the 1920s had degenerated into sluggish gang fights. Injuries were widespread. Officiating was haphazard, often biased. Antiquated rules were loosely interpreted, randomly enforced.

That was when Ray, who had been a four-sport star at the University of Illinois and a successful high-school coach for 20 years, entered the picture by organizing the American Officials Association which began conducting clinics to consider officiating and rules-interpretation problems. A few years later, the National Federation of State High School Athletic Associations asked Ray to write a football code. It was a masterpiece, a model for all future rule books at every level.

Once he joined the NFL, Shorty insisted his officials become absolute masters of rule-book information. He gave them written tests and demanded that they score better than 95 percent every time. At the end of each season, he made recommendations for new rules and urged that others be eliminated. Player safety and speed of play were always prime factors in his proposals. By insisting that officials relay the ball back to the field instead of carrying it back on out-of-bounds situations, Shorty added 12 plays to every NFL game.

Ray took more than 300,000 stopwatch observations during his NFL tenure. He discovered that the faster a game is played, the more time it consumes. "The faster you play, the more plays you create," he explained. "The more plays you create, the more situations you develop in which the clock can be stopped."

When Ray retired because of failing health in 1952, Halas was among many who lauded his efforts. "I've always thought my finest contribution to pro football was bringing Shorty Ray into the NFL."

*Hugh "Shorty" Ray played a unique but valuable role as the NFL Supervisor of Officials for 15 years. Here he is being congratulated by George Halas (left) and NFL commissioner Bert Bell.*

# CLYDE (BULLDOG) TURNER

*Center, linebacker*
*6 ft 2 in, 235 lb*
*Born in Sweetwater, Texas,*
*November 10, 1919*
*Hardin-Simmons University*
*1940–52 Chicago Bears*

Clyde "Bulldog" Turner excelled as a premier center-linebacker for the Chicago Bears for 13 seasons. Yet had it not been for a strange but fortunate set of circumstances while he was still a college player at Hardin-Simmons University, he might never have had the chance to play in the NFL.

Pro football scouting was in the Neanderthal stages in the late 1930s. Most teams relied on football magazines with their traditional pre-season all-America selections, and players from little-known colleges simply weren't included. Yet Turner was eagerly sought by not one but two NFL teams.

A Hardin-Simmons fan tipped off Frank Korch, a Bears scout, about Turner's abilities during his junior season. After watching Turner in the East-West game a year later, Korch convinced George Halas the Bears should draft him. Meanwhile, Detroit owner Dick Richards was so sure he had convinced Turner to turn down offers from any other NFL team he did not even bother to draft the big center. Detroit eventually was fined $5000 for tampering with a player already on another team's draft list.

For the Bears, acquiring the 20-year-old Turner in the first round of the 1940 draft proved to be a master stroke. For both the Bears and Turner, the 1940 season marked the beginning of a period of dominance of their particular specialties, the Bears in winning championships and Turner in becoming the best all-round center in pro football. Turner ended Mel Hein's long reign by winning all-NFL acclaim in 1941 and five more times in the 1940s.

As a linebacker who was blessed with halfback speed, Turner in 1942 led the league in interceptions with eight. He was universally recognized as one of the smartest players in the league with a rare ability to diagnose a play on the field in a split second. On offense, he was a flawless snapper and an exceptional blocker who could also play guard or tackle.

Never was his versatility more evident than in 1944 when he was asked to fill in as a ball-carrier in an emergency situation. He consistently ground out long gains, including a 48-yard touchdown romp. Three years later against Washington, Turner came up with what he called the favorite play of his career. Using quick feints and changes of speed to perfection, the big linebacker returned an interception 96 yards for a touchdown.

*"Bulldog" Turner, was the dominant player at his position in the 1940s. He was named all-NFL six times. A superior pass defender, he had eight interceptions in 1942.*

INTERCEPTION RECORD

| Year | Number | Yards | Average | TD | Year | Number | Yards | Average | TD |
|------|--------|-------|---------|----|------|--------|-------|---------|----|
| 1940 | No records available | | | | 1950 | 0 | 0 | 0.0 | 0 |
| 1941 | 1 | 12 | 12.0 | 0 | 1951 | 0 | 0 | 0.0 | 0 |
| 1942 | 8* | 96 | 12.0 | 1 | 1952 | 0 | 0 | 0.0 | 0 |
| 1943 | 0 | 0 | 0.0 | 0 | TOTALS | 16 | 289 | 18.1 | 2 |
| 1944 | 2 | 44 | 22.0 | 0 | | | | | |
| 1945 | 0 | 0 | 0.0 | 0 | | | | | |
| 1946 | 1 | 15 | 15.0 | 0 | | | | | |
| 1947 | 2 | 103 | 51.2 | 1 | | | | | |
| 1948 | 2 | 19 | 9.5 | 0 | | | | | |
| 1949 | 0 | 0 | 0.0 | 0 | * Led NFL | | | | |

# CHUCK BEDNARIK

*Center, linebacker*
*6 ft 3 in, 230 lb*
*Born in Bethlehem, Pa., May 1,*
*1925*
*University of Pennsylvania*
*1949–62 Philadelphia Eagles*

*Chuck Bednarik continued to play center on offense and linebacker on defense long after platoon football had abolished the 60-minute player, returns an interception against the Washington Redskins.*

No NFL player in the 1950s was immune to bone-jarring contact with the Philadelphia Eagles' Chuck Bednarik because the rough-and-tumble 235-pounder played on both the offensive and defensive units long after the two-way player in pro football had largely faded from the scene.

Bednarik's ability to excel both as a center and middle linebacker was particularly evident in 1960, his twelfth season, when, at the age of 35, he responded to an injury-induced emergency by playing 394½ minutes in a 12-game season. He finished the campaign with a 58-minute performance, capped by a game-saving tackle in the Eagles' NFL championship victory over Green Bay. With just seconds remaining, the Packers' Jimmy Taylor appeared to be heading for a winning touchdown until the last Eagle in his path, Bednarik, bear-hugged him to the ground as time ran out.

As an offensive center, big Chuck was a bulldozing blocker, both on rushing and passing plays. On defense, he was a true scientist in his field and the kind of tackler who could literally stop even the finest enemy runners "on a dime."

One such tackle not only gave the Eagles a crucial victory in 1960 but also put the New York Giants' Frank Gifford out of action for more than a year. When Bednarik, realizing that a win was assured but not knowing how seriously his opponent was injured, erupted into a wild victory dance, the crowd roared its violent disapproval. Films of the play proved, however, that Chuck's tackle, while indicative of his "play for keeps" philosophy, was clean in every way.

Had World War II not been a factor, Chuck might have given up football after high school, where he was considered to be adequate on the gridiron but exceptional in basketball and baseball. After a 30-mission tour as a B-24 waist gunner with the US Air Force that saw him win the Air Medal, Chuck decided he wanted to play football at the University of Pennsylvania. There he was a two-time consensus all-America center. In 1949, he was the Eagles' bonus draft choice.

Bednarik soon proved he could be an outstanding pro as well as a durable one. He missed his first two games as a rookie and then only one more in 14 seasons. Starting in 1950, he was an all-NFL choice seven straight years, once as a center and six times as a linebacker. He also starred in eight Pro Bowls.

The attitude Chuck displayed as a rookie fighting for a spot on the Eagles squad provides an insight into the reasons for his lasting success in pro football. "I always played with a certain amount of cockiness," Bednarik admitted. "You must have absolute confidence in football. You must feel that you are the best at your position at all times!"

INTERCEPTION RECORD

* Led NFL

| Year | Number | Yards | Average | TD | Year | Number | Yards | Average | TD |
|------|--------|-------|---------|-----|------|--------|-------|---------|-----|
| 1949 | 0 | 0 | 0.0 | 0 | 1957 | 3 | 51 | 17.0 | 0 |
| 1950 | 1 | 9 | 9.0 | 0 | 1958 | 0 | 0 | 0.0 | 0 |
| 1951 | 0 | 0 | 0.0 | 0 | 1959 | 0 | 0 | 0.0 | 0 |
| 1952 | 2 | 14 | 7.0 | 0 | 1960 | 2 | 0 | 0.0 | 0 |
| 1953 | 6 | 116 | 19.3 | 1* | 1961 | 2 | 33 | 16.5 | 0 |
| 1954 | 1 | 9 | 9.0 | 0 | 1962 | 0 | 0 | 0.0 | 0 |
| 1955 | 1 | 36 | 36.0 | 0 | TOTALS | 20 | 268 | 13.4 | 1 |
| 1956 | 2 | 0 | 0.0 | 0 | | | | | |

Punting: 12 punts, 40.3-yard average

Punt returns: 2 returns, 26 yards, 13.0-yard average, 0 touchdowns

Kickoff returns: 4 returns, 57 yards, 14.3-yard average, 0 touchdowns

# CHARLES W. BIDWILL SR

*Owner-administrator*
*Born in Chicago, Ill.,*
*September 16, 1895; died*
*April 19, 1947, at age of 51*
*Loyola University of Chicago*
*1933–47 Chicago Cardinals*

Charles Bidwill Sr, who owned the Chicago Cardinals for 15 seasons from 1933 to 1947, is a perfect example of a pioneer whose dedication, determination and love for the game kept pro football alive during its difficult early years. Even though the Cardinals, who exist today in St Louis as one of only two remaining charter franchises of the NFL—the other being the Chicago Bears—never enjoyed even one financially successful season during Bidwill's tenure, Charley's faith in pro football never waivered.

"Blue Shirt Charley," as he was known for the obvious reason he always wore a blue shirt, had been a long-time Bears fan before he purchased his own NFL team for $50,000 in 1933. Bidwill had, in fact, intervened with cash and the acquisition of a loan to prevent George Halas from losing his Chicago Bears team after the 1932 season. Even though the Cardinals and the Bears were natural cross-town rivals, Charley's love for the Bears remained constant through the years.

Perpetually overshadowed by the Bears, the Cardinals were continual losers both on the field and at the box office in the years prior to and during World War II. The end of the war brought another problem for Bidwill. It came in the form of the All-America Football Conference (AAFC) and new Chicago rivals, the Rockets. But it was Charley who delivered the AAFC one of its most stunning defeats when he signed everybody's all-America, Charley Trippi of Georgia, to a then-unprecedented $100,000 contract.

It wasn't just the signing but Bidwill's staging of the announcement that made things doubly hard on the AAFC. Trippi signed with Bidwill right after the Sugar Bowl on January 1, 1947, but the team owner persuaded him to pretend to the rival New York Yankees that they still had a chance. Just when the Yankees were about to announce they had signed the prized halfback, Bidwill called a press conference in Chicago to break the stunning news.

Trippi was the final link in Blue Shirt Charley's so-called "Dream Backfield"—Paul Christman, Pat Harder, Marshall Goldberg and Trippi. This quartet would lead the Cardinals to their finest achievements—an NFL championship in 1947 and a Western Division title in 1948.

Sadly, Bidwill, struck down suddenly by pneumonia in April, 1947, was not around to savor these triumphs. Still, he has never been forgotten and long-time NFLers even today speak admiringly of his contributions to pro football and the league. As his sons said when they spoke out for his election to the Hall of Fame: "We feel our father should have been one of the first in the Hall. Without people like him, there would be no NFL today!"

*Charles Bidwill Sr died suddenly in 1947 and could not enjoy his greatest triumph, the NFL title his Chicago Cardinals won later that year. During the Depression years of the 1930s, he was a leader among the determined men who fought to keep the NFL alive.*

# PAUL BROWN

*Coach*
*Born in Norwalk, Ohio,*
*September 7, 1908*
*Miami University of Ohio*
*1946–62 Cleveland Browns*

When Paul Brown organized the Cleveland team in the new All-America Football Conference (AAFC) in 1946, he immediately started doing many things no one else had ever tried. He hired full-time staff on a year-round basis. He became the first to measure a player's learning capabilities by the use of intelligence tests, to use classroom techniques extensively, to set up complete statistical film studies and then to grade his players from what he had found.

From the strategic standpoint, Paul began the practice of calling plays from the sideline through the use of alternating messenger guards. He developed detailed pass patterns to pick holes in any defense and then went to work to perfect the kind of defense that could stand up to any passing attack. He was the first to shift some running backs to defense because "they were too good to waste on offense."

Paul's coaching career began at Severn Prep in Maryland in 1930 and it took him to his Alma Mater, Massillon, Ohio, High School and to Ohio State before a service call put him in charge of the Great Lakes Naval Training Station team. At every stop, his teams enjoyed exceptional success.

While Brown was still at Great Lakes, Mickey McBride, the owner of the new Cleveland team, offered Paul the most lucrative coaching contract ever up to that time if he would make the jump to pro football. McBride's offer—$20,000 a season plus 15 percent of the profits—proved to be a bargain because the Browns under Coach Brown quickly became the dominant team in pro football.

In four years, Cleveland won all four AAFC titles and amassed a staggering 47–4–3 regular-season record. Many feel that Brown was a major reason for the demise of the AAFC because he developed such superior teams; fans throughout the league simply lost interest.

Then came the merger of 1950. NFL stalwarts eagerly awaited the come-uppance of the Browns when they met the Philadelphia Eagles, the 1949 NFL title-holders, in the season opener, but the Browns stunned the Eagles, 35–10, and went on to win the 1950 championship. Cleveland won divisional titles its first six years in the NFL and added two more NFL crowns in 1954 and 1955. In Paul's 17 years as coach of the Browns, he experienced only one losing season, 1956. After the 1962 season, however, new Cleveland owner Art Modell decided a change was in order. For the next five years, Paul Brown was out of football.

By the time he re-emerged as head coach and general manager of the new Cincinnati Bengals in 1968, his permanent place in history had already been assured. In 1967, he was accorded his sport's highest honor, election to the Pro Football Hall of Fame.

*Paul Brown was a highly successful coach in high school, college and service football but his record in his first 10 years as the Cleveland Browns coach was his best ever.*

---

COACHING RECORD

| Year | Won | Lost | Tied | Division finish |
|---|---|---|---|---|
| 1946* | 12 | 2 | 0 | 1st |
| 1947* | 12 | 1 | 1 | 1st |
| 1948* | 14 | 0 | 0 | 1st |
| 1949* | 9 | 1 | 2 | 1st |
| 1950† | 10 | 2 | 0 | Tie 1st |
| 1951† | 11 | 1 | 0 | 1st |
| 1952† | 8 | 4 | 0 | 1st |
| 1953† | 11 | 1 | 0 | 1st |
| 1954† | 9 | 3 | 0 | 1st |
| 1955† | 9 | 2 | 1 | 1st |
| 1956† | 5 | 7 | 0 | 4th |
| 1957† | 9 | 2 | 1 | 1st |
| 1958† | 9 | 3 | 0 | Tie 1st |
| 1959† | 7 | 5 | 0 | 2nd |
| 1960† | 8 | 3 | 1 | 2nd |
| 1961† | 8 | 5 | 1 | 3rd |
| 1962† | 7 | 6 | 1 | 3rd |
| TOTALS‡ | 167 | 53 | 8 | |

POST-SEASON RECORD

1946 AAFC Championship: Cleveland 14, New York Yankees 9
1947 AAFC Championship: Cleveland 14, New York Yankees 3
1948 AAFC Championship: Cleveland 49, Buffalo 7
1949 AAFC Divisional Playoff: Cleveland 31, Buffalo 21
1949 AAFC Championship: Cleveland 21, San Francisco 7
1950 NFL Divisional Playoff: Cleveland 8, New York Giants 3
1950 NFL Championship: Cleveland 30, Los Angeles Rams 28
1951 NFL Championship: Los Angeles Rams 24, Cleveland 17
1952 NFL Championship: Detroit 17, Cleveland 7
1953 NFL Championship: Detroit 17, Cleveland 16
1954 NFL Championship: Cleveland 56, Detroit 10
1955 NFL Championship: Cleveland 38, Los Angeles Rams 14
1957 NFL Championship: Detroit 59, Cleveland 14
1958 NFL Divisional Playoff: New York Giants 10, Cleveland 0

* In AAFC

† In NFL

‡ Career totals include post-season games

Note: Paul Brown also coached the Cincinnati Bengals from 1968 to 1975 *after* he had been elected to the Pro Football Hall of Fame. His eight-year record with the Bengals was 55–56–1.

# BOBBY LAYNE

*Quarterback
6 ft 2 in. 190 lb
Born in Santa Anna. Texas.
December 19. 1926: died
December 1. 1986 at age of 59
University of Texas
1948 Chicago Bears: 1949 New
York Bulldogs: 1950–8 Detroit
Lions: 1958–62 Pittsburgh
Steelers*

During his 15 pro football seasons, Bobby Layne was an all-NFL caliber quarterback who did well statistically but who was exceptional in the intangibles—leadership, determination, competitiveness, guts, *esprit de corps*. It was something that can't be taught to athletes—they either have it or they don't—and Layne had it in abundance.

Layne left pro football with a legend that may never be exactly duplicated. Bobby's story deals with sterling accomplishments on the field but also with his penchant for enjoying every moment off the field, even if on occasion that meant a big night on the town just hours before a crucial game. While it is likely some of Layne's off-the-field activities have been exaggerated, there is no question he did not subscribe to the norm when it came to the general rules of football-team deportment.

So it may be that Layne's pro football success hinged on the relationship he developed with a wise and understanding coach, Raymond "Buddy" Parker, who understood what made Bobby tick. Parker and Layne did not get together in Detroit until 1951 but once they did, the Lions clicked as no other Detroit team had ever done before or has done since. The Lions won divisional and NFL titles in 1952 and 1953 and a divisional crown in 1954.

In both title victories, Layne was a key figure, but it was in the 1953 game that Layne enjoyed his greatest—and certainly most famous—afternoon. The Browns held a 16–10 advantage with time running out when Detroit got the ball for one last chance at its own 20. "Awright, fellers," Layne told the Lions in the huddle. "Y'all block and ol' Bobby'll pass you raht to the champeenship. Ol' Bobby will get you six big ones." And six big ones he got, in just 60 seconds. He completed four of his first six passes in the

historic drive and then heaved a 33-yard clincher to little-used end Jim Doran. Layne's old high-school teammate, Doak Walker, kicked the extra point and Detroit had a 17–16 victory.

Parker left the Lions to coach in Pittsburgh in 1957. A year later, Layne also went to the Steelers in a trade. The Parker–Layne duo provided the Steelers with some of their finest seasons ever up to that time but the championship that Layne promised he would produce before he retired was not to be.

Doak Walker once said admiringly of his teammate: "Bobby never lost a game. Some days, time just ran out on him." That's the way it was with his vow to bring the Steelers a title. He didn't really break his promise. Time just ran out on Bobby Layne.

*Bobby Layne won widespread acclaim as a quarterback who could come through under pressure during his starring years with the Detroit Lions and Pittsburgh Steelers.*

## PASSING RECORD

| Year | Attempts | Completions | Percentage passes completed | Yards | TD | Interceptions |
|---|---|---|---|---|---|---|
| 1948° | 52 | 16 | 30.7 | 232 | 3 | 2 |
| 1949† | 299 | 155 | 51.8 | 1796 | 9 | 18 |
| 1950‡ | 336¶ | 152 | 45.2 | 2323¶ | 16 | 18 |
| 1951‡ | 332¶ | 152¶ | 45.8 | 2403¶ | 26¶ | 23¶ |
| 1952‡ | 287 | 139 | 48.4 | 1999 | 19 | 20 |
| 1953‡ | 273 | 125 | 45.8 | 2088 | 16 | 21 |
| 1954‡ | 246 | 135 | 54.9 | 1818 | 14 | 12 |
| 1955‡ | 270 | 143 | 53.0 | 1830 | 11 | 17 |
| 1956‡ | 244 | 129 | 52.9 | 1909 | 9 | 17 |
| 1957‡ | 179 | 87 | 48.6 | 1169 | 6 | 12 |
| 1958‡§ | 294 | 145 | 49.3 | 2510 | 14 | 12 |
| 1959§ | 297 | 142 | 47.8 | 1986 | 20 | 21¶ |
| 1960§ | 209 | 103 | 49.3 | 1814 | 13 | 17 |
| 1961§ | 149 | 75 | 50.3 | 1205 | 11 | 16 |
| 1962§ | 233 | 116 | 49.8 | 1686 | 9 | 17 |
| TOTALS | 3700 | 1814 | 49.0 | 26,768 | 196 | 243 |

Career passing rating: 63.2

## RUSHING RECORD

| Year | Attempts | Yards | Average | TD |
|---|---|---|---|---|
| 1948° | 13 | 80 | 6.1 | 1 |
| 1949† | 54 | 196 | 3.6 | 3 |
| 1950‡ | 56 | 250 | 4.5¶ | 4 |
| 1951‡ | 61 | 290 | 4.8 | 1 |
| 1952‡ | 94 | 411 | 4.4 | 1 |
| 1953‡ | 87 | 343 | 3.9 | 0 |
| 1954‡ | 30 | 119 | 4.0 | 2 |
| 1955‡ | 31 | 111 | 3.6 | 0 |
| 1956‡ | 46 | 169 | 3.7 | 5 |
| 1957‡ | 24 | 99 | 4.1 | 0 |
| 1958‡§ | 40 | 154 | 3.9 | 3 |
| 1959§ | 33 | 181 | 5.5 | 2 |
| 1960§ | 19 | 12 | 0.6 | 2 |
| 1961§ | 8 | 11 | 1.4 | 0 |
| 1962§ | 15 | 25 | 1.7 | 1 |
| TOTALS | 611 | 2451 | 4.0 | 25 |

° With Chicago Bears
† With New York Bulldogs
‡ With Detroit Lions
§ With Pittsburgh Steelers
¶ Led NFL

Scoring: 25 touchdowns, 120 extra points, 34 field goals, 372 points

# DAN REEVES

*Owner, administrator*
*Born in New York City, June 30,*
*1912; died April 15, 1971, at age*
*of 58*
*Georgetown University*
*1941–5 Cleveland Rams; 1946–71*
*Los Angeles Rams*

On January 14, 1946, Dan Reeves announced he was moving his Cleveland Rams football team to Los Angeles. This was shocking news because, less than a month earlier, the Rams had won the NFL championship. No established major-league franchise in any sport ever before had called a West Coast city home. Air travel was still in its early stages and Los Angels was 2000 long, hard land miles away from the nearest NFL city. Most important, Reeves' fellow NFL owners were dead set against the move!

But Reeves, who along with a partner had bought the Rams in 1941, was just as determined his club would never play in Cleveland again. Attendance in the Ohio lakeshore city had been less than sensational and only 32,178 showed up to see the Rams defeat the Washington Redskins, 15–14, for the 1945 NFL championship. The last straw for Reeves was the city's decision to triple the stadium rent for the title game.

It took a bitter fight and even a threat to withdraw from the NFL before Reeves could convince his colleagues he meant business. Once the move was made, the Rams had to fight a life-and-death struggle with the rival Dons of the All-America Football Conference (AAFC). Reeves had lost money in trickles in Cleveland but his initial losses in Los Angeles came in tidal waves.

The AAFC folded in 1949 just as the Rams were embarking on a string of outstanding seasons on the field. Boasting some of football's most glamorous stars, the Rams won four divisional titles in seven years and the NFL championship in 1951. The effect at the gate was astounding. Topped by a crowd of 102,368 for a San Francisco 49ers game in 1957, turnouts in the Los Angeles Coliseum surpassed 80,000 on 22 occasions during the Rams' first two decades in California.

The innovative Reeves made several other significant contributions to pro football. He instituted the famed "Free Football for Kids" program that enabled youngsters to enjoy the game in their formative years and then, hopefully, become ardent fans as adults. His signing of the ex-UCLA great, Kenny Washington, in the spring of 1946 marked the first time a black player had been hired in the NFL since 1933. Dan's experimentation in the early days of television provided the groundwork for pro football's current successful TV policies. He was also the first to employ a full-time scouting staff.

For all of the great legacies to pro football the farsighted Dan Reeves left behind, his original move to the Pacific Coast will always rank as the most daring and most significant accomplishment. Every enterprise must have its pioneer, a person who is willing to venture into the unknown with the courage of his convictions. For professional football, Dan Reeves was that man!

*Dan Reeves made a lasting mark in pro football but he is most remembered for moving the Cleveland Rams to Los Angeles in 1946. Reeves is pictured with one-time Rams coach George Allen.*

# KEN STRONG

*Halfback*
*5 ft 11 in, 210 lb*
*Born in West Haven, Conn.,*
*August 6, 1906; died October 5,*
*1979, at age of 73*
*New York University*
*1929–32 Staten Island Stapletons;*
*1933–5, 1939, 1944–7 New York*
*Giants; 1936–7 New York Yanks*
*(AFL)*

Ken Strong's most publicized performance in 14 years of pro football came in the 1934 NFL championship game. Playing on a frozen Polo Grounds field, the New York Giants resorted to the use of basketball shoes in the second half to upset the previously undefeated Chicago Bears. Strong contributed 17 points on two touchdowns, four extra points and a field goal. For almost 30 years, his mark stood as an NFL title-game scoring record.

Strong could do everything—run, block, pass, catch passes, punt, placekick and play defense with the very best. Still, for all his brilliance, he had a tumultuous, checker-board pro career that saw him start with the little-known Staten Island Stapletons, play with the Giants three different times, join a rival league, survive a blackball by the NFL and retire for four years before returning to action a final time.

Ken had been everyone's all-America at New York University and it was widely assumed he would begin his NFL career with the Giants. But when the New York coach tried to sign Strong for $3000 instead of the $4000 team owner Tim Mara had authorized, Ken joined the Stapletons instead.

Strong also was interested in a professional baseball career and he signed a New York Yankees contract. In those days, it was fairly common for a great athlete to play both professional baseball and football, with football being worked in after the baseball season was over. Ken enjoyed an excellent minor league season in 1931 but a wrist injury, complicated by faulty surgery, left him unable to throw well enough from the outfield to continue playing baseball. He had no choice but to concentrate on football. However, after the 1932 season, the Stapes folded.

When Strong asked the Giants for a job, he was rebuffed by Mara, who was still bitter over Ken's initial decision to go to Staten Island. After lengthy bargaining, Strong signed for the $3000 he had originally turned down. In both 1933 and 1934, Ken was a major factor in his team's march to the NFL championship game. In 1934, he was a unanimous all-NFL choice. In 1936, the NFL introduced the college-player draft and the net effect was that most teams, already hard hit by the Depression, reduced the salaries of all veterans in view of the guaranteed influx of new talent from the colleges each year. Strong was offered just $150 a game, a substantial cut from his 1935 salary.

So Ken jumped to the New York Yanks of the rival American Football League (AFL). The NFL considered this action to be "extremely disloyal" and suspended him for five years. The AFL folded, the NFL reneged and the Giants welcomed Strong back for the 1939 season. After just one year, Ken retired.

Four seasons later, the Giants, hard-pressed by wartime manpower shortages, convinced Strong to return as a kicking specialist. It was understood that he would wear no shoulder pads and he seldom took off his wristwatch when he went on the field.

Because his young son had never seen him do anything but kick, Ken asked to carry the ball one last time in the final game in 1947. Trailing 31–0, the Redskins agreed to go along with the plan but a rookie, unaware of the situation, blasted the 41-year-old Strong to the ground. Ken consoled himself that his son had at least seen him carry the ball until he learned, with much consternation, that Ken Jr had a cold and had missed the game.

*A New York University all-America, Ken Strong first joined the Giants in 1933, moved to a rival league in 1936, returned in 1939, retired in 1940 and then came back for a final time in 1944.*

## SCORING RECORD

| Year | TD | Extra points | Field goals | Total |
|------|----|----|----|----|
| 1929° | 4 | 9 | 0 | 33 |
| 1930° | 7 | 8 | 1 | 53 |
| 1931° | 7 | 5 | 2 | 53 |
| 1932° | 4 | 6 | 1 | 33 |
| 1933† | 6 | 13 | 5 | 64§ |
| 1934† | 6 | 8 | 4 | 56 |
| 1935† | 1 | 11 | 4 | 29 |
| 1936–7‡ | No records available | | | |
| 1938 | Did not play | | | |
| 1939† | 0 | 7 | 4 | 19 |
| 1940–3 | Retired | | | |
| 1944† | 0 | 23 | 6§ | 41 |
| 1945† | 0 | 23 | 6 | 41 |
| 1946† | 0 | 32 | 4 | 44 |
| 1947† | 0 | 24 | 2 | 30 |
| TOTALS | 35 | 169 | 39 | 496 |

° With Staten Island Stapletons

† With New York Giants

‡ With New York Yanks (AFL)

§ Led NFL

Note: Complete statistics for Strong in other categories not available

# JOE STYDAHAR

*Tackle*
*6 ft 4 in. 230 lb*
*Born in Kaylor, Pa., March 17,*
*1912; died March 23, 1977, at age*
*of 65*
*University of West Virginia*
*1936–42, 1945–6 Chicago Bears*

By 1936, knowledgeable football observers realized that George Halas was seeking only the finest talent for his building program that would produce the powerful Chicago Bears teams that dominated pro football in the early 1940s. So it was somewhat of a surprise when the NFL staged its first-ever college draft before the 1936 season and Halas' first pick was a tackle from little-known West Virginia by the name of Joe Stydahar.

It was not that the 6 ft 4 in, 230-lb Stydahar did not have the credentials to be a blue-chip pro. As a West Virginia senior, he was named to all-Eastern, Little all-America and all-America squads. He also played in the East-West Shrine game and the College All-Star classic prior to joining the Bears. But pro football teams of that era did not have sophisticated scouting techniques and there was no way a tackle from the ''sticks'' should be that well known. As it turned out, a Bears end, West Virginia alumnus Bill Karr, tipped off the Bears coach to the talents of Stydahar.

In many ways, ''Jumbo Joe'' was the epitome of the Bears' overpowering strength at that time. Fearless and huge by 1940 standards, Stydahar possessed incredible power and remarkable speed. Flaunting his disdain for superstition by wearing jersey number 13, he was a 60-minute performer who often shunned the use of a helmet until NFL rules forced him to comply. From 1937 through 1940, he was picked at left tackle on the official all-NFL team.

Stydahar's tenure as an active player became synonymous with Chicago Bears championships. Starting with his rookie season in 1936, Jumbo Joe was a fixture for seven years until he was called into the US Navy following the 1942 season. He returned in 1945 to play for two more years. During that period, the Bears won three NFL championships and five Western Division titles. In Joe's final game, the 1946 Bears defeated the New York Giants, 24–14. It was the last major triumph of the Bears' dynasty years.

Unlike many athletic stars, Stydahar did not play service football, so when he talked to Halas about rejoining the team in 1945, he told the Bears leader to put down any figure he felt was right on his contract. ''I'm just about washed up as a player,'' Joe told Halas. ''Besides I haven't played for three years.'' Halas offered $8000, twice as much as Stydahar had ever been paid.

''That's the kind of a guy Halas was,'' Joe remembered with great appreciation. ''George was like a second father to me. I really didn't know anything about football until I played for him. Whatever success I had, I owe to him.''

*Joe Stydahar from little-known West Virginia was a key member of the powerful Chicago forward wall for nine years.*

# EMLEN TUNNELL

*Defensive back*
*6 ft 1 in, 200 lb*
*Born in Bryn Mawr, Pa., March 29,*
*1925; died July 22, 1975, at age*
*of 50*
*University of Toledo, University of*
*Iowa*
*1948–58 New York Giants;*
*1959–61 Green Bay Packers*

*Emlen Tunnell left Iowa because he didn't like playing defense but he made his mark with the New York Giants as a defensive and special teams star. He had 79 career interceptions.*

During the 11 years Emlen Tunnell played with the New York Giants, he was known as that team's "offense on defense." Never was this tag more appropriate than in the 1952 season. Deacon Dan Towler of the Rams led NFL rushers with 894 yards and a splendid 5.7 yard-per-carry average but Tunnell accounted for 923 yards on just 52 carries for a spectacular 17.8-yard average. Yet Em did not play even one down as an offensive back. Instead, the slippery star amassed 411 yards on punt returns, 364 yards on kickoff returns and another 149 yards on seven interceptions.

Almost everyone would sooner or later ask the Giants coach, Steve Owen, why Tunnell, so obviously talented as a runner, did not play on offense. "He's more valuable to us right where he is," Owen would answer firmly. "With Em on defense, we have the potential to get the ball on any play in the entire game!"

This was lofty praise for a young athlete who, a decade earlier, had suffered a broken neck as a freshman gridder at the University of Toledo. Tunnell was told he would never play again and both the Army and Navy considered him unfit for service. He did spend three years in the US Coast Guard.

At the war's end, Em migrated to the University of Iowa, where he outlasted hordes of returning veterans to win a varsity spot, primarily as a defensive player. Since Tunnell preferred to play offense, he decided to leave Iowa after the 1947 season, even though he had a year of eligibility remaining.

Most pro teams thought Emlen would play a third year at Iowa so he was not drafted in 1948. Deciding to seek a pro job on his own, he dropped in to the Giants' office to visit the club owner, Tim Mara. Pleased with Tunnell's enthusiasm, Mara offered him a $5000 contract plus $1000 in bonuses. Em thus became the first black to play for the Giants. He later was the first black to be elected to the Pro Football Hall of Fame.

Even though Em proved to be an exceptional special teams player, it was on defense that he made his lasting mark. The umbrella defense that made the Giants so successful in the 1950s was basically a 4–1–6 alignment with two defensive ends dropping back to team with four defensive backs on passing situations. As the safety, Tunnell played at the top, or back, of the alignment. Always a major contributor to his teams' defensive successes, Em intercepted a then-record 79 passes in his 14 seasons with the Giants and the Green Bay Packers.

Teammate Frank Gifford still raves about Tunnell's performances. "There was rarely a game in which I wasn't amazed by his 'reading' of plays and his cat-like reactions. At first I thought he was just lucky. Then I realized he was just great."

INTERCEPTION RECORD

| Year | Number | Yards | Average | TD |
|---|---|---|---|---|
| 1948° | 7 | 116 | 16.6 | 1 |
| 1949° | 10 | 251 | 25.1 | 2‡ |
| 1950° | 7 | 167 | 23.9 | 0 |
| 1951° | 9 | 74 | 8.2 | 0 |
| 1952° | 7 | 149 | 21.3 | 0 |
| 1953° | 6 | 117 | 19.5 | 0 |
| 1954° | 8 | 108 | 13.5 | 0 |
| 1955° | 7 | 76 | 10.9 | 0 |
| 1956° | 6 | 87 | 14.5 | 0 |
| 1957° | 6 | 87 | 14.5 | 1 |
| 1958° | 1 | 8 | 8.0 | 0 |
| 1959✝ | 2 | 20 | 10.0 | 0 |
| 1960✝ | 3 | 22 | 7.3 | 0 |
| 1961✝ | 0 | 0 | 0.0 | 0 |
| TOTALS | 79 | 1282 | 16.2 | 4 |

PUNT RETURN RECORD

| Year | Number | Yards | Average | TD |
|---|---|---|---|---|
| 1948° | 12 | 115 | 9.6 | 0 |
| 1949° | 26 | 315 | 12.1 | 1 |
| 1950° | 31 | 305 | 9.8 | 0 |
| 1951° | 34‡ | 489‡ | 14.4 | 3 |
| 1952° | 30 | 411‡ | 13.7 | 0 |
| 1953° | 38‡ | 223‡ | 5.9 | 0 |
| 1954° | 21 | 70 | 3.3 | 0 |
| 1955° | 25 | 98 | 3.9 | 1 |
| 1956° | 22 | 120 | 5.5 | 0 |
| 1957° | 12 | 60 | 5.0 | 0 |
| 1958° | 6 | 0 | 0.0 | 0 |
| 1959✝ | 1 | 3 | 3.0 | 0 |
| 1960✝ | 0 | 0 | 0.0 | 0 |
| 1961✝ | 0 | 0 | 0.0 | 0 |
| TOTALS | 258 | 2209 | 8.6 | 5 |

° With New York Giants

✝ With Green Bay Packers

‡ Led NFL

Kickoff returns: 46 returns, 1215 yards, 26.4-yard average, 1 touchdown

Rushing: 17 attempts, 43 yards, 2.5-yard average, 0 touchdowns

Scoring: 10 touchdowns, 60 points

# CLIFF BATTLES

*Halfback*
*6 ft 1 in, 201 lb*
*Born in Akron, Ohio, May 1,*
*1910; died April 28, 1981, at age*
*of 70*
*West Virginia Wesleyan College*
*1932 Boston Braves; 1933–6*
*Boston Redskins; 1937*
*Washington Redskins*

*Cliff Battles won the NFL individual rushing title as a rookie in 1952. After the Redskins moved to Washington, he teamed with Sammy Baugh to form a lethal passing-running duo.*

In 1937, owner George Preston Marshall moved his Redskins team from Boston to Washington. He brought with him the NFL's premier running back, Cliff Battles, and quickly added a sensational rookie passer, Sammy Baugh. It didn't seem out of the question that the Battles–Baugh ground and air threat would provide misery for other NFL teams for years to come.

This was not to be, however. Inexplicably, Marshall, who had paid Battles $3000 a year, starting with his rookie campaign, refused to consider a raise, even though Cliff had been a three-time official all-NFL selection and the league's leading rusher in 1932 and 1937. After the season, the exasperated Battles accepted a $4000 job as an assistant coach at Columbia University.

Inadvertently, Baugh may have been a catalyst in Battles' premature retirement. Sammy himself was thinking of quitting pro football for baseball, even though he had enjoyed a marvelous rookie season. Marshall was expending all of his efforts in trying to re-sign his ace passer. Battles later admitted that this concentration of effort by Marshall on Baugh with little or no time left to negotiate with him was a considerable factor in his eventual retirement.

Ironically, it was the same Marshall who had used progressive measures to first sign the Phi Beta Kappa standout from tiny West Virginia Wesleyan. Although Cliff's team was overwhelmed in a game against Georgetown, Marshall saw in Battles the fullback power and the halfback speed that would make him a superstar for his new NFL team in Boston. He sent his envoy with instructions to sign Battles or "don't come back."

Cliff played on just-average teams in Boston but his play was anything but average. He won the NFL rushing title in his rookie 1932 campaign. A year later, he became the first player ever to rush for more than 200 yards in a game. Throughout his career Cliff threatened to go all the way every time he touched the ball.

In 1937, the championship race was nip-and-tuck, with the issue to be decided by a Redskins–Giants clash in New York's Polo Grounds on the season's final day. The morning of the game, thousands of Redskins fans rode to New York in special trains bearing the names of their heroes. The happy entourage marched up Broadway behind the 55-piece Redskins band that Marshall had garbed in buckskins and long Indian headdresses. The fans' exuberance mounted as the Redskins won, 49–14. In what proved to be his final regular-season game, Battles enjoyed a spectacular day. He scored three touchdowns on scrimmage runs of 4 and 73 yards and an interception return of 76 yards. In the process, he clinched the league rushing championship.

A week later, Cliff ran 43 yards on the game's first play and scored the first touchdown as the Redskins defeated the Chicago Bears, 28–21, for their first NFL championship.

Celebrating Redskins fans couldn't possibly have known they had seen their incomparable running star play for the last time. In the years that followed, Baugh established record after record, even without the aid of Battles' long-distance running thrusts, and loyal boosters could only ponder "what might have been."

RUSHING RECORD

| Year | Attempts | Yards | Average | TD |
|------|----------|-------|---------|-----|
| 1932* | 148 | 576§ | 3.9 | 3 |
| 1933† | 146 | 737 | 5.0§ | 3 |
| 1934† | 103 | 511 | 5.0 | 6 |
| 1935† | 84 | 310 | 3.7 | 1 |
| 1936† | 176 | 614 | 3.5 | 5 |
| 1937‡ | 216§ | 874§ | 4.0 | 5 |
| TOTALS | 873 | 3622 | 4.1 | 23 |

\* With Boston Braves

† With Boston Redskins

‡ With Washington Redskins

§ Led NFL

# ART DONOVAN

*Defensive tackle*
*6 ft 3 in. 265 lb*
*Born in The Bronx, N. Y., June 5,*
*1925*
*Boston College*
*1950 Baltimore Colts; 1951 New*
*York Yanks; 1952 Dallas Texans;*
*1953–61 Baltimore Colts*

Art Donovan made the 1950 Baltimore Colts as a 25-year-old rookie but there must have been many days when he wished he hadn't. The hapless Colts became the New York Yanks in 1951 and the Dallas Texans in 1952. In three years, defensive units of which Art was a member yielded a staggering 1269 points in 36 games. His teams' cumulative record was 3–31–2.

But in 1953, Donovan returned to Baltimore to play for a new Colts team. Under the guidance of Weeb Ewbank, the Colts steadily advanced toward championship contention and Donovan developed even more rapidly into one of the finest defensive tackles ever.

Donovan, son of the famous boxing referee, was smart, strong and quick. He rushed the passer, read the keys, closed off the middle, split the double-team blocks and followed the flow of the play. From 1954 to 1957, he was all-NFL four straight years. He also played in five consecutive Pro Bowls.

As great as Art was on the field, he was at least as valuable as a morale-builder. Lovable, laughable, certainly one of the most universally popular players in NFL annals, Artie was the pressure safety valve whenever team tensions built up.

The perpetual brunt of Colt jokes, Artie would feign anger, shout down his tormentors with Marine-acquired language and threaten to punch someone. Then there would be a smile, the tension would ease and the Colts were a happier team because of Artie. Even his well-publicized weight problems turned out to be a team morale-lifter. Artie reported to camp at 309 lb in 1954 but his contract was soon amended to call for a heavy fine if he reported over 270 lb in future seasons. Weigh-in time with Donovan involved was always a festive occasion in Baltimore.

When it became apparent that he would not make the team in 1962, Artie gracefully retired. Two weeks later, in the season-opener, Baltimore fans were ready with a special day for Donovan. There were the usual features—the presentation of a car, numerous other gifts, reading of telegrams from dignitaries and the retirement of Donovan's number 70 jersey.

Choked with emotion, sentimental Artie thanked the city and the team that had done so much for him. "Up in heaven there is a lady who is happy that the city of Baltimore was so good to her son—a kid from The Bronx," he sobbed. And 55,000 fans cried right along with Artie Donovan.

*Defensive tackle Art Donovan was the first player from the*
*Baltimore Colts to be elected to the Hall of Fame.*

# ELROY (CRAZYLEGS) HIRSCH

*Halfback, end*
*6 ft 2 in, 190 lb*
*Born in Wausau, Wisc., June 17, 1923*
*University of Wisconsin, University of Michigan*
*1946–8 Chicago Rockets (AAFC); 1949–57 Los Angeles Rams*

In a crucial game midway into the 1951 NFL season, the Los Angeles Rams found themselves trailing the Chicago Bears, 14–0, and deep in a hole on their own 9-yard line. Quarterback Bob Waterfield faked a handoff, stepped back a few paces and threw far downfield. Meanwhile, Elroy Hirsch took off at the snap and was running full-throttle at midfield. Waterfield's pass was well over his head but Elroy gathered in the ball on his fingertips and raced for a 91-yard touchdown. The Rams went on to an important 42–17 victory.

It was a patented "Elroy Hirsch special," a sizzling shocker that was repeated 17 times that year. Besides his 91-yard bomb, Elroy had scoring catches from such distances as 34, 44, 47, 53, 70, 72, 76, 79, and 81 yards. Such long-distance devastation had never before been seen in the NFL.

It wasn't just the number of long-gainers but the way he did the job that set Hirsch apart from all others. "Crazylegs," a nickname that a sportscaster coined while he was in college, had a unique running style that made him famous. When running downfield, his muscular legs seemed to gyrate in six different directions at once. As teammate Norm Van Brocklin once said, "You've heard of people who zig or zag. Well, Elroy also has a 'zog' and a couple of 'zugs.'"

Pro football success did not come easily to Hirsch, even though he was an all-America halfback at both Wisconsin and Michigan before he joined the Chicago Rockets of the new All-America Football Conference (AAFC) in 1946.

Hirsch described his three seasons in Chicago as "frightful." There was a rapid change of coaches, an unending string of losses, a number of injuries and finally a fractured skull in 1948. Some doubted that Elroy would ever play again but he stubbornly kept to his rehabilitation schedule and slowly worked back into playing condition. He was fitted with a custom-made helmet molded from light, extra-strong plastic with added padding protecting the critical area around his right ear.

When his AAFC contract expired, Hirsch happily joined the Rams. After a year spent mostly on the bench in 1949, Elroy was shifted to end by new coach Joe Stydahar in 1950. For a while, Hirsch, not familiar with the nuances of end play, was like a duck out of water. Hard work eventually paid off and, a year later, he became a primary contributor to the Rams' march to the NFL title.

As the Hirsch legend grew, it was only natural to compare Crazylegs to the other great receivers of pro football. Many insisted he was the best ever but Hirsch modestly downgraded his own case. "I'm just a busted-down, retreaded halfback who happened to get lucky."

*Even Elroy Hirsch wondered if he would ever play again after he suffered a fractured skull in 1948. But he got a new lease of life with the Los Angeles Rams when he switched from halfback to end.*

## RECEIVING RECORD

| Year | Number | Yards | Average | TD |
|------|--------|-------|---------|-----|
| 1946° | 27 | 347 | 12.9 | 3 |
| 1947° | 10 | 282 | 28.2 | 3 |
| 1948° | 7 | 101 | 14.4 | 1 |
| 1949† | 22 | 326 | 14.8 | 4 |
| 1950† | 42 | 687 | 16.4 | 7 |
| 1951† | 66‡ | 1495‡ | 22.7‡ | 17‡ |
| 1952† | 25 | 590 | 23.6 | 4 |
| 1953† | 61 | 941 | 15.4 | 4 |
| 1954† | 35 | 720 | 20.6 | 3 |
| 1955† | 25 | 460 | 18.4 | 2 |
| 1956† | 35 | 603 | 17.2 | 6 |
| 1957† | 32 | 477 | 14.9 | 6 |
| TOTALS | 387 | 7029 | 18.2 | 60 |

## RUSHING RECORD

| Year | Attempts | Yards | Average | TD |
|------|----------|-------|---------|-----|
| 1946° | 87 | 226 | 2.6 | 1 |
| 1947° | 23 | 51 | 2.2 | 1 |
| 1948° | 23 | 93 | 4.0 | 0 |
| 1949† | 68 | 287 | 4.2 | 1 |
| 1950† | 2 | 19 | 9.5 | 0 |
| 1951† | 1 | 3 | 3.0 | 0 |
| 1952† | 0 | 0 | 0.0 | 0 |
| 1953† | 1 | –6 | –6.0 | 0 |
| 1954† | 1 | 6 | 6.0 | 0 |
| 1955† | 0 | 0 | 0.0 | 0 |
| 1956† | 0 | 0 | 0.0 | 0 |
| 1957† | 1 | 8 | 8.0 | 0 |
| TOTALS | 207 | 687 | 3.3 | 3 |

° With Chicago Rockets (AAFC)

† With Los Angeles Rams

‡ Led NFL

Interceptions: 15 interceptions, 251 yards, 16.7-yard average, 0 touchdowns

Punt returns: 21 returns, 286 yards, 13.6-yard average, 1 touchdown

Kickoff returns: 21 returns, 566 yards, 27.0-yard average, 0 touchdowns

Passing: 22 attempts, 12 completions, 156 yards, 1 touchdown, 1 interception

Scoring: 66 touchdowns, 9 extra points, 405 points

# WAYNE MILLNER

*End*
*6 ft 0 in, 191 lb*
*Born in Roxbury, Mass.,*
*January 31, 1913; died*
*November 19, 1976, at age of 63*
*Notre Dame University*
*1936 Boston Redskins; 1937–41,*
*1945 Washington Redskins*

When Wayne Millner joined the Boston Redskins in 1936, the news so excited the team's new coach, Ray Flaherty, he promised to resign if "we don't win the championship with that big Yankee playing end." The Redskins did win the Eastern Division title that year and Millner, a star on both offense and defense, was a big contributor. For the next few seasons during which the Redskins, who moved to Washington in 1937, won two more divisional titles and one NFL championship, Wayne became the favorite target of the brilliant passer, Sammy Baugh. The two combined for many a blockbuster play during some of the Redskins' finest seasons.

The 1937 championship showdown with the Chicago Bears provides a good example. With the Bears ahead, 14–7, Baugh opened up the second half with a 55-yard bomb to Millner. Chicago forged back ahead but the Baugh–Millner combo clicked again, this time for a 78-yard touchdown. The winning score came on another Baugh pass, that one to Ed Justice, while Millner, as a decoy, attracted the attention of the Bears defenders. Wayne wound up the day with eight catches and 181 yards gained.

Millner was among the last of the outstanding two-way ends. When he wasn't catching Baugh's passes, he was blocking for him. He was competitive, determined, and known for his cat-like reflexes and his sure hands. He was respected as a "money player," at his best when the stakes were the highest and the pressure the greatest.

Teammate Cliff Battles, the Redskins' premier ball-carrier, testified to Millner's talent as a blocker. "I always knew if I could get out into the open, Wayne would be there to block for me. His involvement in the play determined whether or not I would get away for a long run."

If Millner thrived on pressure in the NFL, it no doubt came naturally to him. During his three star-studded seasons at Notre Dame, he was involved in many tight situations and many big games. His biggest moment came in the Notre Dame–Ohio State clash in 1935, still referred to as one of the most memorable college games in history. Wayne's touchdown catch in the dying seconds enabled the Irish to win, 18–13.

Millner, who entered the Navy after the 1941 season, wound up his career in 1945 with 124 receptions, the best ever figure for a Redskin up to that time. Had he played for any other pro team, he

might have captured more headlines but the Redskins had Baugh who gained most of the publicity. There may also have been one other factor. So often did Millner deliver under pressure, the press and fans and even his own coaches came to take his clutch performances for granted.

*Highly touted by his coach when he joined the Redskins in 1936, Wayne Millner combined with the fabled Sammy Baugh to give his team a lethal offensive weapon.*

### RECEIVING RECORD

| Year | Number | Yards | Average | TD |
|------|--------|-------|---------|-----|
| 1936° | 18 | 211 | 11.7 | 0 |
| 1937† | 14 | 216 | 15.4 | 2 |
| 1938† | 18 | 232 | 12.9 | 1 |
| 1939† | 19 | 294 | 15.5 | 4 |
| 1940† | 22 | 233 | 10.6 | 3 |
| 1941† | 20 | 262 | 13.1 | 0 |
| 1942–4 | In US Navy | | | |
| 1945† | 13 | 130 | 10.0 | 2 |
| TOTALS | 124 | 1578 | 12.7 | 12 |

° With Boston Redskins

† With Washington Redskins

# MARION MOTLEY

*Fullback*
*6 ft 1 in. 238 lb*
*Born in Leesburg. Ga.. June 5.*
*1920*
*South Carolina State College.*
*University of Nevada*
*1946–53 Cleveland Browns; 1955*
*Pittsburgh Steelers*

During their first decade, beginning in 1946, when the Cleveland Browns dominated two pro football leagues, the most visible element in their deadly effective attack was the pin-point passing of Otto Graham. Yet many experts will tell you that neither Graham nor the Browns would have been nearly so successful had it not been for the contributions of a 238-lb fullback named Marion Motley.

Marion was a devastating pass-protecting blocker, perhaps the best ever at his position. From this key element of a successful aerial attack, the Browns invented the "trap" play which was to prove a back-breaker for numerous Cleveland opponents over the years.

The play called for Graham to drop back to pass but to hand off to Marion when the enemy rush line drew close. Motley in turn would barrel straight ahead and, if necessary, over opponents who stood in his way. Once the Motley reputation was established, defenses could never concentrate solely on Graham again.

Blessed with speed as well as power, Motley did much more than just serve as Graham's bodyguard. He was the leading rusher in the four-year history of the All-America Football Conference (AAFC) and the NFL ball-carrying champion in 1950. When Otto had trouble finding receivers, he knew Marion would be close at hand to catch a short pass and turn it into a big gain. He even returned kickoffs, particularly in his AAFC years.

It was no accident that Motley wound up in Cleveland because he had crossed paths often with coach Paul Brown. Marion played his high-school football just across the street from the present site of the Pro Football Hall of Fame. His Canton McKinley teams lost only three games, all to Brown-coached Massillon high-school elevens, in three seasons. In the Navy during World War II, Motley was a member of the Great Lakes Navy team that upset Notre Dame, 39–7, in 1945. His coach was Paul Brown.

"Our club was badly hit by transfers and discharges in 1945," Brown recalls. "The only reason I still had Motley was that no one realized how good he was."

With the Cleveland Browns, people—fans, teammates and opponents alike—quickly found out just how good Marion really was. Motley, who was one of only two blacks—the other was teammate Bill Willis—to play in the AAFC in 1946, also played linebacker as well as fullback his first two seasons. When he settled down to playing only on the offensive unit, he became even tougher.

Blanton Collier, a Cleveland assistant in the 1940s, insisted Motley was "the greatest all-around football player I ever saw." Four decades later, many qualified observers still unhesitatingly second that assessment.

*While other stars grabbed the headlines, fullback Marion Motley was extremely important as a devastating pass blocker and a constant threat on the Browns' famed "trap play."*

| RUSHING RECORD | | | | |
|---|---|---|---|---|
| Year | Attempts | Yards | Average | TD |
| 1946* | 73 | 601 | 8.2 | 5 |
| 1947* | 146 | 889 | 6.0 | 8 |
| 1948* | 157 | 964§ | 6.1 | 5 |
| 1949* | 113 | 570 | 5.0 | 8 |
| 1950† | 140 | 810¶ | 5.8 | 3 |
| 1951† | 61 | 273 | 4.5 | 1 |
| 1952† | 104 | 444 | 4.3 | 1 |
| 1953† | 32 | 161 | 5.0 | 0 |
| 1954 | Did not play | | | |
| 1955‡ | 2 | 8 | 4.0 | 0 |
| TOTALS | 828 | 4720 | 5.7 | 31 |

| RECEIVING RECORD | | | | |
|---|---|---|---|---|
| Year | Number | Yards | Average | TD |
| 1946* | 10 | 188 | 18.8 | 1 |
| 1947* | 7 | 73 | 10.4 | 1 |
| 1948* | 13 | 192 | 14.8 | 2 |
| 1949* | 15 | 191 | 12.7 | 0 |
| 1950† | 11 | 151 | 13.7 | 1 |
| 1951† | 10 | 52 | 5.2 | 0 |
| 1952† | 13 | 213 | 16.4 | 2 |
| 1953† | 6 | 47 | 7.8 | 0 |
| 1954 | Did not play | | | |
| 1955‡ | 0 | 0 | 0.0 | 0 |
| TOTALS | 85 | 1107 | 13.0 | 7 |

| KICKOFF RETURN RECORD | | | | |
|---|---|---|---|---|
| Year | Number | Yards | Average | TD |
| 1946* | 3 | 53 | 17.7 | 0 |
| 1947* | 13 | 322 | 24.8 | 0 |
| 1948* | 14 | 337 | 24.1 | 0 |
| 1949* | 12 | 262 | 21.8 | 0 |
| 1950† | 0 | 0 | 0.0 | 0 |
| 1951† | 0 | 0 | 0.0 | 0 |
| 1952† | 3 | 88 | 29.3 | 0 |
| 1953† | 3 | 60 | 20.0 | 0 |
| 1954 | Did not play | | | |
| 1955‡ | 0 | 0 | 0.0 | 0 |
| TOTALS | 48 | 1122 | 23.4 | 0 |

* With Cleveland Browns (AAFC)

† With Cleveland Browns (NFL)

‡ With Pittsburgh Steelers

§ Led AAFC

¶ Led NFL

# CHARLEY TRIPPI

*Halfback, quarterback*
*6 ft 0 in, 185 lb*
*Born in Pittston, Pa.,*
*December 14, 1922*
*University of Georgia*
*1947–55 Chicago Cardinals*

As a two-time all-America from the University of Georgia, Charley Trippi became a key figure in the inter-league battling between the All-America Football Conference (AAFC) and the NFL in 1946. The AAFC's New York Yankees were so sure they had signed him, they called a press conference in New York to announce the happy news. But while the newsmen gathered in the Big Apple, Cardinals owner Charles W. Bidwill Sr announced in Chicago he had signed Trippi to a four-year contract worth $100,000. For those days, the size of the contract was stunning news and a big breakthrough in the AAFC–NFL war.

Trippi's acquisition completed Bidwill's quest for a "Dream Backfield." Although Bidwill did not live to see it, Charley became the game-breaker in a talented corps that included Paul Christman, Pat Harder, Marshall Goldberg and, later, Elmer Angsman.

Never was Trippi more magnificent than in the 1947 NFL championship game when the Cardinals defeated the Philadelphia Eagles, 28–21. Playing on an icy field in Chicago, Charley wore basketball shoes for better traction and carried 14 times for 206 yards. He added 102 yards on two punt returns. His touchdowns came on a 44-yard scrimmage run and a 75-yard punt return.

Trippi could and would do anything on a football field. He played as a left halfback for four seasons before switching to quarterback for two years. Charley then moved back to offensive halfback for one campaign before changing almost exclusively to the defensive unit in 1954 and 1955. He also was the Cardinals' punter and he excelled on the punt and kickoff return teams.

Charley's gridiron career began on a modest note in the small mining town of Pittston, Pennsylvania, where his father, an Italian immigrant, was a grocer. "I used to have to sneak out for football practice," he recalls, "because my father disliked the game with a passion. He insisted I would never play." His father finally relented but still saw his son play only twice.

Turned down by Fordham because he was too small, Charley went to Georgia to play college football. After starring in the 1942 Rose Bowl, Trippi left for the Air Force, where he played for the Third Air Force Gremlins eleven. He was back at Georgia by mid-1945. A year later, he steered the Bulldogs to their first undefeated season and a Sugar Bowl victory.

Due to relaxed regulations during the war years, Charley played in five College All-Star classics, two while at Georgia, two while in the service and a fifth as a Cardinal in 1948. Like so many of the things Trippi did on a football field, this was a rare achievement that can never be equalled.

*Charley Trippi signed a $100,000 contract with the Chicago Cardinals in 1947. In the next nine seasons, he served the Cardinals as a halfback, a quarterback and a defensive specialist.*

## RUSHING RECORD

| Year | Attempts | Yards | Average | TD |
|------|----------|-------|---------|-----|
| 1947 | 83 | 401 | 4.8 | 2 |
| 1948 | 128 | 690 | 5.4 | 6 |
| 1949 | 112 | 553 | 4.9 | 3 |
| 1950 | 99 | 426 | 4.3 | 3 |
| 1951 | 78 | 501 | 6.4 | 4 |
| 1952 | 72 | 350 | 4.9 | 4 |
| 1953 | 97 | 433 | 4.5 | 0 |
| 1954 | 18 | 152 | 8.4 | 1 |
| 1955 | 0 | 0 | 0.0 | 0 |
| TOTALS | 687 | 3506 | 5.1 | 23 |

## RECEIVING RECORD

| Year | Number | Yards | Average | TD |
|------|--------|-------|---------|-----|
| 1947 | 23 | 240 | 10.4 | 0 |
| 1948 | 22 | 228 | 10.4 | 2 |
| 1949 | 34 | 412 | 12.1 | 6 |
| 1950 | 32 | 270 | 8.4 | 1 |
| 1951 | 0 | 0 | 0.0 | 0 |
| 1952 | 5 | 66 | 13.2 | 0 |
| 1953 | 11 | 87 | 7.9 | 2 |
| 1954 | 3 | 18 | 6.0 | 0 |
| 1955 | 0 | 0 | 0.0 | 0 |
| TOTALS | 130 | 1321 | 10.2 | 11 |

## PASSING RECORD

| Year | Attempts | Completions | Percentage passes completed | Yards | TD | Interceptions |
|------|----------|-------------|------------------------------|-------|-----|---------------|
| 1947 | 2 | 1 | 50.0 | 49 | 0 | 1 |
| 1948 | 8 | 4 | 50.0 | 118 | 1 | 0 |
| 1949 | 2 | 0 | 0.0 | 0 | 0 | 0 |
| 1950 | 3 | 1 | 33.3 | 19 | 0 | 0 |
| 1951 | 191 | 88 | 46.1 | 1191 | 8 | 13 |
| 1952 | 181 | 84 | 46.4 | 890 | 5 | 13 |
| 1953 | 34 | 20 | 58.8 | 195 | 2 | 1 |
| 1954 | 13 | 7 | 53.8 | 85 | 0 | 3 |
| 1955 | 0 | 0 | 0.0 | 0 | 0 | 0 |
| TOTALS | 434 | 205 | 47.2 | 2547 | 16 | 31 |

Punt returns: 63 returns, 864 yards, 13.7-yard average, 2 touchdowns

Kickoff returns: 66 returns, 1457 yards, 22.1-yard average, 0 touchdowns

Punting: 196 punts, 40.4-yard average

Interceptions: 4 interceptions, 93 yards, 23.3-yard average, 1 touchdown

Scoring: 37 touchdowns, 222 points

# ALEX WOJCIECHOWICZ

*Center, linebacker*
*6 ft 0 in, 235 lb*
*Born in South River, N. J.,*
*August 12, 1915*
*Fordham University*
*1938–46 Detroit Lions; 1946–50*
*Philadelphia Eagles*

He was an expert with the knitting needles and fun to be around, the comic relief of the team. But that was off the field. On the gridiron, he was all business, one of the last of pro football's authentic iron men. His name was Alexander Francis Wojciechowicz, whose play for 13 seasons in the NFL was every bit as tough for opponents to endure as his name itself was difficult to spell and pronounce.

A three-sport star and all-state gridder at his hometown South River high school in New Jersey, "Wojie" gained national prominence for the first time as the pivotman of the famous "Seven Blocks of Granite" Fordham lines of the late 1930s. Flanking Wojie at the guards were Vince Lombardi and another all-America of the day, Mike Franco. Wojie himself was a virtually unanimous all-America choice in both 1936 and 1937. He was Detroit's number 1 draft choice in 1938. In his very first week as a pro, he earned his iron-man tag by playing in four games in seven days—the College All-Star game, the New York All-Star game, a Lions intra-squad scrimmage and a Detroit–Pittsburgh pre-season opener. By the time the regular season began, Wojie was firmly entrenched as a regular.

On offense, he was a play-every-down center. When the other team had the ball, Alex backed up the line. He was a sure tackler with good range in the secondary. In 1944, he intercepted seven passes, a Lions record for several years.

After eight-and-one-half seasons in Detroit, Wojciechowicz was suddenly waived midway through the 1946 campaign. The Philadelphia Eagles immediately claimed him. Coach Greasy Neale, convinced that Wojie should play only one way, installed him as the key man in the defense that would bring the Eagles three divisional and two NFL championships in the next three-and-one-half years. Thus Wojie's burning desire to play on a championship team, never realized in Detroit, was at last satisfied.

By the time Wojie had joined the Eagles, Neale had devised the "chug," a strategy to neutralize the effectiveness of the T-formation by delaying the progress of the offensive ends downfield by whatever means necessary. Wojciechowicz became a master at chugging. As one opponent described, "Wojie's

chugging technique involves hands and feet and arms and maybe even fingernails, plus some conversation."

The Eagles coach also cited an example of just how tough Wojciechowicz really was on pass defense. "The Redskins had Bones Taylor in 1948 and, in our opener, he caught five touchdown passes," Neale recounted. "So the next time we played Washington, I put Wojie on Bones. He never caught a pass that day and he never caught a pass against us the next three years. Wojie made sure of that!"

In spite of his all-around excellence over a long period of time—when he retired, only Sammy Baugh surpassed Wojie in years of service in pro football—Wojciechowicz never made an all-NFL team. Two other Hall of Famers, Clyde "Bulldog" Turner and Mel Hein, always seemed to grab these honors. But as a pivotman, Wojie had one particular distinction no one could match. His stance when he lined up to center the football was an amazing 5 ft 4 in, the widest of any center ever in the NFL.

*Famed for his unusually wide center stance, Alex Wojciechowicz excelled for the Detroit Lions and Philadelphia Eagles for 13 seasons. He enjoyed his finest years when he saw duty exclusively as a linebacker for the Eagles' championship teams of the late 1940s.*

### INTERCEPTION RECORD

| Year | Number | Yards | Average | TD |
|---|---|---|---|---|
| 1938–40° | No records available | | | |
| 1941° | 0 | 0 | 0.0 | 0 |
| 1942° | 2 | 5 | 2.5 | 0 |
| 1943° | 2 | 14 | 7.0 | 0 |
| 1944° | 7 | 88 | 12.6 | 0 |
| 1945° | 0 | 0 | 0.0 | 0 |
| 1946°† | 0 | 0 | 0.0 | 0 |
| 1947† | 1 | 3 | 3.0 | 0 |
| 1948† | 1 | 2 | 2.0 | 0 |
| 1949† | 2 | 26 | 13.0 | 0 |
| 1950† | 1 | 4 | 4.0 | 0 |
| TOTALS | 16 | 142 | 8.9 | 0 |

° With Detroit Lions

† With Philadelphia Eagles

Note: Interception statistics were not kept in the NFL until the 1941 season

# ALBERT GLEN (TURK) EDWARDS

*Tackle*
*6 ft 2 in, 260 lb*
*Born in Mold, Wash.,*
*September 28, 1907; died January*
*12, 1973, at age of 65*
*Washington State University*
*1932 Boston Braves; 1933–6*
*Boston Redskins; 1937–40*
*Washington Redskins*

A 6 ft 2 in, 260 lb professional tackle today attracts no more than passing attention but in the 1930s when Albert Glen "Turk" Edwards was anchoring the offensive and defensive lines of the Boston and Washington Redskins, a player of his dimension stood out like the Rock of Gibraltar.

Edwards typified overwhelming strength and power, rather than speed, yet he was agile enough to get the job done as well as or better than all but a mere handful of stars who have played his position. Like so many of his era, Turk was an iron man—in one 15-game season in Boston, he played all but 10 minutes of the entire campaign.

Edwards was an all-America tackle at Washington State as a junior and his block of a punt and subsequent return for a touchdown against Oregon State enabled the Cougars to preserve an unbeaten season and earn a trip to the 1931 Rose Bowl. Upon graduation a year later, Edwards received offers from three NFL teams—the Boston Braves, the New York Giants and the Portsmouth Spartans. It was before the days of the draft so Turk

chose the highest offer—$1500 for 10 games from the Braves, a new club just getting started under owner-president George Preston Marshall. In 1933 they became the Boston Redskins and in 1937 the team moved to Washington.

The big tackle responded with eight superior campaigns. He won official all-NFL honors his first two seasons in 1932 and 1933 and then again in 1936 and 1937. The Redskins prospered, too, with divisional championships in 1936, 1937, and 1940 and the overall NFL crown in 1937.

An injury forced Edwards' retirement in 1940, but Turk stayed on with the Redskins as an assistant coach for five seasons and three more years as head coach. Altogether, as a player and coach, Edwards was employed by Marshall and the Redskins for 17 years.

Almost unbelievably, the seemingly indestructible Edwards was felled for keeps at a coin-tossing ceremony! It was early in the 1940 season when the Redskins met their closest rival, the New York Giants. Mel Hein, the Giants' captain, was Turk's best friend. Both had been all-Americans at Washington State and each was the best man at the other's wedding. The two exchanged pleasantries, called the flip of the coin, shook hands, wished each other "good luck" and pivoted toward their respective benches.

Edwards never made it. When Turk caught his spikes in the turf, his often-injured knee simply gave way. One of pro football's greatest playing careers thus ended on a bizarre, never-to-be-repeated note.

*"Turk" Edwards was a fixture on the lines of the excellent Redskins teams of the 1930s. Incredibly, his career ended in 1940 when he was injured at a pre-game coin-toss ceremony.*

# EARLE (GREASY) NEALE

*Coach*
*Born in Parkersburg, W. Va.,*
*November 5, 1891; died*
*November 2, 1973 at age of 81*
*West Virginia Wesleyan College*
*1941–50 Philadelphia Eagles*

Pro football enshrinement was accorded Earle "Greasy" Neale because, as head coach of the Philadelphia Eagles for a decade, he led that team to its greatest successes. Once a perennial NFL doormat, the Eagles under Neale finished second three times and won three divisional and two NFL championships. His 10-year won–lost total was an excellent 63–43–5. In his six best seasons, Greasy's mark was a sensational 48–16–3.

Yet the Greasy Neale story actually is a maze of sub-careers, all worthy of attention. In capsulized form, Neale at one time or another captained and coached his Parkersburg, W. Va., high-school team; starred for the West Virginia Wesleyan eleven; played pro football in Canton under an assumed name; batted .357 as a Cincinnati Reds outfielder in the infamous "Black Sox" World Series; had a varied coaching career at six different colleges; and coached the semi-pro Ironton, Ohio, Tanks to four wins in five games with NFL teams in 1930. On a dare, Neale, at 39, played a full 60 minutes at end in the Tanks' 16–15 upset of their nearby NFL rivals, the Portsmouth Spartans.

In 1941, Alexis Thompson, the new Eagles owner, lured Neale back into the pro ranks. The new mentor, always one to keep up with the football times, recognized the power of the T-formation. One of his first acts was to obtain films of the Chicago Bears' 73–0 slaughter of Washington in the 1940 title game. Greasy spent long hours learning the finer points of the T so that, when the Philadelphia building program was ready, so too would the Eagles be ready on the field.

By 1944, Neale had the Eagles in second place, their highest finish ever up to that time. Three years later, they won their first divisional title via a 21–0 playoff victory over Pittsburgh but then lost to the Chicago Cardinals, 28–21, in the NFL title game.

But the Eagles bounced back with championship shutout triumphs, 7–0 over the Cardinals in the snow in 1948 and 14–0 over the Los Angeles Rams in the rain in 1949. No other club has ever won two straight NFL titles by shutouts. Thus Neale, considered to be one of pro football's leading offensive coaches, also put together one of the NFL's best-ever defensive units.

A year later, the Eagles, growing older and beset with injuries, slipped to a 6–6 mark, their lowest in seven years. As proof that sports memories can be short, Greasy was fired. What could not be forgotten, however, was that Neale, in his 10 seasons at the helm, made the Eagles for the only extended period in their history the premier eleven of the NFL.

## COACHING RECORD

| Year | Won | Lost | Tied | Division finish |
|------|-----|------|------|-----------------|
| 1941 | 2 | 8 | 1 | 4th |
| 1942 | 2 | 9 | 0 | 5th |
| 1943* | 5 | 4 | 1 | 3rd |
| 1944 | 7 | 1 | 2 | 2nd |
| 1945 | 7 | 3 | 0 | 2nd |
| 1946 | 6 | 5 | 0 | 2nd |
| 1947 | 8 | 4 | 0 | Tie 1st |
| 1948 | 9 | 2 | 1 | 1st |
| 1949 | 11 | 1 | 0 | 1st |
| 1950 | 6 | 6 | 0 | Tie 3rd |
| TOTALS† | 66 | 44 | 5 | |

## POST-SEASON RECORD

1947 NFL Divisional Playoff: Philadelphia 21, Pittsburgh 0
1947 NFL Championship: Chicago Cardinals 28, Philadelphia 21
1948 NFL Championship: Philadelphia 7, Chicago Cardinals 0
1949 NFL Championship: Philadelphia 14, Los Angeles 0

*Co-coach of combined Phil-Pitt (Eagles-Steelers) team

†Career totals include post-season games, but does not include 1943 merged-team record

*Earle "Greasy" Neale became the Philadelphia Eagles coach in 1941. In the next 10 years, the Eagles finished second three times and first three times in the NFL East. They were NFL champions by shutout scores in 1948 and 1949.*

# LEO NOMELLINI

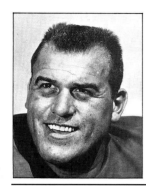

*Offensive–defensive tackle
6 ft 3 in, 284 lb
Born in Lucca, Italy, June 19,
1924
University of Minnesota
1950–63 San Francisco 49ers*

To many a chagrined opponent, it must have seemed that Leo Nomellini was around the NFL for an awfully long time. He was, too, for he didn't miss a game for the San Francisco 49ers for 14 years from 1950 to 1963. Altogether, Leo played in 174 consecutive regular-season games and, counting 10 Pro Bowl appearances, 266 pro contests overall.

The 49ers joined the NFL in 1950 when the All-America Football Conference merged with the older league. One of their first items of business was to select Nomellini as their first-ever NFL draft choice. It proved to be a master selection. ''The Lion'' became one of the few ever to be named to an all-NFL team both on offense and defense. He was all-league on the offensive unit twice and on the defensive platoon four times.

Nomellini had everything needed to be an all-time great—size, speed, agility, aggressiveness and dedication to the game. He was one of the best pass rushers the NFL has seen and it wasn't often the foe probed his area on the ground. On offense, he was a fine pass blocker and adept at opening holes in enemy lines. He was willing to play either way or both ways and, in 1955, went virtually 60 minutes every game when injuries created a severe personnel problem for the 49ers.

The achievement of all-time gridiron greatness is a far cry from the impoverished days Leo knew as a youth. Born in Italy, Nomellini came to Chicago's tough West Side as an infant. He had to pass up high-school sports so that he could work a full shift in a foundry to help support his family.

Shortly after Pearl Harbor, Leo joined the Marines and it was as a member of the Cherry Point, North Carolina, Leatherneck team in 1942 that Nomellini got his first taste of football. Later, he saw combat service in the South Pacific and at Okinawa.

With or without high-school experience, football players of Nomellini's potential are hard to hide. On his return from service, the University of Minnesota offered him a football scholarship. Freshmen were eligible to play on the varsity in 1946 so, in the first college game Leo ever saw, he was a starting guard for the Gophers. Later, he was a two-time all-America tackle.

Then came Leo's exceptional tenure in the pros. Like a fine wine, The Lion seemingly improved with age until finally retiring at the age of 39. After 14 years of battering the opposition in every way a tackle can, Nomellini had proven that he was, as his foes often contended, both indestructible and incomparable.

*Leo Nomellini was the first draft pick the San Francisco 49ers in 1950. He did not miss even one game throughout his 14-year career.*

# JOE PERRY

*Fullback*
*6 ft 0 in, 200 lb*
*Born in Stevens, Ark., January 27, 1927*
*Compton, Calif., Junior College*
*1948–60, 1963 San Francisco 49ers; 1961–2 Baltimore Colts*

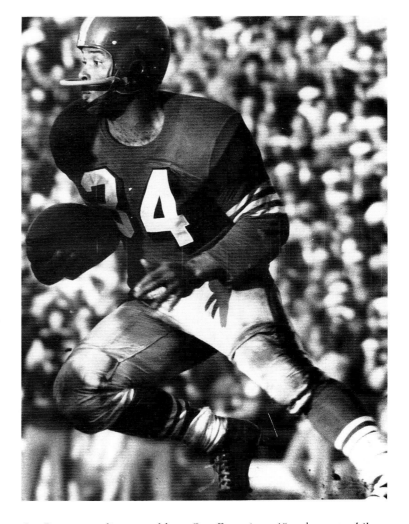

*Joe Perry was discovered by a San Francisco 49ers' scout while he was playing service football in the Navy. Although he had played no college football, he became an instant hit in the pros.*

Like many who become great at a certain endeavor, Joe Perry might well have been outstanding in a completely unrelated field had not fate carved out the circumstances that were to lead him to pro football immortality.

Joe's first love was music and his chosen profession was engineering. His first athletic triumphs came in track and field in high school. He also played basketball and baseball and embraced football on the sly because his mother, fearing injury, strongly opposed his gridiron participation. As it was, in Perry's first high-school scrimmage, he suffered a broken ankle. Eventually, his mother accepted his interest in football and became his staunchest fan.

Perry put Compton, Calif., Junior College on the map with 22 touchdowns one autumn but before he could play another year, military service intervened and, indirectly, paved Joe's way into the pro football world. John Woudenberg, a San Francisco 49ers tackle, first spotted Perry playing for the Alameda Naval Station team. "Just point him in the right direction and watch him go," Woudenberg told an interested but skeptical 49ers owner, Tony Morabito. But Morabito did make Perry an offer.

"It wasn't as good as some of the offers I had received from the 14 or so colleges that had contacted me," Joe recalls, but for a variety of financial and personal reasons, he decided to turn pro.

Joe got his famous nickname, "The Jet," in his second season when 49ers quarterback Frankie Albert marveled at his quick starts. "I'm telling you, when that guy gets a handoff," Albert insisted, "his slip-stream darn near knocks you over. He's strictly jet-propelled."

In his rookie season, Perry's unusual speed caused some problems. For some reason, his junior college coach had tutored him against cutting and twisting so Joe came to the pros as an extremely fast, but straight-ahead running back. Perry adjusted quickly, however, and, for almost a decade, teamed with Hugh McElhenny to give the 49ers a knockout punch on the ground. His

9723 rushing yards in combined AAFC–NFL play placed him second behind only Jim Brown at the time he retired.

After two seasons with the Baltimore Colts in 1961 and 1962, the 49ers brought Perry back for one final season in 1963, in the hope that he could see action in at least three games to qualify for an NFL pension. Joe played in nine, as it turned out. As 49ers president Victor Morabito explained, "Perry deserves the best. He never gave us anything less than all of himself all the years he was with us!"

## RUSHING RECORD

| Year | Attempts | Yards | Average | TD |
|------|----------|-------|---------|-----|
| 1948° | 77 | 562 | 7.3 | 10§ |
| 1949° | 115 | 783§ | 6.8 | 8§ |
| 1950° | 124 | 647 | 5.2 | 5 |
| 1951° | 136 | 677 | 5.0 | 3 |
| 1952° | 158 | 725 | 4.6 | 8 |
| 1953° | 192‡ | 1018‡ | 5.3 | 10‡ |
| 1954° | 173‡ | 1049‡ | 6.1 | 8 |
| 1955° | 156 | 701 | 4.5 | 2 |
| 1956° | 115 | 520 | 4.5 | 3 |
| 1957° | 97 | 454 | 4.7 | 3 |
| 1958° | 125 | 758 | 6.1 | 4 |
| 1959° | 139 | 602 | 4.4 | 3 |
| 1960° | 36 | 95 | 2.6 | 1 |
| 1961† | 168 | 675 | 4.0 | 3 |
| 1962† | 94 | 359 | 3.8 | 0 |
| 1963° | 24 | 98 | 4.1 | 0 |
| TOTALS | 1929 | 9723 | 5.0 | 71 |

## RECEIVING RECORD

| Year | Number | Yards | Average | TD |
|------|--------|-------|---------|-----|
| 1948° | 8 | 79 | 9.9 | 1 |
| 1949° | 11 | 146 | 13.3 | 3 |
| 1950° | 13 | 69 | 5.3 | 1 |
| 1951° | 18 | 167 | 9.3 | 1 |
| 1952° | 15 | 81 | 5.4 | 0 |
| 1953° | 19 | 191 | 10.1 | 3 |
| 1954° | 26 | 203 | 7.8 | 0 |
| 1955° | 19 | 55 | 2.9 | 1 |
| 1956° | 18 | 104 | 5.8 | 0 |
| 1957° | 15 | 130 | 8.7 | 0 |
| 1958° | 23 | 218 | 9.5 | 1 |
| 1959° | 12 | 53 | 4.4 | 0 |
| 1960° | 3 | −3 | −1.0 | 0 |
| 1961† | 34 | 322 | 9.5 | 1 |
| 1962† | 22 | 194 | 8.8 | 0 |
| 1963° | 4 | 12 | 3.0 | 0 |
| TOTALS | 260 | 2021 | 7.8 | 12 |

° With San Francisco 49ers

† With Baltimore Colts

‡ Led NFL

§ Led AAFC

Kickoff returns: 31 returns, 737 yards, 23.8-yard average, 1 touchdown

Scoring: 84 touchdowns, 6 extra points, 1 field goal, 513 points

# ERNIE STAUTNER

*Defensive tackle*
*6 ft 2 in, 235 lb*
*Born in Prinzing-bei-Cham,*
*Bavaria, April 20, 1925*
*Boston College*
*1950–63 Pittsburgh Steelers*

Bavarian-born Ernie Stautner migrated with his family to Albany, New York, when he was three. His introduction to football came on the grade school sandlots but when he came home one day with ankles so badly battered he had to see a doctor, his father's order was quick in coming: "No more football and no more complaining."

Ernie interpreted the order to mean "If I don't complain then he won't know I am playing football." A few years later, he convinced his parents of the value of a good Catholic education at Ascension Institute in Albany. The school just happened to have an outstanding football team. To account for his time in football practice, he got a job in a dime store. He explained his continual face cuts and bruises as "just another fight at school, Papa." But when he made the all-Albany team as a junior, his secret was out. Fortunately, family pride came to the rescue and saved Ernie's gridiron career.

After service in the US Marines, Stautner was turned down by Notre Dame and wound up as a four-year regular at Boston College. Now Stautner had another goal—to play pro football—but New York Giants coach Steve Owen explained: "You are too small for the pros, son. Our smallest tackle is 248 lb and you are not anywhere near that size."

The Pittsburgh Steelers decided to take a chance on the smaller-than-average lineman and picked him in the third round of the 1950 draft. For the next 14 years, Stautner was a fixture at defensive tackle, a folk hero with the long-suffering Steelers fans and a major factor in Pittsburgh's defense, one of the most punishing in the NFL. During that period, Ernie played in nine Pro Bowls.

No team ever had a more willing performer. Always ready to play anywhere just as long as he was playing, he often switched to defensive end or even on to the offensive line when the occasion demanded. By modern-day standards, he was too small to be a defensive lineman but he had, in overwhelming abundance, such invaluable assets as a competitive nature, grim determination and the will to win.

Honed to razor-sharp playing condition at all times, Stautner was extremely durable, missing only six games in 14 seasons—not that Ernie was never hurt, but he kept right on playing, even with such assorted injuries as broken ribs, shoulders, hands and noses too numerous to count. It was almost as though Ernie were still a kid who felt he had to hide his football injuries from Papa Stautner so that he could keep on playing!

*Ernie Stautner was a major fixture in Pittsburgh's strong defense, one of the NFL's best, for 14 seasons.*

# The SEVENTIES

Pro Football Hall of Fame visitors in the 1970s were greeted in the entrance lobby by the statue of Jim Thorpe, the first big-name American athlete to play pro football. During the decade, the Hall expanded twice, in 1971 and 1978, and its membership was expanded to 102 with 43 new enshrinees, most of them from the post-World War II era.

# JACK CHRISTIANSEN

*Defensive back*
*6 ft 1 in, 185 lb*
*Born in Sublette, Kan.,*
*December 20, 1928; died June 29,*
*1986, at age of 57*
*Colorado State University*
*1951–8 Detroit Lions*

*Jack Christiansen was dangerous both as a defensive backfield ace and a punt and kickoff return specialist that most NFL teams had a rule: "Don't pass in Chris's area and don't kick to him."*

The Jack Christiansen story is a perfect illustration of the adage that the path to greatness is not always a direct one. Raised in an Odd Fellows Orphanage in Canon City, Colo., Jack was the victim of a chance shooting accident as a high-school senior. His left arm was so severely injured he was sure he would never play football again, so during his freshman year at Colorado State, he contented himself with being a very good sprint man on the the college track team.

As a sophomore, Jack was coaxed out for football against the advice of his doctors. When the regular safety was injured in the season opener, Jack got into the lineup. From that time on, he was a regular and an all-conference standout. As he was destined to be in the pros, "Chris" was a defensive ace and a return specialist, and also outstanding on offense but his size—6 ft 1 in and 162 lb—seemed to preclude the possibility of a pro football career.

Despite these apparent drawbacks, Lions alumnus Dutch Clark and rookie Thurman McGraw, a one-time college teammate, both recommended Christiansen highly, so the Lions drafted him in the sixth round in 1951. From the start, Jack enjoyed spectacular success. In a crucial contest against Los Angeles as a rookie, he scored twice on punt returns of 69 and 47 yards. In the next six seasons, the Lions won four divisional and three NFL championships and Chris was an all-NFL pick six straight years. He also played in five Pro Bowls in that period.

Christiansen, who even today is still prominent in the punt return record book, was so effective at this specialty that he caused an entire pro league to change its defensive ways. "By the time I came into the league," Jim David, Jack's teammate both in college and the pros, relates, "the other teams had gone to the spread punt formation in order to contain Chris."

As effective as Christiansen was on the specialty units, his forte was defense, where he was the key man for the defensively powerful Lions of the 1950s. He was so much the boss that they called the Lions' deep four "Chris' Crew." It was a unit that continually thwarted the enemy's aerial thrusts and Jack contributed 46 interceptions to the cause.

Just as NFL teams had adjusted to protect against Chris on punting plays, so too did they alter their passing patterns whenever they played Detroit. Many clubs had a standard rule when meeting the Lions—don't throw in Christiansen's area and don't punt to him.

For a guy who thought his gridiron days were over even before he finished high school, Jack Christiansen did indeed go a long way in the football world.

| INTERCEPTION RECORD | | | | |
|---|---|---|---|---|
| Year | Number | Yards | Average | TD |
| 1951 | 2 | 53 | 26.5 | 0 |
| 1952 | 2 | 47 | 23.5 | 0 |
| 1953 | 12* | 238* | 19.8 | 1* |
| 1954 | 8 | 84 | 10.5 | 1 |
| 1955 | 3 | 49 | 16.3 | 0 |
| 1956 | 8 | 109 | 13.6 | 0 |
| 1957 | 10* | 137 | 13.7 | 1 |
| 1958 | 1 | 0 | 0.0 | 0 |
| TOTALS | 46 | 717 | 15.6 | 3 |

* Led NFL

| PUNT RETURN RECORD | | | | |
|---|---|---|---|---|
| Year | Number | Yards | Average | TD |
| 1951 | 18 | 343 | 19.1 | 4* |
| 1952 | 15 | 322 | 21.5* | 2* |
| 1953 | 8 | 22 | 2.8 | 0 |
| 1954 | 23 | 225 | 9.8 | 1* |
| 1955 | 12 | 87 | 7.3 | 0 |
| 1956 | 6 | 73 | 12.2 | 1* |
| 1957 | 3 | 12 | 4.0 | 0 |
| 1958 | 0 | 0 | 0.0 | 0 |
| TOTALS | 85 | 1084 | 12.8 | 8 |

| KICKOFF RETURN RECORD | | | | |
|---|---|---|---|---|
| Year | Number | Yards | Average | TD |
| 1951 | 11 | 270 | 24.5 | 0 |
| 1952 | 16 | 409 | 25.6 | 0 |
| 1953 | 10 | 183 | 18.3 | 0 |
| 1954 | 5 | 102 | 20.4 | 0 |
| 1955 | 7 | 169 | 24.1 | 0 |
| 1956 | 6 | 116 | 19.3 | 0 |
| 1957 | 4 | 80 | 20.0 | 0 |
| 1958 | 0 | 0 | 0.0 | 0 |
| TOTALS | 59 | 1329 | 22.5 | 0 |

Rushing: 20 attempts, 143 yards, 7.2-yard average, 2 touchdowns

Scoring: 13 touchdowns, 78 points

# TOM FEARS

*End*
*6 ft 2 in, 215 lb*
*Born in Los Angeles, Calif.,*
*December 3, 1923*
*University of Santa Clara,*
*University of California at Los*
*Angels (UCLA)*
*1948–56 Los Angeles Rams*

Tom Fears was the first pass receiver in pro football to catch an awesome number of forward passes. He led the NFL in receiving his first three seasons, during which he totalled 212 receptions, more than anyone except Don Hutson had caught in an entire career up to that time. Yet when Tom first reported to camp in 1948, he was ticketed to be a defensive specialist. In his first game, he intercepted two passes and returned one for a touchdown. Rams coach Clark Shaughnessy wisely and immediately decided Tom's running and catching talents could best be utilized on the attack unit.

Fears soon became an integral part of the revolutionary "three-end" formation which placed a speed-burning halfback 10 yards to the outside of the tight end and Fears 10 yards to the outside of the right tackle. With the defenses opened up for the pin-point passes of the Rams quarterbacks, the result was a prolific point outburst and Fears was one of the ringleaders of the assault.

In nine seasons, Tom caught 400 passes but his biggest day came in 1950 when he gathered in 18 passes in a 51–14 defeat of Green Bay. That still is an all-time single-game record. The fact

*Tom Fears was a pass-receiver who became an integral part of the Rams' "three-end" offense. Here he takes one of his 400 career receptions for big yards against the Chicago Bears.*

that this exceptional performance came against a downtrodden team was out of keeping with the Fears image because Tom, as a rule, saved his finest heroics for the biggest games.

In a 1950 playoff for the Western Division crown, Fears caught three touchdown passes in a 24–14 win over the Chicago Bears. A year later in the NFL title game against Cleveland, Tom's 74-yard touchdown reception proved to be the game-winner. The list of big-game accomplishments is long.

Fears was a matchless clutch performer but he must also be remembered as one of the most precise pattern-runners the pro game has seen. Tom could not depend on speed or shiftiness to fool the defense so he worked at outsmarting the opposition not only before and during the catch, but after he got the ball as well. Fiercely determined, he was always tough to bring down.

Fears was also a standout in his pre-NFL years. He was an all-Southern California end in high school, a two-year star at Santa Clara and captain of the famous Second Air Force Superbombers team in 1944 and 1945. He finished his college career with two all-America-type seasons at UCLA in 1946 and 1947.

The player selection system during the war years was a mixed-up affair. The Rams, then based in Cleveland and apparently not realizing that Tom had two more years of college football, drafted him in 1945, a full three years before he could join the team. As it turned out, the Rams agreed, Fears was worth waiting for.

| RECEIVING RECORD | | | | | * Led NFL |
|---|---|---|---|---|---|
| Year | Number | Yards | Average | TD | Interceptions: 2 |
| 1948 | 51* | 698 | 13.7 | 4 | interceptions, 37 yards, |
| 1949 | 77* | 1013 | 13.2 | 9* | 18.5-yard average, |
| 1950 | 84* | 1116* | 13.3 | 7 | 1 touchdown |
| 1951 | 32 | 528 | 16.5 | 3 | |
| 1952 | 48 | 600 | 12.5 | 6 | Scoring: 39 touchdowns, 12 |
| 1953 | 23 | 278 | 12.1 | 4 | extra points, 1 field goal, |
| 1954 | 36 | 546 | 15.2 | 3 | 249 points |
| 1955 | 44 | 569 | 12.9 | 2 | |
| 1956 | 5 | 49 | 9.8 | 0 | |
| TOTALS | 400 | 5397 | 13.5 | 38 | |

# HUGH MCELHENNY

*Halfback,*
*6 ft 1 in, 198 lb*
*Born in Los Angeles, Calif.,*
*December 31, 1928*
*University of Washington*
*1952–60 San Francisco 49ers;*
*1961–2 Minnesota Vikings; 1963*
*New York Giants; 1964 Detroit*
*Lions*

When Hugh McElhenny first decided to play pro football, he figured he would stay around "about three years, just long enough to get a down payment on a house, a car, an investment. . . ." He wound up playing 13 seasons and his career-long accomplishments were so outstanding he was widely known as "The King!"

In his prime, McElhenny was the scourge of the pro ranks, a master open-field runner, an artist on the draw play, a dangerous pass receiver, a workhorse on the return teams. He had the sudden bursts of blinding speed, the change of pace, the fake, the sidestep . . . you name it, The King had it!

When he retired after the 1964 season, he was one of only three players to have gained more than 11,000 yards carrying the football. Of Hugh's 60 career touchdowns, only 38 came on rushing plays, strong evidence of his versatility.

After three touchdown-filled years at the University of Washington, McElhenny was the 49ers' number 1 draft choice in 1952. It quickly proved to be a happy selection for all concerned. Hugh ran 42 yards for a touchdown on his first play in pre-season. He had the longest punt return of 1952—94 yards—and the longest scrimmage play—89 yards. To cap his brilliant first season, he scored two touchdowns in the Pro Bowl. Hugh was a widespread

choice for Rookie of the Year honors and one selection tabbed him Player of the Year.

From the 49ers' standpoint, he helped in an even more significant way. "When Hugh joined the 49ers in 1952," then-general manager Lou Spadia recalled, "it was questionable whether our franchise could survive. McElhenny removed all doubts. That's why we call him our franchise-saver!"

In 1961, Hugh moved to the new Minnesota Vikings team where he enjoyed what he felt was his finest season, "taking everything into account." He totalled 1067 combined yards and earned a sixth trip to the Pro Bowl.

Two years later, McElhenny realized one of his biggest ambitions—that of playing on a championship team—with the New York Giants. "Hugh's knees were shot and I could use him only sparingly," Giants coach Allie Sherman reported. "Still he made valuable contributions. We knew he would always give us his very best."

For the major part of Hugh's career, his best was just that—the best! There were many excellent backs in the NFL during McElhenny's time but to a host of the game's keenest observers, Hugh McElhenny was truly The King—the greatest of them all!

*Hugh McElhenny flashes his peerless running form in a San Francisco 49ers clash with the Chicago Bears.*

## RUSHING RECORD

| Year | Attempts | Yards | Average | TD |
|---|---|---|---|---|
| 1952° | 98 | 684 | 7.0¶ | 6 |
| 1953° | 112 | 503 | 4.5 | 3 |
| 1954° | 64 | 515 | 8.0¶ | 6 |
| 1955° | 90 | 327 | 3.6 | 4 |
| 1956° | 185 | 916 | 5.0 | 8 |
| 1957° | 102 | 478 | 4.7 | 1 |
| 1958° | 113 | 451 | 4.0 | 6 |
| 1959° | 18 | 67 | 3.7 | 1 |
| 1960° | 95 | 347 | 3.7 | 0 |
| 1961† | 120 | 570 | 4.8 | 3 |
| 1962† | 50 | 200 | 4.0 | 0 |
| 1963‡ | 55 | 175 | 3.2 | 0 |
| 1964§ | 22 | 48 | 2.2 | 0 |
| TOTALS | 1124 | 5281 | 4.7 | 38 |

° With San Francisco 49ers

† With Minnesota Vikings

‡ With New York Giants

§ With Detroit Lions

¶ Led NFL

## RECEIVING RECORD

| Year | Number | Yards | Average | TD |
|---|---|---|---|---|
| 1952° | 26 | 367 | 14.1 | 3 |
| 1953° | 30 | 474 | 15.8 | 2 |
| 1954° | 8 | 162 | 20.3 | 0 |
| 1955° | 11 | 203 | 18.5 | 2 |
| 1956° | 16 | 193 | 12.1 | 0 |
| 1957° | 37 | 458 | 12.4 | 2 |
| 1958° | 31 | 366 | 11.8 | 2 |
| 1959° | 22 | 329 | 15.0 | 3 |
| 1960° | 14 | 114 | 8.1 | 1 |
| 1961† | 37 | 283 | 7.6 | 3 |
| 1962† | 16 | 191 | 11.9 | 0 |
| 1963‡ | 11 | 91 | 8.3 | 2 |
| 1964§ | 5 | 16 | 3.2 | 0 |
| TOTALS | 264 | 3247 | 12.3 | 20 |

## PUNT RETURN RECORD

| Year | Number | Yards | Average | TD |
|---|---|---|---|---|
| 1952° | 20 | 284 | 14.2 | 1 |
| 1953° | 15 | 104 | 6.9 | 0 |
| 1954° | 8 | 78 | 9.8 | 0 |
| 1955° | 7 | 10 | 1.4 | 0 |
| 1956° | 15 | 38 | 2.5 | 0 |
| 1957° | 10 | 41 | 4.1 | 0 |
| 1958° | 24 | 93 | 3.9 | 0 |
| 1959° | 0 | 0 | 0.0 | 0 |
| 1960° | 0 | 0 | 0.0 | 0 |
| 1961† | 8 | 155 | 19.4 | 1 |
| 1962† | 5 | 43 | 8.6 | 0 |
| 1963‡ | 13 | 74 | 5.7 | 0 |
| 1964§ | 1 | 0 | 0.0 | 0 |
| TOTALS | 126 | 920 | 7.3 | 2 |

## KICKOFF RETURN RECORD

| Year | Number | Yards | Average | TD |
|---|---|---|---|---|
| 1952° | 18 | 396 | 22.0 | 0 |
| 1953° | 15 | 368 | 24.5 | 0 |
| 1954° | 8 | 210 | 26.3 | 0 |
| 1955° | 9 | 189 | 21.0 | 0 |
| 1956° | 13 | 300 | 23.1 | 0 |
| 1957° | 0 | 0 | 0.0 | 0 |
| 1958° | 2 | 31 | 15.5 | 0 |
| 1959° | 0 | 0 | 0.0 | 0 |
| 1960° | 0 | 0 | 0.0 | 0 |
| 1961† | 2 | 59 | 29.5 | 0 |
| 1962† | 7 | 160 | 22.9 | 0 |
| 1963‡ | 6 | 136 | 22.7 | 0 |
| 1964§ | 3 | 72 | 24.0 | 0 |
| TOTALS | 83 | 1921 | 23.1 | 0 |

# PETE PIHOS

*End*
*6 ft 1 in., 210 lb*
*Born in Orlando, Fla., October 22, 1923*
*University of Indiana*
*1947–55 Philadelphia Eagles*

Pete Pihos was one of the last of the truly great iron men of pro football. In nine seasons with the Philadelphia Eagles, Pete missed just one game. Yet for a great percentage of his career, he was a two-way performer. He was the only player to be named to the all-NFL team before the days of the two-platoon selections and then to be named to both the offensive and defensive units after all-league selections became two-way affairs.

Pihos did not have great speed yet he was a consistently outstanding pass receiver. What he lacked in pace, he made up for with extreme desire. Any defender who battled "The Golden Greek" for a pass was bound to get the worst of it physically. Pete played it clean but very hard and, after he caught a pass, he ran like a bulldozing fullback.

This is understandable because at the University of Indiana, Pihos was an all-America choice as both an end and a fullback. He was drafted by the Eagles in 1945 even though they knew that he would have to spend the next two years in the service.

Unlike many stars of the past, Pihos did "cash in" on his gridiron prowess, at least by 1947 standards, even in his rookie season. "I signed, with bonus, for $17,000," Pihos revealed. "Charley Trippi was the high man at the time with $25,000. The All-America Football Conference was after both of us."

For the Eagles, the $17,000 proved to be money well spent. After Pete joined the team in 1947, the Philadelphia club went on the greatest rampage in its history. The Eagles won three straight divisional championships and NFL titles by shutout scores in both 1948 and 1949. For all three powerhouses, Pihos was a near 60-minute player.

The greatest demonstration of Pete's versatility came later in his career. In 1952, injuries to the Eagles forced Pihos to move to defensive end on a full-time basis. He was named all-NFL. A year later, he was back on the offensive platoon as captain and a full-time offensive specialist for the first time. He responded by winning three straight NFL pass receiving titles with records of 63, 60, and 62 catches. He was named to the all-NFL offensive team each year, making a total of six honors in his nine pro seasons.

Pete retired after the 1955 season while definitely still in top form. This is appropriate because that was the status Pihos enjoyed throughout his career—a top player at the top of the pro football galaxy.

| RECEIVING RECORD | | | | |
|---|---|---|---|---|
| Year | Number | Yards | Average | TD |
| 1947 | 23 | 382 | 16.6 | 7 |
| 1948 | 46 | 766 | 16.7 | 11 |
| 1949 | 34 | 484 | 14.2 | 4 |
| 1950 | 38 | 447 | 11.8 | 6 |
| 1951 | 35 | 536 | 15.3 | 5 |
| 1952 | 12 | 219 | 18.3 | 1 |
| 1953 | 63° | 1049° | 16.7 | 10° |
| 1954 | 60° | 872 | 14.5 | 10 |
| 1955 | 62° | 864° | 13.9 | 7 |
| TOTALS | 373 | 5619 | 15.1 | 61 |

° Led NFL

Scoring: 63 touchdowns, 378 points

*Pete Pihos catches a pass for a long-gainer against the Los Angeles Rams. He began his NFL career as a 60-minute player, then became a defensive specialist before winding up on the offensive unit.*

# JIM BROWN

*Fullback*
*6 ft 2 in, 228 lb*
*Born in St Simons, Ga.,*
*February 17, 1936*
*Syracuse University*
*1957–65 Cleveland Browns*

Jim Brown was a superb craftsman whose primary job was to run with the football for the Cleveland Browns. For nine seasons, this powerful ball-carrier with surprising speed and subtle elusiveness did this better than any player ever, past or present. Not only did he retire at the age of 30 at the peak of his career, but he also left behind a record book clogged with Jim Brown notations.

The Georgia native was more than just a one-of-a-kind running back. He caught passes, returned kickoffs, and even threw three touchdown passes. His 12,312 rushing yards and 15,459 combined net yards put him in a class by himself in the years he played.

Jim was a unanimous all-NFL pick eight times, missing only the 1962 season. He played in nine Pro Bowls in nine years. He was the Pro Bowl's Most Valuable Player twice and closed out his career with a three-touchdown outburst in the 1966 Pro Bowl. The *Sporting News* named him both Rookie of the Year and Player of the Year in 1957. In both 1958 and his final 1965 campaign, he was the Jim Thorpe trophy winner as the NFL's Most Valuable Player.

It is fitting that Brown finished his gridiron career winning an award-named after an all-around athlete like Thorpe, who had been nominated the best American athlete of the first half of the twentieth century. Like Thorpe, Brown was good at everything he tried and some even debate whether football was really his best sport. Jim once scored 55 points in a high-school basketball game. At Syracuse University, he was all-America in both football and lacrosse and a letterman in basketball.

Brown was also outstanding in track events. As a college sophomore, he finished fifth in the national decathlon championships and his marks actually surpassed those of Thorpe in six of the 10 events.

Jim selected football as his career sport, however, and thus became the Cleveland Browns' number 1 draft pick in 1957. Even though coach Paul Brown was traditionally reluctant to use rookies as regulars, Jim Brown was a regular and a star from day one.

In the summer of 1966, while working on a movie set in England, Jim stunned the sports world with his announcement

*Jim Brown, in nine years, rushed for 12,312 yards, led the NFL in rushing eight times, played in nine straight Pro Bowls, was Rookie of the Year in 1957 and Player of the Year three times.*

that he was retiring. Fans still ponder what heights he might have reached had he stayed on the firing line a few more seasons.

As exceptional as Brown's statistics were, his durability may have been even more amazing. Despite a constant pounding from defenses always stacked against him personally, he never missed a game in nine years. As one admiring opponent once said, "That Brown. He says he isn't Superman. What he really means is that Superman isn't Jimmy Brown!"

---

**RUSHING RECORD**

| Year | Attempts | Yards | Average | TD |
|---|---|---|---|---|
| 1957 | 202 | 942° | 4.7 | 9° |
| 1958 | 257° | 1527° | 5.9 | 17° |
| 1959 | 290° | 1329° | 4.6 | 14° |
| 1960 | 215 | 1257° | 5.8 | 9 |
| 1961 | 305° | 1408° | 4.6 | 8 |
| 1962 | 230 | 996 | 4.3 | 13 |
| 1963 | 291° | 1863° | 6.4° | 12° |
| 1964 | 280° | 1446° | 5.2° | 7 |
| 1965 | 289° | 1544° | 5.3 | 17° |
| TOTALS | 2359 | 12,312 | 5.2 | 106 |

**RECEIVING RECORD**

| Year | Number | Yards | Average | TD |
|---|---|---|---|---|
| 1957 | 16 | 55 | 3.4 | 1 |
| 1958 | 16 | 138 | 8.6 | 1 |
| 1959 | 24 | 190 | 7.9 | 0 |
| 1960 | 19 | 204 | 10.7 | 2 |
| 1961 | 46 | 459 | 10.0 | 2 |
| 1962 | 47 | 517 | 11.0 | 5 |
| 1963 | 24 | 268 | 11.2 | 3 |
| 1964 | 36 | 340 | 9.4 | 2 |
| 1965 | 34 | 328 | 9.6 | 4 |
| TOTALS | 262 | 2499 | 9.5 | 20 |

° Led NFL

Passing: 12 attempts, 4 completions, 117 yards, 3 touchdowns, 0 interceptions

Kickoff returns: 29 returns, 648 yards, 22.3-yard average, 0 touchdowns

Scoring: 126 touchdowns, 756 points

# BILL HEWITT

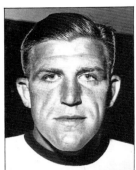

*End*
*5 ft 11 in, 191 lb*
*Born in Bay City, Mich.,*
*October 8, 1909; died January 14,*
*1947, at age of 37*
*University of Michigan*
*1932–6 Chicago Bears; 1937–9*
*Philadelphia Eagles; 1943 Phil–Pitt*

Bill Hewitt is most often remembered for his stubborn refusal to wear a helmet. He finally donned headgear in his eighth pro season in 1939 but only because new NFL rules left him no choice. While an interesting sidelight, this should not overshadow the fact that Hewitt was one of the finest two-way ends ever to play football at any level.

Bill was a terror on offense but absolutely peerless on defense. An "iron-man" performer who averaged more than 50 minutes playing time each game, Hewitt had a zest for competition and a record for making the biggest plays in the toughest situations that set him apart from most other pros of his time.

Bristle-thatched, granite-chinned and happy-go-lucky, Bill was affectionately known by his teammates as "Stinky." He was always conjuring up new gimmicks to foil the opposition. One of his special plays called for a jump pass from fullback Bronko Nagurski to Hewitt who in turn would lateral to another end, Bill Karr, racing toward the goal line. It was this play, the "Stinky Special," that gave the Bears a victory in the NFL's first championship game in 1933.

On defense, Hewitt became the first player to make the masses take their eyes off the football just to watch him stymie the opponent. Because he had a jet-propulsion start at the snap of the ball, the fans tabbed him "The Offside Kid," because they couldn't fathom anyone reacting so quickly without being offside. They were also fascinated by the finality of his tackling and his uncanny knack of diagnosing enemy plays.

Hewitt, who died in an automobile accident in 1947, was the first to admit he wasn't much of a player either in high school or at the University of Michigan. Once he reached the NFL, it was a different story. In just his second season, 1933, Bill was named to the NFL's official all-league team. He repeated the honor in 1934 and 1936 and, in 1937, when he was with the Philadelphia Eagles, he became all-NFL a fourth time. It marked the first time a player had been all-NFL on two different teams.

With the Bears, Bill was showcased on one of the most powerful teams in pro football. He no doubt would have attracted attention, no matter where he played. He wasn't overly large, but he was made of granite, with a thick neck, a barrel chest, and

tremendous arms. "Bill Hewitt is three parts gorilla and one part Englishman," someone once wrote. He might well have added, "And he was one whale of a football player."

*Bill Hewitt excited Chicago Bears' fans with dynamic performances both on offense and defense. After moving to Philadelphia in 1937, he became the first player to be named all-NFL on two different teams.*

RECEIVING RECORD

| Year | Number | Yards | Average | TD |
|---|---|---|---|---|
| 1932° | 4 | 44 | 11.0 | 1 |
| 1933° | 16 | 274 | 17.1 | 2 |
| 1934° | 10 | 151 | 15.1 | 5 |
| 1935° | 5 | 80 | 16.0 | 0 |
| 1936° | 15 | 358 | 23.9 | 6 |
| 1937† | 16 | 197 | 12.3 | 5 |
| 1938† | 18 | 237 | 13.2 | 4 |
| 1939† | 15 | 243 | 16.2 | 1 |
| 1940–2 | Did not play | | | |
| 1943‡ | 2 | 22 | 11.0 | 0 |
| TOTALS | 101 | 1606 | 15.9 | 24 |

° With Chicago Bears

† With Philadelphia Eagles

‡ With Phil-Pitt

Scoring: 25 touchdowns, 150 points

# FRANK (BRUISER) KINARD

*Tackle*
*6 ft 1 in, 218 lb*
*Born in Pelahatchie, Miss.,*
*October 23, 1914; died*
*September 7, 1985, at age of 70*
*University of Mississippi*
*1938–44 Brooklyn Dodgers;*
*1946–7 New York Yankees (AAFC)*

Any modern-day NFL player most likely would have to be strong, tall, and weigh at least 275 lb to qualify for the nickname "Bruiser." But five decades ago, a pro football luminary called Bruiser Kinard heaped misery on the opposition for nine seasons and yet, at the start of his NFL career, weighed only 195 lb. Even in his last pro season, Kinard checked in at only 218 lb.

His play was as his name implies—bruising—and he was a perennial all-star, the best of his time at his job. Kinard had the signal distinction of being the only one of more than 100 NFL players who moved to the All-America Football Conference (AAFC) to win all-league honors in both the NFL and AAFC. He was all-NFL in five of his seven seasons with the Brooklyn Dodgers and all-AAFC in 1946 with the New York Yankees.

The Dodgers of the immediate pre-World War II years were a dominant factor in the NFL, missing divisional titles by only one game in both 1940 and 1941. Brooklyn boasted of several quality players but Kinard proved to be the mainstay. When Bruiser moved to the AAFC after a year in the Navy in 1945, he filled the same role with the Yankees, who won divisional titles in both 1946 and 1947.

Like most great athletes, Bruiser had a burning desire to play and to succeed. On many offensive plays, he was the key blocker. A particular Dodger favorite was a shovel pass that depended on Bruiser for success. On defense, he was a smothering tackler who had the speed to range all over the field to stifle the enemy.

Tough and durable, Kinard rarely needed a rest and 60-minute iron-man performances were his rule rather than the exception. Just once was he sidelined and it was doctor's orders that put him on the bench. After suffering a hand wound that took several stitches to close, Bruiser practiced all week, fully intending to play, until gangrene set in and put playing out of the question.

Kinard, who had been a two-time all-America tackle at the University of Mississippi before Dodger coach Potsy Clark drafted him in the second round in 1938, retired after the 1947 season and returned to his beloved "Ole Miss." He served the Rebels as an assistant coach, interim head coach and athletic director but, through it all, his famous nickname stayed with him.

When contacted by Hall officials as to whether he would prefer his given name "Frank" or his nickname "Bruiser" on his Pro Football Hall of Fame ring, he replied without hesitation, "Better make it Bruiser. If my ring said Frank, no one would know it was mine."

*"Bruiser" Kinard was a perennial all-league tackle, a 60-minute workhorse and a key member of the Brooklyn Dodgers.*

# VINCE LOMBARDI

*Coach*
*Born in Brooklyn, N. Y., June 11,*
*1913; died September 3, 1970 at*
*age of 57*
*Fordham University*
*1959–67 Green Bay Packers; 1969*
*Washington Redskins*

*The Green Bay Packers were at the lowest ebb in their history when Vince Lombardi took over the head coaching reins in 1959. Lombardi quickly transformed the Packers into big winners.*

At the age of 45, when most pro football luminaries have made their mark and passed from the scene of a young man's game, Vince Lombardi was embarking on the dual adventure of being head coach and general manager of the Green Bay Packers, an opportunity that would make him a pro football immortal. His previous NFL experience consisted of a five-year stint as Jim Lee Howell's number 1 lieutenant with the New York Giants.

Amazingly, Vince basked in the limelight for only one decade. Cancer struck him down just as he seemingly was about to create a "second miracle," the rejuvenation of the Washington Redskins. In remarkably few years, Lombardi became the symbol of excellence for an entire sport populated by dozens of progressive, highly capable leaders.

There have been few teams in pro football history in a more downtrodden state than the Packers were when Lombardi was first approached about the coaching job in 1959. Vince had gained a reputation with the Giants for his stylish, thorough and imaginative craftsmanship on offense. He seemed to have all the credentials to be a successful head coach.

Lombardi insisted on a five-year contract to give his building program a fair chance but he set his plan into action at his very first team meeting. "I have never been on a losing team, gentlemen, and I do not intend to start now!" Almost as if the statement were an irreversible command and they had no other choice, the Packers improved from 1–10–1 in 1958 to 7–5 in 1959. The next eight years, the Packers were in a class by themselves, winning six divisional and five NFL championships and achieving victories in Super Bowls I and II.

In 1968, Vince retired as the Packers coach but retained his general manager's duties. He found the hours "out of action" boring and, in 1969, moved to Washington, where the Redskins were as woebegone as the Packers had been 10 years earlier. Remarkably, in his first season with the Redskins, Lombardi created an equally amazing result—a 7–5–2 record.

Lombardi was noted as a tough task-master but he earned the universal respect of his players. Even today, former Giants,

Packers and Redskins will voice their appreciation for what Vince did for their football careers. A typical example is Sonny Jurgensen.

"Just working under Vince Lombardi was the greatest opportunity I ever had," the Redskins quarterback remembers. "He made so much sense. You were really prepared when you got out on the field. In five days, I learned more from him than I had in 12 years of pro football."

---

COACHING RECORD

| Year | Won | Lost | Tied | Division finish |
|------|-----|------|------|-----------------|
| 1959* | 7 | 5 | 0 | 3rd |
| 1960* | 8 | 4 | 0 | 1st |
| 1961* | 11 | 3 | 0 | 1st |
| 1962* | 13 | 1 | 0 | 1st |
| 1963* | 11 | 2 | 1 | 2nd |
| 1964* | 8 | 5 | 1 | 2nd |
| 1965* | 10 | 3 | 1 | 1st |
| 1966* | 12 | 2 | 0 | 1st |
| 1967* | 9 | 4 | 1 | 1st |
| 1968 | Did not coach | | | |
| 1969† | 7 | 5 | 2 | 2nd |
| TOTALS‡ | 105 | 35 | 6 | |

POST-SEASON RECORD

1960 NFL Championship: Philadelphia 17, Green Bay 13
1961 NFL Championship: Green Bay 37, New York Giants 0
1962 NFL Championship: Green Bay 16, New York Giants 7
1965 NFL Divisional Playoff: Green Bay 13, Baltimore 10
1965 NFL Championship: Green Bay 23, Cleveland 12
1966 NFL Championship: Green Bay 34, Dallas 27
Super Bowl I: Green Bay 35, Kansas City 10
1967 NFL Divisional Playoff: Green Bay 28, Los Angeles 0
1967 NFL Championship: Green Bay 21, Dallas 17
Super Bowl II: Green Bay 33, Oakland 14

* With Green Bay Packers

† With Washington Redskins

‡ Career totals include post-season games

# ANDY ROBUSTELLI

*Defensive end*
*6 ft 0 in, 230 lb*
*Born in Stamford, Conn.,*
*December 6, 1925*
*Arnold College*
*1951–5 Los Angeles Rams;*
*1956–64 New York Giants*

I n a sense, Andy Robustelli's pro football career began at a 1950 Arnold–St Michael's college game in Winooski, Vermont. Playing for Arnold College, Andy made tackles, caught passes, blocked a punt and ran back a kickoff for a touchdown. Late in the game, he suffered a broken leg, the only serious injury in his grid career. The Rams' scout in the stands, Andy DeFillippi, had seen enough, however, to send rave notices back to Los Angeles.

The Rams drafted Andy in the 19th round in 1951 but Robustelli and his wife seriously weighed the pro football offer of $4250 on a make-it basis against a high-school coaching job. His doubts became even stronger when his coach, Joe Stydahar, told Andy his only chance to make the team was as a defensive end. Up to that time, Andy had felt he was best as an offensive player. He was so unsure of himself that he didn't unpack his bags for the first two weeks of training camp.

But after the Rams' first all-out scrimmage when Robustelli knocked down ball-carriers, smothered passers and left blockers sprawled on the turf, he not only unpacked his bags but settled down for a 15-year stay in the NFL. Andy proved himself to be extremely durable as well as talented. He missed just one game, and that was in his rookie season. After five excellent seasons in Los Angeles, Robustelli was traded to the New York Giants in 1956.

Andy, happy to be playing near his home in Stamford, Connecticut, was even better in a Giants uniform. Seven times in his 14-year career Robustelli was named to the all-NFL team. Seven times he performed in the prestigious Pro Bowl. In 1962, he was the Maxwell Club's choice as the NFL Player of the Year.

Andy, a genuinely modest athlete as well as a great team leader, was one of the finest pass-rushing ends the game has seen. Not only did he possess unusual athletic skills blended nicely with a fierce competitive spirit, but he was a thinking player as well.

"You've got to know when to rush," Andy explained. "Over-anxiety can hurt you. Knowing when comes with experience and nothing else. But there is only one way to play this game and that is as hard and as tough as you can."

To Giants coach Allie Sherman, this was the key to Robustelli's success. "Watch Andy on the field," he pointed out, "and you'll be studying a real master. Terrific speed of mind, hands and feet make him the best. But without burning desire, he would be just an average football player."

*Defensive end Andy Robustelli of the New York Giants aborts the plans of Los Angeles Rams running back Jon Arnett in a scene typical of his exceptional defensive play throughout his career.*

# Y. A. TITTLE

*Quarterback*
*6 ft 0in, 200 lb*
*Born in Marshall, Tex.,*
*October 24, 1926*
*Louisiana State University*
*1948–50 Baltimore Colts;*
*1951–60 San Francisco 49ers;*
*1961–4 New York Giants*

Y. A. Tittle was about as welcome as a bill collector when he joined the New York Giants in mid-August, 1961. The Giants were a veteran, close-knit group, proud of their past successes. They knew that Tittle, who had excelled for both the Baltimore Colts and the San Francisco 49ers, would be battling a team favorite, 40-year-old Charley Conerly, for the quarterback job. The Giants may have feigned cordiality to their new teammate but, for weeks, "Yat" was the loneliest guy in town.

As the 1961 season started, Tittle and Conerly shared the quarterbacking duties but as the Giants moved nearer to the NFL Eastern Division crown, it became more and more evident that Tittle was the guy making it all possible. By the time he was named the NFL's Most Valuable Player, the cold-shoulder treatment from the Giants had long since evaporated.

In 1962, Tittle played even better with 33 touchdown passes and a career-high 3224 yards. A year later, his TD figure went up to a staggering 36, he completed a sensational 60.2 percent of his passes and again was named NFL Player of the Year. As one New York writer put it, "Yat had a marvelous season in 1961, a superb one in 1962 and an even more magnificent one in 1963!"

Tittle's contributions as a Giant far exceeded his mere statistics, impressive as they may have been. "Y. A. has the enthusiasm of a high-school kid," another Giants great, Frank Gifford, said. "He loves to play. This is great for our young players. When they see a 36-year-old man so fired up, they have to get fired up, too."

A 13-year pro veteran when he joined the Giants, Tittle had already enjoyed considerable individual success but his prime

goal, that of playing on and contributing strongly to a championship team, had eluded him. The Colts tied for the All-America Football Conference divisional title in his rookie 1948 season. The 49ers in 1957 battled to a division tie with Detroit, only to fall victim to a 24-point rally that negated a three-touchdown performance by Y. A.

A terrific competitor who was always willing to play "hurt," Yat led the Giants to divisional titles in 1961, 1962, and 1963. Even though they failed to win the overall NFL crown, those were the "glory years" in New York when Tittle was at the helm.

When he stepped down after the 1964 season, Y. A.'s number 14 Giants jersey was retired. Perhaps no other athlete had ever earned such a tribute in so short a time. It is ample testimony to the greatness of his short-lived tenure in New York but, in a larger sense, also a deserved reflection on his entire 17-year pro career, during which Y. A. Tittle always ranked among the best.

*Y. A. Tittle (left), who led the New York Giants to division titles in 1961, 1962, and 1963, talks over strategy with head coach Allie Sherman. Tittle was a two-time NFL Player of the Year.*

PASSING RECORD

| Year | Attempts | Completions | Percentage passes completed | Yards | TD | Interceptions |
|---|---|---|---|---|---|---|
| 1948° | 289 | 161 | 55.7 | 2522 | 16 | 9 |
| 1949° | 289¶ | 148 | 51.2 | 2209 | 14 | 18¶ |
| 1950† | 315 | 161‖ | 51.1 | 1884 | 8 | 19 |
| 1951‡ | 114 | 63 | 55.3 | 808 | 8 | 9 |
| 1952‡ | 208 | 106 | 51.0 | 1407 | 11 | 12 |
| 1953‡ | 259 | 149 | 57.5 | 2121 | 20 | 16 |
| 1954‡ | 295 | 170 | 57.6 | 2205 | 9 | 9 |
| 1955‡ | 287 | 147 | 51.2 | 2185 | 17‖ | 28‖ |
| 1956‡ | 218 | 124 | 56.9 | 1641 | 7 | 12 |
| 1957‡ | 279 | 176‖ | 63.1‖ | 2157 | 13 | 15 |
| 1958‡ | 208 | 120 | 57.7 | 1467 | 9 | 15 |
| 1959‡ | 199 | 102 | 51.3 | 1331 | 10 | 15 |
| 1960‡ | 127 | 69 | 54.3 | 694 | 4 | 3 |
| 1961§ | 285 | 163 | 57.2 | 2272 | 17 | 12 |
| 1962§ | 375 | 200 | 53.3 | 3224 | 33‖ | 20 |
| 1963§** | 367 | 221 | 60.2‖ | 3145 | 36‖ | 14 |
| 1964§ | 281 | 147 | 52.3 | 1798 | 10 | 22 |
| TOTALS | 4395 | 2427 | 55.2 | 33,070 | 242 | 248 |

RUSHING RECORD

| Year | Attempts | Yards | Average | TD |
|---|---|---|---|---|
| 1948° | 52 | 157 | 3.0 | 4 |
| 1949° | 29 | 89 | 3.1 | 2 |
| 1950† | 20 | 77 | 3.9 | 2 |
| 1951‡ | 13 | 18 | 1.4 | 1 |
| 1952‡ | 11 | −11 | −1.0 | 0 |
| 1953‡ | 14 | 41 | 2.9 | 6 |
| 1954‡ | 28 | 68 | 2.4 | 4 |
| 1955‡ | 23 | 114 | 5.0 | 0 |
| 1956‡ | 24 | 67 | 2.8 | 4 |
| 1957‡ | 40 | 220 | 5.5 | 6 |
| 1958‡ | 22 | 35 | 1.6 | 0 |
| 1959‡ | 11 | 24 | 2.2 | 0 |
| 1960‡ | 10 | 61 | 6.1 | 0 |
| 1961§ | 25 | 85 | 3.4 | 3 |
| 1962§ | 17 | 108 | 6.4 | 2 |
| 1963§ | 18 | 99 | 5.5 | 2 |
| 1964§ | 15 | −7 | −0.5 | 1 |
| TOTALS | 372 | 1245 | 3.3 | 39 |

Career passing rating: 74.4

° With Baltimore Colts (AAFC)

† With Baltimore Colts (NFL)

‡ With San Francisco 49ers

§ With New York Giants

¶ Led AAFC

‖ Led NFL

** Official NFL individual passing champion

Scoring: 39 touchdowns, 234 points

# NORM VAN BROCKLIN

*Quarterback*
*6 ft 1 in, 190 lb*
*Born in Eagle Butte, S. D.,*
*March 15, 1926; died May 2,*
*1983, at age of 57*
*University of Oregon*
*1949–57 Los Angeles Rams;*
*1958–60 Philadelphia Eagles*

One of the most colorful and competitive performers that pro football has seen, Norm Van Brocklin blazed a sometimes stormy, but always eventful path in his 12 NFL seasons. His difficulties began the day he was selected number 4 by the Los Angeles Rams in the 1949 draft. The problem, from Van Brocklin's standpoint, was that the Rams already had a brilliant quarterback, Bob Waterfield, who was also destined for the Hall of Fame.

As a result, "The Dutchman" saw only brief action until the final game of his rookie season when he threw four scoring passes to beat Washington. But the next year, new coach Joe Stydahar opted to alternate his two great passers. Waterfield played in the first and third quarters, Van Brocklin in the second and fourth. Dutch won the 1950 NFL passing title and repeated this feat two years later. In between, Waterfield edged out Norm in the season's finale to win the 1951 individual title. It was a situation that neither quarterback could possibly like.

Even though Norm missed the passing crown in 1951, he hit the record books that year with a 554-yard outburst against the New York Yanks. In the 1951 NFL title game, it was his 73-yard pass to Tom Fears that enabled the Rams to defeat the Browns, 24–17.

Even after Waterfield retired, Van Brocklin still had to fight other quarterbacks for a regular job in Los Angeles. Finally, just before the 1958 campaign, Norm was traded to the Philadelphia Eagles.

If Dutch had been stymied in his desire to be a "coach on the field" while with the Rams, this was not the case in Philadelphia, where Buck Shaw gave him a free hand with the offense. "If it's the game plan you want, see Dutch," an Eagle once told a writer seeking out Shaw for an interview about a coming game.

Behind Van Brocklin, the Eagles finished second in 1959 and then won it all in 1960. By defeating Green Bay in the NFL finale, Norm became the only man to beat Vince Lombardi in a championship game during the latter's years in Green Bay. Van Brocklin's exceptional season earned him unanimous all-NFL selection and several Most Valuable Player trophies. A month after the title game, he bowed out as an active player with a three-touchdown blitz in his eighth Pro Bowl game.

A short time later, The Dutchman was hired as the first head coach of the new Minnesota Vikings team. There he was certain to face frustration. But as the people who hired him knew, Van Brocklin had often faced adversity and had always prevailed.

*Playing with the Philadelphia Eagles, Norm Van Brocklin launches a bullet pass in action against the New York Giants.*

PASSING RECORD

Career passing rating: 75.1

| Year | Attempts | Completions | Percentage passes completed | Yards | TD | Interceptions |
|------|----------|-------------|------------------------------|-------|-----|---------------|
| 1949° | 58 | 32 | 55.2 | 601 | 6 | 2 |
| 1950°§ | 233 | 127 | 54.5 | 2061 | 18 | 14 |
| 1951° | 194 | 100 | 51.5 | 1725 | 13 | 11 |
| 1952°§ | 205 | 113 | 55.1‡ | 1736 | 14 | 17 |
| 1953° | 286 | 156 | 54.5 | 2393 | 19 | 14 |
| 1954°§ | 260 | 139 | 53.5 | 2637‡ | 13 | 21 |
| 1955° | 272 | 144 | 52.9 | 1890 | 8 | 15 |
| 1956° | 124 | 68 | 54.8 | 966 | 7 | 12 |
| 1957° | 265 | 132 | 49.8 | 2105 | 20 | 21‡ |
| 1958† | 374‡ | 198‡ | 52.9 | 2409 | 15 | 20 |
| 1959† | 340 | 191 | 56.2 | 2617 | 16 | 14 |
| 1960† | 284 | 153 | 53.9 | 2471 | 24 | 17 |
| TOTALS | 2895 | 1553 | 53.6 | 23,611 | 173 | 178 |

° With Los Angeles Rams

† With Philadelphia Eagles

‡ Led NFL

§ Official NFL individual passing champion

Rushing: 102 attempts, 40 yards, 0.4-yard average, 11 touchdowns

Punting: 523 punts, 42.9-yard average

Scoring: 11 touchdowns, 66 points

# LAMAR HUNT

*League founder, owner*
*Born in El Dorado, Ark., August 2, 1932*
*Southern Methodist University*
*1960–2 Dallas Texans:*
*1963–present day Kansas City Chiefs*

Almost three decades ago, in January 1959, a young man, totally frustrated in his repeated attempts to buy an NFL franchise, hit upon the idea of founding a new professional football league to rival the established league. The young man was Lamar Hunt, a 26-year-old civic-minded sports enthusiast and prosperous oil man living in Dallas, Texas.

Lamar first approached K. S. "Bud" Adams Jr of Houston, who had also been trying to acquire an NFL team. Several others joined in and, with its organizational meeting on August 14, 1959, the American Football League (AFL) was born. A year later in September, 1960, the AFL began to play. Few gave it much of a chance but its eventual David-and-Goliath-like success in its costly battle with the established NFL is one of sport's most fascinating stories.

It would be incorrect to say that everything good that happened in the AFL before, during and after the fierce inter-league struggle was Hunt's doing. Lamar, however, was a leader in many of the forceful moves the league made and he was a busy participant in the cloak-and-dagger activities that became commonplace in the competition for players. As an example, Hunt once signed defensive stalwart Aaron Brown on a commercial jet flying to New York. NFL agents waiting on the ground to meet Brown went away empty-handed.

By having a winning team and a solid organization right from the start, Lamar gave the AFL added strength. His original Dallas Texans team had to battle the newly established Cowboys head-to-head. Even though the contest was a dead-even affair, Hunt, after three seasons, wisely moved his team to Kansas City. During the AFL's 10-year lifetime, the Texans/Chiefs had the best won–lost record (87–48–5) of any original AFL team. They won three championships, played in the first Super Bowl and, in the last game ever played by an AFL team, upset the Minnesota Vikings in Super Bowl IV. The AFL vs NFL portion of the Super Bowl series thus ended in a 2–2 tie.

It is not surprising that, when merger talks reached the serious stage, Hunt was the AFL representative chosen to meet with NFL emissaries to work out the final details. As announced in June, 1966, the AFL paid $18 million in indemnities and agreed to give up its name, but it won what it had set out to win—total equality, a common draft, inter-league competition and a season-ending championship game. It was more than anyone, friend, foe or even Hunt himself, had thought possible when the AFL began its odyssey. The league's survival and success is a lasting tribute to the man who turned a flickering thought into brilliant reality and changed forever, and undoubtedly for the better, the professional football world.

*Lamar Hunt (right), founder of the American Football League, chats with NFL commissioner Pete Rozelle after the 1966 merger that ended the costly inter-league football war of the 1960s.*

# GINO MARCHETTI

*Defensive end*
*6 ft 4 in. 245 lb*
*Born in Smithers, W. Va.,*
*January 2, 1927*
*University of San Francisco*
*1952 Dallas Texans; 1953–64,*
*1966 Baltimore Colts*

Gino Marchetti terrorized NFL quarterbacks with his vicious pass rushes for 14 seasons with the Baltimore Colts. He was selected to play in 11 straight Pro Bowl games and named to all-NFL teams seven years. In 1969, one panel named him the finest defensive end in the NFL's first 50 years.

There were few clues during Marchetti's younger days to presage such gridiron greatness. The product of an Italian immigrant family who counseled him against playing such a "rough sport," Gino showed little football acumen until he was a senior at Antioch, Calif., High School, where he was the team's Most Valuable Player. A year later, Marchetti was in the US Army, fighting in the pivotal "Battle of the Bulge" in Belgium.

After the war, Gino organized a semi-pro team in Antioch. This led him to Modesto Junior College and then to the University of San Francisco, where he developed into the finest tackle on the Pacific coast. The New York Yanks picked him in the second round of the 1952 draft.

Marchetti's pro career started on a disconcerting note, however. Before his rookie season, the Yanks moved to Dallas as the Texans. Then a year later, they folded. Gino's contract was assigned to Baltimore, a new franchise in a city where the original Colts had failed three years earlier. But the new Colts quickly built toward championship status and Marchetti steadily acquired superstar proportions. As a hint of things to come, he played in his first Pro Bowl after his initial campaign in Baltimore.

Gino became an all-round brilliant defender, best as a pass rusher, but also adept at stopping the run. He was often double-teamed and even triple-teamed but that only served to make the Colts rush line more effective. Gino was respected for his always clean but hard play. The team captain through much of his career, he was a tremendous favorite with Baltimore's rabid fandom.

Marchetti was determined to retire before he lost his great effectiveness. He was coaxed out of quitting in 1963 but he did retire a year later. In November 1966, he responded to a Colts emergency and returned for four games during which, for the first time ever, he turned in an only average performance. Some viewed his return from retirement as a mistake but it did bring into sharp focus how much of a loyalist Gino really was.

"I'm not making a comeback," Marchetti explained. "I'm doing them a favor. If the Colts think I can help, I have to give it a try. Everything I have I owe to them!"

*Gino Marchetti was universally feared for his sterling pass rushing abilities but he was also effective in stopping the running game. Here he nails Los Angeles Rams running back Jon Arnett.*

# OLLIE MATSON

*Halfback*
*6 ft 2 in. 220 lb*
*Born in Trinity, Tex., May 1, 1930*
*University of San Francisco*
*1952, 1954–8 Chicago Cardinals;*
*1959–62 Los Angeles Rams; 1963*
*Detroit Lions; 1964–6*
*Philadelphia Eagles*

When Ollie Matson first signed to play with the Chicago Cardinals in 1952, he was hailed as "The Messiah," the fleet-footed ball-carrier who would lead the Cardinals out of the NFL wilderness. Seven years later, when traded by the Cardinals to the Los Angeles Rams for a stunning total of nine players, he was tabbed as the star who would give the Rams a long-awaited championship.

Through no fault of his own, Ollie did neither. Certainly, more than most games, football is a team endeavor and Matson never had the supporting cast to back up his brilliance. In 14 seasons, the combined record of the four clubs for which he played was a dismal 58–117–5. Only two of his 14 teams had better than .500 records.

It was Ollie's burden that enemy defenses could almost always concentrate on him alone. Yet his career record is exceptional. He gained 12,884 yards—more than $7\frac{1}{4}$ miles—on rushing, receptions and returns. He scored 39 touchdowns running, 23 on receptions, nine on kick returns and one on a fumble recovery. Only a handful of NFL greats ever exhibited such versatility.

After an all-America senior season at the University of San Francisco, Matson became the Cardinals' number 1 draft pick in 1952 but Ollie, who had been an outstanding sprinter in high school, first wanted to try out for the United States Olympic team. He returned from Helsinki with a bronze medal from the 440-meter race and a gold medal from the 1600-meter relay event.

Back in football pads, Matson set the NFL on fire. He shared Rookie of the Year honors with the 49ers' Hugh McElhenny. After a year in the Army in 1953, he continued to shine with the Cardinals. He was all-NFL four straight years and played in the

Pro Bowl after his first five campaigns.

When the NFL title the Rams so eagerly anticipated slipped out of their grasp in the early 1960s, Matson was sent first to Detroit for a year and then to the Philadelphia Eagles in 1964. There he was re-united with his college and first pro coach, Joe Kuharich.

Two seasons later, Ollie enjoyed one final starring day that helped to lead the Eagles to a 9–5 record, the best ever for a Matson team. With the 49ers leading, 20–7, Ollie replaced the injured Tim Brown, ran with bone-crushing effort and capped off a big rally with a leaping touchdown catch for a 35–34 victory.

It was a fitting climax to one of the finest careers, achieved in spite of a multitude of frustrations, that the NFL has known.

*Ollie Matson possessed Olympic running speed which he used to good advantage in his 14-season career with four teams. Here he breaks into the open for big yardage for the Chicago Cardinals.*

## RUSHING RECORD

| Year | Attempts | Yards | Average | TD |
|------|----------|-------|---------|-----|
| 1952* | 96 | 344 | 3.6 | 3 |
| 1953 | In US Army | | | |
| 1954* | 101 | 506 | 5.0 | 4 |
| 1955* | 109 | 475 | 4.4 | 1 |
| 1956* | 192 | 924 | 4.8 | 5 |
| 1957* | 134 | 577 | 4.3 | 6 |
| 1958* | 129 | 505 | 3.9 | 5 |
| 1959† | 161 | 863 | 5.4 | 6 |
| 1960† | 61 | 170 | 2.8 | 1 |
| 1961† | 24 | 181 | 7.5 | 2 |
| 1962† | 3 | 0 | 0.0 | 0 |
| 1963‡ | 13 | 20 | 1.5 | 0 |
| 1964§ | 96 | 404 | 4.2 | 4 |
| 1965§ | 22 | 103 | 4.7 | 2 |
| 1966§ | 29 | 101 | 3.5 | 1 |
| TOTALS | 1170 | 5173 | 4.4 | 40 |

## RECEIVING RECORD

| Year | Number | Yards | Average | TD |
|------|--------|-------|---------|-----|
| 1952* | 11 | 187 | 17.0 | 3 |
| 1953 | In US Army | | | |
| 1954* | 34 | 611 | 18.0 | 3 |
| 1955* | 17 | 237 | 13.9 | 2 |
| 1956* | 15 | 199 | 13.3 | 2 |
| 1957* | 20 | 451 | 22.6 | 3 |
| 1958* | 33 | 465 | 14.1 | 3 |
| 1959† | 18 | 130 | 7.2 | 0 |
| 1960† | 15 | 98 | 6.5 | 0 |
| 1961† | 29 | 537 | 18.5 | 3 |
| 1962† | 3 | 49 | 16.3 | 1 |
| 1963‡ | 2 | 20 | 10.0 | 0 |
| 1964§ | 17 | 242 | 14.2 | 1 |
| 1965§ | 2 | 29 | 14.5 | 1 |
| 1966§ | 6 | 30 | 5.0 | 1 |
| TOTALS | 222 | 3285 | 14.8 | 23 |

## KICKOFF RETURN RECORD

| Year | Number | Yards | Average | TD |
|------|--------|-------|---------|-----|
| 1952* | 20 | 624 | 31.2 | 2 |
| 1953 | In US Army | | | |
| 1954* | 17 | 449 | 26.4 | 1 |
| 1955* | 15 | 368 | 24.5 | 0 |
| 1956* | 13 | 362 | 27.8 | 1 |
| 1957* | 7 | 154 | 22.0 | 0 |
| 1958* | 14 | 497 | 35.5¶ | 2¶ |
| 1959† | 16 | 367 | 22.9 | 0 |
| 1960† | 9 | 216 | 24.0 | 0 |
| 1961† | 0 | 0 | 0.0 | 0 |
| 1962† | 0 | 0 | 0.0 | 0 |
| 1963‡ | 3 | 61 | 20.3 | 0 |
| 1964§ | 3 | 104 | 34.7 | 0 |
| 1965§ | 0 | 0 | 0.0 | 0 |
| 1966§ | 26 | 544 | 20.9 | 0 |
| TOTALS | 143 | 3746 | 26.2 | 6 |

## PUNT RETURN RECORD

| Year | Number | Yards | Average | TD |
|------|--------|-------|---------|-----|
| 1952* | 9 | 86 | 9.6 | 0 |
| 1953 | In US Army | | | |
| 1954* | 11 | 100 | 9.1 | 1 |
| 1955* | 13 | 245¶ | 18.8¶ | 2¶ |
| 1956* | 5 | 39 | 7.8 | 0 |
| 1957* | 10 | 54 | 5.4 | 0 |
| 1958* | 0 | 0 | 0.0 | 0 |
| 1959† | 14 | 61 | 4.4 | 0 |
| 1960† | 1 | 0 | 0.0 | 0 |
| 1961† | 0 | 0 | 0.0 | 0 |
| 1962† | 0 | 0 | 0.0 | 0 |
| 1963‡ | 0 | 0 | 0.0 | 0 |
| 1964§ | 2 | 10 | 5.0 | 0 |
| 1965§ | 0 | 0 | 0.0 | 0 |
| 1966§ | 0 | 0 | 0.0 | 0 |
| TOTALS | 65 | 595 | 9.2 | 3 |

* With Chicago Cardinals

† With Los Angeles Rams

‡ With Detroit Lions

§ With Philadelphia Eagles

¶ Led NFL

Passing: 15 attempts, 5 completions
119 yards, 0 touchdowns,
1 interception

Interceptions: 3 interceptions, 51 yards,
17.0-yard average,

Scoring: 73 touchdowns, 438 points

# CLARENCE (ACE) PARKER

*Quarterback*
*5 ft 11 in, 168 lb*
*Born in Portsmouth, Va., May 17,*
*1912*
*Duke University*
*1937–41 Brooklyn Dodgers; 1945*
*Boston Yanks; 1946 New York*
*Yankees (AAFC)*

*The Brooklyn Dodgers of the early 1940s were perennial championship contenders and "Ace" Parker, a triple-threat star from Duke, was a major contributor to his team's successes.*

"Ace" Parker never really intended to play pro football when he completed his college career as an all-America tailback at Duke University in 1936. His ambition was to be a major-league baseball player and he signed a contract with the Philadelphia Athletics. After the 1937 baseball season, however, Ace joined the Brooklyn Dodgers of the NFL, still expecting to play out just one season and then return to baseball.

History now records that the 1937 season wasn't "the end of it" for the multi-talented fireball. Parker stayed with the Dodgers until a service call interrupted his career in 1942 and then returned for a 1945 season with the Boston Yanks and a brilliant final campaign with the New York Yankees of the All-America Football Conference in 1946.

Interestingly, it was baseball—and not the huge NFL linemen whom Parker faced every weekend—that proved to be the biggest stumbling block in his grid tenure. Broken ankles suffered on the diamond twice endangered his football career. In 1940, Ace won the NFL's Most Valuable Player award, even though he had suffered a broken left ankle in a summer baseball game. For the first three weeks of the season, he had to wear a 10-lb brace that extended from his ankle to his knee.

Ace wasn't exceptionally fast anyway, so he just continued doing what he had always done—running, passing, catching passes, punting, placekicking, returning punts and kickoffs and playing defense. Few will remember that the Dodgers of the early 1940s were constant contenders for Eastern Division supremacy in the NFL. Time and time again, Parker led the Dodgers to victory in a fashion that smacked of story-book fiction, not real-life heroics.

There was, for instance, the game in 1940 on Ace Parker Day in Brooklyn when the tremendous competitor was involved in every score in a 14–9 win over the Cardinals, or the time two weeks later when Ace ruined Mel Hein Day at the Polo Grounds by accounting for all the points in a 14–6 upset of the New York Giants.

Parker did the same thing to the Giants a year later. He contributed a touchdown-saving tackle, a touchdown pass and a 61-yard run that set up the winning score to end a six-game winning streak of the cross-town rivals.

"Somewhere in the dim past there might have been another back who could have done those things, but permit me to doubt it," Associated Press reporter Gayle Talbot wrote. "The brand of football the professionals play today is terrible in its demands but Ace Parker is its master."

## PASSING RECORD

| Year | Attempts | Completions | Percentage passes completed | Yards | TD | Interceptions |
|------|----------|-------------|------------------------------|-------|-----|---------------|
| 1937° | 61 | 28 | 45.9 | 514 | 1 | 7 |
| 1938° | 148 | 63 | 42.6 | 865 | 5 | 7 |
| 1939° | 157 | 72 | 45.9 | 977 | 4 | 13 |
| 1940° | 111 | 49 | 44.1 | 817 | 10 | 7 |
| 1941° | 102 | 51 | 50.0 | 642 | 2 | 8 |
| 1942–4 | In US Service | | | | | |
| 1945† | 24 | 10 | 41.7 | 123 | 0 | 5 |
| 1946‡ | 115 | 62 | 53.9 | 763 | 8 | 3 |
| TOTALS | 718 | 335 | 46.7 | 4701 | 30 | 50 |

## RUSHING RECORD

| Year | Attempts | Yards | Average | TD |
|------|----------|-------|---------|-----|
| 1937° | 34 | 26 | 0.8 | 1 |
| 1938° | 93 | 253 | 2.7 | 2 |
| 1939° | 104 | 271 | 2.6 | 5 |
| 1940° | 89 | 306 | 3.4 | 3 |
| 1941° | 85 | 301 | 3.5 | 0 |
| 1942–4 | In US Service | | | |
| 1945† | 18 | −49 | −2.7 | 0 |
| 1946‡ | 75 | 184 | 2.5 | 3 |
| TOTALS | 498 | 1282 | 2.6 | 14 |

° With Brooklyn Dodgers

† With Boston Yanks

‡ With New York Yankees (AAFC)

Receiving: 8 receptions, 229 yards, 28.6-yard average, 3 touchdowns

Scoring: 20 touchdowns, 25 extra points, 1 field goal, 148 points

Punting (1939–46): 150 punts, 38.3-yard average

Interceptions (1940–6): 7 interceptions

Punt returns (1941–6): 24 returns, 238 yards, 9.9-yard average, 0 touchdowns

Kickoff returns (1945–6): 2 returns, 27 yards, 13.5-yard average, 0 touchdowns

Note: Statistics for punting, interceptions, punt returns and kickoff returns available only for the years indicated

# RAYMOND BERRY

**End**
**6 ft 2 in, 187 lb**
**Born in Corpus Christi, Tex.,**
**February 27, 1933**
**Southern Methodist University**
**1955–67 Baltimore Colts**

variety of helpers—teammates, coaches, groundskeepers, writers, schoolboys and even his wife, Sally.

Raymond also practiced covering his own fumbles every day "just in case." This was one effort that was seemingly wasted—of the 631 times he handled the ball, Berry fumbled just once!

*Most observers felt Raymond Berry did not have the natural talents to become a standout pass receiver in the NFL. But he used hard work and stern determination to develop into an all-time great.*

I f there were ever a self-made superstar, Raymond Berry would be that man. He lacked the speed and height normally associated with great pass receivers but combined the tools he did have—unusual jumping ability and fantastic hands—with a dogged sense of purpose to attain a level of proficiency in his 13 seasons with the Baltimore Colts that few ever realize. Using his keen mind to perfect a scientific approach to the art of pass receiving, Raymond was truly a pioneer in refining a specialized gridiron skill.

Berry's hard work reaped huge rewards. He retired with 631 receptions, a record at that time. He was a game-saving hero many times but never was he better than in the Colts' overtime NFL title win over the New York Giants in 1958. Raymond caught 12 passes for 178 yards, scored one touchdown and made several critical catches to keep the Colts alive both in regulation time and in overtime.

The years when Baltimore was atop the NFL heap were also Berry's finest. In 1958, 1959, and 1960, he led the NFL in receiving, earned all-NFL honors and played in three of his five Pro Bowls. In 1961, he amassed a career-high 75 catches.

To understand fully the unbelievable Raymond Berry saga, it is necessary to go back to Paris, Texas, High School where, although his dad was the head coach, Raymond didn't play as a regular until he was a senior. Berry went to junior college for a year before moving to Southern Methodist. With the Mustangs, he caught only 33 passes and scored just one touchdown in three years.

For some reason, the Colts drafted Berry as a future choice in 1954 but, when he reported to camp in 1955, he was given little chance to make the team. Somehow he managed to stay on, and in his second season he began to pair up with another rookie, quarterback Johnny Unitas. Soon the Unitas–Berry aerial duo was the most lethal in pro football. Raymond caught almost 600 of Johnny U's passes the next 11 seasons.

In his relentless drive for perfection, Berry, by actual count, developed 88 maneuvers for getting around defenders and to the ball. Insistent on practicing every move each week, he enlisted a

RECEIVING RECORD        ° Led NFL

| Year | Number | Yards | Average | TD |
|------|--------|-------|---------|-----|
| 1955 | 13 | 205 | 15.8 | 0 |
| 1956 | 37 | 601 | 16.2 | 2 |
| 1957 | 47 | 800° | 17.0 | 6 |
| 1958 | 56° | 794 | 14.2 | 9° |
| 1959 | 66° | 959° | 14.5 | 14° |
| 1960 | 74° | 1298° | 17.5 | 10 |
| 1961 | 75 | 873 | 11.6 | 0 |
| 1962 | 51 | 687 | 13.5 | 3 |
| 1963 | 44 | 703 | 16.0 | 3 |
| 1964 | 43 | 663 | 15.4 | 6 |
| 1965 | 58 | 739 | 12.7 | 7 |
| 1966 | 56 | 786 | 14.0 | 7 |
| 1967 | 11 | 167 | 15.2 | 1 |
| TOTALS | 631 | 9275 | 14.7 | 68 |

# JIM PARKER

*Tackle, guard*
*6 ft 3 in, 273 lb*
*Born in Macon, Ga., April 3, 1934*
*Ohio State University*
*1957–67 Baltimore Colts*

From the moment Jim Parker joined the 1957 Baltimore Colts as their number 1 draft pick, he was considered a cinch for pro football stardom. Jim had been a two-way tackle, an all-America and the Outland Award winner as the nation's top lineman at Ohio State. His coach, Woody Hayes, confided that Parker's best shot in the pros would be on defense but the Colts' mentor, Weeb Ewbank, had Jim tabbed from the start as an offensive lineman.

The Colts at the time were just evolving as an NFL power and the premier passer in the game, Johnny Unitas, was the guy who made the Baltimore attack click. Even though Ohio State concentrated on the running game and Parker had little experience in pass blocking, Ewbank was sure Jim could do the job.

"It didn't take me long to learn the one big rule," Parker remembers. "Just keep 'em away from John. Coach Ewbank told me at my first practice: 'You can be the most unpopular man on the team if the quarterback gets hurt.' I couldn't forget that!"

Obviously, Parker didn't forget and he earned a number of nicknames in the next few years—"Johnny Unitas' Bodyguard," "The Mother Hen," "The Den-Mother," "The Guardian," "Jumbo Jim." Almost any nickname that meant Jim did his job superbly well would have been appropriate.

The fact that he was assigned to protect such a famous teammate may explain why Parker seemed to attract more publicity than is usually accorded to offensive linemen. Another reason is that he was such an exceptional craftsman. In an out-of-the-ordinary twist, Jim divided his career almost evenly between left tackle and left guard. Each job had its distinct set of responsibilities. Even the opponents were different. As a tackle, he went head-to-head against the faster, more agile defensive ends. At guard, his daily foes were the bigger and stronger defensive tackles.

Parker handled both positions in all-pro fashion. He was all-NFL four times as a tackle and four years as a guard. From 1959 to 1966, he played in eight straight Pro Bowls. He later became the first man who played solely as an offensive lineman to be elected to the Pro Football Hall of Fame.

When injuries cut his effectiveness in 1967, Jim, rather than hamper a team that might be championship-bound, stepped down as an active player. "I can't help the team and I won't deprive 40 guys of their big chance," he said.

Parker was, first and foremost, a team player. This act, which might have cost him a lucrative Super Bowl check, was typical of the unselfishness Jim always displayed on the field of play.

*Jim Parker leads a Baltimore Colts running back in action against the Los Angeles Rams. Parker's primary assignment was to protect the Colts' ace passer, Johnny Unitas.*

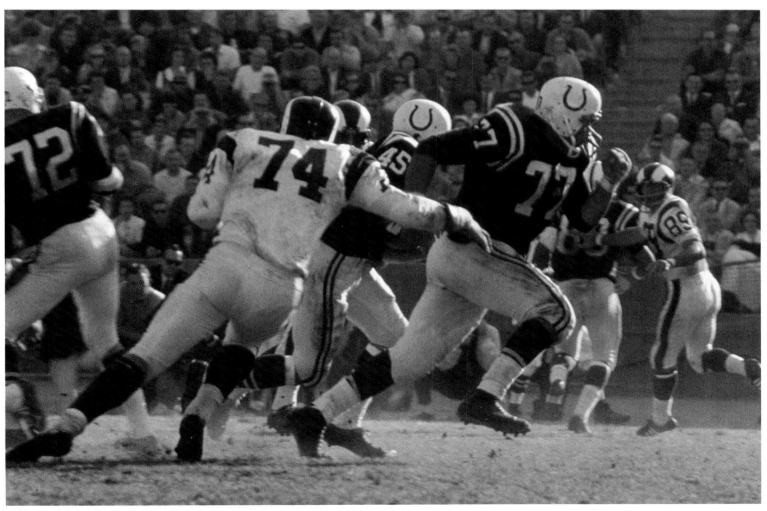

# JOE SCHMIDT

*Middle linebacker*
*6 ft 0 in, 222 lb*
*Born in Pittsburgh, Pa.,*
*January 18, 1932*
*University of Pittsburgh*
*1953–65 Detroit Lions*

Because he had a long history of injuries when he was playing at the University of Pittsburgh, Joe Schmidt was not highly regarded when the time came for pro football. Only at the insistence of assistant coach Buster Ramsey, who had seen Joe play well in the Senior Bowl, did the Lions pick him in the seventh round of the 1953 draft. He was virtually ignored when he reported to his first training camp.

Since even no-name rookies might take jobs away, Schmidt didn't get a warm reception from his new Lions teammates, either. When Dick Flanagan, a popular Detroit linebacker, was traded, Bobby Layne, the superb field general and team spokesman, sidled up to Joe and warned, "Flanagan's gone now. You'd better be good, rookie!"

Schmidt quickly proved he was more than just good but it wasn't until mid-season that Layne and the other Lions finally accepted him into their ranks. When, one day, they invited the outcast for a beer, Joe knew he was officially regarded as a Lion.

Within two seasons, Schmidt was an all-pro and the honors came regularly the rest of his career. He was named all-NFL eight straight years, selected for nine consecutive Pro Bowls and picked by his teammates as the Most Valuable Lion four times.

To many, Joe was the ideal middle linebacker. As the Detroit defensive captain, a job he held for nine years, he barked split-second assignments to his defensive cohorts. He was a ferocious tackler and fast enough to move laterally along the scrimmage line to follow a run or to drop back to cover a pass. He was strong enough to power through a potential blocker to crumble any enemy sortie.

His greatest talent may well have been his uncanny knack of seemingly always knowing what the opposition was going to do. To deprive the offense of its advantage of surprise, Joe studied every foe constantly. He learned what to expect from each opponent at a particular point in the game.

Schmidt's defensive calls featured a lot of blitzing. "I'd say about 75 per cent of our defensive rushes include some kind of red dog," Schmidt once conceded. "It confuses the offense and keeps them off balance."

A remark by John Henry Johnson, who had been both an opponent and a teammate of Schmidt, pin-pointed Joe's contributions on the gridiron: "He is always in the way." For a linebacker who was paid to be just that, it was the ultimate compliment.

| INTERCEPTION RECORD | | | | |
|---|---|---|---|---|
| Year | Number | Yards | Average | TD |
| 1953 | 2 | 51 | 25.5 | 0 |
| 1954 | 2 | 13 | 6.5 | 0 |
| 1955 | 0 | 0 | 0.0 | 0 |
| 1956 | 1 | 7 | 7.0 | 0 |
| 1957 | 1 | 8 | 8.0 | 0 |
| 1958 | 6 | 69 | 11.5 | 0 |
| 1959 | 1 | 17 | 17.0 | 0 |
| 1960 | 2 | 46 | 23.0 | 1 |
| 1961 | 4 | 38 | 9.5 | 1 |
| 1962 | 1 | 3 | 3.0 | 0 |
| 1963 | 0 | 0 | 0.0 | 0 |
| 1964 | 0 | 0 | 0.0 | 0 |
| 1965 | 4 | 42 | 10.5 | 0 |
| TOTALS | 24 | 294 | 12.3 | 2 |

*Considered by many to be the perfect middle linebacker, Joe Schmidt captained the Detroit Lions for nine seasons. He was all-NFL eight years and played in nine straight Pro Bowls.*

# TONY CANADEO

*Halfback*
*5 ft 11 in, 195 lb*
*Born in Chicago, Ill., May 5, 1919*
*Gonzaga University*
*1941–4, 1946–52 Green Bay*
*Packers*

Although Canadeo played his last NFL game in 1952, he never really left the Packers. At one time, he was a commentator on Green Bay's TV games. When the city staged a stadium building fund drive in the mid-1950s, Tony was one of the leaders. Today, he still serves his beloved Packers as a member of the team's board of directors and its executive committee.

Tony Canadeo from little-known Gonzaga University was an unsung seventh-round choice of the Green Bay Packers in 1941 but it wasn't long before he earned the reputation of being a budding superstar who could—and would—do anything on a football field. He played offense and defense, rushed with the pigskin, threw passes, caught passes, returned punts and kickoffs, punted and intercepted passes. In 11 years, he amassed 8682 yards on 1487 multi-categoried sorties, averaging 5.8 yards every time he touched the football. Putting it another way, he accounted for almost 75 yards in each of the 116 games he played.

Canadeo's NFL tenure, interrupted by a service call in 1945, was split into two distinct segments, pre-war and post-war. In the 1941–4 period, Green Bay was a perennial powerhouse and one of pro football's most pass-minded elevens. Tony first understudied the veteran Cecil Isbell and then became the Packers' number 1 passer in 1943, when he was named to the official all-NFL team.

When Tony returned from the Army in 1946, the Packers no longer were contenders and Ward Comp was firmly entrenched in Canadeo's old passing role. So Tony became a heavy-duty running back and, predictably, came through with flying colors. In 1949, he became only the third player to rush for more than 1000 yards in a season. He won all-NFL acclaim for a second time.

For all his exceptional native ability, Tony never looked the part of a football player, let alone a great one. Small by pro standards, Canadeo was neither particularly fast nor elusive. Because he was prematurely gray, he was popularly known as "The Gray Ghost of Gonzaga."

But Tony employed the attributes of most great athletes—determination, courage and tenacity—to attain Hall-of-Fame stature. Two decades later, he had to call on these same traits to survive in the face of a potentially deadly kidney ailment. Canadeo was undergoing semi-weekly treatments on a dialysis machine and not really doing well when, in 1972, he underwent a kidney transplant. His son Robert, a Bronze Star winner in Viet Nam, was the donor. The operation was a total success.

RUSHING RECORD

| Year | Attempts | Yards | Average | TD |
|------|----------|-------|---------|-----|
| 1941 | 43 | 137 | 3.2 | 3 |
| 1942 | 89 | 272 | 3.1 | 3 |
| 1943 | 94 | 489 | 5.2 | 3 |
| 1944 | 31 | 149 | 4.8 | 0 |
| 1945 | In military service | | | |
| 1946 | 122 | 476 | 3.9 | 0 |
| 1947 | 103 | 464 | 4.5 | 2 |
| 1948 | 123 | 589 | 4.8 | 4 |
| 1949 | 208 | 1052 | 5.1 | 4 |
| 1950 | 93 | 247 | 2.7 | 4 |
| 1951 | 54 | 131 | 2.4 | 1 |
| 1952 | 65 | 191 | 2.9 | 2 |
| TOTALS | 1025 | 4197 | 4.1 | 26 |

Receiving: 69 receptions, 579 yards, 8.4-yard average, 5 touchdowns

Passing: 268 attempts, 105 completions, 1642 yards, 16 touchdowns, 20 interceptions

Punt returns: 45 returns, 509 yards, 11.3-yard average, 0 touchdowns

Kickoff returns: 71 returns, 1626 yards, 22.9-yard average, 0 touchdowns

Interceptions: 9 interceptions, 129 yards returned, 14.3-yard average, 0 touchdowns

Punting: 45 punts, 37.0-yard average

Scoring: 31 touchdowns, 186 points

*As he did so many times during his career with the Green Bay Packers, Tony Canadeo breaks into the clear in NFL action of the late 1940s. Tony began his Packers tenure as a passing specialist but wound up as a heavy-duty running back.*

# BILL GEORGE

*Middle linebacker*
*6 ft 2 in, 230 lb*
*Born in Waynesburg, Pa.,*
*October 27, 1930; died*
*September 30, 1982, at age of 51*
*Wake Forest College*
*1952–65 Chicago Bears; 1966 Los*
*Angeles Rams*

I t can be debated whether Bill George, during his 14-year tenure with the Chicago Bears, was the first to play regularly as a middle linebacker. What cannot be disputed are his innovative contributions to the position and the quality of his play.

Bill began his NFL career in 1952 as a middle guard in the standard five-man defensive front of the day. Two years later against the Eagles, George made a mid-game adjustment which permanently changed defensive strategy in the NFL. On passing plays, Bill's job was to bump the center and then drop back. This particular day, the Eagles were completing numerous passes right over George's head. Bill discussed the situation with defensive captain George Connor and they agreed he would omit the center bump and drop back immediately. On the second play, Bill got his first of 18 pro interceptions. It wasn't long before most teams were doing the same thing with their middle guards.

Within three years, the wire services substituted a third linebacker for the middle guard on all their all-league selections. George, who had been a two-time all-NFL middle guard, became instead an all-league linebacker six times in the next seven years. He also played in eight straight Pro Bowls.

During most of Bill's career, the Bears' defensive coordinator was Clark Shaughnessy, a noted football tactician who devised literally hundreds of defensive variances that drove enemy quarterbacks wild. It became George's responsibility not only to learn the complicated system but to make it work on the field. In 1956, he became the Bears' defensive signal-caller and, for most of the next decade, he carried out his job to near-perfection.

George also helped to put an end to the shotgun formation San Francisco used to terrorize NFL defenses in the early 1960s. He did the job simply by moving back into the line, barreling past the 49ers center at the time of the snap and getting to the quarterback almost simultaneously with the ball. When other teams followed Bill's lead, the 49ers curtailed the use of their once-lethal weapon.

Chicago was a blitzing team in those years and George was one of the best and a strong proponent of the tactic. "You've got to put pressure on the good quarterbacks," Bill insisted. "Once we went into a three-man line with eight players in the secondary to face Johnny Unitas and he picked us to pieces. You just can't let the good quarterbacks get set."

*After two years as the Bears' middle guard, Bill George shifted into what became a new position—middle linebacker. As the defensive signal-caller he made the Bears' complicated system work.*

## INTERCEPTION RECORD

| Year | Number | Yards | Average | TD |
|------|--------|-------|---------|-----|
| 1952* | 0 | 0 | 0.0 | 0 |
| 1953* | 0 | 0 | 0.0 | 0 |
| 1954* | 2 | 9 | 4.5 | 0 |
| 1955* | 2 | 13 | 6.5 | 0 |
| 1956* | 2 | 9 | 4.5 | 0 |
| 1957* | 0 | 0 | 0.0 | 0 |
| 1958* | 1 | 5 | 5.0 | 0 |
| 1959* | 2 | 20 | 10.0 | 0 |
| 1960* | 1 | 12 | 12.0 | 0 |
| 1961* | 3 | 18 | 6.0 | 0 |
| 1962* | 2 | 26 | 13.0 | 0 |
| 1963* | 1 | 4 | 4.0 | 0 |
| 1964* | 2 | 28 | 14.0 | 0 |
| 1965* | 0 | 0 | 0.0 | 0 |
| 1966† | 0 | 0 | 0.0 | 0 |
| TOTALS | 18 | 144 | 8.0 | 0 |

* With Chicago Bears

† With Los Angeles Rams

Scoring: 0 touchdowns, 14 extra points, 4 field goals, 26 points

# LOU GROZA

*Offensive tackle, placekicker*
*6 ft 3 in, 250 lb*
*Born in Martins Ferry, Ohio,*
*January 25, 1924*
*Ohio State University*
*1946–59, 1961–7 Cleveland*
*Browns*

When Lou Groza retired in 1968, it was truly the end of an unforgettable era for the Cleveland Browns. The last remaining member of the original 1946 Browns team, the big offensive tackle and placekicking artist played 21 years, more than any other pro player up to that time. He had been a major contributor to one of history's most remarkable gridiron dynasties.

Most fans remember Groza primarily as an exceptional kicker, the first specialist who became so proficient that the Browns started thinking of making field goals, instead of touchdowns, when the going was rough and time was running short.

Lou, however, prefers to think of himself first as a tackle who just happened to be the Browns' field-goal kicker because "I had the talent." It is true that he was one of pro football's finest offensive tackles, particularly in the middle years of his long tenure. Groza was named all-league six of the first eight years Cleveland was in the NFL. In 1954, he was the *Sporting News* NFL Player of the Year. He played in the Pro Bowl nine years. Six times he was a starting tackle.

In 1946, 33-man rosters prevented any team from carrying a specialist, but Groza was almost that, doing all of the kicking and playing on the scrimmage line only occasionally. Late in his second season, Lou made "the first team" and he didn't give up that cherished status until 1959. He sat out the entire 1960 season with a back injury and then returned in 1961 at the age of 37 for seven more campaigns as a kicker only.

Regardless of their abilities, offensive linemen rarely make the headlines so, whether he preferred it or not, a lion's share of Groza's fame was generated by his placekicking achievements. In 21 years, "The Toe," as he quickly became known, tallied 1608

points and for years ranked as the all-time top scorer. Starting in his rookie season, Lou gained attention not only because of his scoring totals but also because of the methods he employed on every attempt. Groza devised a 6-foot measuring tape, stretched from the spot where the ball would be held to the point where he would stand, to remind him of how many steps to take before kicking the football.

During his career, Groza played in three divisional championships and 13 All-America Football Conference or NFL title games. In those games, he scored every field goal and all but one extra point the Browns recorded. No kick was more dramatic than his 16-yard field goal with time running out that gave the Browns a 30–28 win in their first NFL championship game in 1950. It was Lou's most famous kick, arguably his most important and, by The Toe's own admission, "my biggest thrill in pro football."

*Lou Groza scored 1608 points and earned the nickname, "The Toe," because of his accurate placekicking talents. But he prefers to be remembered as an offensive tackle who was all-NFL six times.*

## SCORING RECORD

° Led AAFC
† Led NFL

| Year | TD | Extra points | Field goals | Total points |
|------|-----|------|------|------|
| 1946 | 0 | 45° | 13° | 84° |
| 1947 | 0 | 39 | 7 | 60 |
| 1948 | 0 | 51 | 8 | 75 |
| 1949 | 0 | 34 | 2 | 40 |
| 1950 | 1 | 29 | 13† | 74 |
| 1951 | 0 | 43† | 10 | 73 |
| 1952 | 0 | 32 | 19† | 89 |
| 1953 | 0 | 39 | 23† | 108 |
| 1954 | 0 | 37 | 16† | 85 |
| 1955 | 0 | 44† | 11 | 77† |
| 1956 | 0 | 18 | 11 | 51 |
| 1957 | 0 | 32 | 15† | 77 |
| 1958 | 0 | 36 | 8 | 60 |
| 1959 | 0 | 33 | 5 | 48 |
| 1960 | Injured—did not play | | | |
| 1961 | 0 | 37 | 16 | 85 |
| 1962 | 0 | 33 | 14 | 75 |
| 1963 | 0 | 40 | 15 | 85 |
| 1964 | 0 | 49 | 22 | 115 |
| 1965 | 0 | 45 | 16 | 93 |
| 1966 | 0 | 51 | 9 | 78 |
| 1967 | 0 | 43 | 11 | 76 |
| TOTALS | 1 | 810 | 264 | 1608 |

# DICK (NIGHT TRAIN) LANE

*Cornerback*
*6 ft 2 in, 210 lb*
*Born in Austin, Tex., April 16, 1928*
*Scottsbluff, Nebr., Junior College*
*1952–3 Los Angeles Rams; 1954–9 Chicago Cardinals; 1960–5 Detroit Lions*

Cardinals in 1954. Six years later, he was sent to Detroit where he enjoyed his finest years. Dick was all-NFL only in 1956 during his Cardinal days but, with the Lions, he won all-League honors four straight years. His only two Pro Bowl starts came as a Lion. With 68 career interceptions, Dick in 1969 was selected as the best cornerback in the first 50 years of the NFL.

Had he not found his post-Army job in an aircraft factory, lifting big sheets of oil-covered metal into bins, so totally unsatisfactory, Dick Lane almost certainly would never have played pro football.

Unhappy and depressed, Lane was out job-hunting—for any job, not necessarily a football one—when he chanced into the Los Angeles Rams office one day in 1952 to ask about a tryout. All he had for credentials was a battered scrapbook which chronicled his minimal experiences in high school, junior college and the Army. The defending-champion Rams were loaded at every position but coach Joe Stydahar saw just enough "good press" in the scrapbook to offer Lane a trial.

At first Dick was tried at offensive end but with future Hall of Famers Tom Fears and Crazylegs Hirsch set as first-teamers, his chances didn't look good. His brief offensive tenure did spawn the famous nickname that followed him through his career. Lane spent a great deal of time consulting with Fears, who was continually playing the hit record, "Night Train," on his phonograph. One day, a teammate entered the room, saw Dick and blurted out, "Hey, there's Night Train," and "Night Train Lane" it was from then on.

Once Stydahar moved Lane to defense, he quickly made an impression. Blessed with outstanding speed, exceptional agility and reflex action, plus a fierce determination to excel, Night Train set the NFL on fire as a rookie. He intercepted 14 passes in a 12-game schedule, a record that still stands. Besides being a constant threat to steal the pass, Lane also became known as a violent tackler. Almost all NFL secondary alignments were man-to-man during Lane's career and Dick was one of the very best.

As his career developed, Lane also became known as a gambler who was willing to take chances in spite of the risks. "Sure, Dick gets burned once in a while," Joe Schmidt, the Lions team captain, admitted. "But he comes up with the big play a lot of times, too. I'd say, percentage-wise, he's way ahead of the game."

Lane played two years with the Rams before being traded to the

### INTERCEPTION RECORD

| Year | Number | Yards | Average | TD |
|------|--------|-------|---------|-----|
| 1952° | 14§ | 298§ | 21.3 | 2§ |
| 1953° | 3 | 9 | 3.0 | 0 |
| 1954† | 10§ | 181§ | 18.1 | 0 |
| 1955† | 6 | 69 | 11.5 | 0 |
| 1956† | 7 | 206 | 29.4 | 1 |
| 1957† | 2 | 47 | 23.5 | 0 |
| 1958† | 2 | 0 | 0.0 | 0 |
| 1959† | 3 | 125 | 41.7 | 1§ |
| 1960‡ | 5 | 102 | 20.4 | 1 |
| 1961‡ | 6 | 73 | 12.2 | 0 |
| 1962‡ | 4 | 16 | 4.0 | 0 |
| 1963‡ | 5 | 70 | 14.0 | 0 |
| 1964‡ | 1 | 11 | 11.0 | 0 |
| 1965‡ | 0 | 0 | 0.0 | 0 |
| TOTALS | 68 | 1207 | 17.8 | 5 |

° With Los Angeles Rams

† With Chicago Cardinals

‡ With Detroit Lions

§ Led NFL

Punt returns: 4 returns, 14 yards, 3.5-yard average, 0 touchdowns

Receiving: 8 receptions, 253 yards, 31.6-yard average, 1 touchdown

Scoring: 7 touchdowns, 1 safety, 44 points

*Dick Lane joined the Los Angeles Rams as an unheralded free agent in 1952 and won the NFL interception title as a rookie. Besides being a gambling pass-stealer, he earned the reputation of being a violent tackler. He was all-NFL five times and played in six Pro Bowls.*

# ROOSEVELT BROWN

*Offensive tackle*
*6 ft 3 in, 255 lb*
*Born in Charlottesville, Va.,*
*October 20, 1932*
*Morgan State College*
*1953–65 New York Giants*

In the 27th round of the NFL's 1953 player draft, the New York Giants picked a 19-year-old black all-America tackle from little-known Morgan State College. His name was Roosevelt Brown. The Giants signed him to a $2700 contract and sent him a train ticket for the two-day trip to summer camp in Minnesota. His mother, not trusting "train food," packed him a box of fried chicken and potato salad for the journey. Brown arrived in camp dressed in a neat dark suit that had been his college graduation present. He was carrying a cardboard suitcase and an umbrella. Only a handful of rookies in all NFL history ever looked less like a football player.

"Rosey" didn't even know the proper stance for an offensive lineman. He also had the sociological problem of never having played with or against a white player, let alone under a white coach. But Brown did have the physical dimensions to play tackle. Giants coach Steve Owen felt anyone of his size deserved a "good look," which meant a scrimmage session against Arnie Wein-meister, the rugged all-pro defensive terror. Weinmeister battered Brown all over the field but Rosey stuck out the day and ran a few laps after practice. Owen was impressed.

Brown did have one big advantage—he had no fear of being cut. "I thought once they signed me that meant I had made the team," he explained. "The 1951 NFL championship game which I heard on radio was the extent of my pro football knowledge."

Within weeks, Rosey had won a starting offensive tackle job and he held it for 13 years until phlebitis forced his retirement after the 1965 season. Brown did all of the things a tackle is supposed to do and he did them superbly well. He was a classic pass blocker and, on running plays, he could make the blocks that opened gaping holes in the enemy ranks. He had the speed and mobility to get upfield on the long-gainers and to protect the quarterback when he began to scramble.

For eight straight years from 1956 through 1963, Brown was a virtually unanimous all-NFL choice. He was named to the Pro Bowl 10 straight seasons. In the Giants' 47–7 victory in the 1956 NFL championship, Rosey was named Lineman of the Game.

In spite of his many honors, Brown often lamented the comparatively obscure role of an offensive lineman. "There is self-satisfaction and we have to make that do," he said. "When the newspapers tell which back ran 50 yards but don't tell who made the blocks, that hurts. After all, he had to have blocks, he couldn't go far without them."

*Roosevelt Brown didn't even know he could be cut when he joined the New York Giants in 1953. He soon moved into a starting offensive tackle job, which he held for 13 years.*

# GEORGE CONNOR

*Tackle, linebacker*
*6 ft 3 in, 240 lb*
*Born in Chicago, Ill., January 21, 1925*
*Holy Cross University, Notre Dame University*
*1948–55 Chicago Bears*

When George Connor joined the Chicago Bears in 1948, he stood 6 ft 3 in, weighed 240 lb, had a 53-inch expanded chest measurement and a 37-inch waist. He was a hard core of solid muscle and, as the noted sports writer Grantland Rice once observed, "the closest thing to a Greek god since Apollo."

On the gridiron, George was among the very best. In college, he was all-America one year at Holy Cross and twice at Notre Dame. In eight years with the Bears, he was all-NFL at offensive tackle, defensive tackle and linebacker. In 1951 and 1952, he was named all-league on both offense and defense by different wire services.

While George was an outstanding tackle, he made his biggest mark in pro football as a linebacker, a position he inherited through sheer necessity in an emergency situation.

The Philadelphia Eagles were riding roughshod over the NFL in 1949. One play, an end sweep with two guards and a fullback leading Steve Van Buren, had caused particular damage. In strategy sessions before their game with the Eagles, the Bears coaching staff hit upon the idea of shifting a big, fast and mobile lineman like Connor into a linebacking spot. The experiment worked. George played a major role in blunting the Philadelphia attack and the Bears' 38–21 victory ruined an otherwise perfect season for the Eagles. From that moment on, the prototype for the ideal NFL linebacker had been established—he should be just like George Connor!

Wherever he played, Connor was regarded as one of the smartest of all NFL performers. He was a pioneer in the art of reading "keys." (Keys are football jargon for the tips that the movements of offensive players will provide for the alert defender so he can tell a split-second ahead of time the way a play is going.)

Like any Hall of Famer, Connor enjoyed many outstanding days in the NFL but perhaps his most dramatic display came in the 1952 Pro Bowl. With the opposition driving deep in his team's territory late in the game, George threw Dub Jones for a loss on first down, thwarted Eddie Price on the next play, sacked Otto Graham on third down and batted down Otto's fourth-down pass into the end zone to cancel the enemy threat.

When injuries forced Connor to retire before the 1956 season, the Bears' head man, George Halas, responded, "We set high standards for Connor as a player and he exceeded them. He parlayed leadership and intelligence and fine ability into one of the great careers of our time!"

*George Connor was an all-America at both Holy Cross and Notre Dame and, with the Chicago Bears, he was all-NFL at offensive tackle, defensive tackle and linebacker.*

# DANTE LAVELLI

*End*
*6 ft 0 in, 199 lb*
*Born in Hudson, Ohio,*
*February 23, 1923*
*Ohio State University*
*1946–56 Cleveland Browns*

crowd, you could be sure "Glue Fingers" would come down with the ball.

Through the 10 seasons they worked together, Graham was Lavelli's biggest fan. "We had a lot of great receivers on the Browns but, when it came to great hands, there was nobody like 'Old Spumoni.' As a competitor, he had few peers."

*Dante Lavelli had to beat out five experienced challengers when he joined the Cleveland Browns in 1946. Lavelli won a regular's job and, in the next 11 years, he caught 386 passes.*

When Dante Lavelli reported to the Cleveland Browns summer camp in 1946, he was faced with the problem of being an unheralded rookie on a squad loaded with some of the finest gridiron talent of the time. He was by far the least experienced of five players vying for the right end job on the new All-America Football Conference (AAFC) team. One candidate was a tested professional. Two were former college stars who had excelled on outstanding service teams. The fourth, John Yonaker, was a "can't-miss" 225-pounder from Notre Dame. Dante, on the other hand, had been a high-school quarterback, an Ohio State freshman halfback and had played end only three games in 1942 before leaving for Army service in World War II.

But after the 1946 summer skirmishing was over, the first three candidates had been cut, Yonaker had been moved to defense and Lavelli reigned supreme as the Browns' first-string right-side receiver. Dante quickly proved to coach Paul Brown that his decision had not been a mistake. He led the AAFC in receptions, made the all-league team and caught the winning touchdown pass in the first AAFC title game against the New York Yankees.

There were many more highlights in Lavelli's career. He was all-AAFC again in 1947 and, after the Browns joined the NFL in 1950, he was all-league two more years and a starter in three of the first five Pro Bowl games. In the 1950 NFL championship game, Dante caught 11 passes and scored two touchdowns as the Browns edged the Los Angeles Rams in a classic 30–28 struggle.

For a full decade, Lavelli was the favorite target of the Browns' great quarterback, Otto Graham. All but 20 of Dante's 386 career receptions came with Otto at the helm. Like any great pass-catch team, the two spent long hours learning the other's every habit.

Dante worked hard on his patterns but once there was even a hint things weren't going right, he would take off downfield and yell for the ball. More than once, Dante's penetrating voice provided a homing signal for Graham and the pair clicked for many long-gainers after a play had apparently been contained by the defense. Setting Lavelli apart from all other pass catchers were his great hands. When Dante went up for the football in a

RECEIVING RECORD                                    ° Led AAFC

| Year | Number | Yards | Average | TD |
|------|--------|-------|---------|-----|
| 1946 | 40° | 843° | 21.1 | 8 |
| 1947 | 49 | 799 | 16.3 | 9 |
| 1948 | 25 | 463 | 18.5 | 5 |
| 1949 | 28 | 475 | 17.0 | 7 |
| 1950 | 37 | 565 | 15.3 | 5 |
| 1951 | 43 | 586 | 13.6 | 6 |
| 1952 | 21 | 336 | 16.0 | 4 |
| 1953 | 45 | 783 | 17.4 | 6 |
| 1954 | 47 | 802 | 17.1 | 7 |
| 1955 | 31 | 492 | 15.9 | 4 |
| 1956 | 20 | 344 | 17.2 | 1 |
| TOTALS | 386 | 6488 | 16.8 | 62 |

# LENNY MOORE

*Flanker, running back*
*6 ft 1 in, 198 lb*
*Born in Reading, Pa.,*
*November 25, 1933*
*Pennsylvania State University*
*1956–67 Baltimore Colts*

As they pondered the 1956 player draft, the Baltimore Colts were aware of Lenny Moore's exceptional football ability but they were concerned that his long, sparse frame could not stand the pounding of pro football. Before making a choice, they decided to call the Penn State coach one more time. "Go tell Weeb Ewbank," Joe Paterno, then a Penn State assistant, commanded, "not to miss this guy because if he does, it will be the greatest mistake he could ever make."

So the Colts picked Lenny number 1 and, just as Paterno had predicted, it was a wise choice. He was the 1956 Rookie of the Year and, in his 12-year career, amassed some awesome credentials—12,449 combined net yards, 5174 yards rushing, 363 pass receptions, 678 points on 113 touchdowns.

When Moore first joined the Colts, he was used as a combination flanker–running back but his primary job was to catch passes. Lenny soon teamed with Johnny Unitas to form one of pro football's most lethal aerial combinations. Moore enjoyed his finest years in the late 1950s. In the Colts' drive to their first

championship in 1958, Moore was named all-NFL for the first time and contributed 1633 combined net yards and 14 touchdowns. In the championship game against the New York Giants, he grabbed six passes for 101 yards. One was a 60-yard blockbuster right at the start of the game.

Moore continued to average around 500 yards rushing and 40 to 50 catches a year until the Colts obtained another fine receiver, Jimmy Orr, in 1961. Determined to get more speed into the Colts' backfield, Ewbank moved Moore "inside" and inserted Orr into Lenny's old "outside" spot. Moore made the move gracefully but the transition was not an easy one. His pass reception yardage dropped drastically and his rushing average also went down. He took much more of a physical beating and injuries began to take their toll. In 1963, he played in only seven games.

But Lenny bounced back magnificently in 1964 and enjoyed his finest season ever. He twice played a major role in upsets of the champion Green Bay Packers. He scored at least one touchdown in a record 11 consecutive games and wound up with 20 touchdowns. For the fifth time, he was all-NFL. One wire service named him Comeback Player of the Year; another tabbed him NFL Player of the Year.

Accolades came often for Moore but his high-school coach, Andy Stopper, who presented him at his Hall of Fame enshrinement, perhaps summed it up best. "Lenny is so good that when you tell people how good he is, they think you are lying!"

*Lenny Moore, who excelled both as a running back and a wide receiver with the Baltimore Colts, breaks around right end and into the open field in action against the Minnesota Vikings.*

| RUSHING RECORD | | | | |
|---|---|---|---|---|
| Year | Attempts | Yards | Average | TD |
| 1956 | 86 | 649 | 7.5* | 8 |
| 1957 | 98 | 488 | 5.0* | 3 |
| 1958 | 82 | 598 | 7.3* | 7 |
| 1959 | 92 | 422 | 4.6 | 2 |
| 1960 | 91 | 374 | 4.1 | 4 |
| 1961 | 92 | 648 | 7.0* | 7 |
| 1962 | 106 | 470 | 4.4 | 2 |
| 1963 | 27 | 136 | 5.0 | 2 |
| 1964 | 157 | 584 | 3.7 | 16 |
| 1965 | 133 | 464 | 3.5 | 5 |
| 1966 | 63 | 209 | 3.3 | 3 |
| 1967 | 42 | 132 | 3.1 | 4 |
| TOTALS | 1069 | 5174 | 4.8 | 63 |

| RECEIVING RECORD | | | | |
|---|---|---|---|---|
| Year | Number | Yards | Average | TD |
| 1956 | 11 | 102 | 9.3 | 1 |
| 1957 | 40 | 687 | 17.2 | 7 |
| 1958 | 50 | 938 | 18.8 | 7 |
| 1959 | 47 | 846 | 18.0 | 6 |
| 1960 | 45 | 936 | 20.8 | 9 |
| 1961 | 49 | 728 | 14.9 | 2 |
| 1962 | 18 | 215 | 11.9 | 2 |
| 1963 | 21 | 288 | 13.7 | 2 |
| 1964 | 21 | 472 | 22.5 | 3 |
| 1965 | 27 | 414 | 15.3 | 3 |
| 1966 | 21 | 260 | 12.4 | 0 |
| 1967 | 13 | 153 | 11.8 | 0 |
| TOTALS | 363 | 6039 | 16.6 | 42 |

* Led NFL

Punt returns: 14 returns, 56 yards, 4.0-yard average, 0 touchdowns

Kickoff returns: 49 returns, 1180 yards, 24.1-yard average, 1 touchdown

Passing: 12 attempts, 3 completions, 33 yards, 2 touchdowns, 2 interceptions

Scoring: 113 touchdowns, 678 points

# RAY FLAHERTY

*Coach*
*Born in Spokane, Wash.,*
*September 1, 1904*
*Gonzaga University*
*1936 Boston Redskins; 1937–42*
*Washington Redskins; 1946–8*
*New York Yankees (AAFC); 1949*
*Chicago Hornets (AAFC)*

*Ray Flaherty enjoyed great success as a coach with the Redskins beginning in 1936. In seven seasons with the Redskins, he led his charges to four Eastern Division titles and two NFL championships.*

When coach Ray Flaherty learned the Boston Redskins had signed all-American end Wayne Millner for the 1936 season, he impulsively wired team owner George Preston Marshall: "Please accept my resignation if we do not win the championship." After nine years starring as an NFL player, Ray in his new role didn't realize that coaches normally avoid such rash predictions. The Redskins did not win in 1936 but neither did Flaherty resign.

Ray stayed with the Redskins, who moved to Washington in 1937, until his service call after the 1942 season. In seven years, his teams won two NFL titles and four divisional crowns. After his return to civilian life in 1946, Flaherty led the New York Yankees to two All-America Football Conference divisional championships. His .660 winning percentage based on an 82–41–5 record has been topped by only a handful of coaches.

The most feared team of the late 1930s and early 1940s was the Chicago Bears but in three showdowns in NFL title games, Flaherty's Redskins won twice. Ironically, the 73–0 Chicago win in 1940 is one of history's most remembered games.

Two Flaherty innovations helped the Redskins capture the two NFL championships. In 1937, Ray sensed the Bears would relentlessly pressure Washington's rookie quarterback, Sammy Baugh, so he devised the behind-the-line screen pass. Baugh threw three touchdown passes as the Redskins prevailed, 28–21.

Five years later, Flaherty developed a two-platoon system that created havoc for every NFL defense. Both platoons went two ways but one unit, with Baugh at the controls, featured the forward pass while the second eleven concentrated on a solid running game. Baugh's unit generated two touchdowns, the defense shut off the previously undefeated Bears and Washington won, 14–6. It was Flaherty's last game with the Redskins.

Ray has another distinction—he got along well with Marshall, who had a tendency to "help" with the gridiron masterminding. "I never had any trouble with Mr Marshall," Flaherty insisted. "He came down to the bench one day and I sent him back into the stands. He never came down again."

Under Flaherty's guidance, the Redskins enjoyed the finest years in the franchise's history. Marshall may not have appreciated Ray's insistence on one-man rule on the field, but it was impossible to argue with the results.

---

COACHING RECORD

| Year | Won | Lost | Tied | Division finish |
|------|-----|------|------|-----------------|
| 1936* | 7 | 5 | 0 | 1st |
| 1937† | 8 | 3 | 0 | 1st |
| 1938† | 6 | 3 | 2 | 2nd |
| 1939† | 8 | 2 | 1 | 2nd |
| 1940† | 9 | 2 | 0 | 1st |
| 1941† | 6 | 5 | 0 | 3rd |
| 1942† | 10 | 1 | 0 | 1st |
| 1943–5 | In US Navy | | | |
| 1946‡ | 10 | 3 | 1 | 1st |
| 1947‡ | 11 | 2 | 1 | 1st |
| 1948‡ | 1 | 3 | 0 | 3rd‖ |
| 1949§ | 4 | 8 | 0 | Tie 5th¶ |
| TOTALS** | 82 | 41 | 5 | |

* With Boston Redskins

† With Washington Redskins

‡ With New York Yankees (AAFC)

§ With Chicago Hornets (AAFC)

¶ AAFC had only one division in 1949

‖ Ray Flaherty was released after four games

** Career totals include post-season games

POST-SEASON RECORD

1936 NFL Championship: Green Bay 21, Boston Redskins 6
1937 NFL Championship: Washington 28, Chicago Bears 21
1940 NFL Championship: Chicago Bears 73, Washington 0
1942 NFL Championship: Washington 14, Chicago Bears 6
1946 AAFC Championship: Cleveland 14, New York Yankees 9
1947 AAFC Championship: Cleveland 14, New York Yankees 3

# LEN FORD

*Defensive end*
*6 ft 5 in, 260 lb*
*Born in Washington, DC,*
*February 18, 1926; died March 14,*
*1972, at age of 46*
*Morgan State College, University of*
*Michigan*
*1948–9 Los Angeles Dons (AAFC);*
*1950–7 Cleveland Browns; 1958*
*Green Bay Packers*

Len Ford joined the Los Angeles Dons of the All-America Football Conference (AAFC) in 1948 as a two-way end. He was excellent on defense and a favorite on offense with leaping, one-hand grabs that netted 67 receptions in two years. The Dons' coach, Jimmy Phelan, flatly predicted: "Len can become the greatest all-around end in history. He has everything—size, speed, strength and great hands." While Phelan's assessment proved to be accurate, Ford's pro football career did take a turn that Phelan could not have foreseen.

When the AAFC disbanded after the 1949 season, Ford was placed in a special draft pool. He was quickly grabbed by the Cleveland Browns, who earmarked him for their defensive platoon. It wasn't long before Ford was recognized as the very best of many stars on a unit that allowed the fewest points of any NFL team six of eight years in the 1950–7 period.

Ford developed into such a devastating pass rusher that the Browns changed their whole defensive alignment to take advantage of his rare talents. By using the linebackers behind the two ends and a pair of tackles, Cleveland in effect created the first 4–3 defense. This enabled Ford to line up closer to the ball-handling action and have a better shot at enemy quarterbacks.

Fate in the form of serious injury almost ended Ford's career in his first NFL season. When hit by the elbow of Cardinals fullback Par Harder, Ford suffered a broken nose, two fractured cheek bones and several lost teeth. Len was counted out for the season but plastic surgery, a strenuous rehabilitation program and the use of a specially designed helmet mask made it possible for Ford to return for the 1950 title game with the Los Angeles Rams. Many thought Len would make only a token appearance but he responded with one of his finest games to help Cleveland to a razor-thin 30–28 victory.

During the next five years, Ford was everyone's all-NFL pick each season. He also played in four Pro Bowls. Just as he had been on offense, Lenny was alert for the football, recovering 20 opponents' fumbles in nine NFL seasons. In the 1954 NFL championship game against Detroit, he intercepted two passes as the Browns buried the Lions, 56–10.

From the start, Ford won the respect of his teammates because of his constant all-out effort, even in practice. "Paul Brown used to say: 'You play like you practice.' Well, Lenny delighted in running over our guys," tackle–placekicker Lou Groza once remarked. "He was always hell-bent for leather any time he stepped on a football field."

RECEIVING RECORD

| Year | Number | Yards | Average | TD |
|---|---|---|---|---|
| 1948* | 31 | 598 | 19.3 | 7 |
| 1949* | 36 | 577 | 16.0 | 1 |
| TOTALS | 67 | 1175 | 17.5 | 8 |

* With Los Angeles Dons (AAFC)

*Note:* Ford played exclusively on defense with the Cleveland Browns and Green Bay Packers.

Opponents' fumbles: 20 recoveries, 79 return yards (all with Cleveland)

Interceptions: 3 interceptions, 45 yards (2 with Los Angeles)

*Len Ford played offensive end for the Los Angeles Dons in the All-America Football Conference. But when that league folded, he was quickly picked up by the Cleveland Browns, who made him into a defensive end.*

# JIM TAYLOR

*Fullback*
*6 ft 0 in, 216 lb*
*Born in Baton Rouge, La.,*
*September 20, 1935*
*Louisiana State University*
*1958–66 Green Bay Packers; 1967*
*New Orleans Saints*

When Vince Lombardi took over the Green Bay coaching reins in 1959, Jim Taylor, a rock-hard 216-lb fullback, quickly became the Packers' bread-and-butter guy, the man they looked to for 2 yards for a first down or a single foot at the goal line. As the Packers dynasty grew, so too did Taylor become the symbol of power in the awesome Green Bay attack. Jim was a throwback to the Bronko Nagurski era—he ran with a fierce belligerence no one could match. He caught the short swing passes. He blocked with rugged determination.

The Taylor sting that opponents felt so often came not only from his churning legs and lethal knees but from his free left arm as well. "I use it like this," Taylor demonstrated, while swinging his arm in a choppy, menacing arc. "They don't tackle real low so that arm helps. Maybe you'll get an extra yard or two. Over a season, that's maybe the difference between an 800-yard and a 1000-yard season."

Thousand-yard seasons became a specialty for Taylor, who was destined to become the first player from the Packers dynasty years to be elected to the Pro Football Hall of Fame. He went over 1000 yards five straight seasons beginning in 1960 but reached his zenith in 1962, when he had a career-high 1474 yards and was named the NFL Player of the Year by Associated Press.

Jim was living testimony to the popular football adage "When the going gets tough, the tough get going." Nowhere was this more evident than in the 1962 NFL title game. Playing on a bitter-cold day, Taylor engaged in a personal duel with the New York Giants' outstanding defense, led by all-pro linebacker Sam Huff.

Jim carried 31 times for 85 yards and scored Green Bay's only touchdown in a 16–7 victory. He took a fearful pounding both from the hard-hitting Giants and the frozen ground. He suffered an elbow gash that took seven stitches to close at halftime and a badly cut tongue. At the end, he could scarcely see and he couldn't talk.

"Taylor isn't human," Huff said admiringly. "No human could have withstood the punishment he got today. Every time he was tackled, he kept bouncing up, snarling at us and asking for more!"

Taylor was often compared with Jim Brown, the Cleveland fullback, who played at the same time. There were many different viewpoints but Lombardi's summation was most succinct. "Jim Brown will give you that leg and then take it away from you. Jim Taylor will give it to you and then ram it through your chest!"

*Jim Taylor circles left end for 14 yards and a go-ahead touchdown against the Kansas City Chiefs in Super Bowl I. Taylor was the power man in the Green Bay Packers' awesomely efficient offense.*

| RUSHING RECORD | | | | | RECEIVING RECORD | | | | |
|---|---|---|---|---|---|---|---|---|---|
| Year | Attempts | Yards | Average | TD | Year | Number | Yards | Average | TD |
| 1958° | 52 | 247 | 4.8 | 1 | 1958° | 4 | 72 | 18.0 | 1 |
| 1959° | 120 | 452 | 3.8 | 6 | 1959° | 9 | 71 | 7.9 | 2 |
| 1960° | 230 | 1101 | 4.8 | 11 | 1960° | 15 | 121 | 8.1 | 0 |
| 1961° | 243 | 1307 | 5.4 | 15 | 1961° | 25 | 175 | 7.0 | 1 |
| 1962° | 272 | 1474 | 5.4 | 19 | 1962° | 22 | 106 | 4.8 | 0 |
| 1963° | 248 | 1018 | 4.1 | 9 | 1963° | 13 | 68 | 5.2 | 1 |
| 1964° | 235 | 1169 | 5.0 | 12 | 1964° | 38 | 354 | 9.3 | 3 |
| 1965° | 207 | 734 | 3.5 | 4 | 1965° | 20 | 207 | 10.4 | 0 |
| 1966° | 204 | 705 | 3.5 | 4 | 1966° | 41 | 331 | 8.1 | 2 |
| 1967† | 130 | 390 | 3.0 | 2 | 1967† | 38 | 251 | 6.6 | 0 |
| TOTALS | 1941 | 8597 | 4.4 | 83 | TOTALS | 225 | 1756 | 7.8 | 10 |

° With Green Bay Packers

† With New Orleans Saints

Kickoff returns: 7 returns, 185 yards, 26.4-yard average, 0 touchdowns

Scoring: 93 touchdowns, 558 points

# FRANK GIFFORD

*Halfback, flanker*
*6 ft 1 in, 195 lb*
*Born in Santa Monica, Calif.,*
*August 16, 1930*
*University of Southern California*
*1952–60, 1962–4 New York Giants*

more dynamic role in the Giants' success than did Gifford.

As Giants' executive Jack Mara said, upon Frank's final retirement in 1964: "He gave dignity, tone and class to the entire organization. He was a standout even among stars!"

*Frank Gifford was a standout running back for the New York Giants from 1952 until he was seriously injured in 1960. He sat out a full year and then returned as a flanker in 1962.*

Frank Gifford excelled as a do-everything running back for the New York Giants until, late in his ninth season in 1960, he was felled by a vicious but clean blind-side tackle by the Eagles' great linebacker, Chuck Bednarik. Even though doctors gave him a green light to play again in 1961, he opted to retire.

After a year on the sidelines, Frank decided he wanted to return. In his "second career," Gifford became a flanker where, coach Allie Sherman reasoned, his exceptional receiving talents could be used to their full extent. The move to a new position, particularly after a year's layoff, was difficult but Frank eventually prevailed. He was the NFL Comeback Player of the Year in 1962 and enjoyed three excellent years as a wide receiver.

His return to the NFL may have been somewhat of an uphill struggle but his first nine campaigns with the Giants saw him start at the top and stay there. His only problem was that he was so versatile, the Giants wanted to play him all the time. In 1953, he was pressed into two-way service and even added punt return chores to his offensive and defensive duty. Even for someone of Gifford's stature, two-way service in the era of one-way specialists proved to be too much.

When Vince Lombardi took over the Giants offense in 1954, he immediately claimed Gifford for the exclusive use of his attack unit. "To me, Vince was the difference between my becoming a good pro football player or just another halfback," Gifford insists. "Anything I accomplished in this game, I owe to him. He was a very special man."

Once he settled down to one-unit play, Frank began setting the NFL on fire. He was the NFL Player of the Year in 1956, an all-NFL choice four years and he played in seven Pro Bowls, the first as a defensive back, the next five as an offensive halfback and the seventh as a flanker. No other Pro Bowl star has ever been selected at so many positions.

The Giants won six divisional championships in an eight-year period from 1956 to 1963 and were loaded with many of the great names of pro football. But year in and year out, no one played a

## RUSHING RECORD

| Year | Attempts | Yards | Average | TD |
|------|----------|-------|---------|-----|
| 1952 | 38 | 116 | 3.1 | 0 |
| 1953 | 50 | 157 | 3.1 | 2 |
| 1954 | 66 | 368 | 5.6 | 2 |
| 1955 | 86 | 351 | 4.1 | 3 |
| 1956 | 159 | 819 | 5.2 | 5 |
| 1957 | 136 | 528 | 3.9 | 5 |
| 1958 | 115 | 468 | 4.1 | 8 |
| 1959 | 106 | 540 | 5.1 | 3 |
| 1960 | 77 | 232 | 3.0 | 4 |
| 1961 | Retired—did not play | | | |
| 1962 | 2 | 18 | 9.0 | 1 |
| 1963 | 4 | 10 | 2.5 | 0 |
| 1964 | 1 | 2 | 2.0 | 1 |
| TOTALS | 840 | 3609 | 4.3 | 34 |

## RECEIVING RECORD

| Year | Number | Yards | Average | TD |
|------|--------|-------|---------|-----|
| 1952 | 5 | 36 | 7.2 | 0 |
| 1953 | 18 | 292 | 16.2 | 4 |
| 1954 | 14 | 154 | 11.0 | 1 |
| 1955 | 33 | 437 | 13.2 | 4 |
| 1956 | 51 | 603 | 11.8 | 4 |
| 1957 | 41 | 588 | 14.3 | 4 |
| 1958 | 29 | 330 | 11.4 | 2 |
| 1959 | 42 | 768 | 18.3 | 4 |
| 1960 | 24 | 344 | 14.3 | 3 |
| 1961 | Retired—did not play | | | |
| 1962 | 39 | 796 | 20.4 | 7 |
| 1963 | 42 | 657 | 15.6 | 7 |
| 1964 | 29 | 429 | 14.8 | 3 |
| TOTALS | 367 | 5434 | 14.8 | 43 |

Passing: 63 attempts, 29 completions, 823 yards, 14 touchdowns, 6 interceptions

Punt returns: 24 returns, 118 yards, 4.9-yard average, 0 touchdowns

Kickoff returns: 18 returns, 480 yards, 26.7-yard average, 0 touchdowns

Interceptions: 2 interceptions, 112 yards, 56.0-yard average, 1 touchdown

Scoring: 78 touchdowns, 484 points

# FORREST GREGG

*Offensive tackle, guard*
*6 ft 4 in, 250 lb*
*Born in Birthright, Tex.,*
*October 18, 1933*
*Southern Methodist University*
*1956, 1958–70 Green Bay*
*Packers; 1971 Dallas Cowboys*

Forrest Gregg was respected as one of the most capable and unselfish of all pro football players during his 15 NFL seasons. When he joined the Green Bay Packers in 1956, he wanted to try out for the defensive line but coach Lisle Blackbourn assigned him to offensive tackle, a position Forrest was too small to play by 1956 NFL standards.

Yet Gregg went right to work, not only developing his physical abilities but spending countless hours watching films of the NFL's finest offensive tackles to see how they did their jobs. Forrest knew he could not overpower the monstrous defensive ends he would face so he learned the moves of every opponent and plotted the ways he could finesse them into submission.

In 1961 and again in 1965, when injuries created a crisis on the Packers offensive line, Forrest willingly switched to guard to fill the void. There he had to learn a completely new set of assignments and techniques and acquaint himself with a new group of opponents, the defensive tackles of pro football.

Many thought switching positions would endanger the string of eight straight years beginning in 1960 in which Gregg won all-NFL honors. But it did not. In 1965, Forrest was named as an all-league tackle by one major wire service and as an all-NFL guard by the other! His string of nine straight Pro Bowl appearances also was unaffected by his change in jobs.

As eager as Forrest was to play football—he saw service in a then-record 188 straight games from 1956 until 1971—he actually retired four times before making his fifth retirement stick. He first quit after the 1963 campaign to accept a coaching job at the University of Tennessee. Vince Lombardi couldn't believe anyone as good as Gregg should quit at the age of 30 so he coaxed him back. Gregg started both the 1969 and 1970 seasons as a Packers coach but injury problems each year prompted him to return to the active roster. He retired a fourth time before the 1971 season but was lured back by the Dallas Cowboys when coach Tom Landry issued an SOS for help for an injury-decimated line. After winning his third Super Bowl championship ring in Super Bowl VI, Forrest, at the age of 38, retired for good.

He ended his career knowing that Lombardi, the architect of the Green Bay juggernauts of which Forrest was such an important member, had paid him the highest compliment. In his book, *Run to Daylight*, Vince had written: "Forrest Gregg is the finest player I ever coached!"

*Forrest Gregg was primarily an offensive tackle who played guard in emergencies during the Packers' dynasty years.*

# GALE SAYERS

*Halfback*
*6 ft 0 in, 200 lb*
*Born in Wichita, Kans., May 30,*
*1943*
*University of Kansas*
*1965–71 Chicago Bears*

Like a twisting tornado on the Kansas plains whence he came, the Chicago Bears' Gale Sayers swirled on to the NFL scene in 1965, wreaking havoc and destruction on every opposition defense that stood in his way. The fluid, will-of-the-wisp ball-carrying thrusts of the mercurial Sayers dazzled the pro football world in a manner it had rarely, if ever, experienced in its long history.

There is no telling what heights "The Kansas Comet" might have attained had not fate stepped in to neutralize the flashing feet that no defense could adequately contain. A right knee injury in 1968 was a foreboding of things to come, although Gale underwent a tortuous rehabilitation program and bounced back in 1969 for his second 1000-yard rushing season. A left knee injury sustained in 1970 effectively put a stop to the glittering career after just four-and-one-half seasons.

Incredibly, more than a few pro scouts questioned whether Sayers could make it in the pros. Everyone recognized the Kansas all-American's natural abilities but some doubted the speedster could withstand the pounding he was sure to face in the NFL. Bears coach George Halas didn't share that concern but he did opt to bring his prize rookie along slowly as a confidence-building measure.

Once Sayers got into heavy action, it was the opposition that faced a confidence crisis. Whether he was rushing, receiving, or returning punts and kickoffs, Gale immediately displayed the rocket-like form that soon was to shake up the entire pro football world.

In his first pre-season game against the Rams, Sayers raced 77 yards on a punt return, 93 yards on a kickoff return, and then startled everyone with a 25-yard, left-handed scoring pass.

Midway into his rookie year, he scored four touchdowns, one coming on a 96-yard kickoff return, against Minnesota. Later that year, he tallied a record-tying six touchdowns against San Francisco. In his sensational début season, he amassed 2272 combined net yards and scored a record 22 touchdowns.

Sayers continued to stagger Bears' foes with sizzling performances until the fateful day in 1968 when he was hurt for the first time. Ironically, the "beginning of the end" for Gale came in a game against the 49ers, the team he had ravaged with his 36-point outburst as a rookie.

At 34, Sayers was the youngest player ever elected to the Pro Football Hall of Fame. His term of effective playing time is also the shortest of any Hall of Famer. Those facts stand out as two very strong testimonials to the gridiron greatness that came—and left—so quickly for Gale Sayers.

*For five dazzling seasons, Gale Sayers streaked through enemy defenses with a kind of lethal efficiency rarely, if ever, seen on NFL gridirons. He rushed for more than 1000 yards in 1966 and 1969.*

### RUSHING RECORD

| Year | Attempts | Yards | Average | TD |
|------|----------|-------|---------|-----|
| 1965 | 166 | 867 | 5.2 | 14 |
| 1966 | 229 | 1231° | 5.4 | 8 |
| 1967 | 186 | 880 | 4.7 | 7 |
| 1968 | 138 | 856 | 6.2° | 2 |
| 1969 | 236° | 1032° | 4.4 | 8 |
| 1970 | 23 | 52 | 2.3 | 0 |
| 1971 | 13 | 38 | 2.9 | 0 |
| TOTALS | 991 | 4956 | 5.0 | 39 |

° Led NFL

Passing: 18 attempts, 4 completions, 111 yards, 1 touchdown, 0 interceptions

Scoring: 56 touchdowns, 336 points

### RECEIVING RECORD

| Year | Number | Yards | Average | TD |
|------|--------|-------|---------|-----|
| 1965 | 29 | 507 | 17.5 | 6 |
| 1966 | 34 | 447 | 13.1 | 2 |
| 1967 | 16 | 126 | 7.9 | 1 |
| 1968 | 15 | 117 | 7.8 | 0 |
| 1969 | 17 | 116 | 6.8 | 0 |
| 1970 | 1 | −6 | −6.0 | 0 |
| 1971 | 0 | 0 | 0.0 | 0 |
| TOTALS | 112 | 1307 | 11.7 | 9 |

### PUNT RETURN RECORD

| Year | Number | Yards | Average | TD |
|------|--------|-------|---------|-----|
| 1965 | 16 | 238 | 14.9 | 1 |
| 1966 | 6 | 44 | 7.3 | 0 |
| 1967 | 3 | 80 | 26.7 | 1° |
| 1968 | 2 | 29 | 14.5 | 0 |
| 1969 | 1 | 0 | 0.0 | 0 |
| 1970 | 0 | 0 | 0.0 | 0 |
| 1971 | 0 | 0 | 0.0 | 0 |
| TOTALS | 28 | 391 | 14.0 | 2 |

### KICKOFF RETURN RECORD

| Year | Number | Yards | Average | TD |
|------|--------|-------|---------|-----|
| 1965 | 21 | 660 | 31.4 | 1° |
| 1966 | 23 | 718 | 31.2° | 2° |
| 1967 | 16 | 603 | 37.7 | 3 |
| 1968 | 17 | 461 | 27.1 | 0 |
| 1969 | 14 | 339 | 24.2 | 0 |
| 1970 | 0 | 0 | 0.0 | 0 |
| 1971 | 0 | 0 | 0.0 | 0 |
| TOTALS | 91 | 2781 | 30.6 | 6 |

# BART STARR

*Quarterback*
*6 ft 1 in, 200 lb*
*Born in Montgomery, Ala.,*
*January 9, 1934*
*University of Alabama*
*1956–71 Green Bay Packers*

*In spite of a host of great stars on the Green Bay Packers roster, coach Vince Lombardi insisted his quarterback, Bart Starr, was by far the most valuable player on the team.*

Bart Starr was a 17th-round draft choice of the Green Bay Packers in 1956. Three years later, his playing time was still limited and his football future appeared in doubt. That is when Vince Lombardi took over as the Packers coach.

Many of the new coach's advisors felt that Starr could not help the team but Lombardi, after tireless study of films, found that he liked Bart's mechanics, his arm, his ball-handling technique and, most of all, his great intelligence. The one thing Starr did lack at the time was confidence.

Under Vince's careful nurturing, the Alabama native soon developed the poise he needed to become one of the NFL's great field leaders. In the 1960–7 span, Bart's "won-lost record" was a sizzling 82–24–4 and the Packers won six division, five NFL and the first two Super Bowl championships.

Strangely, for several years, Bart received only minimal fanfare while his more publicized teammates captured the headlines. Maybe this was because Starr, as the ideal leader of Lombardi's balanced precision attack, made it all look so easy. Perhaps it was because some felt, with Green Bay's great array of talent, any quarterback could be successful.

But knowledgeable football men knew who was making the Packers click. As one rival coach said: "I wish there were a way to ban Bart Starr from the games he plays against us. For his team, he is the perfect quarterback."

Because it was a ball-control attack that he led, Starr's passes were limited—remarkably, he never threw as many as 300 passes in any one season. This may have helped to create the illusion he was only an average passer. The records, however, do not bear this out. His career interception avoidance was a superbly low 4.4 percent. Bart led the league in passing three times, was the NFL's Player of the Year in 1966 and the Most Valuable Player in both Super Bowls I and II.

Starr became particularly adept at audibles, the art of changing his calls at the line of scrimmage after he had seen the defensive alignment. Playing a cat-and-mouse game with the enemy, pitting his instant skill against theirs, he changed his call almost 50 percent of the time.

Coach Lombardi was once asked what a quarterback meant to an NFL team. His answer was crisp and to the point—"Everything." Even for the Green Bay powerhouses loaded with sensational stars, that summation still applied. Bart Starr was the guy who put it all together. For the Packers of the 1960s, he was "everything!"

---

**PASSING RECORD**

| Year | Attempts | Completions | Percentage passes completed | Yards | TD | Interceptions |
|------|----------|-------------|-----------------------------|-------|-----|---------------|
| 1956 | 44 | 24 | 54.5 | 325 | 2 | 3 |
| 1957 | 215 | 117 | 54.4 | 1489 | 8 | 10 |
| 1958 | 157 | 78 | 49.7 | 875 | 3 | 12 |
| 1959 | 134 | 70 | 52.2 | 972 | 6 | 7 |
| 1960 | 172 | 98 | 57.0 | 1358 | 4 | 8 |
| 1961 | 295 | 172 | 58.3 | 2418 | 16 | 16 |
| 1962† | 285 | 178 | 62.5° | 2438 | 12 | 9 |
| 1963 | 244 | 132 | 54.1 | 1855 | 15 | 10 |
| 1964† | 272 | 163 | 59.9 | 2144 | 15 | 4 |
| 1965 | 251 | 140 | 55.8 | 2055 | 16 | 9 |
| 1966† | 251 | 156 | 62.2° | 2257 | 14 | 3 |
| 1967 | 210 | 115 | 54.8 | 1823 | 9 | 17 |
| 1968 | 171 | 109 | 63.7° | 1617 | 15 | 8 |
| 1969 | 148 | 92 | 62.2° | 1161 | 9 | 6 |
| 1970 | 255 | 140 | 54.9 | 1645 | 8 | 13 |
| 1971 | 45 | 24 | 53.3 | 286 | 0 | 3 |
| TOTALS | 3149 | 1808 | 57.4 | 24,718 | 152 | 138 |

Career passing rating: 80.5

° Led NFL

† Official NFL individual passing champion

Rushing: 247 attempts, 1308 yards, 5.3-yard average, 15 touchdowns

Scoring: 15 touchdowns, 90 points

# BILL WILLIS

*Middle guard*
*6 ft 2 in. 215 lb*
*Born in Columbus, Ohio.*
*October 5, 1921*
*Ohio State University*
*1946–53 Cleveland Browns*

When Bill Willis first reported to the Cleveland Browns' summer camp in 1946, the fact that he was black undoubtedly aroused more attention than the possibility a potential superstar was joining the new All-America Football Conference (AAFC) team. Ever since the early 1930s, by accident or design, there were no black players in pro football. Bill also was the smallest of the linemen candidates in camp.

Willis quickly erased any doubts he could make the grade. In his first scrimmage, he was stationed across the line from veteran center Moe Scarry. On four straight plays, Bill charged at the instant of the snap, flattened or eluded Scarry and crashed into the quarterback. Scarry protested that no one could react that quickly, that Willis had to be offside. Coach Paul Brown watched a few more plays to be certain everything his new recruit did was legal. After practice, Brown signed Willis to a $4000 contract.

Actually, Willis' appearance in camp was not a surprise to Brown. Bill had played on Brown's 1942 national championship Ohio State team and had written his old coach for a tryout when he heard of the new Cleveland team. Paul assured Willis there was no reason why a black couldn't play in the AAFC but preferred to treat Willis as a drop-in candidate so he waited for two weeks after camp opened before relaying the word to Bill it was time to report.

At first, Willis played both offense and defense but it was as a defensive middle guard that Bill won lasting acclaim. Lightning quickness was his constant trademark but opponents remember he was capable of a solid forearm or a devastating tackle as well. In seven of his eight pro seasons, he was all-league, three times in the AAFC and four years in the NFL. He also played in the first three NFL Pro Bowl games.

In a 1950 playoff game against the New York Giants, Willis had to outrun a Giants halfback who had broken into the open well ahead of the pack to make a game-saving tackle. The ball-carrier, "Choo-Choo" Roberts, ran 44 yards before Bill overtook him at the Cleveland 3-yard line. The Browns went on to win the championship in their first NFL season.

The Browns' press book once boasted that photographers had to shoot Bill at 1/600th of a second to stop the action. At least the photographers did stop him—which opponents rarely did!

*The first black to be signed in the All-America Football Conference, Bill Willis played first as a two-way lineman but eventually settled on the defensive middle guard position.*

# LANCE ALWORTH

*Wide receiver*
*6 ft 0 in, 184 lb*
*Born in Houston, Tex., August 3,*
*1940*
*University of Arkansas*
*1962–70 San Diego Chargers;*
*1971–2 Dallas Cowboys*

Charley Hennigan, himself a record-setting receiver with the Houston Oilers, was particularly strong in his praise. "A player comes along once in a lifetime who alone is worth the price of admission. Lance Alworth was that player."

He was known as "Bambi," the smooth and graceful fawn bounding free and easy among the behemoths of pro football. He was the shining star of the San Diego Chargers, flashing that 9.6 speed, the high jumper's spring and those eager, grasping hands that spelled sudden disaster for even the best-prepared opponent. He was Lance Alworth, the premier pass-catcher of an entire decade and the first superstar from the American Football League (AFL) to enter the Pro Football Hall of Fame.

Alworth's accomplishments are legendary. His 542 career receptions netted 85 touchdowns. He caught at least one pass in every one of the 96 AFL games in which he played. He was all-AFL seven years, a seven-time AFL All-Star game pick and a unanimous choice for the all-time AFL honor eleven. More than any other player, Lance epitomized the glamorous, deadly effective approach to pro football the Chargers exhibited in the 1960s.

To Al Davis, the Chargers assistant coach who foiled the rival NFL by signing Alworth to a $30,000 contract just prior to the 1962 Sugar Bowl game in New Orleans, these rare deeds came as no surprise. "Lance was one of maybe three players in my lifetime who had what I would call 'it'," he recalls. "You could see right away he was going to be special."

Although he was a halfback in college, Lance was considered too small to be a pro running back so he was ticketed for the flanker spot in Sid Gillman's pass-oriented attack. His rookie season, though, was a disappointment because of a freak injury which caused him to miss 10 games but a nine-catch performance against Kansas City early in the 1963 season launched Alworth on his trip to a special niche in history.

In spite of his first-year injury, Lance proved to be an extremely durable player. Although he took a constant pounding from the AFL's desperate defensive platoons, he missed only seven games the remainder of his nine-year stay in San Diego. And he did play hurt. For example, in 1966, he caught 37 passes in a seven-game span even though both arms were in casts because of wrist and hand injuries.

Accolades poured in from every imaginable source when Alworth retired after the 1972 season with the Dallas Cowboys.

| RECEIVING RECORD | | | | |
|---|---|---|---|---|
| Year | Number | Yards | Average | TD |
| 1962° | 10 | 226 | 22.6 | 3 |
| 1963° | 61 | 1205 | 19.8‡ | 11 |
| 1964° | 61 | 1235 | 20.2 | 13‡ |
| 1965° | 69 | 1602‡ | 23.2‡ | 14‡ |
| 1966° | 73‡ | 1383‡ | 18.9 | 13‡ |
| 1967° | 52 | 1010 | 19.4 | 9 |
| 1968° | 68‡ | 1312‡ | 19.3 | 10 |
| 1969° | 64‡ | 1003 | 15.7 | 4 |
| 1970° | 35 | 608 | 17.4 | 4 |
| 1971† | 34 | 487 | 14.3 | 2 |
| 1972† | 15 | 195 | 13.0 | 2 |
| TOTALS | 542 | 10,266 | 18.9 | 85 |

° With San Diego Chargers

† With Dallas Cowboys

‡ Led AFL

Rushing: 24 attempts, 129 yards, 5.4-yard average,
  2 touchdowns

Punt returns: 29 returns, 309 yards, 10.7-yard average,
  0 touchdowns

Kickoff returns: 10 returns, 216 yards, 21.6-yard
  average, 0 touchdowns

Scoring: 87 touchdowns, 524 points

*The first star from the American Football League to be elected to the Pro Football Hall of Fame, Lance Alworth caught at least one pass in every one of his 96 AFL games.*

# WEEB EWBANK

*Coach*
*Born in Richmond, Ind., May 6,*
*1907*
*Miami (Ohio) University*
*1954–62 Baltimore Colts;*
*1963–73 New York Jets*

I n his 20 years as coach of the Baltimore Colts and the New York Jets, Weeb Ewbank made a unique impact on pro football. Most often mentioned is his distinction as the only coach to win championships in both the National and American Football Leagues. His Colts won NFL crowns in 1958 and 1959, and the 1968 Jets followed up their AFL title with a victory in Super Bowl III.

More important than who won or lost is the role these two games played in making pro football the universally popular sport it is today. The Colts' 23–17 overtime win over the New York Giants in 1958 was showcased before millions of television viewers. The dramatic battle is remembered by many as "the greatest game ever played." A decade later, the Jets were pitted against Weeb's first team, the Colts. The stunning 16–7 upset, more than any other factor, assured the competitive viability of the Super Bowl series.

Ewbank's coaching ledger is an unimpressive 134–130–7 but, by discounting his first three building years in both Baltimore and New York, his records become a more respectable and realistic 102–83–3.

With both the Colts and Jets, Weeb inherited young, disorganized teams. With each club, he instituted a patented building program that paid dividends. In both places, Weeb's offenses were destined to center around young and talented quarterbacks, Johnny Unitas in Baltimore and Joe Namath with the Jets. In each situation, Weeb skillfully groomed his prized field leader toward superstardom.

By any yardstick, Ewbank was not a strict coach. He instead developed a reputation for the understanding and realistic way he handled his players. He never screamed at his teams nor did he allow his assistants to do so. He was determined that every player would get a fair chance to make the team. Weeb also learned to adjust to the changing lifestyles of athletes as the disciplined, conservative attitudes of the 1960s evolved into the more liberated modes of the next decade. Training rules and dress codes that would have been enforced on the 1954 Colts were put aside in Ewbank's dealings with the "mod-age" Jets.

When Weeb retired after the 1973 season, Jets center John Schmitt echoed the sentiments of dozens of his former players. "Weeb Ewbank treated us like men and I appreciate that."

*Weeb Ewbank is the only coach to win championships in both the American and National Football Leagues. In 1958, his Baltimore Colts won the NFL title in what many call "the greatest game ever played." A decade later, he led the New York Jets to a stunning 16–7 upset of the Colts in Super Bowl III.*

## COACHING RECORD

| Year | Won | Lost | Tied | Division finish |
|------|-----|------|------|-----------------|
| 1954° | 3 | 9 | 0 | 6th |
| 1955° | 5 | 6 | 1 | 4th |
| 1956° | 5 | 7 | 0 | 4th |
| 1957° | 7 | 5 | 0 | 3rd |
| 1958° | 9 | 3 | 0 | 1st |
| 1959° | 9 | 3 | 0 | 1st |
| 1960° | 6 | 6 | 0 | 4th |
| 1961° | 8 | 6 | 0 | 3rd |
| 1962° | 7 | 7 | 0 | 4th |
| 1963† | 5 | 8 | 1 | 4th |
| 1964† | 5 | 8 | 1 | 3rd |
| 1965† | 5 | 8 | 1 | 2nd |
| 1966† | 6 | 6 | 2 | 3rd |
| 1967† | 8 | 5 | 1 | 2nd |
| 1968† | 11 | 3 | 0 | 1st |
| 1969† | 10 | 4 | 0 | 1st |
| 1970† | 4 | 10 | 0 | 3rd |
| 1971† | 6 | 8 | 0 | 3rd |
| 1972† | 7 | 7 | 0 | 2nd |
| 1973† | 4 | 10 | 0 | 4th |
| TOTALS‡ | 134 | 130 | 7 | |

## POST-SEASON RECORD

1958 NFL Championship: Baltimore 23, New York Giants 17 (overtime)
1959 NFL Championship: Baltimore 31, New York Giants 16
1968 AFL Championship: New York Jets 27, Oakland 23
Super Bowl III: New York Jets 16, Baltimore 7
1969 AFL Divisional Championship: Kansas City 13, New York Jets 6

° With Baltimore Colts

† With New York Jets

‡ Career totals include post-season games

# ALPHONSE (TUFFY) LEEMANS

**Halfback, fullback**
**6 ft 0 in, 200 lb**
**Born in Superior, Wisc.,**
**November 12, 1912; died**
**January 19, 1979, at age of 66**
**University of Oregon, George**
**Washington University**
**1936–43 New York Giants**

Alphonse Emil Leemans—for understandable reasons, he preferred his nickname, "Tuffy"—was a one-man show during his college days at George Washington University. Yet it is doubtful the pros would have been knocking on his door, had it not been for a high-school lad on vacation who caught a terrific Leemans performance against Alabama one autumn. The young man was Wellington Mara, son of the New York Giants president, who reported back to his father that Tuffy was a prospect their team must have. The father listened and Leemans became the Giants' second-round pick in the NFL's first-ever draft in 1936.

Leemans began his post-graduate career by winning Most Valuable Player honors in the College All-Star game. Tuffy had been elected to the all-star squad because of the skullduggery of a Washington sports writer. The scribe reasoned the game sponsor would weigh the thousands of votes that came in for any one player so he wrapped legitimate ballots around bales of hay to assure Leemans' success in the nationwide fan balloting.

Tuffy carried his fast pace from the College All-Star game right into the pro ranks. He led the NFL in rushing as a rookie and was the only first-year man to make the official all-league team. Maybe more than any other player, Leemans for the next seven years was responsible for his team's success at a time when the Giants were perennial contenders. During the "Leeman years," they won three divisional titles and the 1938 NFL championship.

Considering the era in which he played, Tuffy's career statistics were impressive. They are made even more so by two special considerations. One is that Tuffy, who played both halfback and fullback, also passed and caught passes in addition to his ball-carrying duties. A second factor is the Giants of that era utilized a two-platoon alignment that saw equal units divide playing time both on the offensive and defensive teams.

Tuffy played before the years of big salaries. He earned $3500 in his rookie season and reached a top figure of $12,000 as a player–coach in 1943. He didn't even have a shot at the big bonuses available to today's players on winning teams. For instance, his share of the players' pool for the 1941 NFL title game was a mere $288. But Leemans never complained. "I just loved the game," Tuffy insisted. "I know a lot of players back then, myself included, who would have played for nothing."

*Fullback "Tuffy" Leemans slashes 6 yards for the first touchdown in the New York Giants' 23–17 victory over the Green Bay Packers in the 1938 NFL championship game.*

---

**RUSHING RECORD**

| Year | Attempts | Yards | Average | TD |
|------|----------|-------|---------|-----|
| 1936 | 206* | 830* | 4.0 | 2 |
| 1937 | 144 | 429 | 3.0 | 0 |
| 1938 | 121 | 463 | 3.8 | 4 |
| 1939 | 128 | 429 | 3.4 | 3 |
| 1940 | 132 | 474 | 3.6 | 1 |
| 1941 | 100 | 332 | 3.3 | 4 |
| 1942 | 51 | 116 | 2.3 | 3 |
| 1943 | 37 | 69 | 1.9 | 0 |
| TOTALS | 919 | 3142 | 3.4 | 17 |

* Led NFL

**PASSING RECORD**

| Year | Attempts | Completions | Percentage passes completed | Yards | TD | Interceptions |
|------|----------|-------------|------------------------------|-------|-----|---------------|
| 1936 | 42 | 13 | 31.0 | 258 | 3 | 6 |
| 1937 | 20 | 5 | 25.0 | 64 | 1 | 1 |
| 1938 | 42 | 19 | 45.2 | 249 | 3 | 6 |
| 1939 | 26 | 12 | 46.2 | 198 | 0 | 2 |
| 1940 | 31 | 15 | 48.4 | 159 | 2 | 3 |
| 1941 | 66 | 31 | 47.0 | 475 | 4 | 5 |
| 1942 | 69 | 35 | 50.7 | 555 | 7 | 4 |
| 1943 | 87 | 37 | 42.5 | 366 | 5 | 5 |
| TOTALS | 383 | 167 | 43.6 | 2324 | 25 | 32 |

Receiving: 28 receptions, 422 yards, 15.1-yard average, 3 touchdowns

Punt returns: 19 returns, 262 yards, 13.8-yard average, 0 touchdowns

Interceptions: 3 interceptions, 35 yards, 11.7-yard average, 0 touchdowns

Scoring: 20 touchdowns, 120 points

# RAY NITSCHKE

*Middle linebacker*
*6 ft 3 in, 235 lb*
*Born in Elmwood Park, Ill.,*
*December 29, 1936*
*University of Illinois*
*1958–72 Green Bay Packers*

The Packers evolved into the scourge of pro football and Nitschke established himself as one of the key members of the team, treasuring the reputation he earned as one of the hardest-hitting of all pro football players. "You want them to respect you when they run a play," Ray explained. "You want them to remember that you are there!"

*Ray Nitschke was a fierce tackler, cat-like on pass defense and the heart of the oustanding defensive unit of the Green Bay Packers during their "dynasty years."*

During their dynasty years of the early 1960s, the Green Bay Packers had Ray Nitschke at the heart of their defense. A ferocious middle linebacker, he epitomized the hard-hitting tenacity and the cool professionalism of those talented Packers teams. In the mid-1960s, a national sports magazine asked a group of former NFL linebackers to rate the middle linebackers of the day. The panel first determined the skills it would seek in the ideal man—strength, quick reactions, speed, toughness and leadership. Nitschke, the choice as the all-around top man, ranked very high or absolutely top in every category.

On the field, Ray was a savage but clean-playing performer. Wrapped in tape to hide his numerous injuries and his uniform spotted with blood, Nitschke would blast through a cordon of blockers to find the ball-carrier and bring him crashing to the ground. He was cat-like on pass defense as well, as his 25 lifetime interceptions attest.

Off the field, Ray belied the fearsome image he portrayed during a game. In his dark horn-rimmed glasses and traditional business suit, he was thoughtful, intelligent, truly soft-hearted and considerate.

Ray overcame a great deal of adversity to become a success in football and in life. His father was killed when he was 3 and his mother died when he was 13. He was adopted and raised by an older brother.

"I grew up belting other kids in the neighborhood," Ray candidly admits. "My brother was wonderful to me but I never really had any discipline. I felt I was somebody who didn't have anything and I took it out on everybody else."

Athletics provided Nitschke a more viable outlet for self-expression. Ray was an all-state quarterback who could also have played professional baseball. He opted for a football scholarship at the University of Illinois. There he was shifted to the dual role of fullback on offense and linebacker on defense. The Packers eyed him as a middle linebacker when they drafted him in 1958.

## INTERCEPTION RECORD

Kickoff returns: 4 returns, 40 yards, 10.0-yard average, 0 touchdowns

| Year | Number | Yards | Average | TD |
|------|--------|-------|---------|-----|
| 1958 | 1 | 2 | 2.0 | 0 |
| 1959 | 0 | 0 | 0.0 | 0 |
| 1960 | 3 | 90 | 30.0 | 1 |
| 1961 | 2 | 41 | 20.5 | 0 |
| 1962 | 4 | 56 | 14.0 | 0 |
| 1963 | 2 | 8 | 4.0 | 0 |
| 1964 | 2 | 36 | 18.0 | 0 |
| 1965 | 1 | 21 | 21.0 | 0 |
| 1966 | 2 | 44 | 22.0 | 0 |
| 1967 | 3 | 35 | 11.7 | 1 |
| 1968 | 2 | 20 | 10.0 | 0 |
| 1969 | 2 | 32 | 16.0 | 0 |
| 1970 | 0 | 0 | 0.0 | 0 |
| 1971 | 1 | 0 | 0.0 | 0 |
| 1972 | 0 | 0 | 0.0 | 0 |
| TOTALS | 25 | 385 | 15.4 | 2 |

# LARRY WILSON

*Free safety*
*6 ft 0 in, 190 lb*
*Born in Rugby, Ida., March 24,*
*1938*
*University of Utah*
*1960–72 St Louis Cardinals*

At one time or another during Larry Wilson's 13-year tenure, all of the NFL's great quarterbacks felt the sting of the St Louis Cardinals' sterling free safety. If the league's passers weren't being smashed to the ground after a safety blitz, they were watching helplessly as Larry, far downfield, was picking off one of his 52 career interceptions.

When he first joined the Cardinals, Wilson had serious doubts as to whether he could make the team. A two-way star in college, Larry found quickly that offense in the NFL was not for him. A brief try at cornerback on defense had proven disastrous.

What Wilson did not know is that the Cardinals' defensive coordinator, the late Chuck Drulis, had been planning a daring defensive maneuver—soon to become famous as the safety blitz—and he was waiting for just the right man to come along to

try it. Drulis was certain that Larry had the necessary qualities—speed, toughness, sure-tackling ability, dedication and the willingness to take the hard knocks—to make the play work. The tactic called for the safety, ordinarily the back man of the defense, to burst through the offensive line on the snap of the ball, time his charge perfectly and tackle the quarterback before he has time to react.

The play was code-named "Wildcat" in Cardinal terminology. Wilson handled the play so spectacularly well that it wasn't long before people, when they said safety blitz, thought first of Wilson. Larry even acquired the nickname "Wildcat."

Wilson had the reputation of being "the toughest player in the NFL." Fractures, stitches, busted teeth, bumps and bruises by the thousands—the never-say-die dynamo endured them all. In a game against Pittsburgh, Larry demonstrated his greatest courage on a football field. Playing with two broken hands, Wilson ignored doctor's orders and not only played but intercepted a pass for a go-ahead touchdown.

A perennial all-NFL selection who played in eight Pro Bowl games, Larry was an exceptional team leader and widely lauded for his professionalism, consistency and loyalty to his organization.

Pat Summerall, a one-time opponent and now a noted television sportscaster, best summed up Larry Wilson: "You can run out of superlatives in talking about him. He typified everything great you would possibly expect in a pro football player!"

INTERCEPTION RECORD

| Year | Number | Yards | Average | TD |
|---|---|---|---|---|
| 1960 | 2 | 4 | 2.0 | 0 |
| 1961 | 3 | 36 | 12.0 | 0 |
| 1962 | 2 | 59 | 29.5 | 1* |
| 1963 | 4 | 67 | 16.8 | 0 |
| 1964 | 3 | 44 | 14.7 | 1 |
| 1965 | 6 | 153 | 25.5 | 1 |
| 1966 | 10* | 180 | 18.0 | 2* |
| 1967 | 4 | 75 | 18.8 | 0 |
| 1968 | 4 | 14 | 3.5 | 0 |
| 1969 | 2 | 15 | 7.5 | 0 |
| 1970 | 5 | 72 | 14.4 | 0 |
| 1971 | 4 | 46 | 11.5 | 0 |
| 1972 | 3 | 35 | 11.7 | 0 |
| TOTALS | 52 | 800 | 15.4 | 5 |

* Led NFL

Rushing: 5 attempts, 36 yards, 7.2-yard average, 1 touchdown

Punt returns: 3 returns, 26 yards, 8.7-yard average, 0 touchdowns

Kickoff returns: 11 returns, 198 yards, 18.0-yard average, 0 touchdowns

Scoring: 7 touchdowns, 1 safety, 44 points

*Larry Wilson picks up good yardage on one of his 52 career interception returns. Wilson was also famous for his masterful execution of the safety blitz. He gained the deserved reputation of being "the toughest player in the NFL."*

# DICK BUTKUS

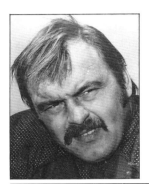

*Middle linebacker*
*6 ft 3 in., 245 lb*
*Born in Chicago, Ill., December 9,*
*1942*
*University of Illinois*
*1965–73 Chicago Bears*

Possessed with a desire to excel that few have ever known, Dick Butkus played as the Chicago Bears' middle linebacker for nine years with only one goal in mind—to be the best!

From the very start, Butkus was just that. A first-round draft choice of the 1965 Bears, he came to camp fretting about his chances of beating out the incumbent middle linebacker, the talented veteran Bill George. Dick's fears were groundless.

Butkus had only one challenger, Bears teammate Gale Sayers, for Rookie of the Year honors. He was named all-NFL for the first of seven times. He played in the Pro Bowl after the 1965 season and for the following seven years. He even figured in the statistical columns with 47 take-aways, 22 on interceptions and 25 on opponents' fumble recoveries.

Dick had drive, meanness, a consuming desire to pursue, tackle, butt and manhandle—anything he could do to thwart the enemy on every play. Still he was a clean player, totally devoted to his career, a man who by his own admission played every game as though it were his last one.

Butkus had the speed and agility to make tackles from sideline to sideline and to cover the best tight ends and running backs on pass plays. He had instinct, strength, leadership and, maybe most important of all, anger.

"When I went out on the field to warm up," Dick acknowledged, "I would manufacture things to make me mad. If someone on the other team was laughing, I'd pretend he was laughing at me or the Bears. It always worked for me."

Born into a large Lithuanian family on Chicago's South Side, Butkus became obsessed with the idea of a pro football career while he was still in grade school. He devoted his entire adolescence and young manhood toward reaching that goal. Dick chose his summer employment, his friends, his college with that thought in mind.

It was inevitable that injuries would eventually come to someone who threw himself so completely into a contact sport such as football. For Dick, it was a right knee in 1970 that didn't totally respond to surgery. Three years later, he limped off an NFL gridiron for the last time.

Still, if Butkus had the chance, he would do it all again. "Few people get to earn a living at what they like to do and there are hazards in any profession," he pointed out. "Football is something I was made for. I gave the game all I could for as long as I could. I guess my only regret is that my career was too short."

*For nine seasons with the Chicago Bears, Dick Butkus played middle linebacker with extreme intensity and effectiveness.*

INTERCEPTION RECORD

| Year | Number | Yards | Average | TD |
|---|---|---|---|---|
| 1965 | 5 | 84 | 16.8 | 0 |
| 1966 | 1 | 3 | 3.0 | 0 |
| 1967 | 1 | 24 | 24.0 | 0 |
| 1968 | 3 | 14 | 4.7 | 0 |
| 1969 | 2 | 13 | 6.5 | 0 |
| 1970 | 3 | 0 | 0.0 | 0 |
| 1971 | 4 | 9 | 2.3 | 0 |
| 1972 | 2 | 19 | 9.5 | 0 |
| 1973 | 1 | 0 | 0.0 | 0 |
| TOTALS | 22 | 166 | 7.5 | 0 |

Kickoff returns: 12 returns, 120 yards, 10.0-yard average, 0 touchdowns

Opponents' fumbles: 25 recoveries, 22 yards returned, 1 touchdown

# YALE LARY

*Safety, punter*
*5 ft 11 in, 189 lb*
*Born in Fort Worth, Tex.,*
*November 24, 1930*
*Texas A&M College*
*1952–3, 1956–64 Detroit Lions*

*Yale Lary made exceptional contributions to the Detroit Lions during his 11-year career. He was a key element on the defensive platoon, a constant threat on returns and a superb punter.*

Detroit Lions fans remember Yale Lary in many different ways. Some think of him as a superb right safety, a key element in Detroit's fearsome defensive platoons in the championship-punctuated years of the 1950s. Others will tell you he was one of history's truly great punters. Still others say it was his breakaway ability on punt returns that set him apart from all the rest.

In reality, every Yale Lary fan is correct in his own private summation because the multi-talented Texan did all those things extremely well during his 11 years with the Lions.

There is no question that Yale's defensive play was a prime factor in his Hall of Fame election. He was named all-NFL four times and he played in nine Pro Bowls. His career mark shows 50 interceptions and he might well have had many more had not opposition passers avoided throwing in his area.

"If I had to pick one defensive back who had everything," quarterback Bobby Layne, Detroit's offensive dynamo, once said, "it would have to be Yale. He was smart but the big thing was his quickness and his ability to recover and intercept after lulling the quarterback into thinking he had an open receiver."

Still, those who remember Lary as a superb punter have plenty of reason to do so. His lifetime punting average of 44.3 yards is one of the absolute best ever. He won three NFL punting titles and missed a fourth by a razor-thin average of 3.6 inches!

The Lions' punting game with Yale in charge was a headache to opponents in another way. One of Lary's favorite ploys was a run from punt formation. He carried the ball only 10 times during his career for a sparkling 15.3-yard average but the mere threat of a Lary run from punt formation kept opponents constantly on edge.

The late George Wilson, Detroit's coach toward the end of the 1950s, remembered Yale yet another way, for his consistent play. "Yale seems to be at his peak every game," Wilson once

marveled. "After eight years many of the best are on their way down but Yale just goes on at an absolute peak level, game after game."

Regardless of exactly how they remember Lary, Lions fans would unanimously agree that his kind comes along only once in a generation. Comparatively small by NFL standards but armed with a big heart and great ability, he did much to make the Lions the scourge of the NFL in the 1950s.

| INTERCEPTION RECORD | | | | |
|---|---|---|---|---|
| Year | Number | Yards | Average | TD |
| 1952 | 4 | 61 | 15.3 | 0 |
| 1953 | 5 | 98 | 19.6 | 0 |
| 1954–5 | In US Army | | | |
| 1956 | 8 | 182 | 22.8 | 1 |
| 1957 | 2 | 64 | 32.0 | 0 |
| 1958 | 3 | 70 | 23.3 | 0 |
| 1959 | 3 | 0 | 0.0 | 0 |
| 1960 | 3 | 44 | 14.7 | 0 |
| 1961 | 6 | 95 | 15.8 | 0 |
| 1962 | 8 | 51 | 6.4 | 0 |
| 1963 | 2 | 21 | 10.5 | 1 |
| 1964 | 6 | 101 | 16.8 | 0 |
| TOTALS | 50 | 787 | 15.7 | 2 |

| PUNT RETURN RECORD | | | | |
|---|---|---|---|---|
| Year | Number | Yards | Average | TD |
| 1952 | 16 | 182 | 11.4 | 1 |
| 1953 | 13 | 115 | 8.8 | 1* |
| 1954–5 | In US Army | | | |
| 1956 | 22 | 70 | 3.2 | 0 |
| 1957 | 25 | 139 | 5.6 | 0 |
| 1958 | 27 | 196 | 7.3 | 1* |
| 1959 | 21 | 43 | 2.0 | 0 |
| 1960 | 1 | 5 | 5.0 | 0 |
| 1961 | 1 | 8 | 8.0 | 0 |
| 1962 | 0 | 0 | 0.0 | 0 |
| 1963 | 0 | 0 | 0.0 | 0 |
| 1964 | 0 | 0 | 0.0 | 0 |
| TOTALS | 126 | 758 | 6.0 | 3 |

| PUNTING RECORD | | |
|---|---|---|
| Year | Number | Average |
| 1952 | 5 | 36.2 |
| 1953 | 28 | 39.7 |
| 1954–5 | In US Army | |
| 1956 | 42 | 40.4 |
| 1957 | 54 | 39.9 |
| 1958 | 59 | 42.8 |
| 1959 | 45 | 47.1* |
| 1960 | 64* | 42.8 |
| 1961 | 52 | 48.4* |
| 1962 | 52 | 45.3 |
| 1963 | 35 | 48.9* |
| 1964 | 67 | 46.3 |
| TOTALS | 503 | 44.3 |

\* Led NFL

Kickoff returns: 22 returns, 495 yards, 22.5-yard average, 0 touchdowns

Rushing: 10 attempts, 153 yards, 15.3-yard average, 0 touchdowns

Scoring: 6 touchdowns, 36 points

# RON MIX

*Offensive tackle*
*6 ft 4 in, 255 lb*
*Born in Los Angeles, Calif.,*
*March 10, 1938*
*University of Southern California*
*1960 Los Angeles Chargers;*
*1961–9 San Diego Chargers; 1971*
*Oakland Raiders*

The most amazing aspect of the Ron Mix story is that he played football at all. In high school, he really wanted to play baseball, was fairly successful in track but somehow ended up playing football, a sport he really hated. Miraculously, Ron did well enough to earn a scholarship to USC. With the Trojans, he gained almost 100 lb, became an excellent offensive tackle and attracted the attention of scouts from both the NFL and the new American Football League (AFL).

Since the Los Angeles Chargers offered a far better contract, Mix opted for the AFL. The fact that he would be playing in his home town was of little consequence because Ron intended to play only long enough "to get a start in life, just a year or two." But as Ron started to improve as a player, he suddenly realized he was really enjoying the game. He decided to stick around.

Nicknamed "The Intellectual Assassin" because, out of uniform, he was articulate, intelligent and modest, Mix on the field started doing his job better than almost anyone else—during his AFL career he was assessed for only two holding penalties. He

was an all-AFL selection eight times as a tackle and once as a guard. He played in seven AFL All-Star games and five of the first six AFL title games. He was unanimously chosen for the AFL's all-time team in 1969.

Particularly early in his career, Mix relied on a fairly basic formula of utilizing his speed and strength to become the AFL's premier offensive tackle. On passing plays, he would pop out at his opponent at the moment of the center snap, hit him, drive him back and continue to attack until the pass was in the air. On running plays, his uncanny balance enabled him to take out the defensive end with a chopping block and proceed downfield where he could wipe out the cornerback.

A film review of the 1963 AFL championship game with Boston showed that, on a twisting, turning 58-yard touchdown run by Paul Lowe, Mix actually blocked out three Patriots during the long play.

As time went by and the caliber of play improved throughout the AFL, Ron found that speed and strength had to be augmented with a variety of new techniques, change-ups and feints that helped him to stay the best at his trade. "I guess you could say I became more coachable," Mix quipped with typically dry humor, "perhaps out of necessity."

But the Chargers coach, Sid Gillman, could see Mix only as one of the very best throughout his career. "Ron Mix is a football coach's football player. He never says a word and he's the hardest worker we have. He's amazing!"

*Ron Mix utilized his speed and strength to become one of the AFL's premier offensive tackles. Remarkably, he was assessed for holding penalties only twice in 10 AFL seasons.*

# JOHNNY UNITAS

*Quarterback*
*6 ft 1 in., 195 lb*
*Born in Pittsburgh, Pa., May 7,*
*1933*
*University of Louisville*
*1956–72 Baltimore Colts; 1973*
*San Diego Chargers*

Rags-to-riches sagas—heartwarming tales of an athlete overcoming formidable roadblocks to achieve stardom—often pop up on the sports scene. Few, if any, are more dramatic or more complete than the climb of Johnny Unitas from the absolute depths to the dizzying heights.

His story is classic American sports folklore. A ninth-round draft choice of the 1955 Pittsburgh Steelers, Unitas was cut before he could throw even one pass in a pre-season game. Still determined, he played semi-pro football for $6 a game. After the season, a fan wrote to Weeb Ewbank, the Baltimore Colts coach, to tell him of "an outstanding prospect" on the Pittsburgh sandlots.

Ewbank signed Johnny for $7000 on a make-it basis. Programmed strictly as a backup, Unitas got his chance in the fourth game when regular quarterback George Shaw was injured. His first pass was intercepted for a Chicago Bears touchdown but from that moment on, Johnny never looked back.

For the next 18 seasons, "Johnny U" ran up a ledger of game-winning exploits seldom matched in NFL annals. Without a doubt, it was his last-second heroics in the 1958 NFL title game, often called "the greatest game ever played," that turned Unitas into a household name among sports buffs.

With two minutes to play, the New York Giants were leading, 17–14, when the Colts started a last-gasp drive at their own 14. "Mr. Clutch" went coolly to work with seven straight passes that set up a game-tying field goal with seven seconds left. A textbook-perfect, Unitas-engineered 80-yard march won the game in overtime. Played before a national television audience, the game gave Unitas his chance to demonstrate to the world all of the marvelous attributes—confidence, courage, leadership, play-calling genius and passing skill—that made him one of the most fabled and followed stars ever. On a greater scale, the game gave pro football the visibility it needed to catapult toward the heights of fan popularity it knows today.

In spite of his massive statistics and numerous honors—40,239 yards and 290 touchdowns passing, all-NFL five years, three-time NFL Player of the Year and 10 Pro Bowls—Unitas was first and foremost a team player. He never criticized his teammates publicly but when someone let him down on the field, many an erring Colt felt Johnny U's sting. His teammates never doubted who was running the show.

As one Colt said when asked how it was on the field with Unitas, "It's like being in the huddle with God."

*Cut by the 1955 Pittsburgh Steelers, quarterback Johnny Unitas rebounded with the Baltimore Colts a year later and soon was recognized as one of the premier passers of all time.*

---

## PASSING RECORD

Career passing rating: 78.2

° With Baltimore Colts

† With San Diego Chargers

‡ Led NFL

Rushing: 450 attempts, 1777 yards, 3.9-yard average, 13 touchdowns

Scoring: 13 touchdowns, 78 points

| Year | Attempts | Completions | Percentage passes completed | Yards | TD | Interceptions |
|------|----------|-------------|-----------------------------|-------|-----|---------------|
| 1956° | 198 | 110 | 55.6 | 1498 | 9 | 10 |
| 1957° | 301‡ | 172 | 57.1 | 2550‡ | 24‡ | 17 |
| 1958° | 263 | 136 | 51.7 | 2007 | 19‡ | 7 |
| 1959° | 367‡ | 193‡ | 52.6 | 2899‡ | 32‡ | 14 |
| 1960° | 378‡ | 190‡ | 50.3 | 3099‡ | 25‡ | 24 |
| 1961° | 420‡ | 229 | 54.5 | 2990 | 16 | 24‡ |
| 1962° | 389 | 222 | 57.1 | 2967 | 23 | 23 |
| 1963° | 410 | 237‡ | 57.8 | 3481‡ | 20 | 12 |
| 1964° | 305 | 158 | 51.8 | 2824 | 19 | 6 |
| 1965° | 282 | 164 | 58.2 | 2530 | 23 | 12 |
| 1966° | 348 | 195 | 56.0 | 2743 | 22 | 24‡ |
| 1967° | 436 | 255 | 58.5‡ | 3428 | 20 | 16 |
| 1968° | 32 | 11 | 34.4 | 139 | 2 | 4 |
| 1969° | 327 | 178 | 54.4 | 2342 | 12 | 20 |
| 1970° | 321 | 166 | 51.7 | 2213 | 14 | 18 |
| 1971° | 176 | 92 | 52.3 | 942 | 3 | 9 |
| 1972° | 157 | 88 | 56.1 | 1111 | 4 | 6 |
| 1973† | 76 | 34 | 44.7 | 471 | 3 | 7 |
| TOTALS | 5186 | 2830 | 54.6 | 40,239 | 290 | 253 |

# The
# EIGHTIES

*In the 1980s, the Pro Football Hall of Fame's all-time attendance
surpassed the 4,000,000 mark with fans coming from every
American state and many overseas nations. Record crowds
turned out for the annual enshrinement ceremonies held on the
front steps of the Hall. Forty-two new members upped the
enshrinee total to 144 by 1988.*

# HERB ADDERLEY

*Cornerback*
*6 ft 1 in, 200 lb*
*Born in Philadelphia, Pa., June 8, 1939*
*Michigan State University*
*1961–9 Green Bay Packers;*
*1970–2 Dallas Cowboys*

Right from his first NFL game with the 1961 Green Bay Packers, Herb Adderley proved to be a "big-play" star who could demoralize his opposition in a variety of ways. As a rookie, he stunned San Francisco with three long kickoff returns. In 1963, Adderley blocked a Minnesota field goal which Green Bay turned into a winning touchdown. In Super Bowl II against the Oakland Raiders, Herb's 60-yard interception return for a touchdown earned him a coveted Super Bowl game ball.

While Adderley excelled on special teams through his first eight years in the NFL, his primary job was to play left cornerback both for the Packers and for the Dallas Cowboys, with whom he played three final seasons. Herb was constantly in the limelight. He was all-NFL five times and played in five Pro Bowls, seven NFL/NFC title games and four Super Bowls, two each with the Packers and Cowboys.

Yet had it not been for injuries on the Packers' defensive unit late in his rookie season, Adderley might not have become one of history's finest cornerbacks. He was an offensive halfback in college and Green Bay's coach, Vince Lombardi, also had programmed Herb to play on offense. But when regular cornerback Henry Gremminger was injured, Herb was called on to take over during the emergency. In his first game on defense, Adderley recorded his first of 48 career interceptions.

Lombardi freely admitted he almost made a major mistake with Adderley. "I was too stubborn to switch him to defense until I had to," Lombardi agreed. "Now when I think of what Adderley means to our defense, it scares me to think of how I almost mishandled him."

Adderley had some doubts of his own about moving to defense but they vanished quickly. "I can honestly say I enjoyed going head-to-head with the best receivers in pro football," he beamed a short time later. "Defense is in my blood now and nothing could make me want to go back to offense."

Herb had a perfect attitude toward his new job. He was a gambler on the field and knew, if his guess was wrong, he could look bad.

*Originally slated for the offensive unit, Herb Adderley was moved to the Green Bay Packers defensive team in an emergency. There he became an all-time great cornerback.*

"You have to recognize that you are going to get beaten once in a while," he pointed out. "You can't dwell on it. You just have to concentrate on not letting the same man beat you again."

Herb also had a special but totally realistic goal. "When people leave the stadium, I want them to say they've just watched one of the best cornerbacks they have ever seen."

| INTERCEPTION RECORD | | | | | KICKOFF RETURN RECORD | | | | |
|---|---|---|---|---|---|---|---|---|---|
| Year | Number | Yards | Average | TD | Year | Number | Yards | Average | TD |
| 1961° | 1 | 9 | 9.0 | 0 | 1961° | 18 | 478 | 26.6 | 0 |
| 1962° | 7 | 132 | 18.9 | 1‡ | 1962° | 15 | 418 | 27.9 | 1‡ |
| 1963° | 5 | 86 | 17.2 | 0 | 1963° | 20 | 597 | 29.9 | 1 |
| 1964° | 4 | 56 | 14.0 | 0 | 1964° | 19 | 508 | 26.7 | 0 |
| 1965° | 6 | 175‡ | 29.2 | 3‡ | 1965° | 10 | 221 | 22.1 | 0 |
| 1966° | 4 | 125 | 31.3 | 1 | 1966° | 14 | 320 | 22.9 | 0 |
| 1967° | 4 | 16 | 4.0 | 1 | 1967° | 10 | 207 | 20.7 | 0 |
| 1968° | 3 | 27 | 9.0 | 0 | 1968° | 14 | 331 | 23.6 | 0 |
| 1969° | 5 | 169‡ | 33.8 | 1 | 1969° | 0 | 0 | 0.0 | 0 |
| 1970† | 3 | 69 | 23.0 | 0 | 1970† | 0 | 0 | 0.0 | 0 |
| 1971† | 6 | 182 | 30.3 | 0 | 1971† | 0 | 0 | 0.0 | 0 |
| 1972† | 0 | 0 | 0.0 | 0 | 1972† | 0 | 0 | 0.0 | 0 |
| TOTALS | 48 | 1046 | 21.8 | 7 | TOTALS | 120 | 3080 | 25.7 | 2 |

° With Green Bay Packers

† With Dallas Cowboys

‡ Led NFL

Scoring: 9 touchdowns, 54 points

# DAVID (DEACON) JONES

*Defensive end
6 ft 5 in, 260 lb
Born in Eatonville, Fla.,
December 9, 1938
South Carolina State College and
Mississippi Vocational College
1961–71 Los Angeles Rams;
1972–3 San Diego Chargers; 1974
Washington Redskins*

David "Deacon" Jones started his NFL career as an obscure 14th-round draft pick of the 1961 Los Angeles Rams but he quickly grabbed the headlines with his crowd-pleasing play. Perhaps more than any other player, Deacon made modern-day pro football fans aware of the fast, tough and mobile defensive linemen who existed to make life miserable for NFL quarterbacks.

Jones was as innovative, quick-thinking and flamboyant out of uniform as he was fabulous on the field. Even before he became a star, he attracted his share of attention. He started by creating his own nickname, Deacon, because, he reasoned, "no one would ever remember a player with the name of David Jones." Then he invented a term for his favorite play, the tackling of a quarterback before he has a chance to get his pass away. Deacon called the play a "sack," because "you need a short term that can fit easily into the newspaper headlines."

For 10 seasons, Deacon teamed with tackle Merlin Olsen to give the Rams a solid all-pro left side for its famous "Fearsome Foursome" defensive front. Among their many contributions, Jones and Olsen perfected the stunt, or loop, a maneuver designed to confuse the defenses and to create a gap for one or the other or both to slide through to sack the passer or to stifle a running play.

Sometimes known as "The Secretary of Defense," Jones was truly adept as a pass rusher. In 1967, for instance, Rams passers were dropped 25 times all year but Deacon by himself sacked the opposition throwers 26 times. He was a consensus all-pro six straight years from 1965 through 1970. He played in eight Pro Bowls and was twice named the NFL Defensive Player of the Year by his fellow NFL players. He was by far the most decorated and honored Ram during the 1960s.

As dedicated as he was to what he saw as "a game of civilized violence," Deacon was also noted for his extremely clean play. "I'm against cheap shots," Jones proclaimed. "You should play clean and shoot square. If you play the game right, you can protect yourself from physical harm."

Jones is living proof this can be true. He missed only three games in 14 pro seasons and ended his career without a "zipper," pro football jargon for surgical stitches, usually in the knee area.

Along with playing excellence, Deacon will be remembered for his cocky, confident, highly quotable utterances. In one statement, he may have made the perfect summation of Deacon Jones, the player and the person. "I'm the best defensive end around," he announced honestly and proudly. "I'd hate to have to play against me!"

*"Deacon" Jones coined the term "sack" for tackling the quarterback because it would fit better in newspaper headlines.*

# BOB LILLY

*Defensive tackle*
*6 ft 5 in, 260 lb*
*Born in Olney, Tex., July 26, 1939*
*Texas Christian University*
*1961–74 Dallas Cowboys*

**B**ob Lilly will always be the number 1 Dallas Cowboy! He was the team's first-ever draft pick (1961), first Pro Bowl selection (1962), first all-NFL choice (1964) and the first who played his entire career with the Cowboys to be elected to the Hall of Fame.

Lilly spent most of his 14 seasons with the Cowboys as a durable, dedicated and devastating defensive tackle. He started as a defensive end, however, and even made the Pro Bowl at that position. But the Dallas coach, Tom Landry, felt that Bob, with his great speed, strength, intelligence and agility, would be better suited at tackle where he would have more freedom to concentrate on the ball-handlers. At defensive end, he had less freedom to move around and improvise.

As the key man in the vaunted "Doomsday Defense" that helped transform Dallas into a dominant NFL power, Bob compiled an awesome list of honors and records. He was selected for 11 Pro Bowls and played in 10 of them. He was a consensus all-NFL choice eight times. Altogether, he played 292 pro games,

including five NFL/NFC championship games and Super Bowls V and VI. In 14 years, he missed just one game, a playoff contest with the Minnesota Vikings in 1973. Bob bounced back from the hamstring pull that kept him out of that game but a neck injury that presaged more permanent damage forced retirement in 1975.

Defensive tackles aren't supposed to score touchdowns, but Bob did—four of them. One came on a 17-yard interception runback, the other three on fumble returns. Altogether, he recovered 16 opponents' fumbles and returned them 109 yards.

Equally effective as a pass rusher or on rushing defense, Lilly continually battled double-team and even triple-team opposition with the center, the guard and sometimes the fullback ganging up on him. He was rarely stopped.

Lilly was so great at pursuit and tracking down his targets that many teams opted to run directly at him, hoping to minimize his pursuing skills. This tactic met with only limited success.

Bob's greatest pro football thrill came in Super Bowl VI, when the Cowboys whipped Miami, 24–3. The win silenced the many critics who insisted Dallas couldn't win the big games after the team had failed in early playoff rounds for several years. Lilly entered the Super Bowl record book himself that day when he sacked Miami quarterback Bob Griese for a massive 29-yard loss.

"Lilly is not enormous but he is strong enough that there isn't any use arguing with him if he gets hold of your jersey," Griese said after the game. "You just fall wherever Bob wants."

*Bob Lilly was the key man in the famed Dallas "Doomsday Defense" for most of 14 seasons. A consensus all-NFL choice eight times, he was selected to 11 Pro Bowls.*

# JIM OTTO

*Center*
*6 ft 2 in. 255 lb*
*Born in Wausau, Wisc., January 5, 1938*
*University of Miami (Fla.)*
*1960–74 Oakland Raiders*

When Jim Otto joined the Oakland Raiders of the new American Football League (AFL) in 1960, most sports experts felt there was little chance that either the league or the team would survive. The prognosis wasn't much better for Otto who, at 205 lb, was considered too small to be a pro football center. Not one team in the established NFL drafted him.

Jim's only chance was the AFL. Armed with two pairs of football shoes, a helmet, two flimsy suitcases and an intense desire to play, Otto reported to the Raiders' camp with a positive "I-intend-to-stay" attitude.

Jim did stay. He immediately embarked on a strength program that increased his playing weight to 255 lb. For the next 15 seasons, he started every regular season and post-season game for the Raiders. He was the only all-league center the AFL ever had and he was also all-AFC three years. He played in all nine AFL All-Star games and the first three AFC–NFC Pro Bowl games. Jim played a total of 308 games as a Raider.

His unique uniform number—00—undoubtedly helped Jim gain the attention he deserved but primarily he received widespread acclaim because he was rapidly becoming a superstar. As Otto developed, so too did his team.

Beginning in 1963 when Al Davis took over as head coach, the Raiders through the rest of Jim's career achieved the best won–lost record in pro football. Oakland won the 1967 AFL championship and seven divisional titles in an eight-year period from 1967 through Jim's final 1974 campaign.

Throughout this period, the well-balanced Raiders could boast of a particularly outstanding offensive line. Otto, a sure-handed ball-snapper and superior blocker, was a tower of strength.

But there was more to Otto's success than technical know-how. People who played with or against him will use such words as pride, dedication, leadership and intelligence. Jim became the ultimate team leader, not in a "rah-rah" way but rather because he was always in the lineup, performing at peak efficiency. Otto was also assigned to call blocking signals for the offensive line. In one season, the Raiders called about 650 plays and Jim was judged to have been wrong only three or four times.

Otto had one more trait—loyalty—that was important to the entire AFL. After his first season, he turned down several offers from NFL teams. He remembered it was the AFL that gave him a chance when the NFL was, collectively, saying "no."

*Playing for the Oakland Raiders, Jim Otto became the only all-league center in the history of the AFL.*

# MORRIS (RED) BADGRO

*End*
*6 ft 0 in, 190 lb*
*Born in Orillia, Wash.,*
*December 1, 1902*
*University of Southern California*
*1927 New York Yankees; 1930–5*
*New York Giants; 1936 Brooklyn*
*Dodgers*

The Red Badgro story is truly lengthy . . . and remarkable. In 1981, at the age of 78, the two-way end from the NFL's pioneer era became the oldest person ever elected to the Pro Football Hall of Fame. The 45-year span between his final game with the 1936 Brooklyn Dodgers and his election also was a record.

The Badgro saga is even more unusual in that he wasn't even sure he wanted to play pro football and, in fact, retired after one year with the 1927 New York Yankees to give pro baseball a try. Red actually played in the major leagues two years with the St Louis Browns but, when he couldn't win a regular job, he decided to give NFL football another look.

"The Yankees had folded so I signed with the Giants for $150 a game," Badgro recalls. "I didn't exactly get rich with that salary but I didn't complain either. Those were Depression days and a dollar went a long way."

During Red's six-year tenure with the Giants, the New York team was a solid championship contender every year and Badgro was one of the team's most honored stars. He was named to an unofficial all-league team in 1930 and then to the official honor eleven in 1931, 1933, and 1934.

Badgro was highly regarded as a sure-tackling defender and an effective blocker on offense but he was also a talented receiver. In 1934, he tied for the NFL's pass-catching crown with 16 receptions, a significant number in those defense-dominated days. He also had the distinction of being the first player to score a touchdown in the NFL championship series that began in 1933. The Bears were ahead, 6–0, on two field goals, when Badgro hauled in a 29-yard toss to give the Giants a 7–6 edge.

Red made many other key catches that were converted into Giants' victories. His 17-yard reception set up a clinching touchdown in a 13–0 victory over the Brooklyn Dodgers in 1930. A year later, his 14-yard catch triggered a New York win over Portsmouth. In 1934, when the Giants marched to a divisional title, Badgro's 15-yard reception was a key play in a long drive for the game's only score in a 3–0 New York win.

Badgro had his big defensive moments as well. Playing against the Boston Redskins in 1935, Red blocked a punt and returned it for a go-ahead touchdown. His own favorite play was a defensive gem against Green Bay when he warded off a blocker and tackled Clarke Hinkle inches short of a winning touchdown.

Badgro had the opportunity to play with and against some of the most legendary stars of early NFL history. It seems he made a definite impression on everyone. Cliff Battles is an example.

"Playing against Red Badgro was an afternoon's work in itself," the Redskins' ace halfback once said. "He was excellent in all departments of the game and an outstanding credit to football."

*"Red" Badgro was one of the most respected stars of the excellent New York Giants' teams of the early 1930s. A sure-tackling defender, he was also an excellent pass receiver on offense.*

# GEORGE BLANDA

*Quarterback–kicker*
*6 ft 2 in, 215 lb*
*Born in Youngwood, Pa.,*
*September 17, 1927*
*University of Kentucky*
*1949–58 Chicago Bears; 1951*
*Baltimore Colts (one game);*
*1960–6 Houston Oilers; 1967–75*
*Oakland Raiders*

The remarkable George Blanda played pro football far longer than any other person. His 26-year, 340-game career was divided into three distinct parts, 10 years with the Chicago Bears followed by seven seasons with the Houston Oilers and nine-years with the Oakland Raiders.

Through most of those 26 seasons, George had two primary assignments—to pass the football and to kick it. On both jobs, he accumulated impressive credentials. He passed for 236 touchdowns and he scored an incredible 2,002 points, most of them by placekicking.

Yet Blanda most likely would have faded unnoticed into retirement had it not been for the 1970 season with the Raiders during which, in a five-game period, George provided Oakland with four wins and one tie with last-second touchdown passes or field goals.

The string started with a three-touchdown passing outburst against Pittsburgh and continued with a 48-yard field goal with three seconds left to tie Kansas City. He then threw a scoring pass and added a 52-yard field goal in the last 96 seconds to whip Cleveland. Next came a touchdown toss that defeated Denver and

a last-instant field goal to upend San Diego. George was named the AFC's Player of the Year and, by the age of 43, he had become a living legend.

George's five-game string of heroics was only a part of his magnificent 1970 season that from beginning to end was story-book in nature. He won a sixth game against the New York Jets with a fourth-quarter conversion and came close to encore game-winners at least two other times. He became the oldest quarter-back to play in a title game. Although the Baltimore Colts won, Blanda accounted for 17 of the Raiders' points. The Associated Press named him the 1970 Male Athlete of the Year.

Blanda's first pro stop in Chicago was not a happy one. He did not become a starter until his fifth season and the next year in 1954 he was shelved by an injury for the only time in his long career. In 1959, Blanda balked at becoming a kicker-only and retired. With 10 years' pro experience, most 31-year-olds would have been happy to call it quits.

But the emergence of the American Football League (AFL) in 1960 gave the highly competitive Blanda another chance to play. For seven years, he bombed Houston's foes with 165 touchdown passes, led the Oilers to the first two AFL titles and won AFL Player of the Year honors for himself in 1961.

In 1967, when Blanda was almost 40, the Oilers decided he was through but the Raiders saw George as a contributing backup passer and a dependable point-maker so they picked him up. George handled both jobs with distinction.

Many fantasized that George would play until he was 50 and he did come close. He was just a month shy of his 49th birthday when he retired in August, 1976. Blanda had experienced a fantasy-land career that almost certainly can never be duplicated. He had captured the fancy of fans of all ages but, for the over-40 set of an entire nation, Blanda had provided a whole new lease on life.

## PASSING RECORD

| Year | Attempts | Completions | Percentage passes completed | Yards | TD | Interceptions |
|---|---|---|---|---|---|---|
| 1949° | 21 | 9 | 42.9 | 197 | 0 | 5 |
| 1950° | 1 | 0 | 0.0 | 0 | 0 | 0 |
| 1951°† | 0 | 0 | 0.0 | 0 | 0 | 0 |
| 1952° | 131 | 47 | 35.9 | 664 | 8 | 11 |
| 1953° | 362¶ | 169¶ | 46.7 | 2164 | 14 | 23 |
| 1954° | 281 | 131 | 46.6 | 1929 | 15 | 17 |
| 1955° | 97 | 42 | 43.3 | 459 | 4 | 7 |
| 1956° | 69 | 37 | 53.6 | 439 | 7 | 4 |
| 1957° | 19 | 8 | 42.1 | 65 | 0 | 3 |
| 1958° | 7 | 2 | 28.6 | 19 | 0 | 0 |
| 1959 | Retired | | | | | |
| 1960‡ | 363 | 169 | 46.6 | 2413 | 24 | 22 |
| 1961‡°° | 362 | 187 | 51.7 | 3330| | 36| | 22 |
| 1962‡ | 418 | 197 | 47.1 | 2810 | 27 | 42| |
| 1963‡ | 423| | 224| | 53.0 | 3003| | 24 | 25| |
| 1964‡ | 505| | 262| | 51.9 | 3287 | 17 | 27| |
| 1965‡ | 442| | 186| | 42.1 | 2542 | 20 | 30| |
| 1966‡ | 271 | 122 | 45.0 | 1764 | 17 | 21 |
| 1967§ | 38 | 15 | 39.5 | 285 | 3 | 3 |
| 1968§ | 49 | 30 | 61.2 | 522 | 6 | 2 |
| 1969§ | 13 | 6 | 46.2 | 73 | 2 | 1 |
| 1970§ | 55 | 29 | 52.7 | 461 | 6 | 5 |
| 1971§ | 58 | 32 | 55.2 | 378 | 4 | 6 |
| 1972§ | 15 | 5 | 33.3 | 77 | 1 | 0 |
| 1973§ | 0 | 0 | 0.0 | 0 | 0 | 0 |
| 1974§ | 4 | 1 | 25.0 | 28 | 1 | 0 |
| 1975§ | 3 | 1 | 33.3 | 11 | 0 | 1 |
| TOTALS | 4007 | 1911 | 47.7 | 26,920 | 236 | 277 |

## SCORING RECORD

| Year | TD | Extra points | Field goals | Total |
|---|---|---|---|---|
| 1949° | 1 | 0 | 7 | 27 |
| 1950° | 0 | 0 | 6 | 18 |
| 1951°† | 0 | 26 | 6 | 44 |
| 1952° | 1 | 30 | 6 | 54 |
| 1953° | 0 | 27 | 7 | 48 |
| 1954° | 0 | 23 | 8 | 47 |
| 1955° | 2 | 37 | 11 | 82 |
| 1956° | 0 | 45¶ | 12 | 81 |
| 1957° | 1 | 23 | 14 | 71 |
| 1958° | 0 | 36 | 11 | 69 |
| 1959 | Retired | | | |
| 1960‡ | 4 | 46 | 15 | 115 |
| 1961‡ | 0 | 64| | 16 | 112 |
| 1962‡ | 0 | 48| | 11 | 81 |
| 1963‡ | 0 | 39 | 9 | 66 |
| 1964‡ | 0 | 37 | 13 | 76 |
| 1965‡ | 0 | 28 | 11 | 61 |
| 1966‡ | 0 | 39 | 16 | 87 |
| 1967§ | 0 | 56| | 20 | 116| |
| 1968§ | 0 | 54| | 21 | 117 |
| 1969§ | 0 | 45| | 20 | 105 |
| 1970§ | 0 | 36 | 16 | 84 |
| 1971§ | 0 | 41 | 15 | 86 |
| 1972§ | 0 | 44¶ | 17 | 95 |
| 1973§ | 0 | 31 | 23 | 100 |
| 1974§ | 0 | 44¶ | 11 | 77 |
| 1975§ | 0 | 44 | 13 | 83 |
| TOTALS | 9 | 943 | 335 | 2002 |

Career passing rating: 60.8

° With Chicago Bears

† With Baltimore Colts (one game)

‡ With Houston Oilers

§ With Oakland Raiders

¶ Led NFL    | Led AFL

°° Official AFL individual passing champion

Rushing: 135 attempts, 344 yards, 2.5-yard average, 9 touchdowns

Punting: 20 punts, 39.0-yard average

# WILLIE DAVIS

*Defensive end*
*6 ft 3 in, 245 lb*
*Born in Lisbon, La., July 24, 1934*
*Grambling College*
*1958–9 Cleveland Browns; 1960–9*
*Green Bay Packers*

Willie Davis got off to a discouraging start in the NFL. He was a 1956 draft pick but Army service intervened and he didn't join the Cleveland Browns until 1958. In his first two seasons, he played briefly at several different positions. Just when he appeared ready for a regular offensive tackle job in 1960, he was traded to Green Bay, then considered to be the Siberia of pro sports. Willie was upset and briefly considered quitting.

However, the Packers coach, Vince Lombardi, quickly assured Davis that Green Bay needed a top-flight defensive end and he thought Willie was the man.

"I consider speed, agility and size to be the three most important attributes in a successful lineman," Lombardi told Davis. "Give me a man who has any two of those dimensions and he'll do OK. Give him all three and he'll be great. We think you have all three."

Davis also possessed the intangibles—dedication, intelligence, leadership—that enabled him to rise a cut above almost everyone else. Willie was an all-NFL selection five times in six years from 1962 to 1967. He played in six NFL title games and the first two Super Bowls. He was a Pro Bowl choice five straight years. He didn't miss even one of 162 games in his 12-year tenure. He recovered 21 opponents' fumbles, just one shy of the record when he retired.

Willie, who grew up in rural Louisiana under the loving care of a mother who shouldered the entire responsibility for raising three young children, readily admits that football turned his life around. And the trade from Cleveland to Green Bay was not only a major factor in Willie's football success but, in a greater sense, a pivotal point in his entire life.

"I had been working my way up in Cleveland and suddenly I was gone," Davis reflects. "I realized how frustrating it would be when I couldn't play football and would have to face the world with a reduced salary and no talents."

Davis went to work to provide himself with the training he would need outside the football world. Willie earned his master's degree in business at the University of Chicago and entered a major company's management training program two years before his Packers career ended.

Willie felt it was important for other black kids to "remember me as a player who moved on to success in business." His preparation and foresight paid off. Today, the business world regards Davis in just the same way as the pro football world did— he is highly respected, successful and one of the best!

*Willie Davis possessed the physical skills – speed, agility and size – and the intangibles – dedication, intelligence, leadership – to be a superior defensive end for the Green Bay Packers.*

# JIM RINGO

*Center*
*6 ft 2 in. 230 lb*
*Born in Orange, N. J.,*
*November 21, 1931*
*Syracuse University*
*1953–63 Green Bay Packers;*
*1964–7 Philadelphia Eagles*

J im Ringo reported to the Green Bay Packers in 1953, took a quick look at all the bigger players in camp and decided he couldn't make the team. He hurried home to Easton, Pa., where he got a cool reception from his wife and father. Both felt he should not give up without trying. ''Besides, where else are you going to make $5250 for four months' work?'' his father queried.

So Jim went back and soon was the regular center in Green Bay. The Packers continued to struggle for the next few years but Ringo grew steadily in ability. Two years before Vince Lombardi arrived to take charge, Jim attained all-pro stature. His first all-NFL selection came in 1957. Altogether, he made the all-NFL team six of 11 years in Green Bay. He was a Pro Bowl starter 10 times and one of the few to start for both the East and West teams in that post-season series.

To be sure, Jim was the last of a vanishing breed, an NFL lineman who wasn't large. He first reported at 211 lb and never weighed more than 235 lb. Ringo reacted to the challenges of much bigger opponents by utilizing his speed and native football intelligence. He was constantly learning from his coaches and teammates, as well as from his game experiences.

Ringo was a quiet but effective leader. He laid down the law, berated players when necessary and instilled the will to win. In short-yardage situations, the Packers regularly called for plays over Jim's center slot.

Possessed with a burning desire to play, Ringo missed only seven games, all in his rookie season, in 15 years. He wound up his career with a string of 182 consecutive games as a starter, including 56 straight with the Eagles.

To achieve this kind of record for durability, Jim had to overcome—more accurately, overlook—a long string of injuries and illnesses. He was constantly hampered by back, knee and neck injuries and such illnesses as mononucleosis, a staph infection and bronchial pneumonia. On the occasions when he had mononucleosis and the staph infection, Jim entered the hospital every Monday, stayed until Friday evening and then played on Sunday. ''It was more a fear of losing my job than any great desire to be a hero,'' Jim modestly insists. ''We had only 33-man squads so there were always plenty of good football players waiting to take my place.''

*This scene – center Jim Ringo over the ball and Bart Starr calling signals – was familiar to Green Bay opponents for many years. Jim was a Pro Bowl starter 10 times.*

# DOUG ATKINS

*Defensive end*
*6 ft 8 in, 275 lb*
*Born in Humboldt, Tenn., May 8,*
*1930*
*University of Tennessee*
*1953–4 Cleveland Browns;*
*1955–66 Chicago Bears; 1967–9*
*New Orleans Saints*

Throughout the 17 years and 205 games that Doug Atkins was wreaking havoc on NFL quarterbacks, opposing linemen faced him with just one thought in mind: "Don't make him mad!"

Everyone knew that holding or tripping Doug was an absolute no-no. When angered, his contemporaries remember, Atkins inflicted the kind of devastation upon enemy lines and quarterbacks that seldom, if ever, has been equalled on any football field. There is a true story about a veteran Los Angeles Rams tackle forcing a rookie guard who had just held Atkins to apologize—and before the next play!

Even when Doug was his natural "easy-going" self, he did his job far better than most defensive ends in the NFL's long history. During almost two decades as a scrimmage-line regular, he felt his primary assignment was to make life miserable for quarterbacks.

"He is the strongest man in football and also the biggest,"

veteran quarterback Fran Tarkenton once said. "When he rushes the passer with those oak-tree arms way up in the air, he is 12 feet tall. If he gets to you, the whole world suddenly starts spinning."

One of Atkins' favorite tricks was to throw a blocker at the quarterback. Another was to hurdle over a blocker to get at the passer. One offensive line star, Jim Parker, a future Hall of Famer himself, even thought of giving up football after a match-up against Doug in his rookie season.

At the University of Tennessee, Atkins was a conference high-jump champion and a scholarship basketball player but the football coach spotted him one day on the basketball court and quickly commandeered Doug for the football team. Reluctantly, Atkins gave football a try and wound up as an all-America tackle as a senior. The Browns made the monstrous Tennessean their number 1 pick in the 1953 NFL draft.

Atkins spent 12 seasons with the Chicago Bears, with whom he was all-NFL three times and an eight-time Pro Bowl choice. By everyone's admission, Doug and the Bears' boss, George Halas, were at odds on a variety of subjects through most of his stay in Chicago. Before the 1967 season, Atkins demanded a trade and got it—with the New Orleans Saints.

When Atkins retired in 1969 after three fine seasons in New Orleans, Saints coach Tom Fears summed up his feelings: "They threw away the mold when they made Doug Atkins. There'll never be another like him!"

*Doug Atkins is in a New Orleans Saints' uniform in this action but he starred with the Chicago Bears for 12 years.*

# SAM HUFF

*Middle linebacker*
*6 ft 1 in, 230 lb*
*Born in Morgantown, W. Va.,*
*October 4, 1934*
*University of West Virginia*
*1956–63 New York Giants;*
*1964–7, 1969 Washington*
*Redskins*

Because his early NFL tenure was spent with a winning team in the multi-media maze of New York, Sam Huff became one of the most publicized of all pro gridders. At the age of 24, he appeared on a *Time* Magazine cover. He was the subject of a television special, "The Violent World of Sam Huff." Almost overnight, he became the symbol of the new glamour era for defensive football.

Sam was flooded with honors. He was named all-NFL four times, picked as the NFL's top linebacker in 1959 and selected for five Pro Bowls, four of them while he was with the Giants.

The relatively new middle linebacker's job called for someone big enough to handle the power runners, fast enough to overhaul swift halfbacks and agile enough to protect against the passer. To these attributes, Huff added a true love for the game and a unique ability to diagnose and disrupt the opponents' plays.

Sam was best known for his hand-to-hand combat near the scrimmage line and for his duels with the likes of Jim Brown and Jim Taylor but he was also adept at pass defense. His 30 pass steals are second best among Hall of Fame linebackers.

In spite of his abundant talents, fate had to intervene several times to keep him out of the West Virginia coal mines. When Sam was a junior at Farmington High School, the University of West Virginia coach came to town to look at a hot prospect but wound up recruiting Sam instead. At the end of Huff's college career, Giants scout Al DeRogatis came to look at an all-America guard named Bruce Bosley. "Bosley is great," DeRogatis wired back, "but there's another guard here who will be even greater. His name is Sam Huff."

Huff was a third-round draft pick in 1956 but, once in camp, things turned sour. Coach Jim Lee Howell agreed that Sam was a quality athlete but admitted he didn't know where to play him. Discouraged, Sam left camp and headed for the airport. There he was intercepted by assistant coach Vince Lombardi who lectured him on the merits of guts and determination and coaxed him back to camp.

Shortly after Sam's return, fate stepped in a final time. Ray Beck, the regular middle linebacker, was injured and Huff, in the emergency, got a chance to fill in. He did the job so well that Beck retired and Sam never had to worry about a regular football job—or the coal mines—again.

| INTERCEPTION RECORD | | | | | |
|---|---|---|---|---|---|
| Year | Number | Yards | Average | TD | |
| 1956° | 3 | 49 | 16.3 | 0 | |
| 1957° | 1 | 6 | 6.0 | 0 | |
| 1958° | 2 | 23 | 11.5 | 0 | |
| 1959° | 1 | 21 | 21.0 | 0 | |
| 1960° | 3 | 45 | 15.0 | 0 | |
| 1961° | 3 | 13 | 4.3 | 0 | |
| 1962° | 1 | 4 | 4.0 | 0 | |
| 1963° | 4 | 47 | 11.8 | 1 | |
| 1964† | 4 | 34 | 8.5 | 0 | |
| 1965† | 2 | 49 | 24.5 | 0 | |
| 1966† | 1 | 17 | 17.0 | 0 | |
| 1967† | 2 | 8 | 4.0 | 0 | |
| 1968 | Retired | | | | |
| 1969† | 3 | 65 | 21.7 | 1 | |
| TOTALS | 30 | 381 | 12.7 | 2 | |

° With New York Giants

† With Washington Redskins

*Middle linebacker Sam Huff was best known for his individual duels with such running backs as Jim Brown and Jim Taylor.*

# GEORGE MUSSO

*Tackle, guard*
*6 ft 2 in, 270 lb*
*Born in Collinsville, Ill., April 8,*
*1910*
*Millikin College*
*1933–44 Chicago Bears*

In the 1930s and early 1940s, the Chicago Bears were true "Monsters of the Midway," dominating and successful and loaded with a galaxy of superstars. At 270 lb, George Musso was the biggest Bear and also one of the best.

From a financial standpoint, he was also the "best buy" in owner–coach George Halas' long career. The shrewd-bargaining Halas had seen enough of Musso in an all-star game in 1933 to offer him a tryout and $90 a game if he made the squad. To seal the deal, he included $5 for expenses—$3 for train fare and $2 for incidentals.

Musso did not play well in early scrimmages so Halas changed his offer to half-salary—$45 a game—while the rookie tried to prove himself. Buoyed by the encouragement of the famous Red Grange, a Bears halfback in 1933, Musso quickly gained confidence. Within two weeks, George not only made the squad but Halas forgot all about the half-salary arrangement.

For the next 12 seasons, Musso was a standout as a middle guard on defense and first a tackle and later a guard on offense. Because of his ability as well as his size, "Big Bear," as he was affectionately known by his teammates, was not easy to overlook on the gridiron. He became the epitome of the powerful line play that made the Bears famous and victorious.

Opponents and Bears alike looked on George as a quality 60-minute performer, an absolute terror on defense and far better than average on offense, particularly as a pass blocker and as a pulling guard on running plays. He became the first player to win all-league honors at two positions. George made it as a tackle in 1935 and as a guard two years later.

Musso also proved to be a leader of unusual magnitude. Elected captain in his fourth season, he held the job the rest of his career. "George was the team captain. His teammates would have it no other way," Grange remembers. "Halas just let him give the pep talks to the players before the big games. Musso had great spirit and his talks really got the guys fired up."

In 1982, when Musso was elected to the Hall 37 years after his final NFL game, he asked his old coach to be his presenter at the induction ceremonies in Canton. When someone asked about Halas' expenses for the trip, Musso had an answer. "I'll just send back the $5 expense money he gave me when I joined the Bears."

*George Musso came to the Chicago Bears in 1933 for just $5 advance money and a $90 per game contract. He stayed for 12 seasons and became a team leader of unusual dimensions. He played middle guard on defense and tackle and guard on offense. He was named all-NFL both as a guard and as a tackle.*

# MERLIN OLSEN

*Defensive tackle*
*6 ft 5 in. 270 lb*
*Born in Logan. Utah.*
*September 15. 1940*
*Utah State University*
*1962–76 Los Angeles Rams*

In a 1967 playoff game against Green Bay, the Los Angeles Rams' devastating defensive line, popularly known as "The Fearsome Foursome," three times stopped the Packers cold, deep in their territory, then blocked a punt and set up a winning touchdown. The next week against Baltimore, the dynamic unit sacked Colts quarterback Johnny Unitas seven times and forced two interceptions.

Absorbing that kind of abuse from the Rams' defensive unit became the expected thing for at least a decade in the 1960s and early 1970s. Through all those years, the leader of the gang proved to be a quiet, unpretentious, but deadly effective defensive tackle named Merlin Olsen.

George Allen, who coached the Rams when Olsen was at his peak, had this to say: "We never had a bad game from Merlin. We always got a good game and more often than not, a great game."

This was the opinion shared by all who saw him play. The league's coaches selected him for the Pro Bowl a record 14 straight years. He was a universal all-NFL choice from 1966 to 1970 and again in 1973.

It is not unusual for even a superstar to experience trouble making the grade early in his career but Olsen, the Rams' first-round draft choice in 1962, was an instant hit. He won the starting left defensive tackle job the third week of his rookie season and never gave it up.

Throughout his career, Olsen skillfully merged his superb physical skills with his "thinking man's" approach to pro football. In his rookie season, Merlin learned that sheer brute strength was not as important in pro football as it had been in college and high school. Headwork counted for at least as much as size and heft. Olsen, a Phi Beta Kappa honor student at Utah State, was amply supplied with brains and brawn. From his first pro scrimmage, Merlin became an avid student of pro football and particularly the intricacies of defensive line play.

Olsen never bought the theory, popular in some circles, that to obtain a proper emotional pitch, a player must actually hate his opponent, at least through the course of the game.

"I believe professionals think too highly of themselves and others in their work to go about hating," Merlin insisted. "How can you feel antagonistic against someone who is great in the profession you have chosen for yourself? If you are motivated by pride and the desire to win, you will want to dominate your opponent, but that is a lot better thing than hatred on which to tie your success."

*Merlin Olsen was a fixture on the Los Angeles Rams' famed defensive line of the 1960s and 1970s.*

# BOBBY BELL

*Linebacker, defensive end
6 ft 4 in, 225 lb
Born in Shelby, N. C., June 17,
1940
University of Minnesota
1963–74 Kansas City Chiefs*

being on the field.

"I think if you had a teamful of Bobby Bells," Stram, who was Bobby's only pro coach, summarized, "you would want to coach forever because you'd win forever."

Bobby Bell was an all-North Carolina high-school quarterback, an all-America tackle at the University of Minnesota, and an excellent defensive end for the Kansas City Chiefs before he settled on the left outside linebacker position. It was a job that earned him a permanent niche in history as the first Chiefs player to be elected to the Pro Football Hall of Fame.

As versatile as he was—Bobby even snapped the football on punts and kickoffs for the Chiefs—outside linebacker did seem to be his perfect position. Bell was built in the shape of an inverted pyramid with massive shoulders tapering down to a 32-inch waist on his 225-lb frame. With a ferocious look on a ruggedly handsome face, he presented a fearsome appearance on the gridiron. Bobby had the ability to match his appearance and the physique and strength both to withstand punishment and to deal out his own punishment in return. He also had exceptional agility and speed—he regularly was timed at 4.5 in the 40-yard sprint.

Bell began his American Football League (AFL) career as a defensive end because that's where the Chiefs needed him most but by Bobby's third season, Chiefs coach Hank Stram decided he had enough defensive line talent to permit Bell to make a permanent move to outside linebacker.

There he gained superstardom, winning all-AFL/AFC (American Football Conference) designation the next eight seasons—he already had been all-AFL once as a defensive end. Bell also played in Super Bowls I and IV and in the last six AFL All-Star games and the first four AFC–NFC Pro Bowls. He was named to the AFL's all-time team in 1969.

"I just like to play football, but if I had to pick one favorite position, it would be outside linebacker," Bell agreed. "It is one of the most challenging positions because you have so many responsibilities. You have to worry about the pass, the run, man-to-man coverage, containing plays, screens and draws.

Bell undoubtedly would have been outstanding on the strength of his God-given talents alone. What made him stand out even more was his superior approach to the game, a willingness to play anywhere, even when he was injured, and his great joy at just

### INTERCEPTION RECORD

| Year | Number | Yards | Average | TD |
|---|---|---|---|---|
| 1963 | 1 | 20 | 20.0 | 0 |
| 1964 | 1 | 4 | 4.0 | 0 |
| 1965 | 4 | 73 | 18.3 | 1 |
| 1966 | 2 | 14 | 7.0 | 0 |
| 1967 | 4 | 82 | 20.5 | 1 |
| 1968 | 5 | 95 | 19.0 | 0 |
| 1969 | 0 | 0 | 0.0 | 0 |
| 1970 | 3 | 57 | 19.0 | 1 |
| 1971 | 1 | 26 | 26.0 | 1 |
| 1972 | 3 | 56 | 18.7 | 1 |
| 1973 | 1 | 24 | 24.0 | 0 |
| 1974 | 1 | 28 | 28.0 | 1 |
| TOTALS | 26 | 479 | 18.4 | 6 |

*Many claimed that Bobby Bell had the athletic ability to play any position in pro football. He started as a defensive end for Kansas City but wound up as a Hall-of-Fame-caliber left outside linebacker.*

157

# SID GILLMAN

*Coach*
*Born in Minneapolis, Minn.,*
*October 26, 1911*
*Ohio State University*
*1955–9 Los Angeles Rams; 1960*
*Los Angeles Chargers; 1961–9,*
*1971 San Diego Chargers; 1973–4*
*Houston Oilers*

Sid Gillman started coaching in college more than 50 years ago when most teams were reluctant to pass more than five or six times a game. The standard opinion was that the running game was a much safer approach. Sid felt otherwise.

"The big play comes from the pass," he insisted. "God bless those runners because they get you the first down, give you ball control and keep your defense off the field. But if you want to ring the cash register, you have to pass."

Gillman's philosophy called for the full use of the field, 53⅓ yards wide and 100 yards long. The goal was to stretch the defensive perimeter and to make it more difficult to cover the five receivers he sent out on every play.

"We wanted people to fear our long game," Sid explained. "Once we threw long successfully, then we could throw short. All five of our receivers ran their patterns with enthusiasm because each knew, as the play developed, he could be the one who got the ball. This made it tough on the defense."

Gillman's first pro job came in 1955 at the age of 43 when he became the Los Angeles Rams' head coach. In his first year, Sid led the Rams to the NFL Western Division crown.

Five years later, when the American Football League (AFL) was founded, Gillman became the head coach–general manager of the Chargers, who played in Los Angeles in 1960 before settling in San Diego the next year.

Gillman's first Chargers elevens were high-scoring, crowd-pleasing, glamour teams that won divisional championships five of the league's first six years and the AFL title in 1963. He was the first coach to win divisional titles in both the AFL and NFL.

Illness forced a temporary retirement in 1969 but he returned to lead the Chargers again in 1971. A dispute with the team's owner, however, prompted his resignation in late season. Except

for a brief stint with the Houston Oilers—he was the AFC Coach of the Year in 1974—Sid's head coaching days were over.

His departure from the Chargers gave cause for those who fought on the AFL side in the inter-league war to assess just what Gillman had done for the young league. They agreed he had given the Chargers image, impetus and respect and, because of this, he had forced an entire league to adopt many of his methods to remain competitive.

"Sid Gillman brought class to the AFL," said Al Davis, a member of the first Chargers staff who later became the AFL commissioner. "Just being a part of Sid's organization was, for me, like going to a laboratory for the highly developed science of organized football."

*Sid Gillman was seen in this familiar sideline scene on the San Diego Chargers sidelines for more than a decade. His pro coaching career began with the Los Angeles Rams in 1955 and ended with the Houston Oilers, when he won AFC Coach of the Year acclaim in 1974. Gillman was noted as an offensive specialist.*

## COACHING RECORD

| Year | Won | Lost | Tied | Division finish |
|------|-----|------|------|-----------------|
| 1955° | 8 | 3 | 1 | 1st |
| 1956° | 4 | 8 | 0 | 5th |
| 1957° | 6 | 6 | 0 | 4th |
| 1958° | 8 | 4 | 0 | 2nd |
| 1959° | 2 | 10 | 0 | 6th |
| 1960† | 10 | 4 | 0 | 1st |
| 1961‡ | 12 | 2 | 0 | 1st |
| 1962‡ | 4 | 10 | 0 | 3rd |
| 1963‡ | 11 | 3 | 0 | 1st |
| 1964‡ | 8 | 5 | 1 | 1st |
| 1965‡ | 9 | 2 | 3 | 1st |
| 1966‡ | 7 | 6 | 1 | 3rd |
| 1967‡ | 8 | 5 | 1 | 3rd |
| 1968‡ | 9 | 5 | 0 | 3rd |
| 1969‡ | 4 | 5 | 0 | 3rd |
| 1970 | Retired—did not coach | | | |
| 1971‡ | 4 | 6 | 0 | 3rd |
| 1972 | Did not coach | | | |
| 1973§ | 1 | 8 | 0 | 4th |
| 1974§ | 7 | 7 | 0 | 2nd |
| TOTALS¶ | 123 | 104 | 7 | |

° With Los Angeles Rams

† With Los Angeles Chargers

‡ With San Diego Chargers

§ With Houston Oilers

¶ Career totals include post-season games

## POST-SEASON RECORD

1955 NFL Championship: Cleveland 38, Los Angeles Rams 14

1960 AFL Championship: Houston 24, Los Angeles Chargers 16

1961 AFL Championship: Houston 10, San Diego 3

1963 AFL Championship: San Diego 51, Boston 10

1964 AFL Championship: Buffalo 20, San Diego 7

1965 AFL Championship: Buffalo 23, San Diego 0

# SONNY JURGENSEN

*Quarterback*
*6 ft 0 in, 203 lb*
*Born in Wilmington, N. C.,*
*August 23, 1934*
*Duke University*
*1957–63 Philadelphia Eagles;*
*1964–74 Washington Redskins*

Sonny Jurgensen riddled enemy defenses with picture-perfect bullets for 18 seasons in the NFL. With Philadelphia for seven seasons and Washington for 11 more campaigns, the talented quarterback accumulated a seemingly endless list of brilliant individual records. Even at the age of 40 in his final 1974 season, Sonny won his third NFL individual passing crown.

Particularly in the nation's capital, Sonny, who was christened with the highly unlikely gridiron name of Christian Adolph Jurgensen III, became a folklore-type hero. Whether the Redskins won or lost, adoring fans knew that Sonny would be providing game-long excitement, throwing long and short, dissecting defenses, arousing his team and working on the clock.

A classic drop-back passer, Jurgensen was respected for his ability to deliver the ball at the last moment under the pressure of a vicious pass rush.

"All I ask of my blockers is four seconds," Sonny explained. "I try to stay on my feet and not be forced out of the pocket. I beat people by throwing, not running. I won't let them intimidate me into doing something which is not the best thing I can do."

Jurgensen's election to the Hall of Fame proved that a great star can win such an honor on the strength of his own merits rather than the success of his teams. In 18 seasons, Sonny played on only eight teams with a better than .500 record. He was a full-time regular on only two. He was a substitute on the 1959 and 1960 Eagles teams and, with four winning Redskins teams, he was hampered by injuries and often out of action completely.

One thing Sonny wanted above all else—to excel in a championship game—eluded him. When the Eagles won in 1960, Jurgensen sat on the bench while the veteran Norm Van Brocklin engineered the victory. With the Redskins 12 years later, Sonny

*Sonny Jurgensen was universally recognized as one of the finest forward passers in pro football history. He continually provided game-long excitement with his defense-dissecting aerials.*

was sidelined with a torn Achilles tendon for both the NFC championship game and Super Bowl VII that followed.

Particularly early in his career, Jurgensen had the reputation of being a curfew-breaking playboy. Sonny did not deny this charge but did defend himself by insisting, "On the field, it is serious business. I am interested in winning."

Noted for his taskmaster approach to coaching, Vince Lombardi nevertheless quickly developed a strong admiration for the fun-loving Jurgensen when he took over the Redskins in 1969. "Jurgensen is a great quarterback," the coach said without hesitation. "He hangs in there under adverse conditions. He may be the best the league has ever seen. He is the best I have seen."

PASSING RECORD

| Year | Attempts | Completions | Percentage passes completed | Yards | TD | Interceptions |
|---|---|---|---|---|---|---|
| 1957° | 70 | 33 | 47.1 | 470 | 5 | 8 |
| 1958° | 22 | 12 | 54.5 | 259 | 0 | 1 |
| 1959° | 5 | 3 | 60.0 | 27 | 1 | 0 |
| 1960° | 44 | 24 | 54.5 | 486 | 5 | 1 |
| 1961° | 416 | 235‡ | 56.5 | 3723‡ | 32‡ | 24‡ |
| 1962° | 366 | 196 | 53.6 | 3261‡ | 22 | 26‡ |
| 1963° | 184 | 99 | 53.8 | 1413 | 11 | 13 |
| 1964† | 385 | 207 | 53.8 | 2934 | 24 | 13 |
| 1965† | 356 | 190 | 53.4 | 2367 | 15 | 16 |
| 1966† | 436‡ | 254‡ | 58.3 | 3209‡ | 28 | 19 |
| 1967†§ | 508‡ | 288‡ | 56.7 | 3747‡ | 31‡ | 16 |
| 1968† | 292 | 167 | 57.2 | 1980 | 17 | 11 |
| 1969†§ | 442‡ | 274‡ | 62.0 | 3102‡ | 22 | 15 |
| 1970† | 337 | 202 | 59.9‡ | 2354 | 23 | 10 |
| 1971† | 28 | 16 | 57.1 | 170 | 0 | 2 |
| 1972† | 59 | 39 | 66.1 | 633 | 2 | 4 |
| 1973† | 145 | 87 | 60.0 | 904 | 6 | 5 |
| 1974† | 167 | 107 | 64.1 | 1185 | 11 | 5 |
| TOTALS | 4262 | 2433 | 57.1 | 32,224 | 255 | 189 |

Career passing rating: 82.625

° With Philadelphia Eagles

† With Washington Redskins

‡ Led NFL

§ Official NFL individual passing champion

Rushing: 181 attempts, 493 yards, 2.7-yard average, 15 touchdowns

Scoring: 15 touchdowns, 90 points

# BOBBY MITCHELL

*Wide receiver, halfback*
*6 ft 0 in., 195 lb*
*Born in Hot Springs, Ark., June 6,*
*1935*
*University of Illinois*
*1958–61 Cleveland Browns;*
*1962–8 Washington Redskins*

*Bobby Mitchell was a running back for the Cleveland Browns for four seasons before moving to Washington, where he became an outstanding wide receiver.*

B obby Mitchell in reality experienced two separate careers during his 11-season tenure in the NFL. At the start, he teamed with the incomparable Jim Brown to give Cleveland one of history's most potent running back combinations. After his 1962 trade to Washington, Bobby became a full-time flanker and one of the best catch-run yardage-makers in pro football. Particularly with the Browns, he was a breakaway threat as a punt and kickoff returner.

When he retired, his record of 14,078 combined net yards was the third highest ever and his 91 touchdowns ranked number 5. Eighteen of his touchdowns came by rushing, 65 on receptions, three on punt returns and five on kickoff returns.

Mitchell quickly gained the reputation of being a big-play man. As a rookie, he had a 98-yard kickoff return. A year later, he rushed for 232 yards in one game and, in another, he scored on a 78-yard punt return. Bobby's big-game, big-play recitation is a long one.

A track star of some note, Mitchell had his sights set on the 1960 Olympics but he had just gotten married and decided, because of financial considerations, he had better listen when the Browns made him an offer. Mitchell did feel he was too small to be a pro running back. He asked the Browns to use him as a wide receiver where he could utilize both his speed and pass-catching talents.

Cleveland, however, had an opening at halfback and that is where Mitchell played. For the next four years, he was excellent at everything he tried—running, catching and returning kicks—but the Browns coveted another big running back and were willing to trade Mitchell to the Redskins for the drafting rights to the heralded Ernie Davis from Syracuse.

Mitchell was a pioneer of sorts in Washington where he became the first black to make the team and prevail for any length of time. This did not affect Bobby's play, however, for he won the NFL receiving title in 1962 with 72 catches. He never caught less than 58 passes his first six seasons in Washington.

Bobby also won his share of post-season honors after he joined the Redskins. He was an all-NFL pick in both 1962 and 1964 and earned three more Pro Bowl bids to go along with his 1960 invitation when he was in Cleveland.

Mitchell retired before the 1969 season. Since he did so many things, he couldn't claim any lifetime statistical leaderships but he could gain great satisfaction in the knowledge that he had the more valuable—and much more unusual—trait of being able to do lethal damage, no matter how he gained possession, every time he carried the football.

## RECEIVING RECORD

| Year | Number | Yards | Average | TD |
|---|---|---|---|---|
| 1958° | 16 | 131 | 8.2 | 3 |
| 1959° | 35 | 351 | 10.0 | 4 |
| 1960° | 45 | 612 | 13.6 | 6 |
| 1961° | 32 | 368 | 11.5 | 3 |
| 1962† | 72‡ | 1384‡ | 19.2 | 11 |
| 1963† | 69 | 1436‡ | 20.8 | 7 |
| 1964† | 60 | 904 | 15.1 | 10‡ |
| 1965† | 60 | 867 | 14.5 | 6 |
| 1966† | 58 | 905 | 15.6 | 9 |
| 1967† | 60 | 866 | 14.4 | 6 |
| 1968† | 14 | 130 | 9.3 | 0 |
| TOTALS | 521 | 7954 | 15.3 | 65 |

## RUSHING RECORD

| Year | Attempts | Yards | Average | TD |
|---|---|---|---|---|
| 1958° | 80 | 500 | 6.3 | 1 |
| 1959° | 131 | 743 | 5.7 | 5 |
| 1960° | 111 | 506 | 4.6 | 5 |
| 1961° | 101 | 548 | 5.4 | 5 |
| 1962† | 1 | 5 | 5.0 | 0 |
| 1963† | 3 | 24 | 8.0 | 0 |
| 1964† | 2 | 33 | 16.5 | 0 |
| 1965† | 0 | 0 | 0.0 | 0 |
| 1966† | 13 | 141 | 10.8 | 1 |
| 1967† | 61 | 189 | 3.1 | 1 |
| 1968† | 10 | 46 | 4.6 | 0 |
| TOTALS | 513 | 2735 | 5.3 | 18 |

## KICKOFF RETURN RECORD

| Year | Number | Yards | Average | TD |
|---|---|---|---|---|
| 1958° | 18 | 454 | 25.2 | 1 |
| 1959° | 11 | 236 | 21.5 | 0 |
| 1960° | 17 | 432 | 25.4 | 1‡ |
| 1961° | 16 | 428 | 26.8 | 1 |
| 1962† | 12 | 398 | 33.2 | 1‡ |
| 1963† | 9 | 343 | 38.1 | 1 |
| 1964† | 3 | 58 | 19.3 | 0 |
| 1965† | 5 | 106 | 21.2 | 0 |
| 1966† | 0 | 0 | 0.0 | 0 |
| 1967† | 0 | 0 | 0.0 | 0 |
| 1968† | 11 | 235 | 21.4 | 0 |
| TOTALS | 102 | 2690 | 26.4 | 5 |

## PUNT RETURN RECORD

| Year | Number | Yards | Average | TD |
|---|---|---|---|---|
| 1958° | 14 | 165 | 11.8 | 1‡ |
| 1959° | 17 | 177 | 10.4 | 1 |
| 1960° | 9 | 101 | 11.2 | 0 |
| 1961° | 14 | 164 | 11.7 | 1 |
| 1962† | 3 | 7 | 2.3 | 0 |
| 1963† | 6 | 49 | 8.2 | 0 |
| 1964† | 0 | 0 | 0.0 | 0 |
| 1965† | 1 | 15 | 15.0 | 0 |
| 1966† | 4 | 21 | 5.3 | 0 |
| 1967† | 0 | 0 | 0.0 | 0 |
| 1968† | 1 | 0 | 0.0 | 0 |
| TOTALS | 69 | 699 | 10.1 | 3 |

° With Cleveland Browns     † With Washington Redskins     ‡ Led NFL

Passing: 3 attempts, 3 completions, 61 yards, 1 touchdown, 0 interceptions

# PAUL WARFIELD

*Wide receiver*
*6 ft 0 in. 188 lb*
*Born in Warren, Ohio,*
*November 28, 1942*
*Ohio State University*
*1964–9, 1976–7 Cleveland*
*Browns; 1970–4 Miami Dolphins*

and had been happy playing for the Browns. He was truly shocked when he was sent to Miami in the blockbuster trade in 1970 but he was particularly elated in 1973 when the Dolphins were playing in Cleveland and 80,000 Cleveland fans gave him a standing ovation when he took the field. To Paul, he was coming home—where he felt he should have been all along.

Although he was one of history's premier wide receivers, Paul Warfield did not deal in big numbers. His 427 catches fall more than 300 short of the all-time leader and more than 100 shy of a dozen others. Yet in many ways, Paul is the model by which great receivers are measured.

Picture a graceful athlete prancing downfield, putting a move on the defender, leaping in the air, gently grasping the football and then streaking downfield. For 13 eventful seasons, that is the way Warfield thrilled millions of excited NFL fans.

Paul had the good fortune to play with two extremely successful teams, the Cleveland Browns at both the start and the end of his tenure and with the Miami Dolphins in the middle. As a result, he was constantly in the big games—four NFL championships, three AFC title games and Super Bowls VI, VII and VIII.

That circumstance also proved to be a personal misfortune for Paul since both the Browns and the Dolphins were ball-control oriented teams who looked on the forward pass more as a threat to make the ground game effective than as a heavy-duty offensive weapon. The 1972 Dolphins, with their perfect 17–0–0 record, provided a splendid example. They rushed 613 times in regular season while passing on only 280 occasions. Paul had just 29 catches and scored only three touchdowns. Still he was considered a key element in the Dolphins' unprecedented success.

"A lot is said about the Miami ball-control offense," one close observer noted. "But the truth is the Dolphins have a very dangerous long-strike, big-play offense. They have the perfect blend. They run enough to set up scoring passes and pass enough to set up touchdown runs. Warfield is a tremendous key to all of this."

Still, Warfield could never completely accept his role in Miami and this was eventually a factor in his "defection" to the World Football League in 1975. When that venture proved to be a disaster, Paul was invited back to the Browns, where he had started his career as a number 1 pick in 1964.

Paul had played both high-school and college football in Ohio

*Paul Warfield breaks free to catch one of the many long forward passes that came his way during his stay with the Miami Dolphins from 1970 to 1974. Warfield first joined the Cleveland Browns in 1964 and wound up back with the Browns in 1976 and 1977.*

RECEIVING RECORD

| Year | Number | Yards | Average | TD |
|------|--------|-------|---------|-----|
| 1964° | 52 | 920 | 17.7 | 9 |
| 1965° | 3 | 30 | 10.0 | 0 |
| 1966° | 36 | 741 | 20.6 | 5 |
| 1967° | 32 | 702 | 21.9 | 8 |
| 1968° | 50 | 1067 | 21.3 | 12§ |
| 1969° | 42 | 886 | 21.1 | 10 |
| 1970† | 28 | 703 | 25.1 | 6 |
| 1971† | 43 | 996 | 23.2 | 11§ |
| 1972† | 29 | 606 | 20.9 | 3 |
| 1973‡ | 29 | 514 | 17.7 | 11 |
| 1974† | 27 | 536 | 19.9 | 2 |
| 1975‡ | Not in NFL | | | |
| 1976° | 38 | 613 | 16.1 | 6 |
| 1977° | 18 | 251 | 13.9 | 2 |
| TOTALS | 427 | 8565 | 20.1 | 85 |

° With Cleveland Browns

† With Miami Dolphins

‡ With Memphis Southmen (World Football League). His receiving record for this year is: 25 receptions, 422 yards, 16.9-yard average, 3 touchdowns

§ Led NFL

Rushing: 22 attempts, 204 yards, 9.3-yard average, 0 touchdowns

Scoring: 86 touchdowns, 516 points

# WILLIE BROWN

*Cornerback*
*6 ft 1 in. 210 lb*
*Born in Yazoo City, Miss.,*
*December 2, 1940*
*Grambling College*
*1963–6 Denver Broncos; 1967–78*
*Oakland Raiders*

Willie Brown joined the Denver Broncos in 1963 as an unheralded, untried free agent who just happened to possess all the natural tools of a perfect cornerback—speed, size, mobility, aggressiveness, determination and a keen football sense. As it turned out, all he needed was a little time and playing experience to become exceptional.

Brown became a starter six games into his rookie season, made the all-AFL (American Football League) team his second year and, by the time Denver traded him to Oakland in 1967, he was a most-coveted and established standout.

It probably is not pure coincidence that, during Brown's tenure in Oakland from 1967 through 1978, the Raiders' 125–35–7 won–lost mark was the best in pro football and the Oakland team appeared in nine AFL/AFC (American Football Conference) title games and Super Bowls II and XI. Prominent among Oakland's many team strengths was a universally respected defensive secondary of which Willie was the unquestioned leader for more than a decade.

Some of his most illustrious opponents spoke of Brown in the most glowing terms. "Some backs you can kind of lean on," Gene Washington, a premier San Francisco pass catcher, once said, "but you can't do that with Willie. He's too strong and too fast."

*Willie Brown joined the Oakland Raiders in his fifth season in 1967. For the next 12 years, Brown anchored the strong Raiders secondary and was regarded as "the greatest cornerback ever."*

After Brown smothered 11 of 12 passes Joe Namath threw to the talented George Sauer one afternoon, the admiring Jets' quarterback remarked, "Willie gives you nothing. Unless you throw a perfect pass, you can't complete it. He's the very best."

Willie also inspired his teammates with his willingness to play hurt. He played with his arm in a cast, a pulled groin muscle and a broken thumb throughout the 1971 campaign. Yet he permitted only 10 receptions in his area while playing every down in a season that saw opponents pass 359 times.

Brown's most-remembered play no doubt was his 75-yard interception return against Minnesota in Super Bowl XI but, during his career, he had 54 steals in regular-season play and seven more in post-season action.

Willie's exceptional play did not go unnoticed. He was named all-league seven times and selected for five AFL All-Star games and four AFC–NFC Pro Bowls.

By the time he retired, more than a few gridiron experts had decided Willie might be the greatest cornerback in his sport's history. One writer summarized those thoughts. "Combine all of Willie's skills and the result is what myths are made of. He is a marvel to watch, a true artist at work."

| Year | Number | Yards | Average | TD |
|---|---|---|---|---|
| 1963* | 1 | 0 | 0.0 | 0 |
| 1964* | 9 | 140 | 15.6 | 0 |
| 1965* | 2 | 18 | 9.0 | 0 |
| 1966* | 3 | 37 | 12.3 | 0 |
| 1967† | 7 | 33 | 4.7 | 1 |
| 1968† | 2 | 27 | 13.5 | 1 |
| 1969† | 5 | 111 | 22.2 | 0 |
| 1970† | 3 | 0 | 0.0 | 0 |
| 1971† | 2 | 2 | 1.0 | 0 |
| 1972† | 4 | 26 | 6.5 | 0 |
| 1973† | 3 | −1 | −0.3 | 0 |
| 1974† | 1 | 31 | 31.0 | 0 |
| 1975† | 4 | −1 | −0.3 | 0 |
| 1976† | 3 | 25 | 8.3 | 0 |
| 1977† | 4 | 24 | 6.0 | 0 |
| 1978† | 1 | 0 | 0.0 | 0 |
| TOTALS | 54 | 472 | 8.7 | 2 |

INTERCEPTION RECORD

* With Denver Broncos

† With Oakland Raiders

Punt returns: 3 returns, 29 yards, 9.7-yard average, 0 touchdowns

Kickoff returns: 3 returns, 70 yards, 23.3-yard average, 0 touchdowns

# MIKE McCORMACK

*Tackle*
*6 ft 4 in. 250 lb*
*Born in Chicago. Ill.. June 21.*
*1930*
*University of Kansas*
*1951 New York Yanks; 1954–62*
*Cleveland Browns*

Although coach Paul Brown often spoke of him as "the finest offensive lineman I ever coached," Mike McCormack spent 10 seasons in the NFL as a largely unknown performer. This is not particularly unusual for a player from "the trenches" whose skills cannot be spotted and appreciated by the fans or even by his coaches until the game films have been carefully studied.

However, as a rookie with the New York Yanks in 1951, McCormack made a lasting impression on the Cleveland Browns' head man. Mike played both as an offensive tackle and a linebacker that year and earned the first of six Pro Bowl invitations.

After his rookie season, McCormack left pro football for a two-year stint in the US Army but in 1953, a full year before Mike would return to civilian life, Brown engineered one of history's truly amazing trades—a 15-player swap—so that McCormack would be wearing a Browns uniform the next time he played on an NFL gridiron.

Brown had McCormack targeted for the right offensive tackle position but that assignment was delayed a year because of the retirement of the superstar middle guard, Bill Willis, before the 1954 season. Called on to fill the void, Mike demonstrated the speed and gridiron instinct necessary to play middle guard, which in reality was the forerunner of the modern middle linebacker position.

By 1955, Brown was able to move McCormack to offensive tackle where he performed with distinction for the next eight seasons. Mike was as adept at opening holes for a running back like Jim Brown as he was at protecting a quarterback like Otto Graham. Just as he had a year before as a middle guard, Mike came through with flying colors in a key job once again.

McCormack was an outstanding field leader and, from 1956 on, served as the Browns' team captain. He was well-liked and respected as a team leader but he was not above taking stern measures if the occasion seemed appropriate. One year, Milt Plum, the Cleveland quarterback, was having a problem staying in his pocket and waiting for the proper moment to release his passes. Exasperated, McCormack interrupted one practice, picked Plum up by the neck, shook him and told him to shape up. Legend has it that the Browns' passing game improved considerably—and quickly.

Mike also recognized that confidence and enthusiasm were two necessary ingredients in developing a winning team. As team captain, he always promoted his own firm conviction: "I never went on a football field when I didn't think my team could win."

*While Mike McCormack was in the US Army in 1953, he became the key man in a 15-player trade that brought him to Cleveland.*

# CHARLEY TAYLOR

*Wide receiver, halfback*
*6 ft 3 in, 210 lb*
*Born in Grand Prairie, Tex.,*
*September 28, 1941*
*Arizona State University*
*1964–75, 1977 Washington*
*Redskins*

the attention of an Arizona State scout.

When it became apparent that Charley was going to occupy a place in the pro football record book, he was asked how he felt. "When you stop playing, nobody remembers you," Taylor answered. "Some won't even believe you played pro ball. But if your name is in the record book, that's proof you did play and people will remember. That really would be nice."

Many coaches and scouts had seen Charley Taylor play college football at Arizona State and they all agreed he was certain to be a standout in professional football. What they did not agree on was where Charley should play.

Some felt he would be a great defensive cornerback while others said he was a natural as a return specialist. The majority, including his first pro coach, Bill McPeak, believed his first shot should come at offensive halfback. So it was as a Rookie of the Year running back that Taylor began his NFL career with the Washington Redskins in 1964.

Charley enjoyed two excellent seasons as a running back and set a personal long-range goal of being a truly outstanding runner, perhaps even of the caliber of Jim Brown. So it is not surprising that Taylor was bitterly unhappy when, midway into the 1966 campaign, Redskins coach Otto Graham reached the conclusion that Charley would be a great split end.

From his performance against Baltimore in his first start as a full-time wide receiver, one could never have guessed that Taylor was in a depressed state. He caught eight passes for 111 yards. The next week against Dallas, Charley tied a team record with 11 receptions. He wound up the season as the NFL's top pass-catcher with 72 receptions.

Slowly Charley began to realize that his new position might also be his ticket to pro football immortality. He could see that, as a pass-catcher, he would have more opportunities to do what he did best—break tackles and race toward the goal line once he found leg room beyond the line of scrimmage.

He led the NFL in receiving again in 1967 and averaged 60 receptions a year until he was sidelined in an injury-plagued season in 1971. Charley wound up his career with 649 receptions, the top total in history up to that time.

Through most of Charley's career, he never seemed to command the attention that normally would accompany a player of his caliber. This was true even after an excellent high-school career when he had to rely on a local booster to bring his talents to

RECEIVING RECORD

| Year | Number | Yards | Average | TD |
|---|---|---|---|---|
| 1964 | 53 | 814 | 15.4 | 5 |
| 1965 | 40 | 577 | 14.4 | 3 |
| 1966 | 72* | 1119 | 15.5 | 12 |
| 1967 | 70* | 990 | 14.1 | 9 |
| 1968 | 48 | 650 | 13.5 | 5 |
| 1969 | 71 | 883 | 12.4 | 8 |
| 1970 | 42 | 593 | 14.1 | 8 |
| 1971 | 24 | 370 | 15.4 | 4 |
| 1972 | 49 | 673 | 13.7 | 7 |
| 1973 | 59 | 801 | 13.6 | 7 |
| 1974 | 54 | 738 | 13.7 | 5 |
| 1975 | 53 | 774 | 14.6 | 6 |
| 1976 | Injured—did not play | | | |
| 1977 | 14 | 158 | 11.3 | 0 |
| TOTALS | 649 | 9140 | 14.1 | 79 |

\* Led NFL

Rushing: 442 attempts, 1488 yards, 3.4-yard average, 11 touchdowns

Passing: 16 attempts, 3 completions, 99 yards, 1 touchdown, 1 interception

Kickoff returns: 5 returns, 133 yards, 26.6-yard average, 0 touchdowns

Punt returns: 5 returns, 63 yards, 12.6-yard average, 0 touchdowns

Scoring: 90 touchdowns, 540 points

*Charley Taylor began his pro career as a running back but was shifted to wide receiver in his third season. There he developed into one of the all-time great pass-catchers. He finished his career in 1977 as the lifetime leader with 649 receptions.*

# ARNIE WEINMEISTER

*Defensive tackle*
*6 ft 4 in, 235 lb*
*Born in Rhein, Saskatchewan,*
*March 23, 1923*
*University of Washington*
*1948 New York Yankees (AAFC);*
*1949 Brooklyn–New York Yankees*
*(AAFC); 1950–3 New York Giants*

Few players have ever dominated their position like Arnie Weinmeister did during his six years in American pro football. He was a rookie with the New York Yankees of the All-America Football Conference (AAFC) in 1948 and finished in the NFL with the 1953 New York Giants before moving on to Canadian football.

Arnie could be described by all the adjectives one would normally associate with a superior defensive tackle—devastating, rugged, aggressive and dedicated. Yet his most outstanding trait was his speed. Weinmeister could outrun any one on the Yankees squad except the speed-burning scatback, Buddy Young. Later, with the Giants, it was standard practice for the coaches to intimidate rookie speedsters by matching them in 100-yard dashes against the big defensive tackle. Arnie never lost.

Because he had the unique ability to diagnose enemy plays and then to range from sideline to sideline to knock down the ball-carriers in open field, Weinmeister was one of the first defensive players to captivate the masses the way an offensive hero does.

"Arnie was bigger than most who played at that time,"

remembers Tom Landry, the long-time Dallas Cowboys coach who was a teammate of Weinmeister for five seasons. "He could operate all over the field because he was probably the fastest lineman in the league. He could also outrun most backs."

Except when they played the Giants, the Cleveland Browns were the dominant team in the NFL in the early 1950s. Stymied by a rugged Giants defense, the Browns were like every other NFL team in one respect—they could not consistently stop Arnie's explosive charge and their passers were constantly forced to get rid of the ball too quickly.

Although Yankees coach Ray Flaherty thought Weinmeister was "the best fullback prospect in the country," Arnie played with the Yankees as a tackle. The Boston Yanks of the NFL also were interested but Arnie accepted the AAFC team's high bid of $8000. "Frankly, if the competition between the leagues had not driven the salaries higher, I would not have played pro football," Arnie insisted.

Seven years later, Weinmeister was involved in another bidding war. This time the Canadian Football League was the "other league." For $15,000, compared to the Giants' offer of $12,000, Weinmeister moved to the British Columbia Lions.

His six-year career in American football is among the shortest of any Hall of Fame member. Still, the board of selectors did not hesitate when it came time to vote for Arnie's election. "Arnie Weinmeister definitely does belong," one voter said. "He was to the defensive tackle spot what Gale Sayers was to halfbacks—in a class by himself!"

*Arnie Weinmeister added unusual speed to the size, dedication and aggressiveness that made him an exceptional defensive tackle. He could outrun most backs in 100-yard dashes.*

# FRANK GATSKI

*Center*
*6 ft 3 in, 240 lb*
*Born in Farmington, W. Va.,*
*March 13, 1922*
*Marshall College, Auburn*
*University*
*1946–56 Cleveland Browns; 1957*
*Detroit Lions*

During his 12 seasons in pro football, Frank "Gunner" Gatski became known as "the silent one." When he did speak, it was usually about his coal-mining experiences in his native West Virginia or perhaps about his favorite pastime, hunting with a bow and arrow. He let his play on the gridiron "speak for itself."

Equally effective as a pass protector or a blocker on running plays, Gatski had the ideal physical requirements to serve as the anchor man on the Browns' line that powered pro football's most lethal attack of the era. With size and strength, he could withstand the fiercest charges of some of the NFL's finest defensive stalwarts.

"He was the best and toughest I ever played against," Hall of Famer Chuck Bednarik of the Philadelphia Eagles said. "As a linebacker, I sometimes had to go over the center but Gatski was an immovable object."

Unless he makes a bad snap, the center is rarely noticed and his name is hardly ever in the record books. Gatski's one statistical entry was a touchdown interception return during a brief stint as a linebacker in his rookie 1946 campaign.

Gunner nevertheless can point with pride to one signal distinction, that of playing in 11 championship games in 12 years in the pros. From 1946 through 1955, the Browns won four All-America Football Conference (AAFC) and three NFL championships and were in three other NFL title games. Frank earned his eighth championship ring when he moved to Detroit in 1957 and helped the Lions whip his old team in the title game.

If one Gatski accomplishment stood out above all others, it was his feat of never missing a game or a practice or even calling a timeout in 20 years of high-school, college and pro football. "You've got to be tough to play football," Gatski explained.

Frank came by his toughness and hard-work ethic naturally. After high school in Farmington, he went to work in the mines, just as everyone who lived in Number Nine Camp was expected to do. A year later, Gatski got a chance to try out for the Marshall College football team. Those who survived the tryouts were given jobs on campus while the others returned to the mines.

It was Gatski's one chance to escape a coal-miner's existence and he made the most of it. From that point on, he truly did let his gridiron performances "speak for themselves."

*Normally a quiet person, Frank Gatski let his playing do the talking during his 12 seasons in the NFL. He never missed a game in 20 years of high school, college and pro football.*

# JOE NAMATH

*Quarterback*
*6 ft 2 in, 200 lb*
*Born in Beaver Falls, Pa., May 31, 1943*
*University of Alabama*
*1965–76 New York Jets; 1977 Los Angeles Rams*

In almost 100 years of pro football, there has been only a handful of players whose lasting effect on how the game is played or how it is accepted by the public far exceeded their considerable achievements on the field.

Joe Namath was such an "impact" player. From the time the touted quarterback from Alabama University signed a reported $400,000 contract with the New York Jets in 1965 until his final pass with the 1977 Los Angeles Rams, "Broadway Joe" attracted universal attention by his every action, whether it be a night on the town or a mind-boggling passing spree on the football field.

As a player, Joe is best remembered for his classic performance in guiding the New York Jets to a stunning 16–7 upset of the Baltimore Colts in Super Bowl III. The "icing on the cake" was Joe's personal "guarantee" of victory a few days earlier. After two easy wins by the NFL the first two years, the epic upset assured the competitive viability of the Super Bowl series.

Of even greater impact was Namath's signing of the contract that launched his pro football career. From the moment Joe signed what was then the most lucrative pro grid contract ever offered, the American Football League (AFL) enjoyed a rising surge of respect in the sports world. Other factors also helped to bring about a merger 18 months later, but Namath's signing without a doubt was the turning point in the costly football war.

In themselves, the inking of an epic contract and one superb game performance should not assure a player of pro football immortality. Namath demonstrated repeatedly that he was a superior quarterback whose only limitation seemed to be the agonizingly long string of injuries that hampered him throughout his career. Joe was producing 300-yard games when such feats were rarities. Among his finest single-game performances was a 266-yard, three-touchdown outburst against Oakland in the 1968 AFL title game that put the Jets into Super Bowl III.

Namath was the 1968 AFL Player of the Year and a unanimous all-pro quarterback in 1972. In 1969, he was named to the AFL's all-time team.

*Joe Namath made big news just by signing a reported $400,000 contract with the New York Jets in 1965. Four years later, he led the Jets to a big upset victory in Super Bowl III.*

Although such things do not appear in the statistics columns Namath was also rich in the intangibles—leadership, play-calling mastery, courage, toughness, competitive spirit and, most of all, the ability to make exciting things happen on the football field.

## PASSING RECORD

| Year | Attempts | Completions | Percentage passes completed | Yards | TD | Interceptions |
|------|----------|-------------|-----------------------------|-------|-----|---------------|
| 1965° | 340 | 164 | 48.2 | 2220 | 18 | 15 |
| 1966° | 471‡ | 232‡ | 49.3 | 3379‡ | 19 | 27‡ |
| 1967° | 491‡ | 258‡ | 52.5 | 4007‡ | 26 | 28 |
| 1968° | 380 | 187 | 49.2 | 3147 | 15 | 17 |
| 1969° | 361 | 185 | 51.2 | 2734 | 19 | 17 |
| 1970° | 179 | 90 | 50.3 | 1259 | 5 | 12 |
| 1971° | 59 | 28 | 47.5 | 537 | 5 | 6 |
| 1972° | 324 | 162 | 50.0 | 2816§ | 19§ | 21 |
| 1973° | 133 | 68 | 51.1 | 966 | 5 | 6 |
| 1974° | 361 | 191 | 52.9 | 2616 | 20 | 22§ |
| 1975° | 326 | 157 | 48.2 | 2286 | 15 | 28§ |
| 1976° | 230 | 114 | 49.6 | 1090 | 4 | 16 |
| 1977✝ | 107 | 50 | 46.7 | 606 | 3 | 5 |
| TOTALS | 3762 | 1886 | 50.1 | 27,663 | 173 | 220 |

Career passing rating: 65.6

° With New York Jets

✝ With Los Angeles Rams

‡ Led AFL

§ Led NFL

Rushing: 71 attempts, 140 yards, 2.0-average, 7 touchdowns

Scoring: 8 touchdowns, 48 points

# PETE ROZELLE

*Commissioner*
*Born in South Gate, Calif.,*
*March 1, 1926*
*University of San Francisco*
*1960–present National Football*
*League*

Pete Rozelle was the 33-year-old general manager of the Los Angeles Rams when he left for the annual NFL meetings in January, 1960. The principal business was to name a new commissioner to replace the popular Bert Bell, who had died three months earlier. After 23 ballots failed to produce a new leader, two NFL owners asked Rozelle to leave the meeting room while they and the other owners had a discussion.

Rozelle was such an unlikely candidate that the press covering the sessions paid little attention as he ventured into the men's room, pretending to wash his hands whenever anyone entered. After a couple of hours, Pete was invited back to the meeting to hear the news he was the NFL's new boss.

The choice of Rozelle as the NFL's number 1 man proved to be the single most important decision in the league's 68-year history. Pete not only "grew into the job," as his backers had predicted, but within a relatively few years, he was universally recognized as the premier commissioner of all professional sports.

The NFL's many problems during Rozelle's tenure are well-documented. Such things as periodic television negotiations, the war with the American Football League and the resulting merger, the development of the Super Bowl into America's premier sports attraction, drug and gambling scandals, player unrest with strikes and threats of strikes, plus the numerous court and legislative challenges that have threatened the organizational structure of the sport have dominated the headlines. Through it all, Rozelle's firm leadership has remained a dominating factor.

A quick insight into the growth experienced during Rozelle's stewardship can be gained through a capsule comparison of the NFL in 1960 and today. In 1960, there were 13 NFL teams and 500 players. Today, 28 teams employ more than 1500 players. NFL attendance grew from 40,106 a game in 1960 to 60,663 in 1986. In 1961, a winning player's championship game share was $5116. Today, a Super Bowl winning player takes home an extra $64,000. Annual NFL per-team TV receipts have increased from $330,000 in 1962 to approximately $17 million today. The list of comparisons could go on and on.

The commissioner's current contract runs through 1991, when he will be 65 and ready for retirement. The adage says that no one is indispensable or irreplaceable. Pete Rozelle may prove to be the exception that proves the rule.

*Pete Rozelle (center), along with Tex Schramm (left) and Lamar Hunt, announce the AFL–NFL merger on June 8, 1966.*

# O. J. SIMPSON

*Running back*
*6 ft 1 in. 212 lb*
*Born in San Francisco, Calif.,*
*July 9, 1947*
*University of Southern California*
*1969–77 Buffalo Bills; 1978–9 San*
*Francisco 49ers*

As a two-time all-America and a Heisman Trophy winner, O. J. Simpson was one of the most heralded rookies ever when he joined the Buffalo Bills in 1969.

Yet Simpson was not an immediate success—he did not even win Rookie of the Year honors. Buffalo teams were comparatively weak at the time but historians are more inclined to cite the curious manner in which the Bills' head coach, John Rauch, decided to utilize his heralded newcomer as the reason for O. J.'s slow start. "That's not my style. I wouldn't build my offense around one back, no matter how good he is," Rauch sharply objected, when observers suggested O. J. might carry the ball 30 or 40 times a game.

Just as Rauch had promised, Simpson was used as a runner, a receiver and on the rugged special teams during his first three years in the NFL. On a kickoff return in 1970, he suffered a serious knee injury.

Not surprisingly, O. J. was pondering an early retirement when the much-traveled coach, Lou Saban, returned to Buffalo for a second term. Lou had a track record of developing strong running games and he immediately made it clear he intended to rehabilitate the Buffalo offense around Simpson. He also recognized that O. J. would need good blockers if he were to fulfill his potential so Saban went to work assembling an exceptionally fine offensive line.

The results began to show in 1972 when O. J. went over 1000 yards rushing for the first time. A year later, Simpson "broke the bank" with more than 200 yards running in three games and an unprecedented season total of 2003 yards. At a press conference following his final game performance, Simpson insisted his "Electric Company" offensive line share the plaudits with him.

Every year in the five-year period from 1972, when Saban turned him loose, through 1976, O. J. rushed for more than 1000 yards, won all-pro honors and played in the Pro Bowl. He won four NFL rushing titles and was named NFL Player of the Year in 1972, 1973, and 1975.

As his career neared its end, it was only natural to compare Simpson with the fabled fullback of another era, Jim Brown, many of whose records O. J. had surpassed. Simpson himself entered the debate. "In his day, Jim Brown was, without a doubt, the finest running back around. But I think today, I am the finest running back around."

All who saw him play will agree with Simpson's personal assessment. "The Juice" most certainly was, during the time he played, "the finest running back around."

## RUSHING RECORD

| Year | Attempts | Yards | Average | TD |
|------|----------|-------|---------|-----|
| 1969* | 181 | 697 | 3.9 | 2 |
| 1970* | 120 | 488 | 4.1 | 5 |
| 1971* | 183 | 742 | 4.1 | 5 |
| 1972* | 292 | 1251‡ | 4.3 | 6 |
| 1973* | 332‡ | 2003‡ | 6.0 | 12‡ |
| 1974* | 270 | 1125 | 4.2 | 3 |
| 1975* | 329‡ | 1817‡ | 5.5‡ | 16‡ |
| 1976* | 290 | 1503‡ | 5.2 | 8 |
| 1977* | 126 | 557 | 4.4 | 0 |
| 1978† | 161 | 593 | 3.7 | 1 |
| 1979† | 120 | 460 | 3.8 | 3 |
| TOTALS | 2404 | 11,236 | 4.7 | 61 |

\* With Buffalo Bills

† With San Francisco 49ers

‡ Led NFL

Receiving: 203 receptions, 2142 yards, 10.6-yard average, 14 touchdowns

Kickoff returns: 33 returns, 990 yards, 30.0-yard average, 1 touchdown

Passing: 16 attempts, 6 completions, 110 yards, 1 touchdown, 0 interceptions

Scoring: 76 touchdowns, 456 points

*O. J. Simpson was considering an early retirement when new coach Lou Saban decided to build the Buffalo Bills offense around the prized running back. Simpson responded with five straight 1000-yard rushing seasons.*

# ROGER STAUBACH

*Quarterback*
*6 ft 3 in, 202 lb*
*Born in Cincinnati, Ohio,*
*February 3, 1942*
*United States Naval Academy*
*1969–79 Dallas Cowboys*

Few players at any level of football ever generated as much excitement as Roger Staubach did every time he took a snap from center. Fans and opposing players alike had little idea as to whether Roger was going to handoff, pass or run.

Many teams were so concerned over Staubach's running skills that they often overlooked his outstanding ability as a forward passer. Roger had an unusually strong arm and his 57.0 career completion percentage will attest to his accuracy.

However, if one characteristic symbolized his daring play more than any other, it was his uncanny ability to lead the Cowboys to come-from-behind victories. He engineered no less than 23 fourth-quarter comebacks that produced victories. Fourteen of them came in the final two minutes or in overtime.

A typical example is the 1972 playoff game against San Francisco that saw the 49ers leading, 28–16, with 70 seconds to play. Making every play count, Roger first threw a 20-yard touchdown pass and, after a successful onside kick, came right back with a 10-yard scoring toss to produce a stunning 30–28 victory.

Staubach was a Cowboys draft pick in 1964 but the Heisman Trophy winner from Navy spent four years in the service during the Viet Nam conflict before reporting to Dallas as a 27-year-old rookie in 1969. Craig Morton was established as the number 1 quarterback at the time and Staubach did not get a chance to start on a regular basis until halfway through the 1971 season.

No pro quarterback ever fared better in his first chance at being a regular. "Roger the Dodger," as he had been known since his Navy days, won the NFL's individual passing championship, NFL Player of the Year acclaim and the Most Valuable Player award in Super Bowl VI.

Once Roger had the starting job, he did not give it up, except when he was injured, for the next nine seasons. During that period, he won four passing titles, was named all-NFC four times and played in four Pro Bowls.

Of even more significance, Roger led the Cowboys to an 85–30

*Roger Staubach was a fine passer, a superb scrambler and a respected team leader. During his nine years as a Cowboys starter, he led his team to its most successful years ever.*

winning record that included eight playoff seasons, four NFC championships and victories in Super Bowls VI and XII.

When Roger won, the Cowboys won—and this they both did over a many-season span with far greater regularity than most who have ever played the game.

---

## PASSING RECORD

| Year | Attempts | Completions | Percentage passes completed | Yards | TD | Interceptions |
|------|----------|-------------|------------------------------|-------|-----|---------------|
| 1969 | 47 | 23 | 48.9 | 421 | 1 | 2 |
| 1970 | 82 | 44 | 53.7 | 542 | 2 | 8 |
| 1971† | 211 | 126 | 59.7 | 1882 | 15 | 4 |
| 1972 | 20 | 9 | 45.0 | 98 | 0 | 2 |
| 1973† | 286 | 179 | 62.6 | 2428 | 23° | 15 |
| 1974 | 360 | 190 | 52.8 | 2552 | 11 | 15 |
| 1975 | 348 | 198 | 56.9 | 2666 | 17 | 16 |
| 1976 | 369 | 208 | 56.4 | 2715 | 14 | 11 |
| 1977 | 361° | 210° | 58.2 | 2620° | 18° | 9 |
| 1978† | 413 | 231 | 55.9 | 3190 | 25 | 16 |
| 1979† | 461 | 267 | 57.9 | 3586 | 27 | 11 |
| TOTALS | 2958 | 1685 | 57.0 | 22,700 | 153 | 109 |

Career passing rating: 83.4       ° Led NFL       † Official NFL individual passing champion

## RUSHING RECORD

| Year | Attempts | Yards | Average | TD |
|------|----------|-------|---------|-----|
| 1969 | 15 | 60 | 4.0 | 1 |
| 1970 | 27 | 221 | 8.2 | 0 |
| 1971 | 41 | 343 | 8.4 | 2 |
| 1972 | 6 | 45 | 7.5 | 0 |
| 1973 | 46 | 250 | 5.4 | 3 |
| 1974 | 47 | 320 | 6.8 | 3 |
| 1975 | 55 | 316 | 5.7 | 4 |
| 1976 | 43 | 184 | 4.3 | 3 |
| 1977 | 51 | 171 | 3.4 | 3 |
| 1978 | 42 | 182 | 4.3 | 1 |
| 1979 | 37 | 172 | 4.6 | 0 |
| TOTALS | 410 | 2264 | 5.5 | 20 |

Scoring: 20 touchdowns, 120 points

# PAUL HORNUNG

*Halfback*
*6 ft 2 in, 220 lb*
*Born in Louisville, Ky.,*
*December 23, 1935*
*University of Notre Dame*
*1957–62, 1964–6 Green Bay*
*Packers*

When Green Bay was dominating the NFL in the 1960s, Paul Hornung was considered by many to be the most important element in the Packers' awesomely efficient offensive machine. Paul was universally lauded for his many talents as a rusher, passer, pass receiver, blocker, kicker and particularly as a guy who could put points on the scoreboard.

Because Hornung did so many things well, he couldn't specialize in any one phase of the game. Only in one category—scoring—did he approach significant totals. Paul led the NFL in scoring three straight seasons. Included was a record 176-point outburst in 1960. He wound up his career with 760 points.

While many of Hornung's tallies came by placekicking, Paul is best remembered as the clutch performer with the "nose for the end zone." When the game was on the line, the Packers invariably gave number 5 the football.

There are plenty of "for instances." In the 1961 NFL title game, Paul was on Christmas leave from the Army when he scored a playoff record 19 points as Green Bay beat the New York Giants, 37–0. In the 1965 finale, he led all rushers and scored the clinching touchdown in a 23–12 win over Cleveland.

In 1965, he tallied five touchdowns in a crucial regular-season contest against the Baltimore Colts and then scored the winning touchdown in a 23–12 victory over Cleveland for the NFL crown.

Pro football success did not come easily nor immediately for Hornung, a Heisman Trophy winner at Notre Dame and a bonus-round pick of the Packers in 1957. For two years, Paul was shuttled between quarterback and halfback with an inept Green Bay eleven. He seriously considered giving up the game.

In 1959, a new coach, Vince Lombardi, installed Hornung at left halfback, a key position in Vince's offense. Secure in knowing for the first time in the pros where he was going to play, Paul developed almost immediately into a true superstar. In both 1950 and 1961, when the Packers began their string of championships under Lombardi, Hornung was the NFL's Most Valuable Player.

Injuries both before and after his year's suspension due to gambling problems in 1963 eventually forced Paul to retire after the 1966 season. Hornung left to Green Bay fans the legend of "The Golden Boy" with the matinee-idol appearance, an alleged high-living lifestyle and extraordinary success on the field. To his teammates, he was simply their leader, from whom they expected the big plays in the big games. Paul rarely disappointed them!

*Paul Hornung played at left halfback, a key position in Vince Lombardi's offense, during the Green Bay Packers' "dynasty years." He was at his absolute best near the goal line.*

## RUSHING RECORD

| Year | Attempts | Yards | Average | TD |
|------|----------|-------|---------|-----|
| 1957 | 60 | 319 | 5.3 | 3 |
| 1958 | 69 | 310 | 4.5 | 2 |
| 1959 | 152 | 681 | 4.5 | 7 |
| 1960 | 160 | 671 | 4.2 | 13° |
| 1961 | 127 | 597 | 4.7 | 8 |
| 1962 | 57 | 219 | 3.8 | 5 |
| 1963 | Suspended—did not play | | | |
| 1964 | 103 | 415 | 4.0 | 5 |
| 1965 | 89 | 299 | 3.4 | 5 |
| 1966 | 76 | 200 | 2.6 | 2 |
| TOTALS | 893 | 3711 | 4.2 | 50 |

## SCORING RECORD

| Year | TD | Extra points | Field goals | Total |
|------|-----|--------------|-------------|-------|
| 1957 | 3 | 0 | 0 | 18 |
| 1958 | 2 | 22 | 11 | 67 |
| 1959 | 7 | 31 | 7 | 94° |
| 1960 | 15° | 41 | 15 | 176° |
| 1961 | 10 | 41 | 15 | 146° |
| 1962 | 7 | 14 | 6 | 74 |
| 1963 | Suspended—did not play | | | |
| 1964 | 5 | 41 | 12 | 107 |
| 1965 | 8 | 0 | 0 | 48 |
| 1966 | 5 | 0 | 0 | 30 |
| TOTALS | 62 | 190 | 66 | 760 |

° Led NFL

Receiving: 130 receptions, 1480 yards, 11.4-yard average, 12 touchdowns

Passing: 55 attempts, 24 completions, 383 yards, 5 touchdowns, 4 interceptions

Kickoff returns: 10 returns, 248 yards, 24.8-yard average, 0 touchdowns

# KEN HOUSTON

*Strong safety*
*6 ft 3 in. 198 lb*
*Born in Lufkin. Tex.,*
*November 12. 1944*
*Prairie View A&M College*
*1967–72 Houston Oilers; 1973–80*
*Washington Redskins*

Ken Houston had been a linebacker in college but the Houston Oilers were thinking of him as a safety when they picked him in the ninth round of the 1967 draft. Ken quickly proved it was a wise choice.

Houston became a regular in his third game and two games later against the New Jets, Ken was off and running with two touchdowns, one a 45-yard scamper with a blocked field goal and the other a 43-yard interception return.

After six excellent seasons with the Oilers, during which Ken established an all-time record by returning nine interceptions for touchdowns, he was swapped to the Washington Redskins for five players, three of whom became instant regulars with the Oilers.

Houston was named all-pro eight years and was selected to play in 12 Pro Bowls. Only Merlin Olsen has been invited to more post-season classics. By the time he retired after the 1980 season, Houston was widely recognized as the premier strong safety of his time, possibly of all time.

While "insiders" had long recognized Ken as a premier player, he had made little impression on the masses. The Redskins' press guide once tabbed him "the NFL's most underrated superstar."

It took just one play and a Monday night television audience to change that. In an October 8, 1973 game against the arch-rival Dallas Cowboys, Washington was leading 14–7, with 16 seconds to play but Dallas had the ball, fourth and goal. Walt Garrison, a power-running fullback, grabbed a short swing pass and pivoted toward the end zone. Houston hit him squarely and stopped him dead in his tracks, inches short of a tying touchdown. Ken was never underrated again.

Houston had all the natural talents to be just what he turned out to be—a sensational strong safety. With a long, fluid stride, he had excellent speed and agility. His rangy, muscular body made him ideal for pass defense and yet helped to make him a punishing tackler. Once he got his hands on the ball, he was a talented runner.

Yet as a child in Lufkin, Ken didn't think of playing football. As a freshman, he played in the school band. "After my freshman year, I decided to go out for football," Houston relates. "I wanted a girl friend and it seemed that only the football players had all the girl friends."

*Ken Houston divided his pro football career between the Houston Oilers and the Washington Redskins. He set the lifetime record with nine interception returns for touchdowns, and was recognized as the premier free safety of his era.*

| INTERCEPTION RECORD | | | | |
|---|---|---|---|---|
| Year | Number | Yards | Average | TD |
| 1967° | 4 | 151 | 37.8 | 2 |
| 1968° | 5 | 160 | 32.0 | 2‡ |
| 1969° | 4 | 87 | 21.8 | 1 |
| 1970° | 3 | 32 | 10.7 | 0 |
| 1971° | 9 | 220 | 24.4 | 4§ |
| 1972° | 0 | 0 | 0.0 | 0 |
| 1973† | 6 | 32 | 5.3 | 0 |
| 1974† | 2 | 40 | 20.0 | 0 |
| 1975† | 4 | 33 | 8.3 | 0 |
| 1976† | 4 | 25 | 6.3 | 0 |
| 1977† | 5 | 69 | 13.8 | 0 |
| 1978† | 2 | 29 | 14.5 | 0 |
| 1979† | 1 | 20 | 20.0 | 0 |
| 1980† | 0 | 0 | 0.0 | 0 |
| TOTALS | 49 | 898 | 18.3 | 9¶ |

° With Houston Oilers

† With Washington Redskins

‡ Led AFL

§ Led NFL

¶ NFL career record

Punt returns: 51 returns, 333 yards, 6.5-yard average, 1 touchdown

Kickoff returns: 3 returns, 53 yards, 17.7-yard average, 0 touchdowns

Scoring: 12 touchdowns, 72 points

# WILLIE LANIER

*Middle linebacker*
*6 ft 1 in, 245 lb*
*Born in Clover, Va.,*
*August 21, 1945*
*Morgan State College*
*1967–77 Kansas City Chiefs*

The next week, in the last game ever played by an AFL team, the Chiefs prevailed over the Minnesota Vikings in Super Bowl IV. Lanier was once again right in the thick of things with a key interception in a defense-dominated upset.

*Nicknamed "Contact" because of his devastating tackling ability, Willie Lanier was the first black to be outstanding at middle linebacker. He was a dynamic defensive leader.*

As the first black in pro football to excel at the demanding middle linebacker position, Willie Lanier was a true pioneer. At 6 ft 1 in and 245 lb with a 34-inch waist, 50-inch chest and 20-inch neck, red-jerseyed number 63 presented an awesome image to any quarterback who lined up against him.

Handsome, quick-smiling and seemingly easy-going off the field, Willie turned into a tiger once the game started. He did his job so effectively for so long that he won all-AFL/AFC (American Football League/Conference) honors seven times and played in eight Pro Bowls.

Ermal Allen of the Dallas Cowboys research and development department once remarked: "You hear a lot about Dick Butkus and Tommy Nobis but this Willie Lanier is really the best middle linebacker in pro football."

In his 11 seasons, Lanier intercepted 27 passes and recovered 15 opponents' fumbles but he was best known for his ability to track down enemy ball-carriers and devastate them with the force of his tackles. He was nicknamed "Contact" because of his powerful hits on the opposition.

Because his fearless assaults on the opposition early in his pro career brought on a series of concussions, Lanier wore a specially padded helmet and eventually learned to play with the safety factor constantly in mind. "Over a period of time, if you attack everyone all out," he admitted, "you will wind up doing more damage to yourself than to anybody else."

Yet Lanier was disciplined, intelligent and obviously much more than just a hitter in his role as quarterback of the defense.

"Playing middle linebacker is sort of a science," Willie pointed out. "The key factor is to make an instantaneous response to a given stimuli. It involves mathematics, geometry and angles. There is, it is true, great joy in exploding into a man, making what they call the big hit. But you cannot do that on every play. You must learn to control your aggressiveness."

Whether it be by a controlled tackle or a fullback-smashing hit, there were many times that Lanier made the critical defensive play for the Chiefs. Best remembered is a stand he led that stopped the New York Jets three straight plays at the Chiefs' 1-yard line and paved the way to win the 1969 AFL championship.

INTERCEPTION RECORD

Fumbles: 15 opponents' fumbles recovered, 21 yards returned

| Year | Number | Yards | Average | TD |
|---|---|---|---|---|
| 1967 | 0 | 0 | 0.0 | 0 |
| 1968 | 4 | 120 | 30.0 | 1 |
| 1969 | 4 | 70 | 17.5 | 0 |
| 1970 | 2 | 2 | 1.0 | 0 |
| 1971 | 2 | 38 | 19.0 | 0 |
| 1972 | 2 | 2 | 1.0 | 0 |
| 1973 | 3 | 47 | 15.7 | 1 |
| 1974 | 2 | 28 | 14.0 | 0 |
| 1975 | 5 | 105 | 21.0 | 0 |
| 1976 | 3 | 28 | 9.3 | 0 |
| 1977 | 0 | 0 | 0.0 | 0 |
| TOTALS | 27 | 440 | 16.3 | 2 |

# FRAN TARKENTON

*Quarterback*
*6 ft 0 in. 185 lb*
*Born in Richmond. Va.,*
*February 3, 1940*
*University of Georgia*
*1961–6. 1972–8 Minnesota*
*Vikings: 1967–71 New York Giants*

In the Minnesota Vikings' first-ever game in 1961, quarterback Fran Tarkenton came off the bench to pass for four touchdowns and run for a fifth in a 37–13 upset of the Chicago Bears. No rookie ever had a more spectacular début.

For the next six seasons with the Vikings, five more with the New York Giants and a final seven back in Minnesota, Fran never let up in his relentless quest of yardage and touchdowns. He wound up his career with a host of records, including passing for 47,003 yards.

Add to that stunning total his 3674 yards rushing—six modern-era Hall of Fame running backs had smaller rushing totals—and you have 50,677 yards—almost *29 miles* or 500 football fields—of offensive progression when Tarkenton handled an NFL football.

In spite of those massive statistics, Tarkenton gained the most attention for his scrambling style during his early years. His actions not only excited the fans but they were also a curiosity inasmuch as the prototype pro quarterback of that day stayed bravely in his pocket of blockers in the face of even the fiercest pass rush.

There are many stories of Fran's classic scrambles. Once, in Los Angeles, Tarkenton twisted, turned and retreated with several Rams in hot pursuit before launching his pass 35 yards behind the scrimmage line. Another time, he scrambled for a full 28 seconds before rifling a touchdown pass downfield.

Tarkenton's unorthodox methods did not meet with universal acclaim. His coach, Norm Van Brocklin, never appreciated Fran's willingness to abandon a game plan. Some of his exasperated foes predicted that, by constantly exposing himself to unnecessary punishment, Tarkenton was inviting career-threatening injuries.

Fran did not miss a game because of injury, however, until bruised ribs forced him out of one game in his 16th season in 1976. A year later, he did suffer a broken leg that caused him to miss five games. He was back for all 16 games in 1978.

In 1967, the Vikings traded Tarkenton to the Giants for four prized draft choices but, five seasons later, the Giants sent him back to Minnesota in another blockbuster trade—this one for two veteran players, a rookie and two élite-round draft picks.

In his second tenure with the Vikings, Tarkenton proved he could lead a winning team. From 1973 to 1978, Minnesota enjoyed a 62–22–2 record and advanced to the Super Bowl three times. Fran's exploits were so spectacular that his coach, Bud Grant, who was not known for superlatives, proudly proclaimed him to be "the greatest quarterback who ever lived."

*In 18 seasons that included two tours with the Minnesota Vikings and a tenure with the New York Giants, quarterback Fran Tarkenton amassed awesome offensive totals.*

## PASSING RECORD

| Year | Attempts | Completions | Percentage passes completed | Yards | TD | Interceptions |
|------|----------|-------------|------------------------------|-------|-----|---------------|
| 1961° | 280 | 157 | 56.1 | 1997 | 18 | 17 |
| 1962° | 329 | 163 | 49.5 | 2595 | 22 | 25 |
| 1963° | 297 | 170 | 57.2 | 2311 | 15 | 15 |
| 1964° | 306 | 171 | 55.9 | 2506 | 22 | 11 |
| 1965° | 329 | 171 | 52.0 | 2609 | 19 | 11 |
| 1966° | 358 | 192 | 53.6 | 2561 | 17 | 16 |
| 1967† | 377 | 204 | 54.1 | 3088 | 29 | 19 |
| 1968† | 337 | 182 | 54.0 | 2555 | 21 | 12 |
| 1969† | 409 | 220 | 53.8 | 2918 | 23 | 8 |
| 1970† | 389 | 219 | 56.3 | 2777 | 19 | 12 |
| 1971† | 386 | 226 | 58.5 | 2567 | 11 | 21 |
| 1972° | 378 | 215 | 56.9 | 2651 | 18 | 13 |
| 1973° | 274 | 169 | 61.7 | 2113 | 15 | 7 |
| 1974° | 351 | 199 | 56.7 | 2598 | 17 | 12 |
| 1975° | 425‡ | 273‡ | 64.2 | 2994 | 25‡ | 13 |
| 1976° | 412 | 255‡ | 61.9 | 2961 | 17 | 8 |
| 1977° | 258 | 155 | 60.1‡ | 1734 | 9 | 14 |
| 1978° | 572‡ | 345‡ | 60.3 | 3468‡ | 25 | 32‡ |
| TOTALS | 6467 | 3686 | 57.0 | 47,003 | 342 | 266 |

Career passing rating: 80.4

° With Minnesota Vikings

† With New York Giants

‡ Led NFL

## RUSHING RECORD

| Year | Attempts | Yards | Average | TD |
|------|----------|-------|---------|-----|
| 1961° | 56 | 308 | 5.5 | 5 |
| 1962° | 41 | 361 | 8.8 | 2 |
| 1963° | 28 | 162 | 5.8 | 1 |
| 1964° | 50 | 330 | 6.6 | 2 |
| 1965° | 56 | 356 | 6.4 | 1 |
| 1966° | 62 | 376 | 6.1 | 4 |
| 1967† | 44 | 306 | 7.0 | 2 |
| 1968† | 57 | 301 | 5.3 | 3 |
| 1969† | 37 | 172 | 4.6 | 0 |
| 1970† | 43 | 236 | 5.5 | 2 |
| 1971† | 30 | 111 | 3.7 | 3 |
| 1972° | 27 | 180 | 6.7 | 0 |
| 1973° | 41 | 202 | 4.9 | 1 |
| 1974° | 21 | 120 | 5.7 | 2 |
| 1975° | 16 | 108 | 6.8 | 2 |
| 1976° | 27 | 45 | 1.7 | 1 |
| 1977° | 15 | 6 | 0.4 | 0 |
| 1978° | 24 | −6 | −0.3 | 1 |
| TOTALS | 675 | 3674 | 5.4 | 32 |

Scoring: 32 touchdowns, 192 points

# DOAK WALKER

*Halfback*
*5 ft 11 in, 173 lb*
*Born in Dallas, Tex., January 1,*
*1927*
*Southern Methodist University*
*1950–5 Detroit Lions*

*Doak Walker was a do-everything contributor in Detroit during the 1950s, when the Lions enjoyed their finest years. Walker scored 534 points in six years and won scoring titles in 1950 and 1955.*

As a three-time all-America and the 1948 Heisman Trophy winner, Doak Walker brought glowing credentials with him when he joined the Detroit Lions in 1950. Yet many NFL scouts honestly felt Doak was too small and while versatile, not a specialist at any phase of the game. They predicted the ''big boys'' would simply overwhelm him.

Walker, polite and soft-spoken, probably did seem like a duck out of water when he joined the swashbuckling Lions, one of pro football's classic tough-talking, beer-drinking, rough-and-tumble teams. Doak did have one big thing going for him—his lifelong friend, Bobby Layne, was the Lions' quarterback and unquestioned team leader.

Doak quickly erased any doubt he belonged in the NFL. He led the league in scoring with 128 points, was named Rookie of the Year, all-NFL and selected to play in the Pro Bowl. He continued to star for five more seasons, winning all-NFL honors three more times and being named to four more Pro Bowls. It is no coincidence that the Lions enjoyed their finest years ever, with three divisional crowns and two NFL titles, while Walker wore the number 37 blue-and-silver jersey.

Just as expected, Walker was a do-everything contributor for the Lions. His career chart showed entries in every possible statistical category—rushing, passing, receiving, punt and kickoff returns, punting, placekicking and even interceptions, for Doak also played defense whenever he was needed.

Walker was particularly efficient at the most important statistic, putting points on the board. In just over five seasons—he was injured during much of the 1952 campaign—Doak tallied 534 points. When he retired, he ranked third among history's top point-makers.

The Texas native had a knack for making the big plays in the most important games. In 1952, he returned from an injury-enforced layoff to throw a 24-yard touchdown pass in the divisional showdown against the Los Angeles Rams. In the NFL title game against Cleveland, Doak rushed for 97 yards and his 67-yard jaunt proved to be the game-winner in a 17–7 decision. A

year later, again facing the Browns, Walker scored the game's first touchdown and then kicked the winning point in a 17–16 squeaker.

After just six seasons and at the peak of his career, Doak decided to retire. The Lions offered a big raise if he would stay but Walker had lucrative business interests in Texas and could make more money by not playing. ''Besides, I want to get out while I'm still healthy,'' he explained, ''and while I can still contribute.''

## RUSHING RECORD

| Year | Attempts | Yards | Average | TD |
|---|---|---|---|---|
| 1950 | 83 | 386 | 4.7 | 5 |
| 1951 | 79 | 356 | 4.5 | 2 |
| 1952 | 26 | 106 | 4.1 | 0 |
| 1953 | 66 | 337 | 5.1 | 2 |
| 1954 | 32 | 240 | 7.5 | 1 |
| 1955 | 23 | 95 | 4.1 | 2 |
| TOTALS | 309 | 1520 | 4.9 | 12 |

Punt returns: 18 returns, 284 yards, 15.8-yard average, 1 touchdown

## RECEIVING RECORD

| Year | Number | Yards | Average | TD |
|---|---|---|---|---|
| 1950 | 35 | 534 | 15.3 | 6 |
| 1951 | 22 | 421 | 19.1 | 4 |
| 1952 | 11 | 90 | 8.2 | 0 |
| 1953 | 30 | 502 | 16.7 | 3 |
| 1954 | 32 | 564 | 17.6 | 3 |
| 1955 | 22 | 428 | 19.5 | 5 |
| TOTALS | 152 | 2539 | 16.7 | 21 |

Kickoff returns: 38 returns, 968 yards, 25.5-yard average, 0 touchdowns

Passing: 28 attempts, 7 completions, 75 yards, 2 touchdowns, 2 interceptions

## SCORING RECORD

| Year | TD | Extra points | Field goals | Total |
|---|---|---|---|---|
| 1950 | 11 | 38 | 8 | 128° |
| 1951 | 6 | 43° | 6 | 97 |
| 1952 | 0 | 5 | 3 | 14 |
| 1953 | 5 | 27 | 12 | 93 |
| 1954 | 5 | 43° | 11 | 106 |
| 1955 | 7 | 27 | 9 | 96° |
| TOTALS | 34 | 183 | 49 | 534 |

° Led NFL

Punting: 50 punts, 39.1-yard average

Interceptions: 2 interceptions, 60 yards, 30.0-yard average, 0 touchdowns

# LARRY CSONKA

*Fullback*
*6 ft 3 in. 235 lb*
*Born in Stow, Ohio, December 25, 1946*
*University of Syracuse*
*1968–74, 1979 Miami Dolphins; 1976—8 New York Giants*

In the early 1970s, the Miami Dolphins amassed a 57–12–1 won–lost record, won three American Football Conference (AFC) championships and two Super Bowls and enjoyed the ultimate experience of an unprecedented 17–0–0 perfect season in 1972.

Coach Don Shula employed a devastating ball-control offense led by two excellent halfbacks and a classic line-smashing fullback, Larry Csonka. Miami ran the ball about two out of every three plays and "Zonk" was the heavy-duty workhorse who had the most carries and the most yards for five straight years. When he wasn't carrying the ball, he excelled as a punishing blocker.

Csonka was at his very best when the stakes were the highest. He was the leading Miami rusher in all three AFC title games, rambled for a game-high 112 yards in Super Bowl VII and then took Most Valuable Player honors in Super Bowl VIII with a record 145 rushing yards that was more than double the rushing total of the badly beaten Minnesota Vikings.

After four years away from Miami with the Memphis Southmen World Football League team and the New York Giants, Larry returned to the Dolphins for an excellent comeback season in 1979, when he ended his career. Eight years later, he still ranked among the top ten rushers of all time but his most awesome statistic is his fumble record—just 21 miscues in 1997 ball-handling opportunities—just one fumble every 95 carries.

At the peak of his career, experts were comparing Larry favorably with the legendary Bronko Nagurski of the 1930s but Zonk always insisted his heroics were "no big deal." "I am a fullback, a power back whose assignment is to establish an inside running game," he explained. "That's my work."

"Fullbacks take a beating. That's also my job," Larry could have added, but didn't. The kind of pounding Larry took—a dozen broken noses, several concussions, a cracked eardrum, a damaged elbow, a banged-up knee—could best be described in a medical journal. In spite of this kind of punishment, Csonka refused to accept medication to ease his pain.

"I don't like to take Novocaine," he insisted. "If I can't control the pain with my head, I shouldn't be playing. I'm willing to play hurt, though. I have an obligation to my teammates to do that. The desire to play, however, must come from within. It is based on pride and determination."

Csonka possessed those qualities in abundance and letting his teammates down is, simply, something that never happened.

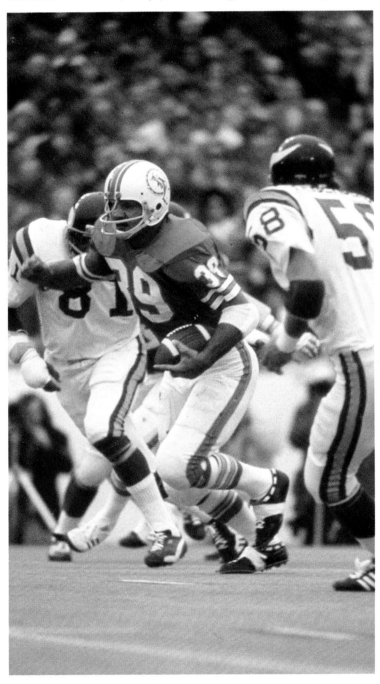

*Larry Csonka charges for big yardage in Miami's victory over the Minnesota Vikings in Super Bowl VIII, in which he won Most Valuable Player honors. Csonka was a three-time 1000-yard rusher.*

RUSHING RECORD

| Year | Attempts | Yards | Average | TD |
|---|---|---|---|---|
| 1968* | 138 | 540 | 3.9 | 6 |
| 1969* | 131 | 566 | 4.3 | 2 |
| 1970* | 193 | 874 | 4.5 | 6 |
| 1971* | 195 | 1051 | 5.4§ | 7 |
| 1972* | 213 | 1117 | 5.2 | 6 |
| 1973* | 219 | 1003 | 4.6 | 5 |
| 1974* | 197 | 749 | 3.8 | 9 |
| 1975† | Not in NFL | | | |
| 1976‡ | 160 | 569 | 3.6 | 4 |
| 1977‡ | 134 | 464 | 3.5 | 1 |
| 1978‡ | 91 | 311 | 3.4 | 6 |
| 1979* | 220 | 837 | 3.8 | 12 |
| TOTALS | 1891 | 8081 | 4.3 | 64 |

* With Miami Dolphins

† With Memphis Southmen (World Football League). His rushing record for this year is: 99 attempts, 421 yards, 4.3-yard average, 1 touchdown

‡ With New York Giants

§ Led NFL

Receiving: 106 receptions, 820 yards, 7.7-yard average, 4 touchdowns

Scoring: 68 touchdowns, 408 points

# LEN DAWSON

*Quarterback*
*6 ft 0 in, 190 lb*
*Born in Alliance, Ohio, June 20,*
*1935*
*Purdue University*
*1957–9 Pittsburgh Steelers;*
*1960–1 Cleveland Browns; 1962*
*Dallas Texans (AFL); 1963–75*
*Kansas City Chiefs*

Selected ahead of even the fabled Jim Brown, Len Dawson was Pittsburgh's number 1 draft pick in 1957 but with veteran quarterbacks always ahead of him, Dawson saw little action. In five years with the Steelers and Cleveland Browns, his record showed just 45 passing attempts.

In 1962 Dawson was released by the Browns and immediately signed by Hank Stram, coach of the Dallas Texans of the American Football League (AFL). Stram had helped coach Dawson when he was a three-year passing and total offense champion at Purdue.

"If I hadn't known him personally," Stram admitted, "I might never have signed him. But I felt he was a diamond in the rough who just needed polishing."

It turned out to be a quick polishing job. Dawson became the regular quarterback before the season began and then won AFL Player of the Year honors while leading the Texans to the AFL title in a 20–17, double-overtime triumph over the Houston Oilers.

The Texans became the Kansas City Chiefs in 1963 but Dawson had found a permanent team. He was the Texans'/Chiefs' regular signal-caller for 14 seasons. He won four AFL individual passing championships and led his team to three AFL titles—more than any other club—and two Super Bowls.

From a technical standpoint, experts rated Dawson as a passer with good range and great accuracy. Noted for his calm, poised approach to every situation, he had the total confidence of his teammates. He was smart, called his own plays and had a special flair for picking the plays that best matched his team's capabilities.

Dawson's finest hour came in Super Bowl IV. He was the game's Most Valuable Player, completing 12 of 17 passes for 142 yards and a game-clinching 46-yard pass-run connection to Otis Taylor, as the Chiefs upset the Minnesota Vikings, 23–7. On

Tuesday before the game, Len was accused of having been involved with a gambler earlier in his career. While the charges were proven to be completely false, Dawson still looks on that week as the most trying of his athletic life.

Super Bowl IV was a personal vindication for Dawson in another way. Four years earlier, he had been the losing quarterback in the Chiefs' 35–10 loss to the Green Bay Packers in Super Bowl I.

"Super Bowl I was a war of the worlds," Dawson reflected. "It was the AFL's chance to prove we belonged but we were embarrassed and I knew we would have to live with that until the time we had the opportunity to play in the Super Bowl again."

*After five years of little activity in the NFL, Len Dawson moved to the AFL, where he became a four-time passing champion. He was named the Most Valuable Player in Super Bowl IV.*

## PASSING RECORD

| Year | Attempts | Completions | Percentage passes completed | Yards | TD | Interceptions |
|---|---|---|---|---|---|---|
| 1957° | 4 | 2 | 50.0 | 25 | 0 | 0 |
| 1958° | 6 | 1 | 16.7 | 11 | 0 | 2 |
| 1959° | 7 | 3 | 42.9 | 60 | 1 | 0 |
| 1960† | 13 | 8 | 61.5 | 23 | 0 | 0 |
| 1961† | 15 | 7 | 46.7 | 85 | 1 | 3 |
| 1962‡‖ | 310 | 189 | 61.0¶ | 2759 | 29¶ | 17 |
| 1963§ | 352 | 190 | 54.0 | 2389 | 26¶ | 19 |
| 1964§‖ | 354 | 199 | 56.2¶ | 2879 | 30 | 18 |
| 1965§ | 305 | 163 | 53.4¶ | 2262 | 21¶ | 14 |
| 1966§‖ | 284 | 159 | 56.0¶ | 2527 | 26¶ | 10 |
| 1967§ | 357 | 206 | 57.7¶ | 2651 | 24 | 17 |
| 1968§‖ | 224 | 131 | 58.5¶ | 2109 | 17 | 9 |
| 1969§ | 166 | 98 | 59.0¶ | 1323 | 9 | 13 |
| 1970§ | 262 | 141 | 53.8 | 1876 | 13 | 14 |
| 1971§ | 301 | 167 | 55.5 | 2504 | 15 | 13 |
| 1972§ | 305 | 175 | 57.4 | 1835 | 13 | 12 |
| 1973§ | 101 | 66 | 65.3 | 725 | 2 | 5 |
| 1974§ | 235 | 138 | 58.7 | 1573 | 7 | 13 |
| 1975§ | 140 | 93 | 66.4 | 1095 | 18 | 8 |
| TOTALS | 3741 | 2136 | 57.1 | 28,711 | 252 | 187 |

Career passing rating: 82.555

° With Pittsburgh Steelers

† With Cleveland Browns

‡ With Dallas Texans

§ With Kansas City Chiefs

¶ Led AFL

‖ Official AFL individual passing champion

Rushing: 294 attempts, 1293 yards, 4.4-yard average, 9 touchdowns

Scoring: 9 touchdowns, 54 points

# JOE GREENE

*Defensive tackle*
*6 ft 4 in., 260 lb*
*Born in Temple, Tex.,*
*September 24, 1946*
*North Texas State University*
*1969–81 Pittsburgh Steelers*

He was called "Mean Joe" Greene. The unwanted nickname came with him to the NFL from college, where his North Texas State team was known as the "Mean Green." Joe would much rather be remembered as the kind of player he portrayed in the famous TV commercial who, after accepting a Coke from a young boy, tossed his number 75 game jersey to the lad. "I just want people to remember me as a good player and not necessarily mean," Joe said when he retired early in 1982.

Joe, however, was much more than just "good." The Steelers of the 1970s could boast of many superstars but Greene was the man who epitomized football as it was played in Pittsburgh in those years. He was the leader of an awesome defensive unit, the cornerstone of the franchise, the force that kept the team together through good days and bad.

Yet when Joe was drafted number 1 in 1969, Steeler fans weren't at all happy. They had envisioned a big-name skill position star and instead were handed an unheralded defensive tackle from a little-known college. Joe himself added to the tension by holding out well into the summer training season. But after just one practice, Greene proved he belonged. Two respected veterans decided to teach the rookie a lesson when Joe lined up against them in a two-way drill.

"Joe grabbed Bruce (Van Dyke) by the neck and me by the shoulder pads," center Ray Mansfield remembers. "It took him about a half-second to get to the quarterback. All of a sudden, we had a player who was head and shoulders above everyone. It was like having a big brother around when the bullies were coming to fight you."

Joe's rapid growth as a player paralleled the Steelers' quick rise to dominance. In 1969, Greene was the NFL's Defensive Rookie of the Year and he also earned his first of 10 Pro Bowl invitations. He was all-pro every year from 1970 to 1977 and the NFL's Most Valuable Defensive Player in both 1972 and 1974. In the same period, the Steelers rose from the depths to win four Super Bowls in six years.

Joe had all the necessary attributes—speed, agility, strength, determination and leadership. At the peak of his career, he could dominate a game almost single-handedly. Even after injuries slowed him in his seventh season, Joe continued to excel by utilizing his experience as a team leader.

As coach Chuck Noll said when Greene retired: "He's the best I've seen. Joe will always be something special!"

*Defensive tackle Joe Greene. Pittsburgh's number 1 draft pick in 1969, rapidly became a star of unusual magnitude.*

# JOHN HENRY JOHNSON

*Fullback
6 ft 2 in, 225 lb
Born in Waterproof, La.,
November 24, 1929
St Mary's College and Arizona
State University
1954–6 San Francisco 49ers;
1957–9 Detroit Lions; 1960–5
Pittsburgh Steelers; 1966 Houston
Oilers*

With an unusual half-crouch running style complete with twists and turns and jack-rabbit speed once he got into the open, John Henry Johnson became the first Pittsburgh Steeler to rush for 1000 yards in one season. Such a feat was a rarity then but John Henry did it twice in 1962 and 1964.

The record shows that Johnson was the number 4 rusher of all time when he retired. What it does not show is that he was even more devastating as a blocker, perhaps the best blocking fullback ever.

"There's far more to playing fullback than just running with the football," John Henry often said. "Everybody wants to run with the ball. But how many times does a back peel off a long run by himself. I'll tell you—absolutely none."

It was that kind of attitude that made Johnson a favorite, particularly among his quarterbacks.

"John Henry is my bodyguard," the Steelers' Bobby Layne insisted. "Half the good runners will get a passer killed if you keep them around long enough. But a quarterback hits the jackpot

*Pittsburgh Steelers fullback John Henry Johnson runs for daylight against the Dallas Cowboys. Johnson became the first Steeler to rush for 1000 yards in one season. He did it twice.*

when he gets a combination runner-blocker like Johnson."

It is ironic that Johnson enjoyed his finest football success with the Steelers, a team he shunned when he was its number 2 draft pick in 1953. When Calgary, of the Canadian Football League (CFL), offered more money, John Henry went north and became the CFL's Most Valuable Player. San Francisco quickly traded with the Steelers for the negotiating rights to Johnson.

With the 49ers, John Henry became the final element in what may have been history's finest backfield. The quartet, known both as "The Million Dollar Backfield" and "The Fabulous Foursome," included three other Hall of Famers, quarterback Y. A. Tittle and running backs Joe Perry and Hugh McElhenny.

In 1954, the 49ers' prized quartet lived up to all expectations. The three running backs finished among the top eight in NFL rushing. Johnson, the rookie, was number 2 with 681 yards, even though he was also the team's blocking specialist.

Injuries, a rapid change of coaches and a 1957 trade to Detroit kept John Henry on hold until he wound up in Pittsburgh in 1960. There, the Steelers gave him the football and turned him loose. The best years of Johnson's football life were at hand.

RUSHING RECORD

| Year | Attempts | Yards | Average | TD |
|------|----------|-------|---------|-----|
| 1954° | 129 | 681 | 5.3 | 9 |
| 1955° | 19 | 69 | 3.6 | 1 |
| 1956° | 80 | 301 | 3.8 | 2 |
| 1957† | 129 | 621 | 4.8 | 5 |
| 1958† | 56 | 254 | 4.5 | 0 |
| 1959† | 82 | 270 | 3.3 | 2 |
| 1960‡ | 118 | 621 | 5.3 | 2 |
| 1961‡ | 213 | 787 | 3.7 | 6 |
| 1962‡ | 251 | 1141 | 4.5 | 7 |
| 1963‡ | 186 | 773 | 4.2 | 4 |
| 1964‡ | 235 | 1048 | 4.5 | 7 |
| 1965‡ | 3 | 11 | 3.7 | 0 |
| 1966§ | 70 | 226 | 3.2 | 3 |
| TOTALS | 1571 | 6803 | 4.3 | 48 |

° With San Francisco 49ers

† With Detroit Lions

‡ With Pittsburgh Steelers

§ With Houston Oilers

Pass receiving: 186 receptions, 1478 yards, 7.9-yard average, 7 touchdowns

Scoring: 55 touchdowns, 330 points

# JIM LANGER

*Center*
*6 ft 2 in, 255 lb*
*Born in Little Falls, Minn.,*
*May 16, 1948*
*South Dakota State University*
*1970–9 Miami Dolphins; 1980–1*
*Minnesota Vikings*

As Minnesota coach Bud Grant prepared his Vikings for their Super Bowl VIII showdown with the Miami Dolphins, he perfected his game plan to stifle his opponent's feared ball-control offense. But he wasn't sure how his team would handle the Dolphins' center, Jim Langer, who many felt was the key to Miami's offensive success. "I believe Jim is the best center we have faced," Grant pondered. "In the games I've seen him play, I don't recall him ever making a mistake. He simply is a fine football player."

Langer was in just his second season as a regular that year but he already was attracting attention as the finest center of his time. His coach, Don Shula, was his strongest advocate and others seemed to agree. Starting in 1973, the press voted him all-pro honors for six straight years. His fellow players elected him to the American Football Conference Pro Bowl squad every year from 1973 to 1978.

Had Jim been able to foresee the rapid rags-to-riches path his pro football career would take, he most likely would have been astounded. Langer was signed as a free agent by the Cleveland Browns but was waived and picked up by the Dolphins in the 1970 summer season. During his first two seasons in Miami, Langer languished on the special teams and as a little-used backup at both center and guard on the offensive line.

In 1972, Shula decided to shift Langer to center full-time and to pit him against the veteran Bob DeMarco in a head-to-head fight for the starting job. Langer won hands down.

Since Jim was starting for the first time, no one knew just how well he would perform. As it turned out, he played every offensive down in Miami's perfect season. On running plays, Jim bowled over his opponents with startling regularity. When the Dolphins set up to pass, he proved to be one of the better pass blockers. A film review after the season revealed that among more than 500 blocking assignments, Langer needed help on only three plays.

Except for the money he missed out on if he had been a high-round draft pick, Langer felt his free-agent start was to his advantage.

"A high draft choice may think a club has money invested in him so he is certain to get a full shot," Langer contended. "Or he may feel he's so good he doesn't have to work at it and then he gets a rude awakening. Being a free agent, I had nothing but a plane ticket. It's human nature. If you come to a team as a top dog, you're not going to scratch your guts out like some guy who has to come up from the bottom."

*Jim Langer began his career as an unheralded free agent but became a regular in his third season with the Miami Dolphins.*

# DON MAYNARD

*Wide receiver*
*6 ft 1 in, 185 lb*
*Born in Crosbyton, Tex.,*
*January 25, 1937*
*Texas Western College*
*1958 New York Giants; 1959*
*Hamilton TigerCats (Canadian*
*Football League); 1960–2 New*
*York Titans; 1963–72 New York*
*Jets; 1973 St Louis Cardinals*

Don Maynard didn't fit the mold of the typical New York athletic hero. He didn't smoke or drink and was rarely seen in public night spots. With cowboy boots and long sideburns, he created a non-hero image that never changed during his 15 seasons on New York gridirons with the Giants, Titans/Jets.

There can be no argument the free-spirited Maynard deserved more attention than he received. Although he caught passes by the bushel in every one of his 10 American Football League (AFL) seasons, he was named all-league just once and to the AFL All-Star game only three times. His one major recognition was his selection to the AFL's all-time team in 1969. Yet his record was exceptional. When he retired, he ranked as the top receiver ever up to that time. Among his many other records was his feat of amassing 100 or more yards receiving in an all-time high 50 games.

Unlike most top receivers, Don was not a precise pattern runner, particularly in his early years. This was partly because Titans and Jets quarterbacks were often scrambling for their lives, which prompted Maynard to abandon any intended pattern and improvise to get himself open.

Jets coach Weeb Ewbank was never thrilled with his free style but with several change-of-pace moves and excellent speed, Don was getting open and making catches, lots of them. When Joe Namath arrived in 1965, Maynard was able to get a little order into his pass-catching life and the number 12 to number 13 pass-catch duo became one of the most exciting in pro football in the late 1960s.

The Namath–Maynard combo was particularly effective in the 1968 season, which culminated in the Jets' upset of Baltimore in Super Bowl III. In the AFL title game against Oakland that led up to the Super Bowl, Don was at his absolute best with six catches for 118 yards and two touchdowns, including the game-winner.

In Super Bowl III, Don didn't catch a pass but still was considered a major factor in the victory. When Namath and Maynard just missed connections on a 60-yard bomb early in the game, the Colts realized that Don's injured leg would not keep him from being a deep threat. When the Colts overreacted to the Maynard menace, Namath was left free to open up the offense in other areas and to seal the Colts' fate. It isn't often a receiver who doesn't catch a pass plays a major role in a big upset but, merely by being on the field, this is exactly what Maynard did in the most important game of his career.

## RECEIVING RECORD

| Year | Number | Yards | Average | TD |
|------|--------|-------|---------|-----|
| 1958° | 5 | 84 | 16.8 | 0 |
| 1959† | Not in NFL | | | |
| 1960‡ | 72 | 1265 | 17.6 | 6 |
| 1961‡ | 43 | 629 | 14.6 | 8 |
| 1962‡ | 56 | 1041 | 18.6 | 8 |
| 1963§ | 38 | 780 | 20.5 | 9 |
| 1964§ | 46 | 847 | 18.4 | 8 |
| 1965§ | 68 | 1218 | 17.9 | 14‖ |
| 1966§ | 48 | 840 | 17.5 | 5 |
| 1967§ | 71 | 1434‖ | 20.2‖ | 10 |
| 1968§ | 57 | 1297 | 22.8‖ | 10 |
| 1969§ | 47 | 938 | 20.0 | 6 |
| 1970§ | 31 | 525 | 16.9 | 0 |
| 1971§ | 21 | 408 | 19.4 | 2 |
| 1972§ | 29 | 510 | 17.6 | 2 |
| 1973¶ | 1 | 18 | 18.0 | 0 |
| TOTALS | 633 | 11,834 | 18.7 | 88 |

° With New York Giants

† With Hamilton TigerCats (Canadian Football League). His receiving record for this year is: 1 reception, 10 yards, 10.0-yard average, 0 touchdowns

‡ With New York Titans

§ With New York Jets

¶ With St Louis Cardinals

‖ Led AFL

Rushing: 24 attempts, 70 yards, 2.9-yard average, 0 touchdowns

Punt returns: 25 returns, 126 yards, 5.0-yard average, 0 touchdowns

Kickoff returns: 15 returns, 349 yards, 23.3-yard average, 0 touchdowns

Scoring: 88 touchdowns, 1 2-point conversion, 530 points

*The first player to be signed by the New York Titans in 1960, Don Maynard caught 72 passes in his initial AFL season. He finished his career with a then-record 633 receptions. Starting in 1965, he teamed with Jets quarterback Joe Namath to provide a talented pass-catch combination.*

# GENE UPSHAW

*Guard*
*6 ft 5 in, 255 lb*
*Born in Robstown, Tex.,*
*August 15, 1945*
*Texas A&I College*
*1967–81 Oakland Raiders*

Gene Upshaw started the trend toward big guards in pro football. Prior to his emergence with the Oakland Raiders in 1967, most pro football guards were "fire-plug" types—stocky and strong but standing only 6 ft 1 in or 6 ft 2 in. Gene, at 6 ft 5 in and 255 lb, could run like a deer. He was intelligent, intense, dedicated and willing to work overtime to take advantage of his natural talents.

For 15 years, Upshaw played his position superbly well. He was deservedly included in the annual rash of season-ending honors. Gene was all-AFL/AFC (American Football League/Conference) eight times. He played in the 1968 AFL All-Star game and six AFC–NFC (National Football Conference) Pro Bowls. He is the only modern player who performed exclusively as a guard to be elected to the Pro Football Hall of Fame.

During the period Upshaw was playing for them, the Raiders excelled. They were champions or near-champions every year and Gene played in 10 AFL/AFC title games and Super Bowls II, XI and XV. In those dominant years, the Raiders featured a well-balanced attack but they were particularly feared for their powerful sweeps around left end. As the team's left guard, Upshaw had the responsibility of getting out in front to lead the rushing convoys and to clear whatever roadblocks might loom in the way.

"That's my play," Upshaw beamed. "That is where I get my satisfaction in football. That's when it comes down to just me and the defensive back. If I get him clean, we're going to make a big gain. If I miss him, we don't get a yard."

Most of all, Upshaw was a team leader who developed a rapport with both the Raiders management and his fellow players. When John Madden became the Oakland coach in 1969, he immediately installed Upshaw as the offensive captain. For many years after that, his Raiders teammates re-elected Gene to that role.

Gene's eventual pro football greatness could not have been predicted in his early years. He did not play football until his senior year in high school and he won a scholarship at Texas A&I only after he got a tryout as a walk-on. But the Raiders managing general partner, Al Davis, had already envisioned Gene in a special role—that of neutralizing the big defensive tackles in pro football—when he made him his number 1 draft pick in 1967.

After an incredible 307 pre-season, regular-season and post-season games in the Oakland Raiders uniform, Upshaw retired in 1982 to the plaudits of the man who brought him into pro football. "Anytime you come into an organization as rookie," Davis said, "and you start all but one game for the next 15 years, you play with some of the greatest players who ever played the game, and you rise above 95 percent of them—you've accomplished something remarkable!"

*For 15 seasons, Gene Upshaw at left guard bulwarked the perennially strong Oakland Raiders defensive line. Upshaw played in 307 pre-season, regular-season and post-season games. He is the first modern era guard to be elected to the Hall of Fame.*

# FRED BILETNIKOFF

*Wide receiver*
*6 ft 1 in, 190 lb*
*Born in Erie, Pa., February 23, 1943*
*Florida State University*
*1965–78 Oakland Raiders*

In Super Bowl XI, the Oakland Raiders' veteran flanker, Fred Biletnikoff, caught four passes for 79 yards against the Minnesota Vikings. Three of his grabs were directly responsible for touchdowns in a 32–14 victory, the Raiders' first-ever Super Bowl triumph. Biletnikoff was named the game's Most Valuable Player, the highlight of his career.

Such performances by the loose-jointed pass-catcher had become commonplace by 1976, Biletnikoff's twelfth season in pro football. But is wasn't always that way for the former Florida State all-America who joined the Raiders of the American Football League as their number 2 draft pick in 1965. The scouting report on Biletnikoff, who caught four touchdown passes in the 1964 Gator Bowl, was that he was blessed with excellent hands and a dedicated work ethic that hopefully would overcome a troublesome deficiency, lack of break-away speed.

Fred's first two seasons were largely unproductive. At first, he even had trouble catching the ball. He did not see action as a wide receiver until the seventh game in his rookie season. Although he responded with a seven-catch, 118-yard production against Boston, his future still wasn't assured. It wasn't until his third season in 1967 that Biletnikoff enjoyed the kind of year the Raiders had originally predicted for him. He caught 40 passes that season and never was below 42 for the next nine years. With 589 career receptions, he was history's fourth-ranked receiver when he retired after the 1978 season.

Fred's success did not come naturally. "Some receivers in the NFL are just gifted. Fred isn't," Raiders coach John Madden once said. "He's had to work very hard for everything he achieved. He is one of the most dedicated athletes I have ever seen." Biletnikoff drove himself relentlessly. He practiced his patterns, gazed at films, studied his opponents hour after hour. His smallest mistake enraged him. And, most of all, he worried. He bit his fingernails until they bled. He gulped antacid to soothe a recurring ulcer. He religiously adhered to a pre-game ritual of smearing his hands with a green, gooey substance to improve his grip.

Through the latter half of his career, friend and foe alike expected Biletnikoff would catch any pass he could reach. As Raiders quarterback Ken Stabler once said: "If I need one guy to catch a ball for me when the pressure is on, then I want Fred."

*Fred Biletnikoff caught more passes—589—and scored more touchdowns—76—than any other Raider in history. The highlight of his career came in Super Bowl XI, when he caught four passes for 79 yards and was named the game's Most Valuable Player.*

RECEIVING RECORD

| Year | Receptions | Yards | Average | TD |
|---|---|---|---|---|
| 1965 | 24 | 331 | 13.8 | 0 |
| 1966 | 17 | 272 | 16.0 | 3 |
| 1967 | 40 | 876 | 21.9 | 5 |
| 1968 | 61 | 1037 | 17.0 | 6 |
| 1969 | 54 | 837 | 15.5 | 12 |
| 1970 | 45 | 768 | 17.1 | 7 |
| 1971 | 61* | 929 | 15.2 | 9 |
| 1972 | 58 | 802 | 13.8 | 7 |
| 1973 | 48 | 660 | 13.8 | 4 |
| 1974 | 42 | 593 | 14.1 | 7 |
| 1975 | 43 | 587 | 13.7 | 2 |
| 1976 | 43 | 551 | 12.8 | 7 |
| 1977 | 33 | 446 | 13.5 | 5 |
| 1978 | 20 | 285 | 14.3 | 2 |
| TOTALS | 589 | 8974 | 15.2 | 76 |

* Led NFL

Scoring: 77 touchdowns, 462 points

183

# MIKE DITKA

*Tight end*
*6 ft 3 in, 225 lb*
*Born in Carnegia, Pa., October 18, 1939*
*University of Pittsburgh*
*1961–6 Chicago Bears;*
*1967–8 Philadelphia Eagles;*
*1969–72 Dallas Cowboys*

Bull-necked, broad-shouldered and tough-minded, Mike Ditka set new standards of excellence for tight ends during his 12 seasons in the NFL. He had no peer as a blocker and gave a new dimension to his position by catching passes in impressive numbers. George Halas, who coached Ditka through six star-studded seasons with the Chicago Bears, insisted he had the best stiff-arm in the NFL.

Ditka was the Bears' number 1 draft pick in 1961 and, during his six years in Chicago, he was viewed by many as a perfect football player. He was named Rookie of the Year in 1961, all-NFL his first four years and a Pro Bowl pick after his first five campaigns. Mike was at his intense best in 1963, when he played a leading role in the Bears' first NFL title in 17 years. His 12-yard catch set up the winning touchdown in the 14–10 victory over the New York Giants in the title game but Ditka contributed key blocks, sensational catches and long runs to avert defeat at least four times during a season that saw the Bears edge the defending-champion Green Bay Packers by a mere half-game for the divisional championship.

Just a decade earlier in Aliquippa, Pennsylvania, Ditka had been a 122-lb high school sophomore struggling to make the team. By the time Mike reached the University of Pittsburgh, he had developed into an all-around star, a linebacker on defense, a fine receiver on offense and one of the nation's finest punters. He was a consensus all-America in 1960.

With the Bears, he ignored injuries to start 84 straight games in six seasons. But when the constant pounding and a feeling that he was not appreciated began to take their toll, Mike was traded to Philadelphia in 1967. Two years later, he moved on to Dallas, where, particularly in 1971, he regained much of his old form. In the Cowboys' first Super Bowl-winning campaign, Ditka scored the first touchdown in pre-season and the team's clinching last tally in Super Bowl VI.

From his first game in 1961 until his finale in 1972, Ditka played football like a man possessed. "I like contact," he said. "And I don't mind getting hit myself."

*Tight end Mike Ditka celebrates a touchdown reception scored for the Dallas Cowboys. He began his career with six outstanding seasons with the Chicago Bears in 1961–6.*

### RECEIVING RECORD

| Year | Number | Yards | Average | TD |
|---|---|---|---|---|
| 1961° | 56 | 1076 | 19.2 | 12 |
| 1962° | 58 | 904 | 15.6 | 5 |
| 1963° | 59 | 794 | 13.5 | 8 |
| 1964° | 75 | 897 | 12.0 | 5 |
| 1965° | 36 | 454 | 12.6 | 2 |
| 1966° | 32 | 378 | 11.8 | 2 |
| 1967† | 26 | 274 | 10.5 | 2 |
| 1968† | 13 | 111 | 8.5 | 2 |
| 1969‡ | 17 | 268 | 15.8 | 3 |
| 1970‡ | 8 | 98 | 12.3 | 0 |
| 1971‡ | 30 | 360 | 12.0 | 1 |
| 1972‡ | 17 | 198 | 11.6 | 1 |
| TOTALS | 427 | 5812 | 13.6 | 43 |

° With Chicago Bears

† With Philadelphia Eagles

‡ With Dallas Cowboys

Scoring: 45 touchdowns, 270 points

# JACK HAM

*Linebacker*
*6 ft 1 in., 225 lb*
*Born in Johnstown, Pa., December 23, 1948*
*Pennsylvania State University*
*1971–82 Pittsburgh Steelers*

Although Ham never sought publicity and was uncomfortable when people told him he was the best, he was one of the most popular Steelers in the 1970s. Admiring rooters formed the "Dobre Shunka" (Slavic for "Great Ham") fan club. Jack once received an ovation at a Sunday evening mass when his presence was announced. "It was just like we were at the stadium," he recalls.

When Ham was honored at a celebrity roast in Pittsburgh, Coach Noll, when called to the podium, could only exclaim: "How do you roast somebody who's perfect?"

Pittsburgh Steelers coach Chuck Noll selected Jack Ham in the second round of the 1971 draft because of his reputation as a big-play college linebacker. Noll had a hunch, which soon proved accurate, the Penn State all-America could fill the same role in the NFL. In his final pre-season game, he intercepted three passes against the New York Giants to win a regular job. Later that year, he single-handedly preserved a victory over the San Diego Chargers with a fourth-quarter interception and a deflection of a potential game-winning toss in the end zone on the game's final play.

At 225 lb, the quiet, unassuming Ham didn't fit the physical description of the typical linebackers of the 1970s who were big enough to shut down power runners and to be dominating on sweeps. But the Steelers were building a fearsome defensive line that could jumble the running game and pressure the passers. Noll, to back up his front four, sought outside linebackers with quickness and intelligence who could stay with the pass receivers but also release to stop the ball-carriers on running plays. Ham proved to be ideal for Noll's building plan.

Considered the premier outside linebacker in the NFL in his peak years, Jack performed at his best under pressure. There was plenty of that as the Steelers moved into perennial title contention. He was a sure-handed tackler and an extremely effective pass defender who possessed an uncanny ability to diagnose and disrupt the opposition's plans. Because of his penchant for blocking punts, he even played on the special teams. Most of all, he was consistent and durable, the ideal team player who played, showered and went home with no uncontrollable ego problems. He missed only five games in his first 10 seasons.

From 1973 through 1979, Jack was a virtually unanimous all-pro choice. In 1975, he was named NFL Defensive Player of the Year. He was also selected for eight Pro Bowls. His trademark was always the big play—two interceptions in the 1974 AFC title game against Oakland that put the Steelers in their first Super Bowl; a blocked punt that prodded his team to victory over Cleveland in 1976. The list is long. His career chart showed 32 interceptions and 19 opponents' fumbles recovered.

*Jack Ham was considered the premier outside linebacker in the NFL during his 12 years with the Pittsburgh Steelers. Known as a big-play star, he ended his career with 32 interceptions and 19 fumble recoveries.*

INTERCEPTION RECORD

| Year | Number | Yards | Average | TD |
|---|---|---|---|---|
| 1971 | 2 | 4 | 2.0 | 0 |
| 1972 | 7 | 83 | 11.9 | 1 |
| 1973 | 2 | 30 | 15.0 | 0 |
| 1974 | 5 | 13 | 2.6 | 0 |
| 1975 | 1 | 2 | 2.0 | 0 |
| 1976 | 2 | 13 | 6.5 | 0 |
| 1977 | 4 | 17 | 4.3 | 0 |
| 1978 | 3 | 7 | 2.3 | 0 |
| 1979 | 2 | 8 | 4.0 | 0 |
| 1980 | 2 | 16 | 8.0 | 0 |
| 1981 | 1 | 23 | 23.0 | 0 |
| 1982 | 1 | 2 | 2.0 | 0 |
| TOTALS | 32 | 218 | 6.8 | 1 |

# ALAN PAGE

*Defensive tackle*
*6 ft 4 in. 225 lb*
*Born in Canton. Ohio. August 7.*
*1945*
*Notre Dame University*
*1967–78 Minnesota Vikings:*
*1978–81 Chicago Bears*

Alan Page, an all-America defensive end on Notre Dame's 1966 national championship team, began his NFL career as the Minnesota Vikings' number 1 draft pick in 1967. He won the starting right defensive tackle job in his fourth game and remained a regular for the rest of his 15-season, 238-game career. In 1972, Page became the first defensive player to be selected the NFL's Most Valuable Player and was the NFC Defensive Player of the Year four other times. He was all-NFL and a Pro Bowl choice every year from 1968 until 1976. Page anchored four Vikings Super Bowl teams during a decade when Minnesota won nine NFC Central crowns.

Page, the first Canton, Ohio, native to enter the Hall of Fame, at his peak could control the flow of a game and at times determine its outcome. He was a big-play superstar who amassed such exceptional career credentials as 24 opponents' fumbles recovered, 28 blocked kicks, 164 sacks and 1431 tackles. Alan lined up as a defensive tackle but, instead of butting heads at the scrimmage line, he used his speed to make tackles from sideline to sideline and his superior intelligence to diagnose and disrupt enemy plays before they could get under way.

Six games into his 12th campaign in 1978, Page and the Vikings abruptly parted company. An independent thinker, Alan had embarked on an extensive running program that improved his agility but reduced his playing weight to 225 lb. Vikings coach Bud Grant decided Page no longer was strong enough to do his job and placed him on irrevocable waivers. Within hours, Page was claimed by the Chicago Bears for the $100 waiver price.

Page never missed a game, starting for the Bears the very next Sunday and then leading the Chicago team in sacks that season and again in 1979. The same year, Alan received a law degree for which he had studied during his playing years. Two seasons later in 1981, Page retired.

Sometimes viewed as a trouble-maker because of his individualistic approach to club rules, Alan was all business on the field. "One thing about Page that always impressed me," Neill Armstrong, who coached him both in Minnesota and Chicago, said, "is that I can never remember a game where he didn't give us his absolute best."

*Alan Page was the first defensive player ever to be named the NFL's Most Valuable Player, named all-NFL nine straight years and picked for the Pro Bowl nine times.*

*Enshrinement day in mid-summer is the highlight of every year at
the Pro Football Hall of Fame. In the colorful surroundings
immediately in front of the Hall, thousands gather to watch and
listen as the game's greatest heroes receive pro football's ultimate
honor in always impressive, and many times highly emotional
ceremonies.*

# INDEX

## AUTHOR'S ACKNOWLEDGEMENTS

No project of this scope can be completed without the interest and assistance of many people. I wish to express my appreciation to Commissioner Pete Rozelle, Don Weiss, Joe Browne and Jim Heffernan of the NFL office, Jim Connelley and Mary Jane McKinney of NFL Properties, Sharon Kuthe and Kevin Terrell of NFL Creative Services and Joe Horrigan and Paula Keller of the Pro Football Hall of Fame. All contributed in a variety of meaningful ways.

Thanks also must be extended to publisher Isabel Moore and my editor, Isobel Greenham, of Octopus Books Ltd. They have proven to be delightful people with whom to work.

Last, but certainly not least, I wish to recognize the dedicated and capable assistance of my wife, Helen, as a researcher, copy-reader and critic. Her contributions were a tremendous and indispensible asset throughout the creation of this book.    DON R. SMITH

## PICTURE ACKNOWLEDGEMENTS

The publishers would like to thank the following organizations and individuals for their kind permission to reproduce the photographs in this book:

John Biever/NFL Photos 138 below, 145 right; Vernon Biever/NFL Photos 131 below, 132 below, 181 right; David Boss/NFL Photos 117 below, 126 below, 142 below, 146 below, 152 below, 162 below; Clifton Boutelle/NFL Photos 159 right, 164 right, 172 right; Tony Duffy/All Sport 2–3; Jerome J. Elder/All Sport 12; Malcolm Emmons/NFL Photos 30, 133 right, 151 below, 179 below; Nate Fine/NFL Photos 19, 41, 154 below, 160 right; James Flores/NFL Photos 129 below; George Gellatly/NFL Photos 175 right; Hall of Fame/NFL Photos 8–9, 16, 66 below, 70 below, 77 right, 88 left; Rod Hanna/NFL Photos 157 right; Fred Kaplan/NFL Photos 135 right; Ed Mahan/NFL Photos 33; Bob Martin/All Sport 15 below; John McDonough/NFL Photos 6–7; NFL Photos 24, 31, 43, 51 right, 54 below, 57 above, 62 below, 63 below, 69 right, 74 left, 76 right, 79 left, 99 below, 121 below, 155 below, 165 below, 167 right; Darryl Norenberg/NFL Photos 141 right, 184 below; Mike Powell/All Sport 1; Pro Football Hall of Fame 9, 10, 11, 13, 14, 15 above, 17, 18, 20, 21, 22, 23, 25, 26, 28, 29, 34, 36, 37, 38, 39, 40, 42, 44, 45, 46, 47, 48, 49, 50, 51 left, 52, 53, 54 above, 55, 56, 57 below, 58, 59, 60, 61, 62 above, 63 above, 64, 65, 66, 67, 68 left, 69 left, 70, 71 right, 72, 73, 74 right, 75, 76 left, 77, 78, 79 right, 80, 81, 82, 83, 84, 85, 86, 87 left, 88, 89 above, 90, 91, 92 left, 93 left, 94, 95, 96, 97, 98 left, 99 above, 100, 101, 102, 103 left, 104, 105 left, 106, 107, 108 left, 109 above, 110, 111 above, 112, 113, 114 left, 115, 116, 117 above, 118, 119, 120, 121 above, 122, 123, 124, 125, 126 above, 127, 128, 129 above, 130 left, 131 above, 132 above, 133 left, 134, 135 left, 136, 137, 138 above, 139, 140 above, 141 left, 142 above, 143 above, 144, 145 left, 146 above, 147, 148 above, 149, 150, 151 above, 152 above, 153, 154 above, 155 above, 156 above, 157 left, 158, 159 left, 160 left, 161 left, 162 above, 163, 164 left, 165 above, 166, 167 left, 168, 169 left, 170 left, 171 above, 172 left, 173 left, 174 above, 175 left, 176 left, 177 left, 178 above, 179 above, 180, 181 left, 182 left, 183 left, 184 above, 185 left, 186 below, 187; Fred Roe 32, 171 below; Frank Rippon/NFL Photos 68 right, 87 right, 89 below, 92 right, 98 right, 103 right, 114 right; Dan Rubin/NFL Photos 130 right; Mr Rubio/NFL Photos 185 right; Carl Skalak Jr/NFL Photos 156 below, 176 right, 178 below; Rob L. Smith/NFL Photos 169 right; Sports Illustrated/NFL Photos 111 below; R.H. Stagg/NFL Photos 148 below, 173 right, 177 right; Vic Stein/NFL Photos 71 left, 93 right, 109 below; Bob Strauss/NFL Photos 27; Tony Tomsie 105 right, 108 right, 140 below, 143 below, 161 right, 170 right, 174 below, 182 right, 183 right, 186 above.